# THE
## COMPLETE BOOK OF BRIDGE

# The
# Complete Book of Bridge

TERENCE REESE

and

ALBERT DORMER

faber and faber

LONDON · BOSTON

First published in 1973
This revised edition first published in 1985
by Faber and Faber Limited
3 Queen Square London WC1N 3AU

Printed in Great Britain by
Redwood Burn Limited
Trowbridge Wiltshire

*British Library Cataloguing in Publication Data*
Reese, Terence
The complete book of bridge
1. Contract bridge
I. Title   II. Dormer, Albert
795.41′5      GV1282.3
ISBN 0-571-13528-5

# CONTENTS

# CONTENTS

## PART II — DEFENSIVE BIDDING

## PART III — ADVANCED BIDDING

# CONTENTS

# FOREWORD TO THE SECOND EDITION

There is no doubt that bridge is the most stimulating card game ever devised. It seems to possess a perfect balance of qualities. It has more human interest than the other great intellectual game, chess. It has luck as well as skill, partnership as well as opposition. It is absorbing but not tiring. Poor players enjoy it as much as good players.

That bridge takes longer to learn and much longer to master than other card games doesn't seem to matter. Mind you, the modern game has one or two drawbacks as well. Those who sit on committees and administer the tournament game have failed to control the spread of conventions to a point where the bidding of international players is often incomprehensible. (For example, a player may make a series of artificial bids whose only function is to extract information from partner.) However, there is no reason why these players should spoil the game for everyone else.

A word about the scope of this book: if there were five grades of player, we would be writing for grades two to four. To write for complete beginners would take another hundred pages, and in any case not many people learn from a book.

The two main divisions of the game, bidding and play, present very different problems. Play is more or less the same for everyone; it is just a question of how one presents the familiar material. Bidding, on the other hand, has endless variations, differently treated in different systems. In the early chapters we describe a method that is both sensible and popular, and later we give an account of specialized systems and conventions.

The contents of this edition are much the same as of the first edition. It was necessary to add an account of one or two new styles, such as the Multicoloured 2◊. The only long section we have left out is the one on conducting a tournament. There are many more professional, or semi-professional, tournament directors than there used to be, so that clubs no longer rely on inexperienced directors.

One final point—concerning "points". The first chapter gives a summary of standard bidding in terms of the point count. But do not misunderstand. Points are useful as a form of shorthand: it is quicker to say that a hand contains ten points, including distribution, than to say that it contains an ace, two queens, and a singleton with adequate trump support. But anyone who thinks that the point count *deter-*

15

*mines* the bid—who thinks along the lines of "I had so-many points, so I had to bid such-and-such"—is beyond hope.

TERENCE REESE
ALBERT DORMER

# PART I

*The Uncontested Auction*

# CHAPTER 1

---

## Point Count

*Valuation of high cards – Valuation of long cards and trump support – Outline of standard openings and responses*

CONSIDERING how many hundreds of ways there are of making the first few bids in bridge, it is rather remarkable that there is so much general agreement on the basic principles of bidding. This is true whatever system you have agreed to play, though of course there are some areas where a radical difference may exist; the opening two-bid is an important example.

In the matter of valuation—deciding what a hand is worth—a still greater uniformity exists. All methods in common use are founded on the familiar 4–3–2–1 count for aces, kings, queens and jacks. All are based on the idea of reaching game with 26 points, a small slam with 33 or 34 points, and so on.

In this chapter we attempt to give the reader a panoramic view of the principal bids and responses in terms of the point count and other features needed for them. We begin with valuation—the process of estimating how many tricks a hand is likely to take. As there are three ways in which tricks can be won—with high cards, with long cards and with trumps—so there are three corresponding elements in the valuation process:

(1) Count first the high-card points:

> Ace = 4 points
> King = 3 points
> Queen = 2 points
> Jack = 1 point

(2) To the high-card points, add points for length:

> *Add 1 point for the fifth card in any suit.*
> *Add 1 point for the sixth card in any suit.*
> *Add 2 points for each subsequent card.*

(3) When raising a trump suit in which the partnership holds at least eight cards, divided 4–4 or 5–3:

> *Add* 3 *points for a void.*
> *Add* 2 *points for a singleton.*
> *Add* 1 *point for a doubleton.*

The general idea is then to make bids that reflect the number of points you hold as well as the other features of the hand. In that way the partners can assess the combined strength of their two hands and select the most suitable final contract. Thus a partnership that can count on at least 26 points in the combined hands should usually bid a game; conversely, when it appears that less than 26 are present in the two hands, the bidding should usually be dropped in the safest part score. The following figures should be committed to memory:

*Points required in the two hands (including length and trump support):*

| | | | | |
|---|---|---|---|---|
| For 3NT or game in a major suit | | | . | 26 |
| For game in a minor suit | . | | . | 29 |
| For any small slam | . | . | . | 33 |
| For any grand slam | . | . | . | 37 |

The three stages of hand valuation are now discussed in detail.

### Valuation of High Cards

The accuracy of the 4–3–2–1 count for valuing high cards can be increased by taking into account the placement of the honour cards. High cards tend to produce more tricks when held in long suits than in short suits. The reason is seen in this example:

(1) A 5 3       (2) A 5 3
    K Q J           K Q J 7

The 10 high-card points in Figure 1 will produce only three tricks; in Figure 2 they will produce four. Equally, length without strength can be a waste of material. No specific adjustment is made to take account of a favourable or unfavourable disposition of the high cards, but this factor may influence a close decision at any point in the auction. Let us say the bidding goes:

| North | South |
|---|---|
| 1◇ | 1♡ |
| 2◇ | ? |

Suppose South holds either of these hands:

(1) ♠ A K 6    ♡ J 8 7 4 3    ◇ 6 2    ♣ K J 7
(2) ♠ A 10 5    ♡ J 8 7 4 3    ◇ K 2    ♣ K J 7

In each case South, with 12 points in high cards, has to choose between the sound rebid of 2NT and a jump to 3NT. At either contract he will surely need to bring in his partner's diamond suit. With hand (1), holding no points in diamonds, he should take the more cautious view; the presence of extra values in the side suits is not sufficient compensation. With (2) the jump to 3NT is a reasonable speculation. Such is the weight in gold of the ◇ K!

The value of a high card may change considerably if the opponents have entered the auction. A holding such as K–x or A–Q, for example, can be looked upon with much more favour when the right-hand opponent has bid the suit than when left hand has bid it.

Finally, aces tend to be of more value than the 4–3–2–1 count indicates, partly because of their usefulness in promoting other high cards in the same suit; a holding such as Q–x–x, for example, is obviously worth more if the ace is in the hand opposite. Jacks, on the other hand, are overvalued, as they have little promotional value.

Despite these minor shortcomings, it is highly unlikely that any other method of valuing a hand will ever become as popular as the 4–3–2–1 count. The inaccuracies often cancel out and there are few hands where they make a great deal of difference. The adjustments we have been discussing should be regarded simply as factors that may sway a close decision.

## Valuation of Long Cards and Trump Support

We saw earlier that points are added for long suits—one for the fifth card in a suit, one more for the sixth card, and two for each subsequent card. This gives a much better indication of the value of a hand than simply counting the high-card points, but it does not always complete the picture.

Length in a suit becomes even more valuable when partner has length in the same suit, enabling it to be selected as the trump suit. Two advantages now accrue: first, the combined length in the two hands makes it that much more likely that the long cards will become winners; secondly, shortages in other suits may now become an asset because extra tricks may be gained by ruffing in one hand or the other.

(1)    9 4          (2)    9 8 4 3
     A K Q 7 2             A K Q 7 2

Counting only the high cards and long cards, each of these combinations would be worth 10 points. Clearly this would be inaccurate, if only because the extra cards in the second example make it more likely that the opposing cards can be drawn. Moreover, if this is the trump suit, dummy's trumps may be put to work at ruffing.

To take account of both factors, a player raising his partner's trump suit may add to the value of his hand three points for any void, two for a singleton, and one for a doubleton. It will be found in practice that a player raising his partner's suit will either have four cards opposite four (or more) or three cards opposite a known five-card suit. In either case the presence of at least eight trumps in the combined hands justifies the addition of extra points according to the 3–2–1 scale.*

♠ Q 10 2  ♡ A J 4 3  ◇ 6  ♣ A K 10 5 3

Suppose you open 1♣ with this 15-point hand and your partner responds 1♡. As you intend to raise with four-card support you add 2 points to the value of your hand to take account of the singleton diamond. Now, with 17 points, you are worth a raise to 3♡ rather than 2♡. If partner responds 1♠ and not 1♡, you would raise this suit also, but to the two level only; you may not add points for the diamond shortage, as you have only three trumps and partner may have only four.

It is necessary to add a warning: when two players are bidding partly on the strength of long suits and neither has any support for his partner, the two hands may be expected to perform below par. When such an unhappy state, termed a " misfit ", is suspected, it is wise to drop the bidding at a lower level than would otherwise have been appropriate.

We now define all the non-specialized bids that may occur on the first round of the auction in terms of the point count and other principal features needed for them. The bids we describe are not

---

* A raise with three trumps, even when a 5–3 fit is present, is not quite as beneficial as a raise with four, and it is advisable to deduct one point from the grand total in this case.

part of any special system. Where the bidding in Acol, the most popular method in Britain, differs from others, we draw attention to this. (Notrump openings and responses are described in a later chapter.)

## Outline of Standard Openings and Responses

| | |
|---|---|
| OPENING BID OF: <br> 1♣, 1♢ <br> 1♡ or 1♠ <br> 13 to 20 points including length | These openings are used on all hands of 13 points or more that lack the requirements for a more specialized opening. A suit of at least four cards is required (exceptionally a three-card minor suit). <br> These openings are not " forcing "; partner may pass with less than 6 points. |

### Responses to opening bid of 1♣, 1♢, 1♡ or 1♠

| | |
|---|---|
| Response in new suit at one level <br> 6 to 18 points including length | These responses indicate at least a four-card suit. They are forcing for one round (that is, they oblige the opener to bid again) unless the responder previously passed. A hand in the upper range (17 or 18 points) is usually worth a jump shift if it contains a strong suit or strong support for opener's suit. In Acol the standard for a jump response is lower. |
| Response of 1NT <br> 6 to 9 points in high cards, occasionally 10 | This response is reserved for moderate hands with no four-card suit that can be bid at the level of one. It is not forcing. In response to 1♣ a bid of 1NT suggests a hand in the upper range, 8 to 10 points. |
| Response in new suit at two level (not a jump) <br> 10 points or more, including length | Similar to a response at the level of one except that the minimum strength is higher. A response of 2♡ over an opening bid of 1♠ is a special case, indicating at least a five-card suit. |

23

| | |
|---|---|
| Jump shift (single jump in a new suit) | This is the most powerful response. It is forcing to game and suggests the possibility of a slam if opener's hand is above a minimum. |

18 points up, including length.

---

### Raise of opener's suit

| | |
|---|---|
| Raise to two level 6 to 10 points, including length and shortages | This is a " limit " bid (that is, non-forcing), based usually on four-card trump support. But a major-suit opening may, as a tactical measure, be raised with three trumps including an honour. |
| Raise to three level 11 to 12 points, including length and shortages | This is normally played as a limit raise guaranteeing at least four trumps. The raise to three of a minor suit emphasizes distributional support, usually with five of the minor. |

*Alternative treatment:* A double raise, 13 to 16 points including length and shortages, may be used as forcing by a player who has not already passed. This is the traditional (but declining) method in North America.

---

| | |
|---|---|
| Raise to four level 13 to 15 points, including length and shortages | This bid is largely pre-emptive in character and is based on very strong trump support. |

---

| | |
|---|---|
| Response of 2NT 11 to 12 points in high cards | The response indicates a notrump type of hand, presumably lacking a major suit that could have been shown at the one level. Most British players use this non-forcing type of 2NT response. Elsewhere it is quite common, however, to treat 2NT as a forcing response, suggesting 13 to 15 points. |

Response of
3NT

13 to 15 points
in high cards

This game bid is best confined to hands of
4–3–3–3 pattern, or possibly 4–4–3–2 with the
doubleton in partner's suit. A response of
3NT on any hand containing ruffing values
makes it difficult to investigate a slam.

Among players who employ a forcing 2NT
response, the direct response of 3NT indicates
a balanced 16 to 18 points.

---

Such are the point-count requirements that govern the first
exchanges between opener and responder in the great majority of
constructive auctions. The general idea is that the first two bids
should be sound. Thereafter valuation, judgment and imagination
play their part.

# CHAPTER 2

## Suit Bids of One and Responses

*Which suit to open – Third and fourth hand openings – The response with 6 to 9 points – The response with 10 to 12 points – The response with 13 points or more – Response by a passed hand*

OPENING bids of 1♣, 1♢, 1♡ and 1♠ are the workhorses of standard bidding. They take care of all hands in the 13 to 20 point range except those suitable for 1NT.

There is a logical basis for the figure of 13: it ensures that a deal will not be passed out when game-going values, usually 26 points in the two hands, are present. Just the same, one should not be too dogmatic about it. There are a few 13-point hands that need not be opened, and several 12-point hands that should be opened. We give two examples of borderline openings:

(1) ♠ K Q 5 4     ♡ 8 3 2      ♢ A 5     ♣ Q J 10 3
(2) ♠ A 4 2       ♡ Q 8 6 5 3   ♢ 9 7     ♣ K Q J

Hand (1) represents a sound opening bid of 1♣ despite the presence of only 12 points. Three factors work in its favour: the points are all in high cards, not distributional; the combination Q–J–10–x is strong; and a safe and constructive rebid exists over any response that partner may make. Hand (2), by contrast, contains 13 points, allowing one for the fifth heart, but it is not an attractive holding for a bid of 1♡. This is because it contains no sound rebid over a response of, say, 2♢, and it is a cardinal principle of bidding that a player who opens with a bid of one in a suit must bid again if his partner responds in a new suit. Also, the high cards in this hand occur in short suits instead of long ones.

### Which Suit to Open

When a player opens with a bid of one his object is not so much to make the bid that gives the best immediate description as the bid that will give the best picture in conjunction with the rebid he intends to make on the second round. Consider this hand:

♠ A 10 4 2   ♡ A K Q 9   ◇ 10 4   ♣ 7 4 3

With 13 points in high cards, this hand must be opened. Clearly the most striking single feature is the fine heart suit, but it would not be right to open 1♡, for if partner responded with 2♣ or 2◇, opener would have no sound rebid. He could not rebid 2♡, because a four-card suit, however strong, may not be rebid unless supported by partner. To follow with 2♠, a higher ranking suit, would suggest a better than minimum hand and also longer hearts than spades. To avoid these difficulties, opener must start with 1♠; then he can bid 2♡ on the next round. This sequence of bidding is consistent with a limited hand containing two biddable suits.

The choice of suit is simplest when the hand contains one or more five-card or longer suits. Then:

*With only one five-card (or longer) suit, bid that suit.*

*With two five-card suits, open with the higher-ranking suit.* (Exception: with clubs and spades the opening is 1♣.)

The choice requires particular care when opener's hand contains no suit of more than four cards. Apart from the necessity of selecting an opening that will leave a sound rebid, there are now two other general objectives: to avoid, if possible, opening the bidding with a weak four-card major suit, and to ensure that a 4–4 major-suit fit, however weak, in the two hands is not " lost ". It will be found that the best bid depends on opener's hand pattern and to some extent on the strength of his hand.

## 4–3–3–3 *Pattern*

With a minimum hand, 13 to 15 points, the normal practice is to open 1♣, regardless of where the four-card suit is located. A rebid of 1NT on the next round will then indicate a hand of this type, not strong enough for a 1NT opening (assuming that you are playing a strong notrump).

♠ A 10 8   ♡ K 10 8   ◇ K J 7 3   ♣ Q 7 4

Open with 1♣ and rebid 1NT over partner's response in hearts or spades. This sequence suggests a balanced hand of 13 to 15 points, as with a stronger hand you would have opened 1NT. Note that this style applies to weak hands only. With a hand too strong for a 1NT opening, 19 or 20 points, opener may have the choice between a four-card major and a short minor. The choice will depend on the holdings in the two suits; a major-suit opening is more attractive on A–K–J–x than on K–J–x–x.

## 4–4–3–2 Pattern

Now the choice depends on the situation of the two four-card suits. It will be found that the best way to ensure a sound rebid is to follow these principles:

(a) *With " touching " suits*, open the higher ranking. With four hearts and four diamonds, for example, open 1♡. Then you can bid diamonds on the next round and your partner can return to your first suit without raising the level of the bidding.

(b) *With " non-touching " suits including a club suit*, open 1♣. Then you are sure to have a suitable rebid over any response from partner.

(1) ♠ A J 7 6   ♡ K Q 10   ◇ Q 7   ♣ Q 8 4 3

(2) ♠ 9 4 3   ♡ K J 9 6   ◇ K 3   ♣ A Q 7 5

Both hands are opened with a bid of 1♣. With (1) opener intends to rebid 1♠ over a response of 1◇ or 1♡. With (2) the idea is to bid 1♡ over a response of 1◇, but 1NT over a response of 1♠. With ♠ K–x–x and only ◇x–x you would raise 1♠ to 2♠.

(c) *With four spades and four diamonds*, open with the suit next in rank above the three-card suit.

(1) ♠ K 10 9 7   ♡ 10 7 3   ◇ A Q J 4   ♣ A 8

(2) ♠ K J 10 3   ♡ 8 2   ◇ K J 10 3   ♣ A J 3

In each case the way to avoid a rebid problem is to open the suit above the trebleton (or below the doubleton, if you prefer to think of it like that). The worst that can happen is that partner responds in your three-card suit and you have to raise it. In (1), for example, you open 1♠. If partner bids 2◇ or 2♡ you can raise to three. (In principle a response of 2♡ over 1♠ promises a five-card suit.) If the response is 2♣ the rebid is, of course, 2◇. With (2) a 1♠ opening would create a problem if partner responded 2♡; 2NT, the only " natural " rebid, would suggest a better hand. Therefore the opening bid is 1◇.

## 4–4–4–1 *Pattern*

This type of pattern is usually easier to handle. You simply open with the suit below the singleton:

(1) ♠ Q J 9 6    ♡ K Q J 4    ◇ 7      ♣ A 10 7 3

(2) ♠ 8        ♡ K 9 8 6    ◇ A J 3 2   ♣ K Q 8 4

Open the first hand with 1♣, the second with 1♡. This ensures that a fit in any suit will be brought to light, for if partner responds in your singleton suit you can continue with a new suit at the most economical level. In (2), for example, the bidding might go:

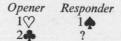

*Opener*    *Responder*

1♡         1♠

2♣         ?

Three suits have been bid and the responder can still introduce a diamond suit at a low level.

There are exceptions to almost every rule in bidding and a player learns to cope with these as he acquires experience. One reason for departing from the principles outlined above is that it is desirable to avoid opening with a weak four-card major suit. This is because although a strong 4–3 trump suit is satisfactory, a moderate 4–3 fit is not. The avoidance of weak four-card major suits affects the choice of opening with this type of hand:

♠ J 9 6 3    ♡ A Q J 4    ◇ A J 9 7    ♣ 4

If the spade suit were more robust it would be normal to open 1♠ which is in effect the suit below the singleton. However, this particular spade holding is somewhat fragile and opener should consider what alternative is available. There is no objection to opening 1♡; partner will no doubt show a spade suit if he has one, while otherwise opener can rebid his hand very satisfactorily in diamonds.

The following example presents a borderline case:

♠ Q 9 7 4    ♡ K 10 7 3    ◇ J 4    ♣ A K 3

There are intrepid souls who would happily open with 1♠, intending to rebid 2♡. The substantial objection to such a sequence is that partner may support the spades on the second round with x–x–x. Therefore the more prudent course of action is to open with the useful three-card club suit. If the clubs and diamonds were reversed we would be more likely to go along with a 1♠ opening, though some players would then prefer 1◇.

There are also exceptions to the rule about bidding a five-card suit before a four-card suit. A case in point occurs when opener has 5–4 in two touching suits and the five-card suit is lower ranking:

♠ 9 5    ♡ A Q 9 7    ◇ K J 6 4 3    ♣ K 3

Suppose you were to open 1◇ and your partner responded 2♣. It would be unsound to bid 2♡ now, as this would be a ' reverse ', suggesting at least 17 points. (To bid two touching suits in the reverse of the normal order always suggests extra strength.) To avoid misleading partner you would have to rebid 2◇, concealing the heart suit. This might not matter, because partners who hold four of a major generally respond in this suit.

It is important to note the reason why a reverse bid should be avoided with a hand of less than 17 points. Partner's new-suit response to an opening bid is unconditionally forcing for one round, but nevertheless it does not guarantee a strong hand: at the one level it may denote no more than 6 points. Clearly, therefore, opener must avoid a sequence which may carry the partnership to the three level unless considerable extra values are present on his side. That, at least, is the original reason for playing strong reverses; they have now become part of the language of bidding.

With more shapely hands it is usually correct to open the major suit whether or not the values for a reverse bid are present. This proves its worth when opponents enter the auction.

♠ 7    ♡ K Q J 8 3    ◇ A K J 7 6 4    ♣ 8

This 17-point hand is strong enough for a 1◇ opening, to be followed by a reverse bid in hearts; indeed, by opening 1◇ and later bidding hearts twice, opener can indicate five hearts and six diamonds. However, the opponents may very well contest in spades, and therefore, to ensure that neither of your suits is shut out, it is advisable to open 1♡.

The reader anxious to come to grips with more challenging aspects of bidding may consider that we have devoted much space to the choice of suit. But it must be emphasized that where a hand offers the choice of two or more bids, it is wise to proceed with caution, for an ill-judged opening may have repercussions later.

## Third and Fourth Hand Openings

In third or fourth position it may be tactically right to open with a little less than the usual values, especially with a biddable spade suit or when a constructive lead can be indicated without risk.

(1) ♠ A Q 8 5 3    ♡ J 4       ◇ A 10 6       ♣ 9 8 4
(2) ♠ 7 3          ♡ K 10 4    ◇ A Q J 10 4   ♣ 10 7 6

Both hands should be passed in first or second position, but either may be opened when partner has passed.

A player who declined to open the bidding is no longer unlimited: it may be assumed that he has no more than 12 points. Therefore the opener in third or fourth position is no longer under compulsion to bid again on the second round. This often affects the choice of opening; for example, it is no longer necessary to open with a three-card club suit on a 4–3–3–3 hand; in most cases opener simply bids the four-card suit and passes partner's response. In general, the opening bid is selected with a view to showing the main feature of the hand.

♠ A 9 4 3    ♡ A Q J 9    ◇ J 8 4    ♣ J 5

In first or second position it would be necessary to open the empty spade suit so as to have a sound rebid of 2♡. In third or fourth position the opener's intention is to pass a response of either 2♣ or 2◇ and therefore it is practicable to open with the much more attractive bid of 1♡, which also ensures that a 4–4 fit in either major will not be overlooked.

We turn next to responses to suit openings of one, treating the responding hand as belonging to one of three categories:

Weak    .    .    .    about 6 to 9 points
Medium  .    .    10 to 12 points
Strong  .    .    .    13 points or more

## The Response with 6 to 9 Points

Responder is under an obligation to keep the bidding open with 6 points, but in the interest of safety he must also keep the bidding low. He aims to select a bid that will advise partner at once of his limitations; a single raise of opener's suit, for example, or a response of 1NT, either of which limits his hand to 9 points. The only other permissible response with a weak hand is a suit bid of one. This bid may properly be made with as few as 6 points but it does not possess the advantage of a clearly defined upper limit.

### Single Raise of Opener's Suit

This bid is always selected when the responder has 6 to 9 points and is fortunate enough to hold four cards in opener's major suit. Holding four-card support, he may now count points for short suits as well as for high cards and length:

♠ J 7 5 3    ♡ 4    ◇ A 8 5 2    ♣ 9 7 3

With 5 points in high cards and one for the doubleton heart, this hand is worth a raise of partner's 1♠ opening.

Although it cannot be assumed initially that the opener has more than a four-card suit, it can be right to offer a single raise with three trumps to an honour. It depends on whether any ruffing value is present, and on what alternative response is available:

(1) ♠ J 10 4    ♡ 8 3    ◇ A K 6 2    ♣ 9 7 5 4
(2) ♠ J 10 4    ♡ J 8 3    ◇ Q 6 2    ♣ A 8 7 5

After 1♠ from partner, a raise to 2♠ is best with the first example, as the hand is not well suited for 1NT. With the second hand the natural response of 1NT is preferred as there is no ruffing value.

The principle of always raising with four trumps does not apply to minor suits. Game in a minor is far away and therefore the responder should introduce his own suits, not only to discover whether a fit is present but also to see whether the necessary guards are held for 3NT. On most hands where the responder has no biddable suit of his own, and no ruffing values, it is best to respond in notrumps.

### 1NT Response

This response covers all hands in the 6 to 9 point range that lack the requirements for a raise of opener's suit and do not contain a major suit which can be bid at the one level. It is not necessary to have notrump distribution:

♠ 8 6    ♡ 10 7    ◇ Q 9 4    ♣ K Q 10 7 5 3

With this hand you bid 1NT over 1♡ or 1♠ despite the 6–3–2–2 pattern. You have too much to pass and too little for a bid of 2♣.

1NT in response to 1♣ is generally played as having a higher range, 8 to 10 points. With 6 or 7 points a response in the four-card suit is usually available; with 3–3–3–4 bid 1◇ over 1♣.

## One-level Response in a New Suit

This is a variable response, ranging from a very strong hand to a minimum containing no more than 6 points. Although it does not have the advantage of a precise upper limit, a one-level response in a major suit may be preferred to 1NT on even the weakest type of responding hand. This is because the discovery of a 4–4 major-suit fit is a primary objective of good bidding.

♠ Q 10 8 2   ♡ 4 2   ◇ K 10 7 3   ♣ J 8 4

Over partner's 1♡ opening the response is 1♠ rather than 1NT. The opener is entitled to assume that responder will show a spade suit if he has one, and if responder fails to do so a 4–4 fit may be bypassed.

Over 1♣ the best response on this hand is 1◇. It is usual for the responder to bid four-card suits " up the line ", as the expression is. With a five-card suit and a four-card suit it is normal to respond at the one level in the longer suit.

The responder often has a choice between supporting opener's minor suit and bidding a major of his own. With a hand in the upper range of strength it is better to introduce the major suit.

♠ Q J 8 7   ♡ A 6 4   ◇ 7 2   ♣ J 9 7 2

Bid 1♠ over partner's 1♣. If on the next round you return to clubs, partner will have no reason to expect a stronger hand.

♠ K 7 3 2   ♡ 9 6 4   ◇ Q J 10 3   ♣ 10 7

With this weaker type of hand a raise of 1◇ to 2◇ is preferred. If you bid spades and then show support for diamonds, partner will gain the impression that you hold better values.

### The Response with 10 to 12 Points

Hands of this strength often present a problem which sometimes does not become apparent until the second round. The prospects of game will depend on the precise strength of opener's hand, yet even his second bid may not define this clearly enough. Nevertheless, the responder will be better placed to make a suitable move if his first response was well chosen.

## Response in a New Suit

With a hand in the 10 to 12 range the responder may make a minimum bid in a new suit at either the one or two level. Since the minimum count for a response at the two level is 10 points, this is a useful descriptive move in itself. It does not necessarily guarantee a five-card suit, except in the case of 2♡ over 1♠.

When the responder has two four-card suits it is usual to select the suit that can be bid more economically.

♠ 10 4   ♡ Q J 8 5   ◇ 8 6 3   ♣ A K 7 3

Bid 1♡ over 1◇, but 2♣ over 1♠.

With suits of unequal length it is a sound practice, provided the hand is worth two bids, to show the longer suit first even when this means responding at the range of two.

♠ A K 10 7   ♡ 10 4   ◇ 8 6   ♣ A 10 7 3 2

Respond 2♣ to 1◇. If opener rebids 2◇ you intend to continue with 2♠, as you will not have given up hope of game. With a weaker hand on which you intended to pass 2◇ you would respond in your four-card major suit initially.

♠ Q J 10 7   ♡ K 4   ◇ 10 4   ♣ Q J 7 4 2

Partner opens 1◇. You have enough for a response of 2♣, but if partner were to continue with 2◇ you would have a borderline decision between 2NT, 2♠ or pass. As your hand is really worth only one bid it is better to select 1♠, the major suit.

With two five-card suits the first response should be in the higher ranking.

♠ K 8 7 6 2   ♡ 4   ◇ A Q 10 7 3   ♣ J 5

Respond 1♠ equally to 1♡ or 1♣. The principle holds good whether or not it is intended to bid both suits.

## Double Raise of Opener's Suit

This bid is nearly always based on at least four trumps. The modern practice, which has long been favoured by most tournament players and has always been an integral part of Acol, is to treat the jump raise as non-forcing, indicating 11 or 12 points (exceptionally, 10). This has distinct advantages in competitive situations. The older practice, still popular in the United States, is to define the bid as forcing when made by a player who has not already passed; the forcing response suggests about 13 to 15 points. All players treat the bid as non-forcing when made by a passed hand.

All suitable responding hands containing four cards in opener's major suit are described by an immediate jump raise, even when the hand also contains length in the other major.

♠ A 10 5 3 2    ♡ Q 10 9 2    ◇ K 6    ♣ 8 3

Raise partner's 1♡ opening to 3♡. You can hardly improve on hearts as a contract, and to introduce the spade suit merely gives the opponents free information, plus the possible chance to compete in one of the minors.

In the case of a minor-suit opening it is better to search first for a major-suit fit and to support opener's suit on the second round.

♠ A 10 8 2    ♡ 8 3    ◇ A Q 10 4    ♣ 7 6 2

Respond 1♠ to 1◇. If opener rebids 2◇ or raises to 2♠, continue with 3◇.

An immediate double raise of a minor-suit opening may have a slightly higher upper limit than the raise of a major.

♠ 5 2    ♡ A J 4    ◇ K Q 7 3    ♣ Q 8 6 5

Over 1◇, 3◇ is best, staying within range of 3NT.

## Response of 2NT

This response indicates a balanced hand of 11 or 12 points, exceptionally 10 points with good intermediates. When played in this style the response is not forcing. Alternatively, 2NT can be played as a forcing response on 13 to 15 points.

### Responding with 13 points or more

With a hand of this strength the responder intends to reach game, the principle being that an opening bid opposite an opening equals a game. But it is not always necessary to signify this with the first response. Sometimes it is better to make a series of forcing responses in new suits until the best final contract can be selected.

## Strong Hands with Support for Opener's Suit

Hands that contain 13 points or more in support of opener's major suit may differ widely and require to be treated in different ways. The general idea is to raise straight to game on hands that are weak defensively, but to go more slowly on hands that are strong in high cards and may produce a slam. These two hands both contain 13 points, but if you were to raise equally to 4♠ in each case the opener would not know where he stood:

(1) ♠ Q J 8 7 2   ♡ 5       ◇ K 10 8 7 3 2   ♣ 7
(2) ♠ A J 8 5   ♡ Q 10 7   ◇ 8 2       ♣ K Q 9 8

With hand (1) it is certainly desirable to raise pre-emptively to 4♠ in order to discourage unwelcome competition. This direct raise is used only on hands of less than opening strength. Supporting hands which contain opening values are expressed by first bidding a new suit and raising to game on the second round. With hand (2), therefore, the response is 2♣, to be followed by 4♠. This is known as a " delayed game raise " and suggests about 13 to 15 points.

## Response of 3NT

This suggests 13 to 15 points. If 2NT is played as forcing, 3NT suggests a balanced 16 to 18.

## The Jump Shift

The jump response in a new suit is the strongest bid available to the responding hand. There is no upper limit. The lower limit, subject to individual style, is usually about 18 points, including distribution, but this may be reduced with good support for opener's suit or with a strong independent suit. Suppose your partner opens 1♡ and you hold:

(1) ♠ 2           ♡ K J 8 5   ◇ K 10 6   ♣ A K 10 7 3
(2) ♠ A K Q 10 3   ♡ 10 5     ◇ A 9 8   ♣ Q J 3

In each case a jump shift is in order. With the first hand, 3♣, followed by support for hearts, tells the whole story and leaves partner to judge whether or not to initiate a slam venture. With the second hand responder bids 2♠ and follows with 3NT.

It is normal to force with most hands of this strength, if only because it is sometimes difficult to " catch up " after failing to force immediately. But it is not essential to force when the best denomination is in doubt. Sometimes a simple response in a suit, to be followed by a change of suit on the next round, is the best way to explore the potentialities of the hand while remaining within range of 3NT.

♠ 8 3   ♡ J 7 6   ◇ A K Q 9   ♣ A K 10 4

In response to partner's 1♠ opening, either 3♣ or 3◇ would be ill-advised. This type of hand calls for gradual development. The best contract may well be 3NT if partner has a heart guard, but partner may not be able to bid notrumps until you have shown both your suits. Therefore it is best to respond 2◇. If opener rebids 2♠ you continue with 3♣, which is 100 per cent forcing.

### Responses by a Passed Hand

The standards for a simple response in a new suit are no different for a passed hand than for the first or second player. However, as the responder is known to be limited, the opener is liable to pass. Therefore the responder avoids bidding weak suits and is more inclined to bid notrumps or raise his partner's suit. Your partner opens 1♠ in third position and you hold:

(1) ♠ 9 6   ♡ Q J 9 5   ◇ A 6 3   ♣ A 10 4 2
(2) ♠ K 8 5   ♡ 6 2   ◇ A J 5 3   ♣ K 10 4 3

If you had not already passed you would make an exploratory bid of 2♣ with each of these hands. After a pass, 2NT is recommended with the first hand, 3♠ with the second. Apart from the fact that 2♣ would be inappropriate on so moderate a suit, it is reasonable to assume that partner's spades will not be unduly weak.

A jump response in a new suit, after a previous pass, is forcing for one round and logically implies some kind of fit for the opener's suit.

### OPENING AND RESPONSES QUIZ

You are the dealer with each of the following hands. What is your call?

(1) ♠ K J 10 2   ♡ 7   ◇ K 10 8 7   ♣ A Q J 4
(2) ♠ Q 9 5 3 2   ♡ A Q J 6 3   ◇ A 4   ♣ 7
(3) ♠ A Q 8   ♡ K Q 8 4   ◇ A J 10 9 6   ♣ 4
(4) ♠ K Q J 2   ♡ A 10 8 7 4   ◇ K 5   ♣ 8 3
(5) ♠ Q 5   ♡ J 8 4 3   ◇ A J 10 8   ♣ A Q J
(6) ♠ A 10 9 7   ♡ 10 8 2   ◇ A K 9 6   ♣ Q 3
(7) ♠ Q J 6 4   ♡ 3 2   ◇ A J 8 4   ♣ K Q 10
(8) ♠ A J 9 4 2   ♡ K Q 10 7 5 3   ◇ 8 3   ♣ -

(1) 1◇. With a three-suited hand you follow the principle of opening the suit below the singleton. This ensures that a 4-4 fit in any suit will not be overlooked.

(2) 1♠. With two touching suits of equal length it is normal to bid the higher-ranking first even if the other is stronger. When you follow with the lower-ranking suit on the second round, partner can, if necessary, choose between the two without raising the level of the bidding.

(3) 1◇. This attractive 17-point hand is strong enough for a reverse. It is therefore right to open with 1◇, intending to bid 2♡ over a response of 1♠, 1NT or 2♣. By adopting this sequence you show a hand of this strength with at least five diamonds and four hearts.

(4) 1♠. Unlike the previous hand, this is not strong enough to justify a reverse bid. If you were to open 1♡ you would not be able to bid spades on the next round, and as it is undesirable to conceal a strong major suit it is better to open 1♠ and rebid 2♡.

(5) 1◇. This bid is selected to avoid the weak heart suit. There will be no rebid problem as you can raise a response of 2♣ to 3♣.

(6) 1♠. If you opened 1◇ and your partner responded 2♣, you would be in a fix: a bid of 2♠ or 2NT would suggest a stronger hand, while 2◇ would suggest at least a five-card diamond suit. Thus you would look in vain for a satisfactory rebid.

A 1♠ opening leaves you well placed over any call your partner may make. If partner bids 2♡, for example, you can raise to 3♡, as partner will have five.

(7) 1◇. This is a case where, with four spades and four diamonds, it is advisable to open 1◇. Whether partner responds in hearts, spades or notrumps, you can handle matters. As you have strength in clubs you can raise a 2♣ response to 3♣. If you were to open 1♠ and your partner responded 2♡, you would have no sound rebid.

(8) 1♠. Although this hand has only 10 points in high cards it must be opened because of the distributional values. Since you intend to show both major suits, but without reversing, you open with spades, even though the heart suit is longer.

Your partner opens 1♣ and the next hand passes. What is your call with each of the following?

(9) ♠ K 8 7 4    ♡ A 10 8 3    ◇ K Q 4    ♣ 10 2

(10) ♠ Q 8 4 2    ♡ Q 9 5 3    ◇ A 7 3    ♣ 9 5

(11) ♠ A Q 9 8    ♡ 9 3 2    ◇ 6 4    ♣ A Q 10 7

(12) ♠ 9 7 4    ♡ K J 6 2    ◇ J 7 6 4    ♣ 8 3

(13) ♠ K 8 7    ♡ A K 10 5    ◇ Q 8 6 3    ♣ K 4

(9) 1♡. With two biddable four-card major suits it is usually a sound policy to respond in the lower ranking. If your partner has a spade suit he has a chance to bid it over 1♡; thus a fit in either major suit will come to light.

(10) 1♡. The embargo against bidding a moderate four-card major suit does not extend to the responding hand. If you bid 1NT with this hand, concealing both major suits, it would be held against you on the Day of Judgment. Remember that 1♡ promises no greater strength than 1NT, and the discovery of a 4–4 major-suit fit is a prime objective of the bidding process.

(11) 1♠. Here you have the values for a jump raise in clubs, but it is more constructive to show a biddable major suit first.

(12) Pass. We will not deny that if you make a practice of bidding 1♡ with this type of hand you will sometimes do very well, but more often you will get too high. It is true that your partner may not enjoy playing the hand in 1♣; but you could get into worse trouble if you were to respond with less than the normal minimum of 6 points.

(13) 2♡. If you bid 3NT with a hand of this strength you may miss a slam in hearts when partner has a four-card heart suit. To respond in diamonds would be misguided, as it is a sound principle to avoid bidding a weak suit with a strong hand.

Your partner opens 1♡ and the next player passes. What is your call with each of the following?

(14) ♠ 8 4    ♡ K Q 10 8    ◇ K J 8 4 3    ♣ 9 6

(15) ♠ 7 4    ♡ Q 7 3 2    ◇ 9 6 2    ♣ K 8 7 3

(16) ♠ A 6    ♡ Q J 8 7 4    ◇ 5    ♣ A Q J 5 3

(14) 3♡. The jump raise of opener's suit shows about 11 or 12 points, including trump support. To bid 2◇ as an initial move with this type of hand simply gives the opponents a chance to enter cheaply; moreover, it may be difficult later (without overbidding) to convince partner that the trump support is so good.

(15) 2♡. This hand may seem hardly worth a bid, but as a matter of tactics it pays to support partner's major suit with even the most slender values when you have four trumps and a probable ruffing value. If your side plays in hearts at any level and goes down, the odds are that you will be saving at least a part score.

(16) 3♣. As you have such strong support for opener's suit, and a fine suit of your own, you are worth a jump shift with slightly less than the usual high-card strength. Your 3♣ is forcing to game and suggests the possibility of a slam if partner has better than a minimum opening.

Your partner opens 1♠ and the next player passes. What is your call with each of the following?

| | | | |
|---|---|---|---|
| (17) ♠ 10 4 | ♡ Q 3 | ◇ K 8 2 | ♣ Q 9 7 5 3 2 |
| (18) ♠ Q J 8 6 3 2 | ♡ 9 4 | ◇ 4 | ♣ K 10 8 5 |
| (19) ♠ K J 5 | ♡ 8 5 3 2 | ◇ Q 8 | ♣ A J 10 3 |

(17) 1NT. Despite the six-card club suit, this is the only sound response on a moderate hand with 6 to 9 points in high cards and no suit that can be bid at the one level. A bid of 2♣ would suggest at least 10 points.

(18) 4♠. The direct raise to game shows strong trump support with limited high-card values. It is not a slam invitation and is aimed partly at shutting out the opponents. Partner is not expected to go on unless his hand is well endowed with controls.

(19) 2♣. This is a case where you do not raise partner immediately, even though you hold very fair support for his suit. Your hand is too strong for 2♠, but a raise to 3♠ is not attractive with only three trumps. Thus the sound course is to bid 2♣, with the intention of supporting spades next time.

# CHAPTER 3

## Opener's Rebid

*Responder has raised opener's suit – Responder has bid no-trumps – Responder has bid a new suit – Responder has made a jump shift*

THE PROBLEM of selecting a suitable rebid differs according to whether partner has made a limited or an unlimited response. If the responder has done anything other than bid a new suit he will have described his hand within narrow limits, as by bidding no-trumps or raising the opener's suit. On these occasions the opener will have a good idea of where the hand ought to be played.

But when the responder has bid a new suit the opener, at his second turn to bid, cannot be sure of the best final contract. He may know the best trump suit if a fit has been found, but he cannot know more, as the responder's hand is virtually unlimited. In most cases the opener's job is to select a rebid that will describe both his point count and his distribution, so that the responder can determine where to play.

### Responder Has Raised Opener's Suit

We deal first with the simplest situation, where opener's major suit has been supported and opener is satisfied that the hand should be played in that suit. There is then a straight problem of valuation. Suppose the bidding begins:

| Opener | Responder |
|--------|-----------|
| 1♠ | 2♠ |
| ? | |

As opener you hold:

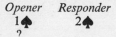
♠ A J 7 3 2   ♡ K Q 6   ◇ A 10 3   ♣ 9 4

You have 15 points, counting one for the fifth spade. Your partner has raised you to 2♠, indicating 6 to 9. It is usually safe to add a point when a five-card suit has been supported, but that still

41

leaves you with 25 at the most. Therefore you simply pass 2♠. The rule is that *you stop bidding as soon as you know that 26 points cannot be present in the two hands.*

Now suppose partner has responded with 3♠, indicating 11 or 12 points. Then you can rely on 26 points even if partner is minimum, so you bid 4♠.

Sometimes you would like your partner's hand to be more precisely defined, and his point count may not be the only consideration. Here is a case where you may reach a sound game contract with slightly less than 26 points.

| Opener | Responder |
|--------|-----------|
| 1♡ | 2♡ |
| ? | |

Opener holds:

♠ 8 5  ♡ A K J 10 3  ◇ A 8 7 3  ♣ K 6

You started out with 16 points and can add one now that your suit has been supported. Game may be there if partner is maximum, and one way of finding out about this would be by pushing forward to 3♡.* As it happens, there is a better bid; game may be possible even if partner has only a moderate raise, provided he has a suitable diamond holding, such as the king or Q–J, or a shortage in diamonds together with adequate trumps. Accordingly, you bid 3◇, which is forcing. This bid in a new suit after a single raise is called a trial bid. It indicates that opener is hopeful of game in his original suit. It invites the responder to bid game not only when he is in the upper bracket of the 6 to 9 point range, but also when he is in the middle to lower bracket and has a suitable holding in opener's second suit.

Sometimes, when opener's suit is raised, he may still not be sure that this is the best denomination. This is often the case when opener's minor suit has been supported.

| Opener | Responder |
|--------|-----------|
| 1♣ | 2♣ |
| ? | |

Opener holds:

♠ A K J 5  ♡ J 6  ◇ 10 8 3  ♣ A K Q 3

---

* Many partnerships use this bid not to show extra strength, but as a pre-emptive manoeuvre to shut out opponents.

For game in a minor suit about 29 points are needed and these cannot be present here even if the responder has a maximum. However, there are other possibilities. The opener should try 2♠, hoping that the responder will either be able to raise the spades or will have sufficient in the red suits to venture 2NT.

After a double raise in a minor suit, opener should not need much encouragement to convert to 3NT.

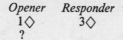

| Opener | Responder |
|--------|-----------|
| 1◇ | 3◇ |
| ? | |

Opener holds:

♠ 9 8 3    ♡ A K 3    ◇ K 10 7 4 3    ♣ K 7

Opener should bid 3NT. He has a minimum in high cards but the broken five-card diamond suit has grown in stature because of the raise. Attempts at scientific exploration, as with a bid of 3♡, tend to work out poorly in these cases. In practical play it is better to take a chance with an unguarded suit than to risk directing the opponents to the best line of defence.

### Responder Has Bid Notrumps

After this type of response the opener will have a good picture of the combined strength but may still be uncertain whether the hand should be played in notrumps or in a suit. This is especially so when the response is 1NT.

#### 1NT Response

The response of 1NT has to do duty on a wide variety of hands, some of which are relatively unbalanced. Opener should not be too ready to assume that his partner's hand will contain tolerance for one or other of his suits. With 16 points or less, opener should be ready to pass when he has no singleton or void and also when he has a 5–4–2–2 pattern. In particular, he should resist the temptation to rebid a suit simply because it is rebiddable.

| Opener | Responder |
|--------|-----------|
| 1♡ | 1NT |
| ? | |

43

Opener holds:

(1) ♠ A 8 3   ♡ A K J 3 2   ◇ Q 2   ♣ J 8 3
(2) ♠ A 4   ♡ A 8 7 5 4 2   ◇ 7 6 3   ♣ K 4

Neither hand has enough points for game and the sole question is whether 2♡ is likely to be safer than 1NT. With (1) a pass is recommended, since the notrump partial will still have chances even if the heart suit cannot be brought in. With (2) opener should remove to 2♡. A heart partial may survive a poor trump break but 1NT is likely to be hopeless if the hearts prove intractable. The principle here is that long, weak suits should be played in a trump contract, but strong suits are likely to prove valuable in notrumps.

After a 1NT response opener may be faced with the question of introducing a secondary suit. A bid in a lower-ranking suit is not forcing and indeed shows no extra strength. It is generally right to remove 1NT on a 5–4–3–1 type, but with 5–4–2–2 the important consideration is whether partner may be expected to have length in the second suit. Compare these two hands:

(1) ♠ K J 7 6 5   ♡ K 4   ◇ A Q 9 2   ♣ Q 8
(2) ♠ 8 5   ♡ 10 2   ◇ K Q J 4 3   ♣ A K 10 4

With hand (1), after an opening bid of 1♠ and a response of 1NT, there are no real grounds for bidding 2◇. Partners are notorious for having a complementary shape in these situations, with length in each of opener's short suits. Hand (2) is different, for after a 1◇ opening and a response of 1NT the responder's failure to bid a major suit suggests that he must have appreciable length in the minors, no doubt including a four-card club suit. It is therefore a sound idea to take out into 2♣. In the same way, when the responder bids 1NT over 1♣ it is safe to conclude that he has support in clubs.

When the opener decides to take his partner out of 1NT he should usually introduce a new four-card suit rather than rebid a five-card suit.

| Opener | Responder |
|--------|-----------|
| 1♠     | 1NT       |
| ?      |           |

Opener holds:

♠ A Q 9 4 3   ♡ 6   ◇ K 10 8   ♣ A 10 7 6

The singleton heart is an evident hazard for notrumps. To take out into 2♠ might be no improvement, but a flexible 2♣ is a much better rebid. As we have noted, this simple takeout does not promise more than a minimum opening; a takeout in a higher-ranking new suit, as in the sequence 1♡–1NT–2♠ would be a reverse, suggesting at least 17 points.

After a response of 1NT opener needs about 17 to 19 points before he can consider game prospects. The most common exploratory move is a raise to 2NT, which has the advantage of affording responder the chance to show delayed support for opener's suit.

| Opener | Responder |
|--------|-----------|
| 1♡ | 1NT |
| ? | |

Opener holds:

♠ K Q ♡ A K 10 9 3 ◇ A 7 6 2 ♣ J 3

With this 18-point hand opener should not give up hopes of game. As 2◇ would give no indication of his strength the choice is between 2NT and 3♡. Apart from the fact that the heart suit is not really long enough for a jump rebid, a raise to 2NT is more promising because the responder, with the values for game, has room to bid 3♡; this would be forcing, not a sign-off.

With 17 to 19 points the opener may make a jump bid in a new suit. This is forcing for one round but does not commit the partnership to game.

| Opener | Responder |
|--------|-----------|
| 1♠ | 1NT |
| ? | |

Opener holds:

♠ A Q J 3 2 ♡ K 10 8 ◇ A K 7 4 ♣ 5

The best bid is 3◇. This forces responder to bid, of course, but the opener is not committed to bidding game after a further limited response. Thus if partner can bid only 3♠, opener may pass. It is up to the responder to show signs of life if he has a suitable hand.

*Jump Response in Notrumps*

After this response, the opener will have a very good idea of the

45

best final spot, for both 2NT and 3NT limit the responder's hand more precisely than a bid of 1NT.

A response of 2NT shows 11 or 12 points, exceptionally an attractive 10; 3NT shows 13 to 15 points and in either case the response suggests a balanced hand. The opener, however, should not rely too much on the presence of a cast-iron stopper in each of the unbid suits, especially when the responder is a passed hand. An exploratory form of action is therefore called for with this type of holding:

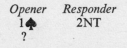

Opener holds:

♠ A 9 8 3 2   ♡ K 2   ◇ A K 7 4   ♣ 9 5

Game will certainly be reached, but the best spot is uncertain; it is not very likely that the hand will be played in diamonds, but if partner has three-card spade support then 4♠ may be safer than 3NT. A bid of 3◇ affords responder the chance to clarify his hand.

If the responder in this situation has useful support for opener's first suit he may show this by going to 4♠—" jump preference ", as it is termed. This will obviously assist opener if his hand is borderline for slam.

A minimum rebid in opener's suit, 1♡–2NT–3♡, is a weak bid, which responder will usually pass. This, at least, is the Acol style. A jump to four of the major suit is a game bid, not a slam suggestion.

Over the response of 3NT, normally 13 to 15 points, a rebid in a major suit is a sign-off, but a takeout into a minor suit may be the beginning of a slam try.

(1) ♠ A J 8 7 3   ♡ K 4   ◇ K 2           ♣ A Q 10 3
(2) ♠ Q J       ♡ K 7   ◇ A Q 10 8 4 3   ♣ A 8 3

Suppose you open 1♠ with hand (1) and partner responds 3NT. You can count on at least 31 points. A slam is possible, so, to test partner's reaction, you bid 4♣. Now 4♠ from partner would be a sign-off; 4◇ or 4♡ would be a cue-bid signifying slam interest. (See Chapter 12.)

With hand (2), after 1◇–3NT, opener should bid 4◇. This time the responder signs off in 4NT if unable to co-operate in a slam venture.

## Responder Has Bid a New Suit

When the responder bids a new suit at the one level he may have anything between 6 to 16 points. When he bids at the two level his lower limit is 10, but the range is still too wide for the opener to be able to judge the partnership's combined strength. Therefore, the opener's object in both cases is to select a rebid that will describe his own hand within narrow limits and thus enable responder to judge where the hand should be played. It is convenient to arrange the opener's rebids according to this scheme:

13 *to* 16 *points*. These are treated as minimum hands for the purpose of selecting a rebid. Opener rebids his own suit or raises his partner's suit at the minimum level, or rebids 1NT. He may also make a minimum bid (not a reverse) in a new suit.

17 *to* 19 *points*. These are " intermediate " hands. Opener may jump rebid his own suit short of game, or double raise partner's suit. He may also make a reverse bid in a new suit. When partner has responded at the range of two a simple bid in a new suit will also be treated as forcing for the moment.

20 *points upwards*. These are game-going hands. Opener either bids game direct or makes a forcing rebid in a new suit. (It is unusual to open one of a suit with more than 20 points, but opener's values may exceed this figure when revalued in support of partner's suit.)

We deal first with hands that present no problem—those containing primary support for the responder's suit.

### Raise of Responder's Suit

When the opener's hand is suitable for a raise of responder's major suit it is right to raise directly. With four-card support, or three cards opposite a known five-card suit, he may add points for ruffing values as well as long suits.

The bidding goes:

| Opener | Responder |
| :---: | :---: |
| 1♣ | 1♡ |
| ? | |

Opener holds:

(1) 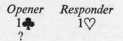 ♠ A Q 8 3   ♡ 10 6 3 2   ◇ 9      ♣ K Q J 3

47

(2) ♠ A K 2   ♡ K J 5   ◇ 5 2   ♣ K J 7 4 3

(3) ♠ 4   ♡ A 9 8 2   ◇ K Q J   ♣ A Q J 6 2

Hand (1) is in the minimum range of 13 to 16 points, even when 2 points are added for the diamond singleton. It therefore qualifies only for a raise to 2♡. Note that a bid of 1♠ would be at best superfluous, for when a 4–4 fit in a major suit has been found there is usually no advantage in disclosing other suits.

With hand (2) it is natural to raise partner's heart response, but with only three-card support you may not add a point for the shortage in diamonds. With 16 points the hand is still in the minimum range and worth a raise to 2♡ only.

In (3) you have 20 points, counting two for the singleton spade. As partner's minimum is 6 points you should raise straight to 4♡. Take away a point or two and the hand, now in the intermediate range, would qualify for a limit raise to 3♡.

There is one common type of hand where the immediate raise of partner's suit is not best:

♠ A Q 10   ♡ 7   ◇ K 10 7 4 3   ♣ A K 8 5

You open 1◇ and partner responds 1♠. With 17 points you are in the " intermediate " range. It may seem that a jump to 3♠ is in order. However, it is a sound principle to avoid a jump raise of partner's suit with only three trumps unless partner is known to have five. As the hand is too strong for a single raise the best temporary move is 2♣. On the next round you indicate support for spades, enabling partner to place you with a hand of this type.

We turn now to another rebid which closely limits the opener's hand: the rebid in notrumps.

### Opener's Rebid in Notrumps

There are two classes of balanced hand that present the opener with an easy rebid on the second round: those in the 13 to 15 range and those in the 19 or 20 range. The first are too weak for an opening bid of 1NT but the picture can be conveyed by a suit opening and a rebid of 1NT. The second type of hand is too strong for a 1NT opening; it is expressed by opening with one of a suit and jumping to 3NT on the next round. (This analysis presupposes a notrump opening of 16 to 18. When a weak notrump of 12–14 is played, a rebid of 1NT is comparatively strong, usually 15–16.)

(1) ♠ K 5     ♡ A Q 10 6     ◇ 7 6 2     ♣ K J 8 5

(2) ♠ A Q 4     ♡ K Q 10     ◇ A 9 8 3     ♣ K J 8

On hand (1) the best plan is to open 1♣ and over 1♠ rebid 1NT, indicating 13 to 15 points. (This is preferable to opening 1♡ and rebidding 2NT over 2◇, which would suggest a stronger hand.) The sequence 1♣—one of a suit—1NT is also employed on 4-3-3-3 hands to indicate 13 to 15 points.

With hand (2) you open 1◇ and jump to 3NT over any minimum response. At worst, you may wind up in 3NT with a combined 25 points. The jump rebid of 3NT may also be made with less in high cards when the hand contains a long, strong minor suit.

The rebid in notrumps is not restricted to balanced hands that are either too weak or too strong for an opening bid of 1NT. It also covers a number of intermediate hands that have the right point count for 1NT, but are not entirely suitable in other respects. Consider this very common type:

♠ 7 2     ♡ A K 10 6 2     ◇ A K 3     ♣ Q J 8

Within this sort of hand you open your five-card major rather than 1NT. If partner responds in your short suit you rebid 2NT, indicating a hand of this strength, while if partner responds in one of your three-card suits various rebids are available. With the hand above, for example, if partner bids 2♣ you can temporize with 2◇. Over a response of 2◇, 3♣ would reflect both the reversing values and the presence of a five-card heart suit. Remember that these changes of suit are forcing after partner has responded at the two level.

It is also normal to rebid 2NT on hands not quite strong enough for a 1NT opening which have been improved by partner's two-level response:

♠ K 2     ♡ Q J 3     ◇ K 10 8 7 2     ♣ A Q 5

With this type of hand you can be quite flexible. You could owe yourself a point and open 1NT, or you could open 1◇, intending to rebid 1NT over 1♡ or 1♠. If partner bids 2♣ over 1◇, however, the extra values implied by the two-level response, combined with your excellent club fit, fully justify a rebid of 2NT. Thus a rebid of 2NT, following a response at the two level, has a slightly lower range than a jump to 2NT after a response at the one level.

*Rebids of Opener's Suit*

A rebid of opener's suit invariably shows at least a five-card suit. A simple rebid suggests a minimum or near minimum opening hand, but sometimes there is no better move with this type of 16-point hand:

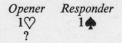

|   Opener   |   Responder   |
| :--------: | :-----------: |
|    1♡      |      1♠       |
|    ?       |               |

Opener holds:

♠ K J   ♡ A Q J 9 3   ◇ K J 7   ♣ 10 8 3

The soundest rebid is 2♡. If partner had responded 2♣ the hand would have been worth 2NT.

Even with a weak hand opener should not rebid his suit when a more constructive move is available.

| (1) | ♠ Q 9 6 3 | ♡ K 2 | ◇ 8 5 | ♣ A K J 9 2 |
| (2) | ♠ 5 | ♡ A J 9 8 3 | ◇ A 10 3 | ♣ Q J 7 4 |

With (1) you open 1♣ and partner responds 1◇ or 1♡. Bid 1♠, not 2♣. The search for a major-suit fit takes precedence over the rebid of a minor suit.

With (2) you open 1♡ and partner responds 1♠. Bid 2♣. Your suit is indifferent but there are greater drawbacks to any other rebid. One advantage of rebidding 2♣ is that you indirectly give a picture of your five hearts, as with 4–4 you would probably have rebid 1NT. With 6–4 you would rebid the major suit.

A jump rebid of opener's suit, indicating 17 to 19 points, is usually based on at least a six-card suit. The jump rebid is not forcing when made over a one-level response but is strongly invitational.

| (1) | ♠ 10 4 | ♡ A K 8 7 4 3 | ◇ A J 2 | ♣ K 6 |
| (2) | ♠ A 6 | ♡ 9 5 | ◇ A 10 3 | ♣ A K J 8 4 3 |

Each of these hands qualifies for a jump rebid after a new-suit response by partner. With hand (1), if the bidding began with 1♡ by opener, 1♠ by responder, the jump rebid of 3♡ would not be forcing; there might be no more than 23 points in the two hands. But if partner had responded with 2♣ or 2◇, indicating 10 points, 3♡ would be forcing. With hand (2) you might rebid 2NT after a 1♡ response from partner; over 1◇, 3♣ would be the only sensible call.

## Opener's Rebid in a New Suit

In some cases it is not convenient for the opener to limit his hand on the second round by means of one of the bids described above. The natural way to develop is to bid a new suit. Such a bid is not forcing after a response at the one level and may be based on a minimum opening unless it takes the form of a " reverse " bid. These are examples of a reverse:

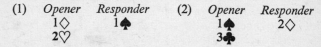

In each case the opener has bid his suits in the reverse of the normal sequence, obliging the responder to bid at the three level if he wants to return to the first suit. Both sequences show at least 17 points and indicate also that the first suit was of at least five cards. The second sequence, where the responder bids at the range of three, is forcing; moreover, it may be assumed that opener will bid again if his partner's next bid is short of a game call.

The three-level rebid in a new suit is a valuable exploratory move for strong hands and is often made on a three-card minor suit:

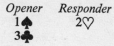

Opener holds:

♠ A Q 9 7 2   ♡ K 6   ◇ 8 4 3   ♣ A K 5

After the encouraging response of 2♡ opener is prepared for game in either hearts, spades or notrumps. The forcing rebid of 3♣ is clearly the best exploratory move. If responder's next bid is either 3♡ or 3♠, opener raises to game. If responder bids either 3◇ or 4♣, opener returns to hearts.

## The Jump Shift by Opener

There are times when opener can be sure that the values for game are present, but is unwilling to make a direct game bid, either because such a bid would not express the full value of his hand, or because he is unsure of the best contract. In either case the solution (unless a simple change of suit would be forcing) is a jump shift. The single jump in a new suit is game-forcing and suggests a count of 20 or more.

♠ A Q J 3 ♡ K 6 ◇ 9 4 ♣ A K Q 5 2

This 20-point hand is not strong enough for a two-bid but becomes strong enough for game when partner responds to 1♣. Over a response of 1♡ or 1◇, opener should jump to 2♠, not just to ensure getting to game, but also to enable partner to take a slam initiative if he has a suitable hand.

With strong support for the responder's suit, opener's hand may become worth even more than 20 points. The best way to convey the information then may be by jumping in a new suit, perhaps a three-card suit, before supporting responder's suit.

♠ K Q J 3 ♡ 7 ◇ A Q 10 5 4 ♣ A K 7

Suppose you open 1◇ with this 20-point hand and partner responds 1♠. Adding 2 points now for the heart singleton, you judge that a straight raise to 4♠ would not tell the whole story, so you jump to 3♣ and bid 4♠ on the next round. This has the advantage of portraying the heart shortage.

### Responder Has Made a Jump Shift

When the responder jumps in a new suit, forcing to game, the opener will generally rebid in the same denomination as over a simple response. Consider this sequence:

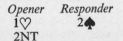

Opener's rebid of 2NT indicates the same strength as 1NT over 1♠, about 13 to 15 points. The same principle does not, however, extend to rebids in a suit. With 17 to 19 points and a six-card suit, for example, opener does not make a jump rebid over his partner's force: he simply rebids his suit at the minimum level.

Opener's jump rebid in a suit has a special meaning in this sequence:

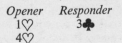

Here 4♡ indicates a solid suit, at least A–K–Q–J–x–x. This is often the key to a successful slam venture and the opportunity for such a bid should not be missed. (There is a negative inference when a suit is rebid, but without a jump.) Conversely, it is wise to avoid bidding a weak suit, or rebidding a moderate five-card suit, in a forcing sequence. In general, the opener should seek to give a picture of where his values lie.

## REBID QUIZ

You open with 1♡ and your partner bids 1NT. What is your rebid with each of the following hands?

(1) ♠ A 8   ♡ K J 9 8 5 2   ◇ A 10 7   ♣ K J

(2) ♠ 7   ♡ A J 7 5 4   ◇ K J 3   ♣ Q J 8 7

(3) ♠ 8   ♡ A K 10 8 7   ◇ A J 2   ♣ A Q 10 8

(1) 3♡. This 18-point hand falls in the intermediate range and qualifies for a jump rebid, which may be passed by partner if he has only 6 or 7 points and no support for hearts.

(2) 2♣. This is preferred to a pass and greatly preferred to 2♡. The responder, in this sequence, may well have length in clubs and a singleton heart. Also, 2♣ gives the picture of five hearts and at least four clubs. (With four of each opener would have passed 1NT.)

(3) 3♣. The jump rebid in a new suit is forcing for one round in this sequence. Partner may be able to bid 4♡ or 3NT, either of which you would pass. If partner bids only 3♡ you pass, as he must be dead minimum with no good fit.

You open 1◇ and partner bids 2NT. What is your rebid with each of the following?

(4) ♠ A 7 6 3   ♡ 9 5 2   ◇ A Q J 10   ♣ A 9

(5) ♠ 2   ♡ Q 7 4   ◇ Q J 8 7 6 5   ♣ A K 4

(6) ♠ 7   ♡ A K J 3   ◇ A K 10 9 4   ♣ K J 10

(4) 3NT. Your partner's bid of 2NT suggests 11 or 12 points. There would be little purpose in bidding 3♠, for with a reasonable four-card spade suit partner would have bid 1♠ over 1◇. A bid of 3♠ would therefore give the impression that you were anxious to play in a suit contract, whereas you are well content with 3NT.

(5) 3◇. The combined assets cannot amount to 26 points, and although you have compensation in the form of a six-card suit you are missing the top cards and may be unable to establish it in time. Game is problematical, so you issue a warning with 3◇.

(6) 3♡. With this powerful hand you expect to make game without difficulty—the only question is whether a slam is there. The most promising exploratory move is 3♡, even though partner is not likely to hold four hearts. Your 3♡ invites partner to show preference for one of your suits, and if he obliges, it will be reasonable to bid a slam after checking on aces. If partner can bid only 3NT over 3♡, you should pass.

You open with 1♣ and your partner bids 1♠. What is your rebid with each of the following?

| | | | | |
|---|---|---|---|---|
| (7) | ♠ K Q 4 | ♡ 7 3 | ◇ Q J 8 | ♣ A J 10 8 7 |
| (8) | ♠ 7 4 | ♡ A J 8 | ◇ K 10 2 | ♣ K Q 9 6 3 |
| (9) | ♠ K J 8 | ♡ A Q 9 2 | ◇ 4 | ♣ A K 10 8 5 |
| (10) | ♠ A J | ♡ 4 | ◇ 10 7 5 2 | ♣ A Q J 8 5 2 |
| (11) | ♠ 10 7 | ♡ K Q 2 | ◇ K Q 10 | ♣ A K J 7 4 |
| (12) | ♠ K 2 | ♡ A 5 3 | ◇ 7 6 | ♣ A K Q 10 3 2 |

(7) 2♠. With no guard in hearts a rebid of 1NT is ruled out and the choice is between 2♣ and 2♠. It is a sound principle to raise partner's major suit rather than rebid your own suit.

(8) 1NT. This rebid suggests 13 to 15 points in high cards, a balanced hand with strength in the unbid suits. The alternative bid, 2♣, would also express a limited hand but would not reflect your holdings in hearts and diamonds.

(9) 2♡. This is a "reverse", suggesting 17 to 19 points. It also indicates that the first suit, clubs, is longer than the second suit. The hand is too strong for 2♠, and a jump to 3♠ with only three trumps does not attract. You intend to support spades later.

(10) 2♣. The rebid of opener's suit shows a limited hand with relatively unbalanced distribution. Partner is warned that game is unlikely unless he has the equivalent of opening values.

(11) 2NT. Now that partner has bid spades, this hand is well suited to a notrump contract. Game will be there unless partner has a bare minimum.

(12) 3♣. It would be unsound to jump to 2NT with no guard in diamonds. The jump rebid in clubs, which is highly encouraging but not forcing, indicates 17 to 19 points and a strong six-card suit.

You open 1♠ and your partner bids 2♣. What is your rebid with each of the following?

| | | | |
|---|---|---|---|
| (13) ♠ A K J 10 8 4 | ♡ 7 2 | ◇ A 3 | ♣ Q 10 8 |
| (14) ♠ A Q J 5 2 | ♡ J 9 7 | ◇ 10 4 | ♣ A Q J |
| (15) ♠ A K J 5 4 | ♡ K 10 5 | ◇ Q J 3 | ♣ J 5 |

(13) 3♠. This hand contains only 14 points in high cards, but the self-supporting suit and favourable holding in responder's suit make it worth much more. The hand should be treated as in the 17 to 19 point range. Since partner's response has been made at the level of two, the jump rebid is forcing to game.

(14) 3♣. The alternative is 2♠. As partner already knows about the spade suit, and doesn't know about the club holding, the raise is recommended. There may be a chance to rebid spades later. Meanwhile, 3♣ is a constructive move, for with a weak opening you would have avoided raising to the three level.

(15) 2NT. You could rebid the spades, but 2NT gives a better impression of the all-round strength.

You open 1◇ and your partner bids 2♠. What is your rebid with each of the following?

| | | | |
|---|---|---|---|
| (16) ♠ A 4 | ♡ K 10 | ◇ A Q J 9 2 | ♣ Q 7 4 2 |
| (17) ♠ Q 6 3 | ♡ A J | ◇ A 10 5 3 2 | ♣ Q J 2 |
| (18) ♠ 10 4 | ♡ 8 3 | ◇ A K Q J 10 7 | ♣ K 10 2 |

(16) 3◇. When partner makes a jump shift and you hold better than a minimum, there is always the possibility of a slam. For this reason alone it would be inadvisable to bid 3♣, as with such a weak suit you could never bid slam with any confidence even if partner supported you. A slam may be there in spades if partner can rebid the suit, or in diamonds; in clubs, only if partner can bid them. Your 3◇ does not limit the hand in any way, because the sequence is game-forcing.

(17) 2NT. It would be a mistake to rebid the diamonds after partner's jump shift, so the choice lies between 2NT and 3♠. All in

all, 2NT gives a better description of the hand—a sound minimum opening, balanced distribution and protection in the unbid suits. If partner raises to 3NT you pass; if he takes any other action you support spades on the next round.

(18) 4◇. After partner's jump shift a jump rebid shows a solid trump suit. On this particular hand, once you've bid 4◇, you've said your piece and can leave matters to partner.

# CHAPTER 4

## Rebids by the Responder

*Opener has rebid his own suit – Opener has rebid in notrumps – Opener has raised responder's suit – Opener has bid a new suit – Opener has shown reversing values – Opener has made a jump shift*

AFTER the first three bids the responder will have learned a great deal about the opener's hand. Frequently he will be able to select the final contract, more especially when opener has rebid his suit, or bid notrumps, or raised responder's suit. In all these cases the opener will have limited his hand and the responder will usually have no difficulty in closing the auction.

The responder may be less sure of his bearings when opener has bid a new suit on the second round—either a simple bid, a reverse or a jump shift. The opener's hand will not then be closely defined. Nevertheless, the responder still looks first for a bid that will represent the combined assets, taking into account what he does know of opener's hand. If no such bid presents itself, the responder endeavours to limit his own hand by bidding notrumps or by making a limit bid in one of the partnership suits.

There are thus six cases to consider—three where the opener has bid a new suit and three where he has made a limiting bid. We take the " limited " cases first.

### Opener Has Rebid His Own Suit

A minimum rebid in opener's own suit suggests a one-suited hand in the 13 to 15 point range, exceptionally 16. The responder's point count, after he has revalued his hand in the light of opener's rebid, will be a guide to his next step.

| *Responder's point count* | *Responder's action after opener has rebid his own suit* |
|---|---|
| **13** points or more | (i) Bid game direct, or |

(With this strength game should be reached unless there is clear evidence of a misfit.)

(ii) make a bid in a new suit, or
(iii) make a jump rebid in a strong six-card suit.

11 or 12 points
(Game will depend on how well the hands fit and whether opener is maximum.)

(i) Raise opener's suit below the game level, or
(ii) bid 2NT, or
(iii) bid a new suit.

10 points or less
(Game is unlikely.)

(i) Pass, or
(ii) rebid a sound six-card suit.

When the opener rebids his suit over a response at the level of one, bypassing 1NT and the intermediate suits, he will usually have a six-card suit.

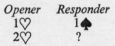

```
          Opener   Responder
            1♡         1♠
            2♡         ?
```

Responder holds:

(1) ♠ A K 9 8 4    ♡ K 5    ◇ J 10 5    ♣ 9 8 3

(2) ♠ Q 10 8 7 3    ♡ 9    ◇ K Q 7 5    ♣ Q 10 2

(3) ♠ A K 7 3    ♡ 7 4 2    ◇ A Q 6    ♣ 8 5 4

In this sequence the opener is unlikely to have concealed a secondary four-card suit and with a 5–3–3–2 pattern he might well have rebid 1NT. Therefore he is likely to have six hearts. In any case, on hand (1) a raise to 3♡ stands out.

On hand (2) it does not appear that the values for game can be present and the responder should therefore pass 2♡. The principle is that when game is unlikely the responder should accept opener's suit unless he has a void or singleton, with a seven-card or sound six-card suit of his own. It is true that on the present hand 2NT might be a better contract than 2♡, but it would not be sound to bid it. In this sequence 2NT does not mean " This may be the safest spot ", but " I have 11 or 12 points and am hopeful of game."

Hand (3) presents a straightforward case. Responder has opening values opposite an opening, so he intends to reach game. Knowing that there are at least eight hearts in the combined hands, he simply raises to 4♡. Athough his own hand is balanced and looks suitable for a notrump contract, the opener is presumably unbalanced.

When there is evidence of a misfit it may be unsafe to contract for game even though responder has 13 points. For example:

| Opener | Responder |
|--------|-----------|
| 1◇ | 1♠ |
| 2◇ | ? |

Responder holds:

♠ A Q 8 6 3 2  ♡ Q  ◇ 3  ♣ K 7 5 4 2

This hand may have no future at all and the wise move is simply 2♠. To bid 3♣, in an attempt to find a better spot, would be unsound, as a new suit at the three level would be forcing.

## Opener Has Made a Jump Rebid in His Own Suit

As this rebid indicates at least 17 points the responder needs about 7 to 9 points for game. When he is in the lower range the game prospects depend on " fit ".

| Opener | Responder |
|--------|-----------|
| 1♡ | 1NT |
| 3♡ | ? |

(1) ♠ Q J 3    ♡ 6 5 2    ◇ A 7    ♣ 10 8 7 4 3
(2) ♠ K 10 2   ♡ 8 3      ◇ Q 8 7 4 2   ♣ K J 3

Hand (1), with very fair support for hearts and a probable ruffing value, is well worth a raise to 4♡. Hand (2) does not fit so well, but the responder, with 9 points in high cards, has too much to pass. He should bid 3NT.

As there is a long way to go for game in a minor suit, responder should raise opener's rebid of 3♣ or 3◇ only when his hand is unsuitable for 3NT and there is a good hope of finding the 29 points needed for game. A bid in a three-card suit is often the best temporary move.

| Opener | Responder |
|--------|-----------|
| 1♣ | 1♠ |
| 3♣ | ? |

Responder holds:

  (1) ♠ K 10 8 7 2    ♡ 8 5 2    ◇ A 10 8    ♣ Q 6

  (2) ♠ A 10 8 6    ♡ Q 4 3    ◇ Q 10 6    ♣ J 9 5

  (3) ♠ A Q 10 8 2    ♡ 9 2      ◇ 6 5 3      ♣ Q 10 6

On hand (1), with 9 points in high cards, the obvious move is 3◇. Responder would like to be in 3NT if opener had a heart stopper, or in 4♠ if opener had three-card support. Failing either, the hand should play safely in 4♣.

Hand (2) also contains the values for 3NT and here the responder should bid it direct. It is often right to treat Q–x–x of an unbid suit as a full guard in this type of sequence, for even when partner has only x–x the odds are against the opponents being able to run five tricks.

With hand (3) responder draws the obvious inference that opener cannot have a sound guard in both red suits, for then he would have rebid 2NT instead of 3♣. However, the responder's hand is worth 10 points in support of clubs, taking account of the ruffing value in hearts, and eleven tricks could just be there. Responder should raise to 4♣, especially as a final contract of 4♠ is not ruled out. With slightly stronger spades and weaker clubs he could bid 3♠, which would be forcing for one round.

## Opener Has Rebid in Notrumps

A rebid in notrumps defines the opener's strength within close limits and says much about his hand pattern. He is unlikely to have concealed a major suit and he cannot hold four cards in responder's major suit. In many cases the ultimate destination will be clear; when it is not, it is important to known which bids are forcing and which are not.

### Opener Has Rebid 1NT

A bid in a new suit by responder is not forcing or even invitational. The bidding goes:

| Opener | Responder |
|--------|-----------|
| 1♣ | 1♠ |
| 1NT | 2◇ (or 2♡) |

In this sequence the responder is indicating a distributional type of hand with at least 5–4 in his two suits. Opener may pass if he is minimum and prefers the second suit.

Since opener's rebid of 1NT shows 13 to 15 points in high cards, responder may raise to 2NT with 11 points, to 3NT with an attractive 12. The raise to 2NT is also the best exploratory move on many hands where the responder has a five- or six-card major suit. The bidding goes:

| Opener | Responder |
|--------|-----------|
| 1◇ | 1♠ |
| 1NT | ? |

Responder holds:

♠ A Q 9 7 3   ♡ K 8 2   ◇ Q 8 2   ♣ 5 3

Here 2NT is the most accurate bid. There is still room for opener to bid 3♠ (forcing) if he has three-card support.

As this raise to 2NT takes care of most hands where responder cannot quite guarantee a game, it is logical to treat any jump rebid in a suit by responder as forcing. It is otherwise impossible to develop many hands where game is sure to be reached but the best spot is uncertain. Thus a jump rebid of responder's own suit is forcing, and so is a jump in opener's suit, as in this sequence:

| Opener | Responder |
|--------|-----------|
| 1♡ | 1♠ |
| 1NT | 3♡ |

Responder may hold this type:

♠ A 10 7 4 3 2   ♡ Q 10 8   ◇ 8 5   ♣ A 10

He should assume that game will be reasonable in one major suit or the other. To cover both possibilities he jumps to 3♡ rather than 3♠.

A bid in a higher-ranking new suit (a reverse) by the responder is forcing in this type of sequence:

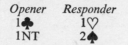

| Opener | Responder |
|--------|-----------|
| 1♣ | 1♡ |
| 1NT | 2♠ |

Responder may hold:

♠ A Q J 8   ♡ K 10 7 6 4 2   ◇ 8 4   ♣ 7

61

Opener should not fail to jump to game now with a suitable hand. A rebid of 2NT would not be forcing; nor would 3♡, though this might encourage partner on the present occasion.

## Opener Has Rebid 2NT

The points shown by opener's rebid of 2NT differ according to whether he has jumped or not.

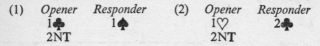

|  | (1) | Opener | Responder | (2) | Opener | Responder |
|---|---|---|---|---|---|---|
|  |  | 1♣ | 1♠ |  | 1♡ | 2♣ |
|  |  | 2NT |  |  | 2NT |  |

In the first sequence opener has about 17 or 18 points, in the second about 15 or 16. In neither case is 2NT forcing, but there are few hands where responder would pass now. In (1) a modest 7 or 8 points would suffice for a raise; in (2) he needs no more than his advertised minimum of 10 points in high cards.

As game will be so close in this type of sequence, any suit bid by the responder now will be forcing, except for a simple rebid in his own suit. Suppose you are the responder in sequence (2) and have one of these hands:

(1) ♠ 5 3      ♡ Q 8 7   ◇ A 6 2   ♣ K J 10 5 4

(2) ♠ K Q 10 4   ♡ 7 4   ◇ 6 3    ♣ A J 9 8 2

(3) ♠ K 3      ♡ 8 2    ◇ 7 4    ♣ K J 9 7 5 4 3

The first two hands are strong enough for 3NT, but game in a major may be safer. With (1) you bid 3♡, with (2) 3♠, both forcing. On hand (3) you would sign off in three of your own suit. Opener is not barred from going to 3NT, but only with a suitable club holding —which means A–x–x, *not* a singleton!

## Opener Has Rebid 3NT

After this rebid, any continuation other than a game bid in responder's own suit is a constructive move.

|  | (1) | Opener | Responder | (2) | Opener | Responder |
|---|---|---|---|---|---|---|
|  |  | 1◇ | 1♠ |  | 1♡ | 2♣ |
|  |  | 3NT | 4◇ |  | 3NT | 4♡ |

In (1) the opener is invited for the moment to select game in spades or in diamonds, but he should not overlook the possibility that responder has a slam in mind. At this point, 4♣ by opener would mean that he had no more to offer. A cue-bid of either 4♡ or 5♣ would indicate slam interest, probably in diamonds.

In (2) responder is reverting to partner's major suit, but here again he is making a forward move. With a moderate supporting hand he would have raised the hearts immediately instead of introducing the diamonds.

When a player who has opened with one of a minor rebids 3NT, his bid is often based on the minor suit itself. Responder should seldom persist with his own suit. After 1♣–1♡–3NT responder should not revert to 4♡ with:

♠ K 9   ♡ J 8 6 5 3 2   ◇ Q 10 6   ♣ 8 4

### Opener Has Raised Responder's Suit

Responder should always feel encouraged when his suit is raised, even though the raise may betoken no more than a minimum opening hand. A responding hand of 11 or 12 points, when initially game was not certain, now attains game stature.

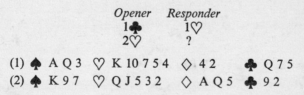

|   | Opener | Responder |
|---|--------|-----------|
|   | 1♣ | 1♡ |
|   | 2♡ | ? |

(1) ♠ A Q 3   ♡ K 10 7 5 4   ◇ 4 2   ♣ Q 7 5
(2) ♠ K 9 7   ♡ Q J 5 3 2   ◇ A Q 5   ♣ 9 2

The extra values arising from the known heart fit bring both these hands within range of game. With (1) responder goes to 4♡, with (2) he jumps to 3NT. In effect, responder is justified in adding a point to the value of his hand when a five-card suit is accorded immediate support; with a broken six-card suit he may add 2 points.

A double raise of responder's major suit, indicating at least 17 points, is highly encouraging but not forcing, as responder may have bid 1♡ or 1♠ on 6 points. When responder has bid at the two level, however, a double raise of his minor suit is forcing.

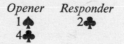

|   | Opener | Responder |
|---|--------|-----------|
|   | 1♣ | 2♣ |
|   | 4♣ |   |

Responder must not pass 4♣. With no interest in a slam he bids either 4♠ or 5♣.

## Opener Has Bid a New Suit

Opener's simple rebid in a new suit has a wide range of strength. It may also be based on many different hand patterns; thus the two hands may fit reasonably well or they may not fit at all. Responder should not hesitate to pass if he has responded on only 6 points, though with a preference for opener's first suit he may return to it without extra strength.

|  | Opener | Responder |
|---|---|---|
|  | 1♣ | 1♡ |
|  | 1♠ | ? |

(1)  ♠ 8 6 2   ♡ Q J 9 5   ◇ K 9 6   ♣ 7 5 4
(2)  ♠ 7   ♡ A J 6 4 3   ◇ 9 8 4 2   ♣ J 10 3

With (1) responder should not bid 1NT as this would suggest about 7 to 10 points. As there cannot be 26 points in the combined hands, he should simply pass 1♠. With (2) he returns to 2♣.

When responder has strength in opener's second suit, a raise will indicate much the same values as a first-round raise to the same level. The bidding goes:

|  | Opener | Responder |
|---|---|---|
|  | 1♣ | 1♡ |
|  | 1♠ | ? |

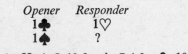

♠ A 9 8 4   ♡ A Q 10 2   ◇ 7 4 3   ♣ 10 6

If the opening bid had been 1♠ the responder, with 11 points, would have raised to 3♠, and that is the right bid now. In close situations the responder is influenced by his holding in opener's first suit; a doubleton honour is the best holding, a singleton (with four trumps in the second suit) is fair, a void is poor, x–x–x tends to be bad.

## Opener Has Shown Reversing Values

When the opener makes a reverse bid he will be in the 17 to 19 range. When the responder has indicated at least 10 points by responding at the range of two, the bidding will clearly reach game level—at least. But if the responder has bid at the one level he may have only 6 or 7 points, and in this case there must be provision for stopping in a suitable part score. We consider this situation first.

## Responder Has Bid at the One Level

Opener's reverse is not forcing and with a minimum 6 or 7 points responder may pass. When he cannot leave partner to play in the second suit he may, without suggesting extra values, give preference to the first suit. A minimum rebid in his own suit is strictly limited, and so is 2NT. Suppose the bidding goes:

| Opener | Responder |
|--------|-----------|
| 1◇ | 1♠ |
| 2♡ | ? |

Responder holds:

(1) ♠ Q 9 6 4 3    ♡ 8 5 2    ◇ 10 7    ♣ K Q 8
(2) ♠ Q J 9 8 6 5    ♡ 10 4 3    ◇ Q 4    ♣ 9 2
(3) ♠ A 8 7 3 2    ♡ 7 5    ◇ 10 6 3    ♣ J 10 6

With (1) the responder is just worth 2NT, which opener may pass with 17 points or occasionally 18. It follows that the responder must jump to 3NT over his partner's reverse whenever he has a sprightly 9 points including a guard in the unbid suit. With (2) the responder's rebid is 2♠, with (3) 3◇.

When the responder, after a reverse, cannot be sure of the best contract he may have recourse to bidding the fourth suit.

| Opener | Responder |
|--------|-----------|
| 1♣ | 1♠ |
| 2♡ | ? |

Responder holds:

♠ A J 6 4 3    ♡ K 10 2    ◇ 8 7 3    ♣ Q 8

With 11 points and excellent holdings in opener's suits, responder must ensure reaching a game, yet he cannot tell whether the hand should be played in 5♣, 4♡, 4♠ or 3NT. The best solution is to bid 3◇, the fourth suit, after which opener's next bid will no doubt point to the best contract. The principle of using a bid of the fourth suit as a " relay " or conventional force, to extract further information from partner, is now common among experienced players.

*Responder Has Bid at the Two Level*

Any bid short of game by the responder is now forcing. This is logical because both players have shown good values and may need time to select the best contract. It would be foolish to oblige the responder to plunge immediately into a game contract after the bidding had developed in this way:

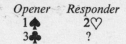

Opener    Responder
1♠          2♡
3♣          ?

Responder holds:

(1) ♠ Q 8   ♡ A J 10 7 5 3   ◇ K 2   ♣ 8 7 4

(2) ♠ 7 5 3   ♡ K Q J 4 2   ◇ A 4 3   ♣ 10 7

(3) ♠ 8 4   ♡ A Q 8 7 3   ◇ A 9 8 2   ♣ 9 6

In (1) the opener is known to have at least five spades and presumably, though not necessarily, a club suit. But nothing is known about his hearts. If the responder had to jump to game he would have difficulty in choosing between 4♡ and 4♠ at this point. It is clearly advantageous to be able to bid 3♡, forcing.

In (2) the responder should not be keen to rebid his hearts, as he has already indicated five of them. The best spot may be 4♣, but 3♠ is sufficient in the forcing situation. If opener signals an independent diamond guard by bidding 3NT, responder will be more than pleased to pass.

With (3) the responder again has ample values for game, but over 3♣ he has no wish to commit himself as between hearts, spades and notrumps. A bid of 3◇ conveys a suitably neutral message. All these rebids may also be used on appreciably stronger hands where responder has visions of a slam.

With sound values it is a good principle to make a jump rebid whenever the correct contract is clearly in view. This may enable opener to look for a slam. Consider these examples:

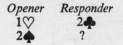

Opener    Responder
1♡          2♣
2♠          ?

Responder holds:

(1) ♠ Q 4    ♡ Q 10 6    ◇ 9 8 2    ♣ A K 7 5 3
(2) ♠ K 5 2    ♡ 9 4       ◇ A Q 8 3   ♣ K J 10 4

With (1) responder should jump to 4♡. A bid of 3♡ would be forcing, but it would be what is sometimes called a "trap bid": over the expected 4♡ responder would be uncertain whether or not to make a slam try. With (2) a bid of 2NT, also forcing, is open to the same sort of objection; far better to express the strength and character of the hand by jumping to 3NT.

## Opener Has Made a Jump Shift

The general approach is the same: as the bidding is sure to continue, the responder, if not yet certain of the best denomination, simply makes a waiting bid.

As the opener's jump shift means that game will be reached even when responder is minimum, slam will be on the horizon whenever he has a few extra points. In such a case responder should avoid a game bid which the opener may pass.

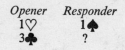

*Opener*    *Responder*
1♡        1♠
3♣        ?

Responder holds:

♠ Q 10 8 3 2   ♡ Q 6   ◇ A K 10   ♣ J 9 4

This is a typical situation where a bid of 3NT, which may seem natural, would in fact be a culpable underbid. Responder has 12 points in high cards and opener has at least 20, including distribution. If opener's hand has been improved by the spade fit the values for slam will surely be present; if not, there may be a slam in hearts, clubs or notrumps. The best move for the moment is 3◇.

## RESPONDER'S REBID QUIZ

Your partner opens 1♣, you respond 1♡, and your partner raises to 2♡. What is your call with each of the following hands?

(1) ♠ 8 3     ♡ A J 7 2    ◇ 10 9 5 2   ♣ A Q 9
(2) ♠ 7 5 3    ♡ K Q 10 8   ◇ K Q 6     ♣ 6 3 2
(3) ♠ 8       ♡ A K 7 4    ◇ 9 5 3 2    ♣ A Q 10 8

(1) 3♣. Game is no more than a possibility, for although you have excellent cards in partner's club suit you have less than opening values and only a moderate heart suit. It is therefore advisable to proceed cautiously. A bid of 3♣ describes the situation well and enables partner to bid 4♡ if he has extra values.

(2) *Pass.* You have less than opening values and partner is unlikely to have sufficient compensating strength. A game contract would be speculative. Rather than jeopardize a safe partial, it is better to pass.

(3) 4♣. The best final contract is likely to be 4♡, but it would hardly be cricket to bid this hand without showing your impressive support for partner's suit. The bid of 4♣ is forcing and might enable partner to arise in his might and bid a slam with a suitable distribution.

Your partner opens 1♣, you respond with 1♠, and your partner rebids 1NT. What is your call with each of the following?

(4) ♠ A Q 8 2   ♡ Q 9 4   ◇ K 10 8   ♣ 9 6 4

(5) ♠ A 10 8 6 2   ♡ 8 7 6 5   ◇ K Q 6   ♣ 4

(6) ♠ Q J 9 8 2   ♡ K J 9 8 3   ◇ 7 6   ♣ 7

(4) *2NT.* Opener has indicated a sound, minimum, balanced hand with about 13 to 15 points. As you have 11 points and good intermediate cards, the raise to 2NT is, if anything, on the cautious side.

(5) *Pass.* It would be unsound to raise to 2NT with only 9 points in high cards, especially with a singleton in partner's suit. You are entitled to add a point for the useful five-card suit, but that does not give you enough. A bid of 2♠ would be injudicious as partner may have a doubleton, conceivably a singleton.

(6) 2♡. This is not the type of hand with which it is advisable to leave partner in 1NT. As you lack high cards, it will probably be easier for you to make 2♡ or 2♠. Your 2♡ shows no extra strength, for a simple change of suit is not forcing in this situation.

Your partner opens 1♣, you bid 1♡, and partner rebids 1♠. What is your call with each of the following?

(7) ♠ K 8 2   ♡ K J 9 6   ◇ J 4 3   ♣ Q 4 3

(8) ♠ 9 6   ♡ A Q 7 5 3   ◇ A K 10 9 2   ♣ 7

(9) ♠ 6 4 3   ♡ A Q 7 5 2   ◇ 8 3   ♣ Q 10 4

(7) 1*NT*. Opener could have as few as 13 points or as many as 18. If he has 16 or more you will want to be in a game with your values, but the best you can do for the time being is to indicate a balanced hand of about 8 to 10 points by bidding 1NT.

(8) 2◇. This hand may certainly be expected to produce a game, on the principle that an opening opposite an opening equals game. 2◇ is forcing as it is the fourth suit.

(9) 2♣. Your heart suit is rebiddable—but it would not be a good idea to do so, as in this sequence your partner could be short in hearts. The sounder course is to show preference for one of partner's suits, in this case clubs, where you assume that some fit exists. If partner has opened a " short club " he can correct to 2♡.

Your partner opens 1♠, you respond 2◇, and partner rebids 2♡. What is your call with each of the following?

(10) ♠ J 8      ♡ K 2      ◇ A J 7 6 4      ♣ J 7 4 2
(11) ♠ K       ♡ 10 8 3    ◇ K J 8 3 2      ♣ A 10 9 6
(12) ♠ Q 4     ♡ J 5 3     ◇ A Q 8 5 2      ♣ A 6 3

(10) 2♠. If you experience an urge to bid 2NT in this type of situation, you should suppress it. The hand is not really strong enough and your holding in the unbid suit, clubs, is far from impressive.

However, partner may have reserves of strength, so you keep the bidding open by giving him a preference bid in his first suit. (Partner may well have more spades than hearts and will rarely have more hearts than spades.) Your hand is not at all unsuitable for a spade contract, and if partner's next bid is 3♠ you intend to bid 4♠.

(11) 2*NT*. This call suggests about 10 to 12 points in high cards, the ♠ K being given its full value as partner has bid the suit. 2NT has the advantage of defining the strength of the hand much more accurately than 3♣.

(12) 3♣. Here you want to know whether partner can rebid one of his suits or show an independent guard in clubs. It is a good moment for bidding the fourth suit.

Your partner opens 1♠, you respond 2♡, and partner rebids 3◇. What is your call with each of the following?

(13) ♠ J 9 8     ♡ A J 8 7 4     ◇ K 4     ♣ 8 3 2

(14) ♠ Q 10 8    ♡ A K 8 5 4    ◇ K 10 2    ♣ 4 3
(15) ♠ J         ♡ K Q 7 5 4    ◇ 10 8 5    ♣ K Q J 9

(13) 4♠. By bidding a new suit at the level of three, opener has indicated a strong hand. At the very least, he should have 17 points, including a five-card spade suit. Although you are minimum in terms of points you should assume that game is certain, your attractive holdings in each of partner's suits being worth the equivalent of at least two extra points.

By jumping to 4♠ you indicate three-card support for spades and imply some sort of fit for diamonds. If partner has values beyond those already expressed, he may be able to proceed further.

(14) 3♠. A slam must be well on the way and you gain time by bidding simply 3♠. You need not fear that this will turn out to be a " trap " bid, because you intend to proceed to 5◇ over 4♠.

(15) 3NT. Opener has indicated more than a minimum opening hand and as you yourself possess almost the equivalent of an opening you may be inclined to think in terms of a slam. But it is very likely that at least one of your K–Q combinations will be opposite a singleton and not pulling its weight, so you should proceed with caution.

Your partner opens 1♠, you raise to 2♠, and partner bids 2NT. What is your call with each of the following?

(16) ♠ 10 9 3 2   ♡ Q 9 7   ◇ K J 10   ♣ Q 8 4
(17) ♠ A J 6 4    ♡ 5 2     ◇ 9 7 4    ♣ A 10 8 4
(18) ♠ J 9 8 6 2  ♡ 9 2     ◇ 8 3      ♣ 10 7 4 3

(16) 3NT. Opener, for his rebid of 2NT, is expected to have 17 or 18 points in high cards and therefore a game is likely. As you have no ruffing values it may be easier to make nine tricks in notrumps than ten in spades.

(17) 4♠. You have the most your partner could reasonably expect for 2♠, and therefore you should certainly accept the game invitation. The only real question is whether to bid 4♠ or 3NT. As you have a ruffing value and four trumps, 4♠ is certain to be an excellent contract.

(18). 3♠. The choice between 3♠ and pass is close, actually. With the lead coming up to him, partner may find 2NT easier than 3♠. On the other hand, there is no risk of a disaster in 3♠.

# CHAPTER 5

## Notrump Openings and Responses

*The 1NT opening – Responding to 1NT – The Stayman convention – The 2NT opening – Responding to 2NT – Stayman over 2NT – The 3NT opening*

AUCTIONS that begin with an opening bid of 1NT tend to be simpler and more accurate than those that begin with one of a suit. This is because a 1NT opening straightaway defines the strength of the hand within 2 points. It also gives an accurate picture of opener's distribution, which can only be 4-3-3-3, 4-4-3-2 or 5-3-3-2. The partner of the notrump bidder, therefore, is able to judge the combined assets at once and can often select the final contract with his first call.

Moreover, if the responder feels the need for further information concerning opener's hand, there are very effective ways in which he can elicit it. In this case the exchange of information is very much one way: the responder knows far more about the combined hands than the opener, and accordingly he is in control right from the start.

The principles of notrump bidding which we now describe do not depend on the precise range of strength shown by the notrump opening. Whether it be 16 to 18 points, a strong notrump, or 12 to 14, a weak notrump, the questions to which the responder addresses himself are the same. Do the combined hands contain 26 points? If not, the bidding should be dropped in the safest partial. Do the hands contain eight cards in either spades or hearts? If so, that may well be the best spot, especially if the suit is divided 4-4. Is it simply a question of whether the opener is minimum or has a little in hand? Responder can discover this by raising to 2NT.

### The 1NT Opening

As a basis, we propose to describe the " strong notrump ", which shows a reasonably balanced hand with 16 to 18 points in high cards.

71

Those are the only hard-and-fast requirements. It is not desirable to reduce the frequency of such a valuable bid by insisting on such luxuries as a guard in every suit.

(1) ♠ 9 7 3   ♡ A J 7 3   ◇ A Q J 8   ♣ A 10

(2) ♠ A Q 8   ♡ K J 7   ◇ K Q 7 4 2   ♣ J 3

In the long run it will be a winning policy to open 1NT with hands of this type. An opening 1◇ will probably lead to the same final contract as 1NT, the difference being that meanwhile the opponents have been told which suit to attack and which to avoid. Also, it is easier for them to overcall 1◇ than 1NT.

At the same time, it is right to recognize that point count is not the whole answer. A plain doubleton is a distinct drawback. And there is a mysterious factor which we call " texture ". What we mean by this is that A–x–x is less good material for notrumps that K–J–9. It will be found that tenace holdings, such as A–Q–x and K–J–x, are especially valuable when held in the declarer's hand in a notrump contract. Consider these examples:

(1) ♠ K J 5   ♡ 10 4   ◇ A Q 3   ♣ A Q 10 7 3

(2) ♠ Q 10 3   ♡ A K J 8   ◇ 7 4 2   ♣ A Q 9

(3) ♠ A 10 8 6   ♡ K 9 8 3   ◇ A Q   ♣ K 7 5

(4) ♠ 7 6 4   ♡ A 10 9 3   ◇ A K 3 2   ♣ K Q

It is sound to open 1NT with the first three hands, each of which is endowed with tenaces. True, there is the possibility of an alternative contract, especially in (2) and (3), but the responder will be able to judge matters at least as well after a 1NT opening as he would after one of a suit.

In (4) there are several features that suggest a suit opening: no tenace holdings, no spade guard, the presence of a biddable heart suit, and a ruffing value. This hand can best be described by opening 1♡ and rebidding 2◇ if partner responds with 2♣. If partner's response is 1♠ opener should be content to rebid 1NT, even though such a sequence normally suggests no more than 15 points. Here a point may be deducted because the club honours are unguarded.

The principles for selecting a notrump opening are just the same when a lower range is used. However, at the cheap end of the market, where a 13 to 15 or 12 to 14 notrump finds favour, it is less important to conform to type. Aficionados of the weaker forms of notrump observe with some justice that when a player opens, say, 1◇ he is simply setting things in motion and not expecting to play in 1◇; so, when they open 1NT, they are just " making a noise " to signal 12 to 14 points in a fairly balanced hand. The opening has, of course, some pre-emptive value.

## Responding to 1NT

A response of either two or four of a major suit is a " sign-off "; that is, a bid which is expected to close the auction. A response of three in any suit is exploratory and forcing.

Deferring for a while any discussion of the Stayman convention, the scheme of responses to a 16–18 1NT is this:

| Responder's point count | Response |
| --- | --- |
| 0 to 7 points | As there cannot be 26 points in the two hands, responder either passes or signs off in two of a suit. |
| 8 to 9 points | Raise to 2NT. |
| 10 to 14 points | With no long major suit, raise to 3NT. With a five-card major, jump to three in the suit. With a six-card major, jump to game. |
| 16 or 17 points | With a balanced hand, raise to 4NT; with an unbalanced hand, bid three of a suit. |
| 18 or more points | Bid a slam, either directly or after investigation. (Note that when you have 17 points opposite your partner's 1NT opening, the opponents cannot have two aces and the chances of their holding the A–K of one suit are very small indeed.) |

For any other type of notrump opening, the same figures apply with suitable adjustments. Note that while the player who opens 1NT may count only his high-card points, the responder may include distributional points when valuing his hand for a suit contract. He may also add a point for a five-card suit when raising the no-trump call.

It will be found that the responder never bids a four-card suit directly over 1NT, and not always a five-card suit; but he should always bid a six-card major suit.

♠ Q 10 8 5 4 2   ♡ K 6   ◇ K 8 7   ♣ 7 5

To the 8 points for high cards the responder adds two for the long spades. Then, with 26 points and at least eight spades in the two hands, he jumps straight to 4♠. With a weaker hand of the same pattern he would sign off in 2♠. This sign-off is to be respected except that occasionally an opener who has a maximum with good controls and trump support may raise to three. Partners who violate a sign-off of 2♡ or 2♠ by bidding 2NT (or, heaven forbid, 3NT) must be taken aside and spoken to quietly, but firmly.

A response of 2♢ is also a sign-off, but 2♣, as we will see shortly, is not. With a weak hand containing a very long club suit it is possible to play in 3♣ by bidding and rebidding the suit.

With a hand containing a five-card major suit and the values for game, the responder has to consider whether a game in the suit is likely to be safer than game in notrumps. This is often a critical decision and one in which the opener's co-operation should usually be invited. This may be done by bidding the suit at the level of three.

♠ K J 10 8 3   ♡ J 10 7   ♢ 2   ♣ A 7 6 4

Partner opens 1NT and you have this hand. If the spades were a minor suit you would raise straight to 3NT, trusting partner to look after your singleton suit. As it is, you bid 3♠, offering partner a choice of game contracts. Opener is expected to raise to 4♠ in most cases where he has three-card support, but if his hand is completely balanced, with all suits protected, he may decide to bid 3NT.

Since the jump response of three in a suit is so likely to elicit a raise from opener, responder should employ the manoeuvre only when he has solid grounds for preferring a suit contract. With the following type he may elect to conceal a five-card major suit:

♠ A 4   ♡ K Q 10 4 3   ♢ 6 5 2   ♣ 8 7 2

One reason for not bidding 3♡ here is that you are not keen to have the opening lead come through your partner's holdings in the minor suits; the chances are that the hand will play better with your partner as declarer. As you have a high card in your short suit, spades, you have no real source of weakness. It is highly improbable that ten tricks in hearts will be easier to make than nine in notrumps, so you should raise to 3NT. With a weak hand of this type it is a borderline question whether to pass 1NT or sign off in 2♡.

A player who opens 1NT will often have a four-card major suit and a hand suited for a trump contract. To investigate that possibility, players use the Stayman convention, which we now describe.

74

## The Stayman Convention

When the opener and responder have a 4–4 fit in either hearts or spades, game in that suit will usually be superior to game in no-trumps. An artificial response of 2♣ may be used after an opening bid of 1NT to ascertain whether such a suit is present. Partner opens 1NT and you hold:

♠ J 10 9 3   ♡ A K 8 2   ◇ K 10 4   ♣ 4 2

You have the values for a raise to 3NT, but if partner has either four hearts or four spades it will be better to play in that suit. To find out, you bid 2♣. This says nothing about your club holding; it requests opener to bid 2♡ or 2♠ if he has four of either. With this hand you would then raise straight to game. Holding no four-card major suit, opener will bid 2◇; you then go to 3NT.

Opener is entitled to assume that a partner who employs the Stayman convention has at least one major suit. Suppose the bidding goes:

| Opener | Responder |
|--------|-----------|
| 1NT | 2♣ (Stayman) |
| 2♡ | 3NT |
| ? | |

Opener holds:

♠ Q 10 8 7   ♡ K 9 7 5   ◇ A 6   ♣ A Q J

Since opener's bid of 2♡ has evidently failed to please, it may be assumed that the responder has a four-card spade suit. Accordingly, opener now bids 4♠.

The Stayman convention may also be employed on hands that are borderline for game or slam. Suppose you have this common type of responding hand:

♠ Q 8 7 5 3   ♡ A J 7   ◇ 5 4   ♣ J 6 3

Your partner opens 1NT, showing 16 to 18 points. You have the right values for a raise to 2NT, but you do not want to overlook the possibility of game in spades if partner has a suitable hand. To display this medium type you begin with 2♣, not so much in the hope of finding partner with four spades, as to convey the range. If partner obliges with 2♠, the extra trick that may be expected from the 5–4 fit will justify a raise to game. If partner bids 2◇ or 2♡ you continue with 2♠, indicating a five-card suit and 8 or 9 points. (Your

75

bidding indicates this number of points because with more you would have bid 3♠ on the previous round and with less you would have either passed 1NT or bid 2♠ direct.) Opener may now pass if minimum or he may advance either in spades or notrumps. Again, suppose your partner opens 1NT and you hold:

♠ A 10 7 3　♡ K 9 8 6　♢ A 10 5　♣ K 3

6NT is improbable with no more than 32 points in the combined hands, but if partner has four cards in either spades or hearts a slam will surely be reasonable, as the 4–4 trump fit will produce at least one extra trick. Accordingly you bid 2♣, intending to make a vigorous attempt for a slam if partner has a fit for either major.

We shall have more to say in Chapter 12 about slam bidding after an opening bid in notrumps. Further conventional sequences for use over 1NT will be found in Chapter 13.

## The 2NT Opening

This bid is not forcing and is reserved for balanced hands of 21 or 22 points. These hands have too much in high cards to be opened with a one bid but they lack the power for a game-forcing opening.

It is frequently asserted that a 2NT opening should not contain an unguarded doubleton suit. Such a holding must be accounted an undesirable feature, it is true, but we have yet to hear of a better bid than 2NT on a hand like this:

♠ A Q J　♡ J 2　♢ A Q 10 8 3　♣ A K J

To open 1♢ with such a powerful hand places too great a strain on the responder, who in consequence may develop the undesirable habit of keeping open your one bids on hands that should properly be passed. The responder should be able to pass a one bid without trepidation whenever he has less than 6 points.

There are other considerations in favour of the 2NT opening. One is that the hand is likely to be played in 3NT and it may be advantageous to conceal the five-card suit. Another is that it is desirable for the stronger hand to become declarer. Should a suit contract be preferable, responder has the means to investigate.

### Responding to 2NT

Any response to 2NT is forcing to game. A bid of 3♢, 3♡ or 3♠ suggests at least a five-card suit and offers opener the choice of game in the suit or in notrumps. It will be found that game in quite a moderate 5–3 major suit fit may be more secure than a game in notrumps, as the weaker hand may be short of entries to develop the long suit. It is important to realize that an opener who has only x–x–x in his partner's suit should be inclined to support it, as in notrumps there may be entry problems; with K–Q–x or better, 3NT may be playable.

It follows that the responder should not hesitate to introduce 3♡ over 2NT with a hand such as this:

♠4    ♡ J 8 7 4 3    ◇ A 8 7    ♣ J 10 6 3

Opener is expected to raise the responder's major suit with three-card support, although he may bid 3NT with a 4–3–3–3 pattern that includes a useful holding in partner's suit.

### Stayman over 2NT

To explore the possibility of a 4–4 fit after a 2NT opening, the Stayman convention is used in a slightly modified form.

3♣ over 2NT, like 2♣ over 1NT, is artificial. But there is a difference in the scheme of responses, arising from the fact that the bidding cannot be dropped below game.

It is now more logical for the 2NT opener to follow what is sometimes known as the " Baron " style.

*With no four-card suit other than clubs:* rebid 3NT.

*With any other pattern:* bid the lowest-ranking four-card suit. In this case the responder follows with his own lowest-ranking four-card suit and the bidding must continue until a fit is found or 3NT is reached. The opener's obligation to show four-card suits ends there.

It is now possible to locate a 4–4 fit in any suit, including a minor. As already noted, the presence of such a trump suit may make the difference between a game contract and a successful slam.

Here are two examples showing how the 3♣ convention works after an opening bid of 2NT:

| (1) | Opener | Responder | (2) | Opener | Responder |
|-----|--------|-----------|-----|--------|-----------|
|     | 2NT    | 3♣        |     | 2NT    | 3♣        |
|     | 3◇     | 3♡        |     | 3♡     | 3♠        |
|     | 3♠     | 3NT       |     | 3NT    | 4♣        |
|     | Pass   |           |     | 6♣     | Pass      |

In (1) 3◇, 3♡ and 3♠ all show genuine suits. No fit having been found, the bidding is allowed to subside in 3NT. In (2) the opener bids 3NT over 3♠ as he has no other suit to show below game level; but when responder advances in clubs the opener is able to support him.

## The 3NT Opening

This bid rarely occurs and there is a divergence of opinion about its use. The older idea is to open 3NT with a balanced hand of about 25 or 26 points, but as such a hand can well be described by opening with an artificial bid of 2♣ and rebidding 3NT, it is wasteful to use two bids for the same hand.

The better method is to open 3NT on a long, solid minor suit, with little or no outside strength. This is known as the 'gambling' 3NT opening. This would be a typical holding:

♠ 9    ♡ 8 5 4    ◇ A K Q 10 8 4 3    ♣ 10 7

In third or fourth position the presence of scattered outside strength would be no disadvantage, but when the bid is made by the first or second player his partner will assume that he has no assets beyond the solid minor suit. The general idea now is that the partner of the player who opened 3NT is in control and decides whether to stand pat or take out into 4♣, which the opener may transfer to 4◇.

As with all advanced conventional bids, if you use this one and partner doesn't understand, it is *your* mistake!

## NOTRUMP BIDDING QUIZ

Your partner opens with 1NT, indicating 16 to 18 points, and you hold each of the following hands. What is your call?

(1) ♠ 10 8 3    ♡ 7 4 2    ◇ J 9    ♣ A Q 10 6 3
(2) ♠ A 10 8 4    ♡ J 10 7 3    ◇ K 7 6 2    ♣ 8
(3) ♠ J 9 8 6 4 2    ♡ 10 7 2    ◇ 6    ♣ 8 5 4
(4) ♠ 8 4    ♡ K 8 7    ◇ 10 5    ♣ Q 10 7 5 4 2

(1) *2NT*. This bid invites partner to raise to 3NT if he has 17 or 18 points, or 16 with a five-card suit. The raise is justified, as you may add a point for the fifth club.

(2) 2♣. This is artificial, asking partner for a four-card major

suit (Stayman convention). If partner responds with either 2♡ or 2♠ you intend to raise to game on the strength of your distributional values. If partner bids 2◇, denying a four-card major suit, you indicate your 8-point hand by bidding 2NT.

(3) 2♠. This hand might well be worthless in notrumps, yet it will surely be worth several tricks with spades as trumps. The 2♠ response promises no more than length in spades, and the notrump opener will normally pass.

(4) *Pass*. This hand might play better in 2♣ than in 1NT, but a bid of 2♣ would be conventional and opener would be bound to respond to it. You would then have to rebid 3♣. Rather than ascend to such a high level, leave partner to do the best he can in notrumps.

Suppose you are South on each of the following hands. What is your call?

(5) ♠ A K 5     ♡ 8 3 2     ◇ A J     ♣ K J 7 5 4

| South | North |
|-------|-------|
| 1NT   | 3♡    |
| ?     |       |

(6) ♠ K 10     ♡ K J 3     ◇ A 7 6 2     ♣ A Q 9 4

| South | North |
|-------|-------|
| 1NT   | 2♣    |
| 2◇    | 2♡    |
| ?     |       |

(7) ♠ 10 9 7 3     ♡ A K J 4     ◇ A 2     ♣ K J 5

| South | North |
|-------|-------|
| 1NT   | 2♣    |
| 2♡    | 3NT   |
| ?     |       |

(8) ♠ J 7 4 3     ♡ A K J     ◇ A K Q 4     ♣ K 8

| South | North |
|-------|-------|
| 2NT   | 3♣    |
| 3◇    | 3♡    |
| ?     |       |

(9) ♠ K 9 8 3  ♡ A 8 7 3  ◊ 4  ♣ K J 8 7

| North | South |
|-------|-------|
| 2NT | 3♣ |
| 3NT | ? |

(5) 4♡. Responder is showing at least a five-card suit and in this sequence you should invariably raise when you hold three-card trump support and a ruffing value. The fact that your trumps are so diminutive makes it all the more necessary to play in partner's suit.

(6) 3♡. Partner's bidding suggests a five-card heart suit and about 8 or 9 points. Your hand is not a maximum in terms of high cards but you have good trump support and a ruffing value. Therefore you should offer a raise.

(7) 4♠. As partner has invoked the Stayman convention he is assumed to have four cards in one of the major suits, evidently spades. In view of your holding in diamonds it is likely that game in a major suit will be safer than game in notrumps. (If partner is short in diamonds, this will be a weakness in notrumps; if long, there will be ruffing values in spades.)

(8) 3♠. Despite your strong heart holding you may not raise the suit, as partner may have only four of them. (If responder had wanted you to raise with three-card support he would have bid 3♡ directly over 2NT.) Equally, you should show your four-card spade suit despite its sketchy nature, for your partner will not raise unless he has four.

(9) 6♣(!). In response to your conventional bid of 3♣ opener has denied length in diamonds, hearts and spades, and must therefore have at least four clubs. With a combined holding of eight trumps you may add 2 points for the diamond singleton, bringing you to a minimum of 34 points in the combined hands, enough for slam.

# CHAPTER 6

## Two-bids

*The 2♣ opening – Responding to 2♣ – Weak two-bids – Responding to weak two-bids – Acol (strong) two-bids – Responding to Acol two-bids – Forcing two-bids*

YOUR opening bid of one in a suit is liable to be passed out when your partner has less than 6 points. When your hand is so powerful that you want him to respond with less than six you must open with a forcing bid. The modern style is to use an artificial 2♣ for all such hands.

In the old Culbertson system all opening suit bids of two were forcing, but that style has been generally abandoned as it makes uneconomic use of bidding space. It is, after all, rare for a player to hold game in his own hand, and when he does, it is not essential to name his real suit at once. It makes sense to open 2♣ on all hands where opener intends to reach game with little or no support from his partner. Opening bids of 2◇, 2♡ or 2♠ can then be used either as weak two-bids for pre-emptive effect or as a means of introducing strongly distributional hands (Acol two-bids).

### The 2♣ Opening

This call is entirely artificial and is unrelated to clubs. Its purpose is to proclaim at once that the values for game (or very nearly) are present, so that neither player will need to jump the bidding later. When a game-forcing situation is established, both players are free to show features of their hands and explore the possibility of a slam at a safe level. These types of hand qualify for a 2♣ opening:

(i) *A balanced hand from 23 points upwards.*
(ii) *A 5–4 hand pattern or a moderate six-card suit and at least 22 points in high cards*, or
(iii) *A strong six-card or moderate seven-card suit and at least 20 points in high cards*, or
(iv) *A strong seven-card suit and at least 18 points in high cards.*

On the second round the opener shows whether his hand is balanced or unbalanced. With a balanced hand containing 23 or 24 points he rebids 2NT, which the responder may pass on complete weakness. With a balanced 25 or 26 points he rebids 3NT. Any other rebid suggests an unbalanced hand and is forcing to game unless, of course, the opponents intervene and are doubled.

(1) ♠ A K Q 3     ♡ K 9 2     ◇ A Q 5     ♣ K Q 9

(2) ♠ A K J 8 6 3 2     ♡ A Q 6     ◇ A 9     ♣ 5

(3) ♠ A     ♡ K J 10 8 3     ◇ A K Q 2     ♣ A J 9

(4) ♠ A K J     ♡ A J 8 6 5     ◇ A 7     ♣ K Q 5

The first three hands are all worth a 2♣ opening, but they are all minimum hands of their kind. With (1) opener intends to rebid not 2♠ but 2NT, indicating 23 or 24 points in a balanced hand. With (2) he is prepared to put his fortunes to the test in 4♠ provided partner has thirteen cards, so he opens 2♣ and rebids 2♠. Hand (3) is just worth 2♣, but with a spade more and a heart or a diamond fewer 2NT would be more accurate.

Hand (4) does not merit a 2♣ opening to be followed by a rebid in hearts. With an additional ten or so you might treat the hand as worth 23 points in high cards, in which case you would open 2♣ and rebid 2NT. As it is, the sounder procedure is to open 2NT, which shows 21 or 22.

### Responding to 2♣

When the responder has fewer than 7 points in high cards he must give the negative response of 2◇. This too is an artificial bid and is used because it is the cheapest possible call over 2♣. Anything else is a positive response.

The cardinal rule for the responding hand is that the bidding must never be allowed to die below game except in this one sequence:

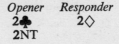

Opener     Responder
2♣         2◇
2NT

Here 2NT is not forcing. Opener is showing a balanced 23 or 24 count and responder may pass on a worthless hand; but he needs only 3 points, or Q–x–x–x–x, for a raise to game.

Note that distributional points are not counted in determining whether responder has the values for a positive response to 2♣. Responder's first duty is to tell partner that he has, or has not, some high cards that will be useful even when the opener has an unbalanced hand. The 2♣ opener may have the firm intention to play in one of his own suits and in that case he would rather find one ace in the responding hand than a long suit headed by the Q–J.

For a positive response *in a suit* the responder requires not just 7 points, but certain high-card combinations, called quick tricks. At the two level one quick trick, an ace anywhere or K–Q in the suit named, is the minimum. At the three level the approximate standard is one and one-half quick tricks; that is, a suit headed by the A–Q, or one headed by the ace or K–Q, with another king elsewhere.

When scattered values, rather than quick tricks, are held the responder may bid 2NT to show a balanced 8 to 9 points, 3NT to show 10 to 11. It is often advisable, however, to begin with 2◇ even when you hold moderate values. Suppose your partner bids 2♣ and you hold:

(1) ♠ Q 10 7  ♡ 5  ◇ Q 9 8 4 3  ♣ K J 6 2
(2) ♠ Q 8 4  ♡ A J 9 8  ◇ 9 7 6 3  ♣ 10 4
(3) ♠ 9 6  ♡ 8 5 2  ◇ Q 7 6  ♣ A Q 8 4 3

On hand (1) neither 2NT nor 3◇ commends itself. It is best to bid 2◇ and await an opportunity to express the value. Hand (2) is borderline; some players would prefer the hearts to be stronger for a positive response—either A–J–10–x or a five-card suit. However, a positive response of 2♡ is reasonable. Hand (3) represents about a minimum for a positive response in a minor suit.*

Rebids by the 2♣ bidder follow a natural path but there is one sequence with a special meaning. This occurs when opener makes a *jump* rebid in any suit over his partner's response.

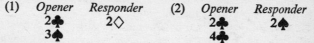

| (1) | *Opener* | *Responder* | | (2) | *Opener* | *Responder* |
|-----|----------|-------------|---|-----|----------|-------------|
| | 2♣ | 2◇ | | | 2♣ | 2♠ |
| | 3♣ | | | | 4♣ | |

In each case the opener is showing a solid suit, at least A–K–Q–J–x–x or A–K–Q–x–x–x–x. This type of rebid does not necessarily promise extra values but it fixes the trump suit and thus enables attention to be concentrated on outside controls. Any subsequent bid in a new suit would be a cue-bid.

* Some systems use what are known as " ace responses " to 2♣. Then 2◇ denies an ace, 2♡, 2♠, 3♣ and 3◇ show the ace of the suit named, 2NT shows about 8 points with no ace, and 3NT shows two aces.

A player who has shown 0 to 6 points by responding negatively should look for an opportunity to describe his hand still more accurately within the limits already shown. For example, with support for opener's suit he has the choice of raising immediately, which is mildly encouraging, or of first making a further negative bid in notrumps. With a notrump-type hand responder may on occasion be able to afford a jump to show modest values. The bidding goes:

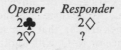

| Opener | Responder |
|--------|-----------|
| 2♣ | 2♦ |
| 2♡ | ? |

Responder holds:

| | | | |
|--|--|--|--|
| (1) ♠ 7 | ♡ J 10 8 2 | ◇ Q 7 5 3 | ♣ K 10 8 3 |
| (2) ♠ 9 4 | ♡ 10 8 7 5 | ◇ 9 8 3 | ♣ K 8 6 2 |
| (3) ♠ 8 3 | ♡ 9 6 4 2 | ◇ 9 7 5 | ♣ J 9 3 2 |
| (4) ♠ Q J 9 | ♡ 8 5 | ◇ J 10 6 2 | ♣ K 8 4 3 |

In (1) the responder could not have a better hand. If he had an ace he would raise to 3♡ to agree the suit and then cue-bid his ace on the next round. As it is, he should raise straight to 4♡, indicating a hand with good support but no ace.

With (2) the responder simply raises to 3♡. With (3) also the responder intends to play in hearts, but to warn partner of the pitiful values he first bids 2NT and then supports hearts on the next round.

With (4) a bid of 2NT would convey nothing and would leave responder with undisclosed values which might be difficult to express later. The proper bid is 3NT. It is most frustrating to hold a " power-house " and feel the dead weight of a partner who will not make any move with this type of responding hand.

When after an opening bid of 2♣ and a negative response of 2♦, the opener rebids 2NT or 3NT, responder, as over a 2NT opening, may make an artificial bid in clubs to inquire for four-card suits.

| Opener | Responder |
|--------|-----------|
| 2♣ | 2♦ |
| 3NT | 4♣ |

4♣ is conventional, with " Baron " responses as described in Chapter 5.

## Weak Two-bids

One advantage of proclaiming all game-going hands by an artificial bid of 2♣ is that 2♢, 2♡ and 2♠ are released for other purposes. It is common in Britain to play strong two-bids, but first we consider the use of these bids as a mild pre-emptive manoeuvre. The requirements favoured by most tournament players are:

(1) A six-card suit headed by at least the Q–J–10.

(2) 6 to 11 points in high cards with, usually, one and one-half or two quick tricks.

(3) Either five or six likely playing tricks, according to vulnerability.

(4) Little or no support for the other major suit.

This last stipulation is necessary because otherwise a responder with a fair hand including length in the unbid major would not know whether to keep the bidding open in the hope of a fit.

The weak two-bid is undoubtedly an effective weapon, but its use requires discipline, especially in first or second position. When disappointing results occur from its use, it is usually because players have ignored the standard requirements, especially the one relating to the strength of the trump suit.

## Responding to Weak Two-bids

Various methods have been suggested for responder. Most players agree on the desirability of treating 2NT as the only forcing response. A bid in a new suit is used by some to deny support for opener's suit and suggest an alternative contract, but we consider it more sensible, on grounds of frequency, to say that a bid of a new suit, while not forcing, is constructive. A direct raise to game serves a dual purpose: it may be based on a strong hand or it may be a pre-emptive manoeuvre. A single raise is usually played as defensive and not an invitation to game.

According to this method, a positive response of 2NT always shows at least the equivalent of an opening bid, although not necessarily a notrump type of hand.

Opener proceeds as follows:

(1) With a minimum hand he simply rebids his suit.

(2) With a solid suit, or a strong suit with a sure re-entry, he raises to 3NT.

(3) With a sound opening hand, but lacking the requirements for (2), he may show a side feature such as K–J–x or Q–x–x–x.

### Acol (Strong) Two-bids

This style of two-bid indicates a powerful suit and is forcing for one round. At least eight playing tricks are required and this means that a six-card suit will usually be present; but the bid can be used with two five-card suits and, exceptionally, with 5–4 in the major suits. Most hands that warrant an opening two-bid contain between 16 to 19 high-card points.

The following hands qualify for an Acol bid of 2♠:

(1) ♠ A K Q J 8 7 3   ♡ 9   ◇ A Q 2   ♣ 6 4

(2) ♠ A Q J 9 3   ♡ A K 10 9 2   ◇ 6   ♣ A 7

(3) ♠ A K J 5 3   ♡ K Q J 9   ◇ A J 8   ♣ 3

Hand (3), with spades and hearts, is the only 5–4 type where an Acol two is recommended.

With a borderline Acol two-bid opener asks himself: " If I open one and am passed out, is there a danger of missing a game? " The following hand is not strong enough for a bid of 2♣ and the choice therefore is between 2♡ and 1♡.

♠ A 6   ♡ A Q J 8 7 4   ◇ A K 8 3   ♣ 10

If partner has two or three hearts and an entry there is likely to be a play for game, so the hand should be opened with 2♡. This commits the partnership to the three level only.

### Responding to Acol Two-bids

The negative response to an Acol two is 2NT. (Some players use a " Herbert " response in the next highest suit.) After a negative response a simple rebid of opener's suit is not forcing but may be raised with one quick trick; very little is required in the way of trump support. A sequence such as 2♠–2NT–3◇ should be kept open to 3♠ at least.

The requirements for a positive response to an Acol two are somewhat higher than to 2♣. Partner should usually respond negatively whenever he holds less than 10 points in high cards, unless he has good support for opener or can bid a suit at the two level; in that case 7 or 8 points may suffice.

When you hold the requirements for a positive response, follow this scheme:

*With trump support and an outside ace* raise to three of opener's suit. Opener's next move will indicate whether he is interested in a slam. Note that Q-x of trumps or x-x-x constitute good trump support.

*With trump support but no outside ace* raise to four of opener's suit to indicate at least 11 points, including distribution; or bid a suit headed by at least the K-J and support opener's suit on the next round.

*Lacking trump support,* show a strong four-card suit at the two level, or a five-card suit at the three level, or jump to 3NT with all suits held.

One of the main advantages of the Acol two is that it copes well with strong two-suited hands where the responder would be likely to pass an opening bid of one. For example:

|  | Opener | Responder |
|---|---|---|
| ♠ | 5 | 10 8 6 4 |
| ♡ | A 8 | 7 6 4 |
| ◇ | A K Q 4 2 | 5 |
| ♣ | A Q 9 5 3 | K 8 7 6 2 |

The bidding goes:

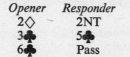

| Opener | Responder |
|---|---|
| 2◇ | 2NT |
| 3♣ | 5♣ |
| 6♣ | Pass |

Clearly East would have to pass an opening bid of 1◇. After his negative response to 2◇ he can safely indicate strong trump support by jumping in clubs.

### Forcing Two-bids

When the artificial 2♣ opening is not employed all two bids in a suit are forcing to game. The requirements for a two-bid are broadly the same as for a 2♣ bid, but the conventional negative response is 2NT. This response should always be given on hands of less than 7 points; some players give a negative response on stronger hands unless a quota of quick tricks, usually 1 or $1\frac{1}{2}$, in present.

Forcing two-bids are extremely inefficient as compared to the artificial 2♣ opening. They use four bids in place of one to introduce strong hands. They fail to provide a satisfactory treatment for hands of 23 to 24 points, which therefore have to be opened with 2NT. Moreover, the 2NT response, as a negative, is inefficient too; it gives the responder no chance to display scattered values and it often leads to the strong hand being displayed on the table, which is usually to the defenders' advantage.

## TWO-BIDS QUIZ

Your partner opens with a conventional game-forcing bid of 2♣. What is your call with each of the following?

| | | | | |
|---|---|---|---|---|
| (1) | ♠ A 10 8 | ♡ J 9 7 6 | ◇ J 7 | ♣ Q 9 6 3 |
| (2) | ♠ A 10 9 7 | ♡ K 4 2 | ◇ 8 3 | ♣ K 8 6 2 |
| (3) | ♠ Q 7 | ♡ 6 5 2 | ◇ A Q J 8 3 | ♣ 8 7 3 |
| (4) | ♠ Q J 8 | ♡ K 9 3 | ◇ 9 7 2 | ♣ A 10 8 3 |

(1) *2NT*. With 8 points in high cards you are over the limit for the conventional negative response of 2◇. As neither of the four-card suits is biddable and the hand contains only one quick trick, 2NT will portray your hand best.

(2) *2♠*. With 10 points in high cards this hand merits a positive response. The only question is whether to bid 2♠ or 2NT. As you hold an ace and two kings, a non-limited response of 2♠ is a better first move than 2NT or 3NT.

(3) *3◇*. If you respond with the negative bid of 2◇, being too mean to jump the bidding, you will never subsequently be able to convince partner that you hold such a strong hand. If you bid 2NT he will never believe that K–x of diamonds is worth five tricks.

(4) *3NT*. In response to 2♣, a suit such as A–10–x–x is biddable only at the two-level. A response of 3♣ would suggest a better suit.

With neither side vulnerable, your partner deals and opens with a weak 2♡ (6 to 11 points). What is your call with each of the following?

| | | | | |
|---|---|---|---|---|
| (5) | ♠ 8 | ♡ 8 4 3 | ◇ A K J 7 2 | ♣ K Q 9 3 |
| (6) | ♠ K 10 4 | ♡ 10 3 2 | ◇ A 8 7 6 3 | ♣ 9 7 |
| (7) | ♠ Q 6 | ♡ 5 | ◇ A 7 4 3 | ♣ A Q J 9 6 2 |
| (8) | ♠ A K 10 4 | ♡ J 6 | ◇ A J 9 7 | ♣ Q 3 2 |

(5) 4♡. Even if partner is in the minimum range you hope to make game for the loss of a spade, a trump and a club. A forcing response of 2NT would serve no useful purpose and might enable the opponents to compete in spades.

(6) 3♡. This may go one down, but the odds are that opponents can make at least nine tricks in their best suit. Remember that the single raise is defensive, not a game try.

(7) 3♣. This is not forcing, but if partner can raise the clubs you may make a game in this suit.

(8) 2NT. With this hand you want to know more about partner's range, so you force with 2NT. If partner bids 3NT, showing solid hearts, you pass; if he bids clubs you convert to 3NT; if he shows a feature in diamonds you may take a chance on 4♡; if he signs off in 3♡, you give up.

With neither side vulnerable, the bidding goes:

| Opener | Responder |
|--------|-----------|
| 2♠ (weak two) | 2NT |
| ? | |

What is your call with each of the following?

(9)   ♠ K Q J 7 3 2    ♡ 8 5    ◇ 9    ♣ K 10 3 2

(10) ♠ A K Q 10 4 3    ♡ 5 4    ◇ 8 6    ♣ 8 4 2

(11) ♠ K J 10 8 3 2    ♡ K 2    ◇ 10 7 6    ♣ 9 3

(9) 3♣. As you are not vulnerable you could be appreciably weaker. Your hand ranks as nearly a maximum 2♠ and therefore a sign-off of 3♠ should be avoided. Instead you show a secondary feature by bidding the clubs.

(10) 3NT. You are justified in offering this raise because the spade suit can be treated as solid. Responder will probably pass or remove to 4♠, according to the nature of his hand. He may, of course, have higher ambitions.

(11) 3♠. This hand must be regarded as in the minimum range and accordingly you simply rebid your suit.

Your partner opens with an Acol 2♡ bid. What is your call with each of the following?

(12) ♠ K J 3    ♡ J 9 2    ◇ 8 7 5 4 3    ♣ 9 6

(13) ♠ 8 6    ♡ Q 4 3 2    ◇ A 10 7 2    ♣ Q J 9

(14) ♠ 10 4    ♡ K 7    ◇ J 8 7 4 3    ♣ K Q J 2

(12) *2NT*. Your hand is very suitable for a heart contract, but before supporting you must give the conventional negative response to show a lack of high cards.

(13) 3♡. This response guarantees trump support and an ace. Having set the trump suit, you intend to cue-bid the ◇ A on the next round unless partner indicates lack of slam interest by simply raising 3♡ to 4♡. In that case you would pass, having little extra to announce.

(14) 3♣. No doubt this hand will be played in hearts, but a direct raise of opener's suit would show an ace. 3♣ is preferred to 3◇ as a positive response to an Acol two should promise at least the king of the suit named.

# PART II

*Defensive Bidding*

# CHAPTER 7

## Overcalls

*The simple overcall – Responding to an overcall – Overcalls in notrumps – The strong jump overcall – The weak jump overcall – The cue-bid overcall – Overcalls in fourth position*

AN OVERCALL is a bid made after the opponents have opened. It differs greatly from an opening bid in terms of strength and in its objectives.

The opening bidder tends to assume, for the moment, that he and his partner hold the balance of power and that it will pay to explore the possibilities of the two hands. A player who overcalls is frequently trying to disrupt this process or suggest a likely lead or sacrifice. With a hand strong enough to offer a good chance of outbidding the opening side he would be more likely to double for takeout (see next Chapter) than to make a simple overcall.

Yet although the role of the overcall is partly negative, it has an important place in the scheme of things. The sound use of overcalls also requires judgment, for here the point count is a much less reliable guide than in the uncontested auction.

### The Simple Overcall

A simple overcall is a bid in a suit at the minimum level, such as 1♡ over 1♣ or 2♢ over 1♠. The upper limit of strength is about equal to a sound but not far from minimum opening; with a stronger hand some other form of action is preferred. There is no formal lower limit and overcalls which have a good tactical purpose are sometimes made on as little as 7 or 8 points.

More important than point count is the strength of the suit and the number of tricks the hand is likely to take. Most overcalls are based on at least a five-card suit, but an overcall at the one level may be made on a sound four-card suit; especially 1♠, which has the virtue of shutting out a response of 1♡.

Since overcalling is closely associated with the takeout double and other forms of competitive action, it may be useful to present an outline of the overall scheme for defensive bidding by second hand after a suit opening.

| *Type of hand* | *Action by second hand* |
|---|---|
| One-suited hand (exceptionally, two-suited), not more than 15 points, including distribution. | Overcall at the lowest level. With a two-suited hand bid the longer suit, or the higher ranking when of equal length. |
| One- or two-suited hand, at least 16 points. | Either double for takeout, or make a strong jump overcall with a six-card suit. |
| Tolerance for the three unbid suits, at least 13 points in high cards. | A takeout double is the only recommended action. |
| Guard in opener's suit, 16 to 18 points in high cards. | Bid 1NT unless the hand is unbalanced and suitable for a takeout double. |

Obviously, this is only a brief sketch of the scheme of defensive bidding. On many hands which possess the superficial requirements for an overcall it may be politic to stay out of the auction. We consider now the tactical reasons that may prompt a simple overcall.

(1) *To obstruct the opponents' bidding.* This is one of the most important aims in competitive bidding. When you have this object in mind you should ask yourself whether an overcall is really likely to thwart the opponents to any extent. For example, with neither side vulnerable, the player on your right opens 1◇ and you hold:

(1) ♠ 7 5   ♡ K J 9 4   ◇ J 6 5   ♣ A J 7 2
(2) ♠ 8 6   ♡ Q 5 2   ◇ 9 4   ♣ A Q 10 8 7 3

With (1) you are not likely to come to any great harm if you bid 1♡, but there is no obstructive value in the manoeuvre: the next player will still be able to make whatever call he intended. But exchange the hearts and spades, and there is then some purpose in overcalling with 1♠, as this at least denies third hand the opportunity to respond 1♡.

With (2) a bid of 2♣ may make it awkward for the next player to introduce either hearts or spades, and this may cause a major-suit fit to be "lost". There is a case for the overcall despite the very meagre values.

(2) *To reach a makable contract.* The general idea in competitive bidding is that most good hands should be introduced with a double, but there are some useful hands which lack the distributional requirements for such a call. The choice may then be between a simple overcall and a pass; the rank of your main suit will usually be the determining factor. With neither side vulnerable, the player on your right bids 1♦ and you hold:

(1) ♠ 8 2   ♡ A J 9 3   ♦ A 5 4 3   ♣ A J 2

(2) ♠ 10 7   ♡ A 7 3   ♦ K J 6 3   ♣ A J 8 4

Hand (1) is a case where an overcall of 1♡ is justified on a four-card suit. The bid has no obstructive value, but as you have the equivalent of a sound opening bid there is a possibility that the hand belongs to your side. You cannot double for takeout as your spade support is non-existent and you have no compensating values. It would be quite unsound to double and then proceed with 1NT over 1♠.

Hand (2) is also unsuitable for a takeout double and not strong enough for 1NT. As it is unsafe to overcall at the two level with a four-card suit you must pass, at any rate for the time being.

(3) *To reach an economical sacrifice.* This motive often prompts an overcall when the opening side is vulnerable and the defending side is not, and especially when the overcaller's suit is spades. A bid of 1♠ may then be justified on as little as this:

♠ Q J 10 4 3   ♡ 7 3   ♦ A 10 8   ♣ 8 6 5

Suppose your partner deals and passes and next hand bids one of a suit. The prospects of saving a vulnerable game at the cost of a modest penalty is attractive enough to justify 1♠. With such a weak hand an overcall is sound only at the one level; to bid at the two level, when the main motive is a sacrifice, would require something like:

♠ K 6   ♡ 8 4 2   ♦ 9 8   ♣ K Q 9 8 6 3

This 10-point hand is just about worth a non-vulnerable bid of 2♣ over 1♠.

(4) *To suggest an opening lead.* This is one of the less important motives for an overcall, but nevertheless, since partner will usually lead your suit, it is a consideration to be borne in mind when other

matters are not decisive. With both sides vulnerable, the dealer bids 1◇ and you hold:

  (1) ♠ 7 4 3    ♡ A Q J 9  ◇ K 9 2  ♣ J 7 5

  (2) ♠ J 7 6 4 3  ♡ K 7     ◇ J 8 4   ♣ A Q 2

  (3) ♠ 9        ♡ Q 10 6 2 ◇ 8 4    ♣ K Q J 6 3 2

With (1) the desire to suggest a heart lead swings the balance in favour of an overcall of 1♡. There is the further possibility that the heart overcall may deter the opponents from bidding 3NT. In (2) your suit is spades and you are more likely to buy the contract, but if you don't, there is the disadvantage that a lead by your partner from either the ace, king or queen could well cost a trick; therefore a pass is better than 1♠. With the third hand an overcall of 2♣ might prove expensive, but against that, (a) you show a sound lead against any contract, and (b) you may stop the opponents from bidding 3NT, because they will not know that you have no fast entry for your club suit.

## Responding to an Overcall

It may seem reasonable, on the surface, to respond to an overcall in similar fashion as to an opening bid, but actually quite a different technique is needed. This is because overcalls have certain constant factors: at least a fair suit may be presumed, and the point-count range is narrower.

An opening bid is often a tentative move to get the ball rolling; it may not even be the opener's best suit. An overcall is usually based on a one-suited hand; whether the partner of the overcaller likes this suit or not, there is seldom much future in looking elsewhere for a fit.

As the overcaller's upper limit is little more than the strength of a minimum opening, the responder should usually give up the quest for game unless he himself has opening values. In most cases he simply passes, but a neutral response, such as a single raise or a minimum bid in notrumps, is not ruled out as a tactical move. Note that a takeout into a new suit, which is not forcing, is not classed as a neutral response: it suggests a dislike for the overcaller's suit. With neither side vulnerable the bidding goes:

| Opponent | Partner | Opponent | You |
|----------|---------|----------|-----|
| 1♣ | 1♠ | Pass | ? |

You hold:

(1) ♠ 9 3　♡ A J 9　◇ A 8 7 4 3　♣ J 6 4
(2) ♠ 7 5　♡ K 10 6　◇ A 10 8 2　♣ Q J 9 3

With (1) you pass. You have less than opening values and can therefore see no prospect of game. You intend to compete to the level of 2♣ if necessary, but it would be misleading to venture into 2♣ freely at this point and your hand is not suitable for either 1NT or 2◇, which would suggest a better suit.

With (2) it is right to bid 1NT, for this describes the hand well. In this case you would not continue with a competitive bid in spades if the opponents reopened; having shown your values you would leave partner to judge, as he would have a better appreciation of the combined hands.

When three-card support is held, it is usually correct to give a direct raise; a two-level overcall is sometimes raised on a doubleton. The bidding goes:

| Opponent | Partner | Opponent | You |
|----------|---------|----------|-----|
| 1♠ | 2♡ | 2♠ | ? |

The following would present a satisfactory raise to 3♡:

♠ 9 5 3　♡ 10 7　◇ K 10 3 2　♣ A K 7 2

A direct raise may also be made on various other hands where tactical considerations, especially vulnerability, enter the reckoning. Suppose that the opponents are vulnerable and you are not. The bidding goes:

| Opponent | Partner | Opponent | You |
|----------|---------|----------|-----|
| 1♣ | 1♠ | Pass | ? |

You might raise to 2♠ with either of these:

(1) ♠ Q 10 3　♡ 7 3　　◇ K J 8 6 4 2　♣ 9 6
(2) ♠ J 8 4 3　♡ A 9 7 6 5　◇ Q J 3　　♣ 8

With (1) the raise is purely tactical; the opponents very probably have a heart fit, perhaps a game, and the raise may either obstruct them or lead to a sacrifice. You do not really expect to register a plus score, but you are not likely to come to much harm.

Hand (2) is much more promising but the simple raise is still sufficient. The possibility of reaching 4♠ is not entirely ruled out, but as it is unlikely that the opponents can make a game, the first consideration must be not to jeopardize the part score that your side can assuredly make. At this vulnerability, the overcaller may be quite weak and you proceed cautiously. At any other vulnerability you would raise to 3♠. Note that your hand is worth 11 points in support of spades, and partner could, in theory, have 15.

### Responding with a Strong Hand

When your partner overcalls and you have the equivalent of a minimum opening bid you may hope, but not necessarily expect, to make a game; it depends on whether the hands fit. With most of these hands you make a jump response, either in partner's suit or in notrumps.

| Opponent | Partner | Opponent | You |
|----------|---------|----------|-----|
| 1♡ | 1♠ | Pass | ? |

| (1) | ♠ 10 7 2 | ♡ A 7 | ◇ A Q 8 5 3 | ♣ K 4 3 |
| (2) | ♠ 9 4 | ♡ K Q 9 | ◇ J 10 4 3 | ♣ A Q 10 6 |

On (1), with opening values and three-card support, you jump to 3♠; with (2) to 2NT. Neither bid is forcing.

When assessing the response to an overcall, the responder must be very conscious of the score. Consider this sequence:

| Opponent | Partner | Opponent | You |
|----------|---------|----------|-----|
| 1◇ | 2♣ | Pass | ? |

You hold:

♠ Q J 8   ♡ A J 6 3   ◇ K J 3   ♣ 10 9 2

Suppose, first, that your side is vulnerable. In that case it would be timorous to bid less than 3NT. Partner is likely to have a sound six-card suit and a high card elsewhere, and you must not expect him to bid the same values twice. Not vulnerable, and especially against vulnerable opponents, partner may have chanced his arm with a motley assortment. Therefore you would bid only 2NT and if doubled you would give serious thought to retreating to 3♣.

As in most competitive situations, when you hope to reach game but cannot be sure of the best contract, a cue-bid in the enemy suit is the great stand-by.

| Opponent | Partner | Opponent | You |
|----------|---------|----------|-----|
| 1♠ | 2♢ | Pass | ? |

You would bid 2♠ now with either of these hands:

(1) ♠ A 7  ♡ A 2  ♢ J 8 4 3  ♣ K Q 10 9 3

(2) ♠ 10 8 2  ♡ A 9 3 2  ♢ K J 3  ♣ A J 6

With the first hand you propose to reach game in any event. With the second you hope that partner, over 2♠, will be able to bid no-trumps. If he bids 3♢ you will raise to 4♢, another strong try for game.

## When Partner's Overcall is Doubled

Players who rescue their partner in this situation merely because they are short in his suit soon go broke, but at the same time Casabianca (the boy who stood on the burning deck) would not necessarily have been a big winner either. The true test is not so much whether your suit may be better than your partner's, but whether your hand is likely to be more useful to him than his to you.

| Opponent | Partner | Opponent | You |
|----------|---------|----------|-----|
| 1♠ | 2♣ | Double | ? |

(1) ♠ 9 7 6  ♡ J 5 2  ♢ A K 8 7 4 3  ♣ 10

(2) ♠ 10 4 3  ♡ A Q 4 3  ♢ J 9 8 6 2  ♣ 7

(3) ♠ Q 9 2  ♡ Q J 9 8 7 2  ♢ 9 3  ♣ 6 2

On the first two hands you should pass the double. Partner's overcall in this situation would be pointless if not based on a good suit, and your hand contains quick tricks that will surely be of assistance. Hand (3), by contrast, can hardly be a great deal of use to partner in 2♣ doubled. You should remove to 2♡, hoping that partner's assets will include one or two quick tricks.

## Overcalls in Notrumps

1NT directly over an opponent's opening shows 16 to 18 points, similar to a strong 1NT opening bid. There must, of course, be a guard in the opponent's suit.

This is a good overcall, for it gives a full picture of your basic values straight away. Therefore you shouldn't be too strict about the hand pattern. With a hand of this strength the only other call is a takeout double, and you should be willing to bid 1NT on quite an eccentric pattern if your hand is not really suitable for a double. After 1♠ on your right, these hands are all best expressed by 1NT:

(1) ♠ A Q J    ♡ 3 2    ◇ K Q J    ♣ K J 8 5 3

(2) ♠ K 7    ♡ J 7    ◇ A K Q 10 5    ♣ K 9 3 2

(3) ♠ K J 8 6 3    ♡ K 5    ◇ K J 2    ♣ A Q 10

On hand (1) there is no sound alternative; a double is most unattractive with such a poor holding in the unbid major suit. With (2) you might bid 2◇ if vulnerable, but 1NT is more dynamic. With (3) a " trap pass " would be in order against vulnerable opponents.

Responses to a notrump overcall follow the same pattern as after a notrump opening. It is possible, too, to use the Stayman convention, proceeding as though the opening bid had not been made. The alternative, and more usual, method is to employ a cue-bid in the opener's suit as a substitute for the Stayman convention. For example:

| Opponent | Partner | Opponent | You |
|----------|---------|----------|-----|
| 1◇ | 1NT | Pass | 2◇ |

This asks partner to show a four-card major or rebid notrumps. The cue-bid in this situation may be based on no more than 7 or 8 points, enough for 2NT, at least when the location of the main enemy strength is known.

### The 2NT Overcall

This bid is often assigned a conventional meaning, the Unusual Notrump described in Chapter 14 being a prime example. When used in a natural sense, 2NT suggests a hand too strong for 1NT and containing a good minor suit. Bid 2NT over 1♠ with this type:

♠ K 10 3    ♡ 8 4 3    ◇ A K Q 9 3    ♣ A Q

With one more diamond the bid would be 3NT. With a stronger and more balanced hand the correct procedure is to double first and bid notrumps on the next round.

## The Strong Jump Overcall

The traditional use of the jump overcall is to show a fairly powerful one-suited hand in sequences like the following:

| (1) | *Opponent* | *Overcaller* | (2) | *Opponent* | *Overcaller* |
|---|---|---|---|---|---|
| | 1♣ | 2♡ | | 1♠ | 3◇ |

The single jump, not forcing, suggests at least a six-card suit. The high-card strength, depending on vulnerability and level, may range from the equivalent of an average opening hand up to about 16 points. With a stronger hand it is better to double first.

In response to a jump overcall it is usual to keep the bidding open with 7 points or more. Two small trumps or a singleton honour are enough for a raise, or even for a jump raise where two or three quick tricks are held. A change of suit is forcing for one round.

| | *Opponent* | *Partner* | *Opponent* | *You* |
|---|---|---|---|---|
| | 1◇ | 2♠ | Pass | ? |

| | | | | |
|---|---|---|---|---|
| (1) | ♠ 8 4 3 | ♡ A 7 | ◇ 10 6 3 2 | ♣ K Q 7 4 |
| (2) | ♠ 8 6 | ♡ J 8 5 | ◇ J 6 4 | ♣ A Q 8 3 2 |

With (1) jump to 4♠. You would bid 3♠ without the ♣K. With (2) bid 3♣, forcing for one round. Partner may be able to bid 4♠ or 3NT.

## The Weak Jump Overcall

The use of a single jump as a pre-emptive manoeuvre, on a hand containing a six-card suit and no more than two quick tricks, is popular with many tournament players, who contend that hands suitable for a strong jump overcall can well be introduced with a takeout double. One point in favour of the weak jump overcall is that it narrows the range of the simple overcall. Suppose the player on your right opens 1◇ and you hold:

| | | | | |
|---|---|---|---|---|
| (1) | ♠ K Q 9 8 6 3 | ♡ 7 3 | ◇ K 4 | ♣ 10 8 4 |
| (2) | ♠ J 2 | ♡ 10 8 | ◇ 9 7 4 | ♣ A Q J 10 5 3 |
| (3) | ♠ 9 3 | ♡ A 2 | ◇ 10 7 2 | ♣ A K 10 4 3 2 |

The first two are suitable for a weak jump overcall. The third hand contains rather too much in the way of quick tricks and qualifies for 2♣. Note that, playing strong jump overcalls, you would have to make a simple overcall with all three hands.

### The Cue-bid Overcall (" direct cue-bid ")

The term " cue-bid " is used to cover several quite different situations. In constructive bidding it means showing an ace when a trump suit has been fixed. In a contested auction, a suit which has been called by the opponents may be cue-bid at any stage to create a forcing situation. We are concerned here with the occasions when second hand makes an immediate, or direct, cue-bid in the suit which has been called on his right.

*Opener*   *Overcaller*
1◇     2◇

The traditional use of this cue-bid is to show a very powerful hand which for one reason or another is not suitable for a takeout double. The cue-bid does not necessarily show a particular holding in the opener's suit. Hands strong enough for a cue-bid do not occur often, and insisting on control limits the use still further. Cue-bid 2◇ over 1◇ on any of the following hands:

(1) ♠ 7     ♡ A K J 8 4 3 2 ◇ 8 6 ♣ A Q J

(2) ♠ K Q J 9 2 ♡ A K 10 9 4   ◇ –   ♣ K Q 5

(3) ♠ K 5     ♡ A 4 2     ◇ J  ♣ A K Q J 9 4 3

With none of these is game a certainty, but a takeout double would be no solution and could work out poorly if a competitive situation developed and partner persisted in bidding his own suit. With (1) you intend to persevere with hearts. With (2) you want to bid both suits and cannot afford the risk that partner may pass a double of 1◇. With (3) you hope partner will be able to bid no-trumps in time; if he can't, the bidding may still die in 4♣.

### Overcalls in Fourth Position

When an opening bid is followed by two passes, competitive action by the fourth player does not require the same values as by second hand.

*Opponent*  *Partner*  *Opponent*  *You*
1♡    Pass    Pass    1♠
                          (or 1NT)

These bids in fourth position promise less than if they were immediate overcalls. The theory is that the third-hand player must be very weak to pass his partner's opening bid, and your partner may have passed with quite a fair hand that was not well suited to immediate competitive action.

The weak jump overcall clearly has no existence in fourth position. The jump is needed for intermediate hands like this:

(1) ♠ K Q J 5 3 2    ♡ 8 7     ◇ A 10 6    ♣ 9 7
(2) ♠ K 7          ♡ 10 9 6   ◇ J 8      ♣ A K Q 9 3 2

In fourth position 1NT shows 11 to 14 points. This too is a good competitive manoeuvre, not only because it is descriptive but also because there is often advantage in forcing the strong opponent, the one who has opened, to make the opening lead. So, 1NT is the best move on most balanced hands in this range, even when no guard is held in opener's suit.

| Opponent | Partner | Opponent | You |
|----------|---------|----------|-----|
| 1♠       | Pass    | Pass     | ?   |

Reopen with 1NT on any of these hands:

(1) ♠ K 4 2   ♡ K J 9 3   ◇ A 7 5      ♣ Q 10 3
(2) ♠ Q 6    ♡ A 7 4     ◇ Q 8 6 3 2  ♣ A Q 5
(3) ♠ J 10 3  ♡ K J 2     ◇ Q J 7 5    ♣ K Q 10

In (1) you have strength in the unbid major but all the same 1NT is better than a double as you do not want the opening lead to come through your ♠K. In either (2) or (3) your chances of a double stop will be better if you play the hand, as you may find partner with A–x–x or K–x–x of spades.

A player who reopens in fourth position is said to " protect " or " balance ". The same sort of tactics may be employed at any stage when both opponents have bid but have faded out at a low level.

| Opponent | You  | Opponent | Partner |
|----------|------|----------|---------|
| 1♡       | Pass | 2♡       | Pass    |
| Pass     | ?    |          |         |

You hold:

♠ 10 7 5 4 3   ♡ 9 4 2   ◇ A 7   ♣ K J 2

A bid of 1♠ on the first round would have been inadvisable, but it is sound tactics to bid 2♠ now. Partner will not place you with more in view of your pass, and the chances of being doubled are slight.

This is a useful principle to bear in mind: *Don't let opponents play in a contract of their own choice at the level of one or two.* Try to push them to the three level at least. Once in six, perhaps, you may push them to game and see them make it; but the part-score swings you will have gained on the other occasions will be ample compensation. We shall have more to say about this aspect of bidding in Chapter 16.

## OVERCALLS QUIZ

With neither side vulnerable, the player on your right opens with 1♣. What is your call with each of the following?

(1) ♠ Q J 8 7 3 2  ♡ A 6  ◇ 8  ♣ 10 7 4 2

(2) ♠ K J 2  ♡ K 6  ◇ K J 9 4  ♣ A J 9 3

(3) ♠ 4 3  ♡ A K J 6  ◇ A 8 2  ♣ J 9 8 2

(1) 1♠. Despite the shortage of high-card strength, you should not allow yourself to be silenced when you have such a robust spade suit. If you were playing weak jump overcalls the hand would qualify for 2♠.

(2) 1NT. This is an ideal hand for 1NT, indicating the equivalent of a normal 1NT opening, with the adverse suit well held. The major-suit holdings are not suitable for a double.

(3) 1♡. This is one of the occasions where an overcall with a four-card suit is recommended. With a sound major suit and 13 points you are averse to being shut out but are not keen to double for takeout with such a weak spade holding.

With neither side vulnerable, the player on your right opens with 1♡. What is your call with each of the following?

(4) ♠ 10 4  ♡ Q J 2  ◇ A K J 8 7  ♣ 8 3 2

(5) ♠ 8 4  ♡ A 6 3  ◇ Q 8 6 3  ♣ A K 7 4

(6) ♠ A K J 8 3  ♡ 10 5  ◇ A 2  ♣ A Q J 3

(4) 2◇. There is a risk in overcalling at the two level, and a pass would not by any means be wrong. At the same time, 2◇ may make it difficult for the next player to introduce the spade suit.

(5) *Pass*. Despite the presence of 13 points in high cards, no form of intervention is safe with this hand. To bid 2♣ on a four-card suit would be highly dangerous. As for a double, it is a sound principle

not to employ this weapon with minimum values when support for the unbid major is lacking.

(6) *Double.* Since an overcall would not reflect the full values, the recommended procedure is to double for takeout. If partner responds 2◇ you intend to bid 2♠, indicating a hand of this type.

You are East, with both sides vulnerable, and the bidding goes:

| South | West | North | East |
|-------|------|-------|------|
| 1◇ | Pass | 1♡ | ? |

What is your call with each of the following?

(7) ♠ K J 8 4 3    ♡ J 8 4    ◇ K 6    ♣ A 7 2

(8) ♠ Q 9 8 6    ♡ A 4    ◇ 8 3    ♣ A K J 8 5

(9) ♠ Q 8 4    ♡ K Q 7 3    ◇ A Q    ♣ J 8 7 2

(7) *Pass.* Here both opponents have bid and it is at least possible that your partner is very weak. If you intervene you may be caught for 800 or more. It is right to pass now. If South bids 2◇ or 2♡, and this comes round to you, then you may think about competing with 2♠.

(8) *Double.* Although your clubs are much stronger than the spades, it is better to double than to bid 2♣. The double suggests interest in the unbid major suit, and this after all represents your best chance of outbidding the opponents.

(9) *Pass.* With so much of your strength in the opponents' suits, the hand is unsuitable for a takeout double. The possibility of doubling on the next round is not excluded if the bidding peters out at a low level. To intervene with 1NT could be to lay your head on the block.

With neither side vulnerable, the player on your left opens with 1◇ and your partner overcalls with 1♠. After a pass by the next player, what is your call with each of the following?

(10) ♠ 6 2    ♡ Q J 6 4    ◇ A Q J    ♣ 10 8 7 2

(11) ♠ 10 7 2    ♡ Q 2    ◇ 9 8 4 3    ♣ A K 9 7

(12) ♠ J 5    ♡ A K 4 3    ◇ J 10 2    ♣ A Q J 7

(10) *1NT.* In response to an overcall, 1NT is forward-going and indicates about 8 to 11 points. With a weaker hand you would pass,

for partner's hand is limited by his failure to double. Partner probably has no more than the equivalent of a modest opening, and he may have less.

(11) 2♠. It would not be constructive to bid 2♣ with this hand. Partner's overcall suggests a one-suited type of hand and if you fail to support him he will fear a misfit. Besides, 2♣ would not be forcing and partner might well pass.

(12) 2◇. With 16 points in high cards, and tolerance for spades, it is reasonable to get your sights on game, but the safest contract is unclear. It may be 4♠ (if partner's spade suit is rebiddable), 3NT (if partner has a diamond bolster), or even 4♡ (if partner has a secondary heart suit). You cannot explore with a simple response in a new suit, as you would over an opening, as such a response would not be forcing in this sequence.

To cover all the possibilities, you cue-bid the opponents' suit. Partner's next bid will suggest where the hand should be played.

With both sides vulnerable, the player on your left opens with 1♠, your partner passes and the next player passes. What is your call with each of the following?

| | | | |
|---|---|---|---|
| (13) ♠ 10 4 | ♡ 9 3 | ◇ K J 7 4 3 2 | ♣ A 8 7 |
| (14) ♠ Q 8 4 | ♡ Q 6 2 | ◇ A Q 10 8 | ♣ J 5 4 |
| (15) ♠ Q J 8 7 6 | ♡ A 5 | ◇ K 2 | ♣ J 10 7 4 |

(13) 2◇. When an opening bid is followed by two passes there is a good chance that the hand belongs to the defending side. Fourth hand is entitled to assume that his partner has fair strength. In this instance, with a six-card minor suit, it is certainly reasonable to compete for the partial.

(14) 1NT. The choice is between trying to defeat 1♠ or bidding 1NT, which is a more attractive call than 2◇ or a double. A pass would have more to commend it if you had four trumps, and 1NT, which in this sequence indicates 11 to 14 points, is preferred.

(15) Pass. The object of bridge is to win points, and in this instance the goal can best be achieved by passing. The opponents are almost certainly in their worst contract, and any form of action would allow them to improve their lot.

You are West, with neither side vulnerable, and the bidding has proceeded:

106

| South | West | North | East |
|-------|------|-------|------|
| *1♣* | *Pass* | *Pass* | *2♦* |
| Pass | ? | | |

What is your call with each of the following?

(16) ♠ K Q 9   ♡ K 8 7   ♦ A 10 4   ♣ Q 6 5 2

(17) ♠ J 7   ♡ J 8 3   ♦ Q 10 4   ♣ A K 7 6 4

(18) ♠ A 7 4   ♡ K 7 6 4 2   ♦ K J 8 7   ♣ 9

(16) 2NT. When partner has reopened in the balancing position you should proceed with caution until his values are confirmed. He may be bidding partly on the strength of your hand. Therefore you should content yourself with 2NT, which suggests 12 to 14 points. Had partner overcalled in second position the hand would have been well worth 3NT.

(17) 3♦. With two quick tricks, trump support, and a ruffing value, you can be hopeful of making 3♦. A bid of 3♣ would be wrong as it would suggest that you had reason to prefer that contract to 2♦ or 3♦.

(18) 4♦. You should not mind bypassing 3NT, because even if partner held a spade stopper the clubs might be wide open. It would not be a mistake to bid 2♠ and follow with diamond support. It is hardly worth mentioning the hearts, for the hand is sure to be worth extra tricks in diamonds.

107

# CHAPTER 8

## Takeout Doubles

*Requirements for a takeout double – Responding to a double – The doubler's rebid – Double in fourth position – Double by a passed hand – Double by a player who has opened – Responsive doubles*

THE PURPOSE of a takeout double is to show a strong hand after an opponent has opened the bidding. The double requests partner to bid his best suit in response. It is an effective and economical way of entering the auction.

It is naturally most important to know when a double is for takeout and when for penalty. A double immediately after an opponent has opened with one of a suit is always for takeout.

| Opener | Opponent |
|--------|----------|
| 1♡ | Double |

This double is for takeout. The initial presumption is that second hand has length in the unbid suits. A double is also for takeout when made immediately after both opponents have bid. Suppose you are fourth hand in this situation:

| Opponent | Partner | Opponent | You |
|----------|---------|----------|-----|
| 1♣ | Pass | 1♡ | Double |

This double too is for takeout, just as if it had been a double of an opening bid. Here the double suggests length in spades and diamonds. The general rule which indicates when a double is for takeout is:

A double of a suit contract at part-score level is for takeout *if made at the first opportunity of doubling and provided partner has not made a bid.*

Note that a takeout double of 1NT is not a takeout request. It is primarily an attempt to exact a penalty.

Later in the chapter we shall see that the takeout double can be employed in a variety of situations, including some where the doubler has opened the bidding. But first we consider the most common form of takeout double, which is when the right-hand opponent has opened with one of a suit.

## Requirements for a Takeout Double

When second hand doubles for takeout he should preferably have length in all three suits not bid by the opener; a 4–4–4–1 or 5–4–3–1 pattern is best, and 4–4–3–2 is acceptable. When this type of pattern is held, a double may be made with no more than 12 points in high cards, exceptionally 11. These hands all present a sound minimum double of a 1♠ opening:

(1) ♠ 7    ♡ A Q 7 4    ◇ Q 10 5 2    ♣ K J 6 3
(2) ♠ 8 3    ♡ K 10 9 4    ◇ K Q 8 2    ♣ A J 6
(3) ♠ 7    ♡ Q 10 7 4 2    ◇ A Q 8 4    ♣ K 9 3

When a hand is too strong for a simple overcall it may be right to double on less favourable patterns such as 5–4–2–2 or 6–3–2–2. But when you do that you must be strong enough to take care of a response by partner in your short suit. You must have enough tricks to let him play opposite your doubleton or you must have a suit of your own which you can bid over his response. There are, it is true, some awkward hands where neither course of action is ideal. For example:

♠ A 7    ♡ K 8 6 5 2    ◇ 8 4    ♣ A K J 6

A double is certainly better than an overcall of 2♡. If partner responds to the double by bidding 2◇ (as partners will) you bid 2♡, though the suit is weak for that sequence. Knowing that you have all-round strength, partner may remove to 3♣.

Like an opening bid, the takeout double has a range of up to about 20 points. But while it is right to open with all hands in the 13–20 range, it is not safe to double on all such hands. A double must either meet certain distributional standards or be based on extra strength.

*With no more than 15 points* the doubler should have at least three cards in each unbid suit. When the opening bid is in a major suit the doubler should have four cards, or at least a strong three-card holding, in the other major. Otherwise a simple overcall or a pass is recommended.

*With* 16 *points or more* a double is the standard move on all unbalanced hands and all balanced hands of more than 18 points. (Balanced hands of 16 to 18 points are shown by a direct overcall of 1NT.)

Whether or not to double with a minimum hand depends largely on which suit has been opened. Suppose you hold this hand:

♠ Q 10 8 2  ♡ K 7  ◇ K 9 2  ♣ A 10 4 3

You have a minimum, but sound, double of 1♡. The distribution is nothing to cheer about, but you can stand any response, and you have an important asset in four cards of the unbid major suit, which partner will bid if he can.

Now suppose that the opening is 1◇. It would be unsound to double with such poor support for hearts. Still less could you consider a double of 1♠.

♠ A 9 8 5  ♡ 3  ◇ K 8 4  ♣ A Q 10 9 7

Here you have a good double of 1♡. A 5–4–3–1 hand represents a more nimble force than 4–4–4–1. But it would still be incorrect to double 1◇ or 1♠; you have a sound alternative in 2♣.

With stronger unbalanced hands, 16 points or more, you may usually double regardless of your pattern. Since your hand will warrant a further bid, your lack of preparedness in one suit will not be fatal.

♠ J 4  ♡ A Q 7 3  ◇ A K 5 4 3  ♣ K 6

With this hand you have an obvious double of 1♣ or 1♠ as you can take care of any development. Over an opening 1♡ or 1◇, however, your best move would be 1NT or, against vulnerable opponents, a trap pass.

♠ A K J 10 5 2  ♡ 9 8 3  ◇ A 6  ♣ K 2

Here you would double first and bid spades over any response. The test with this type of one-suited hand is simply whether it is too strong for a simple overcall; if it is, you double. (We assume in this discussion that you are not playing strong jump overcalls. If you do play such overcalls you will often have an alternative to a double on hands with a long suit.)

## The Double When Both Opponents Have Bid

When the opponents have bid two suits a double asks partner to name one of the other suits, as in this sequence:

| Opponent | Partner | Opponent | You |
|----------|---------|----------|--------|
| 1♣ | Pass | 1♡ | Double |

A double here suggests the values for an opening bid, presumably with length in diamonds and spades. Doubles of this kind are not made on moderate hands unless the vulnerability conditions are favourable for a sacrifice. With only 4–4 in the unbid suits you would need about 14 points in high cards to double in the above sequence.

It is often advisable to pass with quite substantial values when the opponents have bid two suits.

♠ K J 9 3   ♡ A K J 2   ◇ Q 10 3   ♣ 8 4

Suppose the player on your left opens 1♣ and your partner passes. If next hand bids 1◇ you can comfortably double, but if he bids 1♡ or 1♠ you should pass.

A double of an opening 1NT is for penalties rather than takeout, but a double of a notrump *response* is quite different.

| Opponent | Partner | Opponent | You |
|----------|---------|----------|--------|
| 1♡ | Pass | 1NT | Double |

In this situation it is best to double on the same type of hand as if you were sitting directly over the opening suit bidder, except that you would not of course double now on a minimum hand. Partner is not debarred from passing for penalties, but in principle he is invited to respond in one of the unbid suits.

There has to be a point in the auction beyond which all doubles are primarily for penalties. The dividing line is the game level.

| Opponent | Partner | Opponent | You |
|----------|---------|----------|--------|
| 1♠ | Pass | 4♠ | Double |

In this auction the double does not promise trump tricks, but it will usually be left in. The doubler is showing at least four quick tricks and partner is not expected to take out unless he has a very long suit.

A double of 4♡, however, by a player who has not had the opportunity to speak, implies at least tolerance for a takeout into 4♠.

## Responding to a Double

The most important rule is that you must not pass except in the rare case where you have a long strong sequence in opener's suit. We deal with this first because any uncertainty leads to disaster.

| Opponent | Partner | Opponent | You |
|----------|---------|----------|-----|
| 1♡ | Double | Pass | ? |

This is the sort of hand with which you would pass, not because you are weak but because you expect to beat 1♡:

♠ 7  ♡ Q J 10 9 6 2  ◇ 8 4 3  ♣ 9 5 2

Note that your hearts are so strong that you would welcome a trump lead from your partner; and it is virtually a convention that he *should* lead a trump after a penalty pass.

Apart from this case, no matter how weak a hand you hold, you must not pass a takeout double. Suppose you are unfortunate enough to find yourself in this situation:

| Opponent | Partner | Opponent | You |
|----------|---------|----------|-----|
| 1♠ | Double | Pass | ? |

♠ 9 6 4  ♡ 10 5  ◇ 9 7 6 3 2  ♣ 8 5 4

You must bid 2◇. You may not make it, but if you pass, the opponents will be left playing in 1♠ doubled, with overtricks worth 100 or 200 a time. That would be much worse.

If the third hand bids over the double you are relieved of any obligation to enter the auction. The bidding goes:

| Opponent | Partner | Opponent | You |
|----------|---------|----------|-----|
| 1♡ | Double | 1♠ | ? |

Now you bid only when you have some values to show. We return to this subject below.

When responding to partner's takeout double you must distinguish between weak, moderate and useful holdings. With a minimum, obviously, you make a minimum response. This is how you act on better hands:

*With a medium hand* (*usually* 9 *to* 12 *points*) you make a jump response in a suit if most of your values are in the unbid suit. This is not forcing. When you have values in the opener's suit, you bid notrumps.

112

*With a strong hand (usually 13 points or more)* you either jump to game or make a forcing bid in the opponent's suit.

### Responding on Weak Hands (0 to 8 points)

With this type of hand the object is to find a fit at the lowest level. Since a double puts emphasis on the major suits it is often right to respond in a four-card major at the level of one rather than in a five-card minor at the level of two.

| Opponent | Partner | Opponent | You |
|----------|---------|----------|-----|
| 1♢ | Double | Pass | ? |

♠ 5  ♡ Q 8 7 3  ♢ 6 4 3  ♣ J 8 7 4 2

Bid 1♡ rather than 2♣. If partner continues with 1♠, then you may introduce the clubs.

The emphasis on major suits is such that you should often show one when it is not the cheapest response:

| Opponent | Partner | Opponent | You |
|----------|---------|----------|-----|
| 1♠ | Double | Pass | ? |

♠ 8 5 4  ♡ 10 9 7 3  ♢ A 8 6 2  ♣ 9 4

2♡, where you are very likely to have a 4–4 fit, is preferable to 2♢. When slightly stronger, it may be right to bid 2♡ on four cards rather than a five-card minor.

A 1NT response to a double does duty on a wide range of hands which do not fit neatly into the same categories as a suit response. In theory it is a mildly constructive response. Partner doubles 1♠ and you hold:

♠ Q J 8 3  ♡ J 2  ♢ J 4 3  ♣ K 7 6 2

This is the sort of hand your partner will expect when you bid 1NT, which is much more descriptive than a bid of 2♣. Sometimes, however, you will be obliged to reduce the standards:

♠ K 8 7 3  ♡ 10 4 2  ♢ J 6 2  ♣ 10 8 5

In response to a double of 1♠ there is no sensible alternative to 1NT.

When an opponent bids over the double it is right to pass most weak responding hands but advisable to enter when you have anything at all useful to contribute.

| Opponent | Partner | Opponent | You |
|----------|---------|----------|-----|
| 1♡ | Double | 2♡ | ? |

♠ Q 9 4 3   ♡ 8 5 2   ◇ 7 4   ♣ A 9 6 3

Since the doubler is very likely to have strength in the unbid major suit you are fully entitled to mention your spades.

A critical situation occurs when the third player redoubles. This will usually mean that the opening side holds distinctly the balance of the strength. Responses now are directed towards finding a fit at the lowest possible level; it is especially important for the responder to bid the next suit over opener's bid, should he hold it, lest the doubler remove to a higher level. The bidding goes:

| Opponent | Partner | Opponent | You |
|----------|---------|----------|-----|
| 1◇ | Double | Redouble | ? |

You hold:

(1) ♠ 6 3   ♡ 10 8 4 3 2   ◇ J 5 4   ♣ 9 4 2

(2) ♠ 9 8 4   ♡ Q 6 3   ◇ 10 7 2   ♣ 9 7 5 3

(3) ♠ 10 3   ♡ 8 6   ◇ J 5 3   ♣ Q J 9 7 6 2

With (1) bid 1♡ as otherwise partner may be obliged to make some bid at a higher level. With (2) pass. This does not mean that you wish the opponents to play the hand in 1◇ doubled, but that partner is to find his own resting-place. With (3) bid 2♣ without waiting for partner to bid a major. He will realize that you have a long suit.

## Responding on Medium Hands (*9 to 12 points*)

With these values responder may make a jump bid in a suit, encouraging but not forcing. This hand would be typical for a jump to 2♠ after partner had doubled 1♡:

♠ K 10 7 5 3   ♡ A 8 2   ◇ Q 10 8   ♣ 7 4

Observe that although this hand appears to have only 10 points including one for the fifth spade, it can be counted as worth 11. Partner is expected to have support for spades, and therefore a point can be added for the club shortage.

Here are two examples where the decision is close. Partner again doubles 1♡ and you hold:

(1) ♠ K J 6 3  ♡ 8 4 2  ◇ K J 10 6  ♣ J 3

(2) ♠ 9 4 2  ♡ K 4  ◇ Q 8 7 5  ♣ K J 6 2

In (1) you have only 9 points, but the four cards in the unbid major suit are a powerful recommendation. Also, all your points are in the unbid suits; an honour in hearts might well be wasted. You should bid 2♠ rather than 1♠.

In (2) also you have 9 points but you do not have four cards in the unbid major suit. A jump to 3♣ does not appeal, although if you had a slightly better hand, and no guard in the opponent's suit, there would be no alternative. As it is, 1NT, with a little more than partner might expect, is the best solution.

For a conventional way of responding in a competitive situation, see below, *Responsive Double*.


## Responding on Strong Hands (13 points or more)

With these values your hand will usually be worth a game opposite a takeout double. However, the point-count method has to be applied with some imagination, as this example will show. Partner doubles 1♠, next hand raises to 2♠, and you hold:

♠ 8 5 4  ♡ Q J 6 4 3  ◇ A K 4  ♣ 9 6

You have only 11 points, counting one for the fifth heart, but partner is very likely to have heart support and therefore you may add a point for the doubleton club. Now you have 12 points, and as 3♡ would sound " competitive " you take the strain off partner by jumping to 4♡.

When the responder's long suit is a minor he must think first in terms of notrumps. Holding a guard in the opponent's suit it is sometimes in order to bid notrumps with quite an unbalanced pattern. In response to a double of 1♡ you hold:

♠ 8  ♡ Q J 3  ◇ J 6 4  ♣ A K 8 7 3 2

Partner, in view of his double, can surely look after the spade suit, and it is reasonable to gamble on running the clubs. So, jump to 3NT.

A most valuable weapon when the best contract is in doubt is a cue-bid in the enemy suit. In many cases this is the only practical bid. Consider these hands after partner has doubled 1♦ and next hand has passed:

(1) ♠ Q 9 6 2    ♡ A 8 5 4    ♦ 8 3    ♣ A Q 10

(2) ♠ A          ♡ 10 9 2    ♦ 10 7 4    ♣ A K J 7 4 3

(3) ♠ K 8 7 4 3 ♡ 9 4     ♦ A 8 2    ♣ A 10 3

Bid 2♦ on each occasion. On (1) you want to discover partner's better major. On (2) you are too strong for 3♣ (which would be right without the ♠A). On (3) you do not want to plunge unilaterally into 4♠.

## The Doubler's Rebid

When you have doubled you do not have to bid again unless your partner cue-bids the opponent's suit. Indeed, it is usually unwise to bid again unless you have extra values, and even then you may still pass if partner's response has told you that there cannot be 26 points in the two hands. All the same, you are not obliged to pass just because you cannot see a game: sometimes you may bid again with the object of getting to a better part-score contract.

When partner has made a minimum response to your takeout double you must pass unless you have substantial extra values or a sound alternative suit.

♠ 9 6  ♡ K J 10 7  ♦ A K J 8 6  ♣ A 4

Suppose you double 1♠ and partner bids 2♡. With 18 points you are worth a raise to three, but no more. If partner's bid is 2♣ you bid simply 2♦.

When you hold a very strong double, say 20 or 21 points, you may give a jump raise with four-card support, or jump in a new suit. In either case your partner will bid again if he has 5 or 6 points. Suppose you double 1♡, your partner responds 2♦, and you hold:

(1) ♠ K Q 9       ♡ 5    ♦ A Q 8 4 3 ♣ A K 6 2

(2) ♠ A K 10 9 3 2 ♡ 4    ♦ K 8 4     ♣ A K J

(3) ♠ A Q 10 3   ♡ K 6  ♦ Q 7      ♣ A K Q 8 3

Hand (1) is worth 20 points in support of diamonds and therefore you should jump to four. If partner responded in spades your hand would be worth only 18 points and would not justify a jump.

Hand (2) is worth 20 points in its own right and therefore you bid 3♠ over partner's 2◇ response. With hand (3) the best move over 2◇ is 2NT.

*Partner has made a Jump Response in a Suit*

A bid in a new suit by you, the doubler, is now forcing. A raise of partner's suit is not. The bidding goes:

| Opponent | You | Opponent | Partner |
|---|---|---|---|
| 1◇ | Double | Pass | 2♠ |
| Pass | ? | | |

(1) ♠ Q 10 3   ♡ A K 7 5 2   ◇ 9 7   ♣ A Q 6

(2) ♠ A K J 2   ♡ 8 6   ◇ K Q 2   ♣ J 9 7 5

With (1) a game seems likely after partner's encouraging response and so you bid 3♡, indicating a five-card suit. You are pinning your hopes of game on partner having three-card support for hearts, or five spades, or a diamond guard. With (2) do not be misled by the strong spade holding, which was the principal part of the original double. Adding a point for shortness now that a fit has been found, you are just worth a raise to 3♠, for if partner has 11 points there will be 26 in the two hands.

### Double in Fourth Position

Like other calls in the " balancing " position, a takeout double may be made on less than is required in second position. The following would be about the minimum for a double of 1♡ at equal vulnerability:

♠ K 8 3 2   ♡ 6   ◇ Q 10 9 5   ♣ A 9 8 6

A double in the balancing position is passed for penalties much more often than a double in second position. This is because the partner now sits over, instead of under, the opponent; K–J–9–x–x may be worth four tricks instead of perhaps only one. Because of the possibility of a penalty pass, the fourth player should refrain from doubling when his defensive values are anything less than in the example above.

The player in second position must beware of overestimating his

117

hand in response to a double by fourth hand. Suppose you are second hand after this bidding:

| Opponent | You | Opponent | Partner |
|----------|-----|----------|---------|
| 1♠ | Pass | Pass | Double |
| Pass | ? | | |

You hold:

|      |            |            |              |            |
|------|------------|------------|--------------|------------|
| (1) ♠ | J 9 2 | ♡ K Q 6 3 | ◇ 8 5 | ♣ K 8 3 2 |
| (2) ♠ | K J 2 | ♡ Q 7 | ◇ Q 8 3 2 | ♣ Q 8 4 2 |
| (3) ♠ | K J 8 3 2 | ♡ Q 7 | ◇ A 10 2 | ♣ Q 7 3 |

With (1) bid only 2♡. Had partner doubled directly over an opening bid of 1♠ you would have jumped to 3♡, but in the present sequence your partner's hand may be little better than your own.

With (2) bid only 1NT. After a double in the protective position partner will allow for a 1NT response being made on a fair hand.

With (3) a penalty pass is indicated. Partner is expected to have some defensive strength and your strategically placed trump holding should produce a big penalty. After your penalty pass any further double by partner would be for penalties.

### Double by a Passed Hand

A player who has passed originally may double on a suitable hand pattern with quite limited strength. You are the dealer and the bidding goes:

| You | Opponent | Partner | Opponent |
|-----|----------|---------|----------|
| Pass | 1◇ | Pass | 1♡ |
| ? | | | |

It would be quite in order to double with this hand:

♠ A 9 8 6   ♡ A 10 3   ◇ 6   ♣ Q 9 6 4 3

The double is still for takeout because this is your first opportunity to double. The move is reasonable as you have just what partner would expect—not far short of an opening bid, with good support for both unbid suits.

### Double by a Player who has Opened

Takeout doubles are a valuable weapon for the opening side just as they are for the defenders. The bidding goes:

118

| Opener | Opponent | Responder | Opponent |
|--------|----------|-----------|----------|
| 1♣ | Pass | Pass | 2♦ |
| ? | | | |

Opener holds:

♠ A K J 4 2    ♡ Q 6 4 3    ♢ 7    ♣ A K 9

To pass or bid 2♠ would be poor tactics, as the hand is tailor-made for a double. With 17 points in high cards, and a most promising distribution, the chances are that the hand belongs to the opening side, despite partner's pass, and clearly a double leaves partner more room for manoeuvre than any other call. This can be seen by imagining that the responder in this example has one of the following:

| | | | |
|--|--|--|--|
| (1) ♠ 7 3 | ♡ J 9 7 2 | ♢ J 6 3 | ♣ 8 5 3 2 |
| (2) ♠ 5 | ♡ J 9 5 | ♢ J 10 8 4 3 | ♣ J 7 4 2 |
| (3) ♠ 6 | ♡ K 10 8 7 5 2 | ♢ 9 6 5 | ♣ 10 8 3 |

With (1) the responder bids 2♡. This contract will need less luck than 2♠, and the opponents can probably make 2♢ or 3♢. With (2) responder passes his partner's reopening double for penalty. Hand (3) is the one that opener deserves to find if he rebids 2♠ instead of reopening with a double. Responder jumps to 3♡ after a double, is raised to four and makes it. In 2♠ declarer may easily lose control.

A reopening double may be made on less when the responder has been denied the opportunity to bid at the one level.

| Opener | Opponent | Responder | Opponent |
|--------|----------|-----------|----------|
| 1♡ | 2♣ | Pass | Pass |
| Double | | | |

Here the responder may have a few points and so the double could be based on no more than:

♠ Q J 4    ♡ A Q 7 4 2    ♢ K 10 6    ♣ A 3

The double is far better than 2♡, for if the responder has values he is likely to be short in his partner's suit. If partner has fair defence to clubs and can pass the double, a useful penalty may follow.

### Responsive Doubles

When an opening bid is doubled for a takeout and the next player raises to the two or three level, the partner of the doubler may find himself in quite an awkward situation: he may have modest or even fairly substantial values, yet be unable to express them accurately. Suppose you are the fourth player in this sequence:

| Opponent | Partner | Opponent | You |
|----------|---------|----------|-----|
| 1♣ | Double | 3♣ | ? |

You hold:

♠ A 8 4 2    ♡ 10 8 6 3    ◇ K Q 2    ♣ 9 6

You could bid 3♡ or 3♠, but either might be the wrong choice. With a stronger hand you could bid 4♣, but here you do not want to go above the three level if partner has a minimum double.

The solution is the *Responsive Double* convention. This means that a double by fourth hand is not primarily for penalties but shows a desire to contest. The convention applies only when the opener's suit has been raised.

With this hand, therefore, you double 3♣ and your partner bids his best suit. Placing you with a hand of this strength, he may jump to game if he has anything more than a sound minimum double.

Fourth hand will sometimes be deprived of the opportunity to double for penalties, it is true. On the other hand, the responsive double, which guarantees some defensive tricks, may be converted into a penalty double by the second player.

Responsive doubles are usually played up to the level of 3♠, but not beyond.

## TAKEOUT DOUBLE QUIZ

With neither side vulnerable the player on your right opens 1♡. What is your call with each of the following?

(1) ♠ A J 8 3   ♡ 6 4        ◇ Q 8 2   ♣ A K 9 3
(2) ♠ K 10 7   ♡ K J 6 2   ◇ Q 5     ♣ A 10 8 2
(3) ♠ K 10 7   ♡ A Q 9     ◇ K J 2   ♣ A Q 6 4

(1) *Double.* With values equivalent to a sound opening, and support for the unbid suits, it is safe and constructive to double for takeout rather than to overcall in spades.

If you bid 1♠, and partner has a singleton or doubleton, he will not necessarily take you out and you may find yourself in entirely the wrong contract. A double is much more likely to bring to light the most suitable trump suit in the combined hands.

(2) *Pass*. With appreciable strength in the opponent's suit it is sound policy to pass unless you have the equivalent of a strong no-trump opening, about 16 to 18 points. With a lesser hand you have a better chance to gain a plus score by adopting a defensive posture.

(3) *Double*. Your hand is too strong for 1NT, so you double for takeout with the intention of bidding notrumps over partner's response. This sequence will indicate a balanced hand with about 19 or 20 points.

The player on your left opens with 1♡, your partner doubles and the next player passes. What is your call with each of the following?

| | | | | | | | |
|---|---|---|---|---|---|---|---|
| (4) | ♠ J 8 5 2 | ♡ 10 3 | ◇ 10 9 8 4 3 | ♣ Q 7 |
| (5) | ♠ 8 | ♡ K 10 7 3 2 | ◇ K J 8 3 | ♣ J 9 3 |
| (6) | ♠ A 10 9 7 | ♡ 6 4 | ◇ A J 8 3 | ♣ J 10 7 |
| (7) | ♠ 10 7 6 2 | ♡ A 10 7 | ◇ A Q J 8 | ♣ K 4 |
| (8) | ♠ 10 9 | ♡ K 10 3 | ◇ K 7 | ♣ K 10 8 5 3 2 |
| (9) | ♠ 8 2 | ♡ Q J 10 9 5 3 | ◇ A 7 2 | ♣ 8 2 |

(4) 1♠. It is usual to respond to a double by bidding the longest suit, but with a weak hand it is often preferable to show a four-card major suit at the one level than a five-card minor suit at the two level. To pass would be high treason.

(5) 1*NT*. In response to your partner's takeout double, this bid shows useful high-card values with, of course, a sound guard in opener's suit. Besides, 1NT is more constructive than 2◇, which could be based on length in diamonds and nothing else. Your heart suit is not the stuff of which penalty passes are made.

Your partner, in view of his double, is expected to hold strength in the unbid suits, and especially in spades, the unbid major. Thus 1NT is a sound response despite the singleton.

(6) 2♣. This is not forcing to game but it does say that game is likely if partner has a sound double. The jump response tells partner that you are bidding on genuine values, not merely because you are forced to.

(7) 2♡. These values are sufficient for game opposite a double. To make sure of reaching the best contract, which may be either 4♠, 5◇ or 3NT, you cue-bid the opener's suit. Partner then keeps the bidding open until the most suitable game contract has been found.

121

(8) *2NT*. Occasionally a somewhat adventurous course of action is in order when responding to a takeout double. Here partner is expected to have some strength in clubs, in which case your hand will produce a satisfactory number of tricks. So 2NT is more purposeful than 2♣ or 3♣.

(9) *Pass*. With this hand you may get your biggest score by allowing opener to play in 1♡ doubled. Partner is expected to lead a trump if he has one, and this will help you later to pick up the declarer's low trumps.

You are South and the bidding has gone:

| West | North | East | South |
|------|-------|------|-------|
| 1♡ | Double | 2♢ | ? |

What is your call with each of the following?

(10) ♠ Q 9 7 3   ♡ A 7 6 2   ♢ 8 5 4   ♣ 6 2

(11) ♠ 8 7   ♡ A 10 3 2   ♢ Q 8   ♣ K Q 6 5 3

(12) ♠ K 4 2   ♡ 9 5 3   ♢ J 8 4   ♣ A 8 7 3

(10) *2♠*. A free bid in this situation indicates certain assets, but these are strictly limited. Partner is expected to treat a simple intervention at this point as merely an attempt to compete for the partial. He should not assume that you have more than about 7 or 8 points.

You may reasonably hope that your partner has spade support, since he doubled the other major suit.

(11) *3NT*. In this type of competitive sequence it is sometimes necessary to grasp the bull by the horns. You have too much for a 3♣ bid and are entitled to assume that partner will have stoppers in spades and diamonds.

(12) *Double*. Your trump holding is not impressive but partner will have something in diamonds and you must take some action to demonstrate that you hold useful values opposite a double.

You are South and the bidding has gone:

| West | North | East | South |
|------|-------|------|-------|
| 1♢ | Double | 3♢ | ? |

(13) ♠ J 8 7 5 3   ♡ Q 2   ♢ 7 5 3   ♣ K 10 8

(14) ♠ 10 9 8 5   ♡ K 10 7 2   ♢ A 7 3   ♣ Q J

(15) ♠ 10 7 4   ♡ K J 9 7 4 2   ♢ 7 3   ♣ K 9

(13) 3♠. Your hand is certainly nothing to write home about, but you should not be silenced by East's pre-emptive raise. If you pass, your partner will need an exceptionally strong hand to reopen.

(14) 4♢. Game should be there in a major, but if you bid either 3♡ or 3♠ your partner might pass. At the same time, a jump to 4♡ or 4♠ might hit the wrong suit. The solution is to cue-bid the opponents' suit, inviting partner to name the trump suit. The alternative, a responsive double of 3♢, would be the best choice if you were a little weaker.

(15) 4♡. Game is not certain, but you lack space and must take the strain off partner. A mere 3♡ would sound competitive and might be a good deal weaker. Compare with example (13).

You are South and the bidding has gone:

| East | South | West | North |
|------|-------|------|-------|
| 1♠ | Double | Pass | 2♡ |
| Pass | ? | | |

What is your call with each of the following?

(16) ♠ 4  ♡ K J 8 2  ♢ A K 8 2  ♣ A J 7 5

(17) ♣ K Q 2  ♡ A 9 2  ♢ K Q 10  ♣ A Q 8 2

(18) ♠ 10 2  ♡ A K J 8  ♢ K 10 4  ♣ Q J 7 3

(16) 3♡. It would be wrong to bid more strongly. Partner might be very weak and in that case a spade lead and continuation would leave him awkwardly placed on the table. With the 5 or 6 points that would make 4♡ playable he will continue to game.

(17) 2NT. In this sequence 2NT is powerful and forward-going, indicating a hand too strong for an original bid of 1NT. To raise hearts would be unsound as partner might have been constrained to bid a moderate four-card suit.

(18) Pass. To bid 3♡ would be a game try in more senses than one: your hand simply does not warrant it. Partner was forced to bid in response to the double and may have a very poor hand indeed. You have no more than a minimum double and should therefore abandon hopes of game.

# CHAPTER 9

## Pre-emptive Bids

*The opening three-bid – Responding to three-bids – Doubles and overcalls of a three-bid – Responding to doubles and overcalls – Other pre-emptive bids*

PRE-EMPTIVE bids come in all shapes and sizes but all are based on the idea of crowding the auction and making it hard for opponents to judge what to do. The main requirement is a long suit, with little defensive strength. An ideal 3♠ opening, for example, looks something like this:

♠ K Q J 9 8 3 2  ♡ 7  ◇ 10 8 3  ♣ 6 2

The player who pre-empts is prepared to lose up to 500 points to prevent opponents from making a game; that is, two down doubled when vulnerable, or three down doubled when not vulnerable. When you expect to win six tricks with your long suit as trumps you can afford to open with a non-vulnerable three-bid. For a vulnerable three-bid you need seven tricks.

The effectiveness of pre-emptive bids cannot be judged by what happens on individual hands. A player who pre-empts may lose more than he bargained for or he may concede a penalty when the opposition could not have made a game. Against that he will sometimes save a game at no cost at all, as when the opponents finish up in the wrong contract. When this happens the gain is very large, although only a modest 50 or 100 may appear on the score-sheet.

By far the most common form of pre-emptive action is the opening three-bid in a suit.

### The Opening Three-bid

When you open with a three-bid in first or second position your partner's holding is an unknown quantity. You cannot tell whether the hand belongs to the opponents or not. But if your three-bid is based on the right type of hand your partner will know what you have and will be able to assess not only what your side can make but also what the opponents can make.

It is true that opponents will also know what your hand is like, but they may not find it at all easy to judge how the outstanding balance of strength is distributed or where their correct contract lies. Your partner will probably be the only one who knows roughly the situation.

From this emerges an important principle which applies to all auctions where a pre-emptive bid has been made: the *partner* of the player who has pre-empted is the one who makes the decisions—how high to bid, whether or not to save, and so on. To enable him to do his work accurately, it is important that when you pre-empt in first or second position your hand should conform to this pattern:

Less than 13 points (that is, less than the strength for a one-bid); Six probable tricks when not vulnerable, or seven when vulnerable. No secondary major suit.

The reason for this last stipulation is the same as we noted when discussing weak two-bids in Chapter 6. It is impossible for the responder to bid sensibly if he has to allow for a side suit, particularly a major, in the opening hand.

These two hands are ideal for an opening three-bid at suitable vulnerability:

(1) ♠ 7 2      ♡ K Q 10 9 8 3 2    ◇ 10 4    ♣ J 5

(2) ♠ A K J 9 6 5 3    ♡ 4              ◇ 8 3    ♣ 10 7 4

Not vulnerable, open 3♡ on (1), counting the hearts as six tricks; vulnerable, you would have to pass. With (2) you could open with a vulnerable 3♠; not vulnerable, you might venture 4♠. In each case you take a fairly optimistic view about the trick-winning power of your trump suit. That is normal when opening with a pre-empt.

The following hands, for one reason or another, are not quite right for a three-bid in first or second position. Assume in each case that you are not vulnerable:

(3) ♠ A Q 10 9 5 4 2    ♡ 7 3    ◇ A 10 2    ♣ 7

(4) ♠ Q J 3             ♡ Q 7    ◇ 4      ♣ K 9 8 6 4 3 2

(5) ♠ 10 9 6 3    ♡ A K J 8 5 2    ◇ 9 4    ♣ 5

Hand (3) is too strong in high cards for a bid of 3♠, and 4♠ would be precipitous. The right opening is 1♠.

Hand (4) does not contain the quota of six tricks required for a non-vulnerable three-bid. Another point, relevant to all pre-empts, is this: a pre-emptive bid in clubs is not as effective as a bid in a higher-ranking suit, though the risks involved are the same. It is therefore bad business to make a borderline pre-empt in a minor.

On hand (5) the objection to 3♡ is that the hand is playable in spades. If you open 3♡ and miss game in spades you will have to take the blame.


## Three-bids in Third Position

Suppose you are in third position and your partner has passed. The tactical situation is now rather different. If your own hand is weak enough in high cards for you to consider pre-emptive action, then the hand surely belongs to the opponents. It is no longer important for partner to know how many tricks your hand is worth: it is simply a question of what risks you should be prepared to take in an attempt to crowd the opponents.

Earlier it was remarked that while a pre-empt will sometimes cost you points although the opponents could not have made a game, it may also save a game without costing anything. This is when it pushes opponents into the wrong contract. Most experts believe that this last factor is the more important of the two. In third position they are prepared to take considerable risks, especially at favourable vulnerability. Not vulnerable against vulnerable, it is reasonable to open three with any of these hands:

(1) ♠ 7    ♡ Q J 9 7 6 4 3    ◇ 10    ♣ J 10 9 2
(2) ♠ K 10 8 7 5 4 2    ♡ 6    ◇ Q J 3    ♣ 8 4
(3) ♠ A 8    ♡ 5 4    ◇ A Q J 8 6 4 3    ♣ J 2

With hand (1) you take the optimistic view that the hearts will provide five tricks and the useful club holding one more.
Hand (2) represents about the minimum for a three-bid under

the most favourable circumstances, justified only because the suit is spades.*

Hand (3) would be too strong for a three-bid in first or second position, but after partner has passed the strong pre-empt may be good tactics.

## Three-bids in Fourth Position

In fourth position three-bids are made on hands on which you expect to make your call if the outstanding strength is equally divided, but where you would not welcome competition. Again, it may be right to open three of a minor on a hand where in first or second hand you would open with a bid of one.

(1) ♠ 8 3    ♡ 9 4   ◇ K J 7    ♣ A K J 10 6 2

(2) ♠ Q J 10 8 6 4  ♡ 5   ◇ A Q 7 4  ♣ 8 2

After three passes an opening bid of 3♣ is quite a sensible move on hand (1). Clearly partner has some values, but there is a danger that the opponents may be able to compete in the major suits. Partner is expected to pass 3♣ if he has no more than his fair share of the outstanding points, but a response of 3NT is not ruled out. On hand (2) you might try to snatch a part score with an opening 3♠.

## Responding to Three-bids

We have seen that after a three-bid by first or second hand the responder is in a good position to judge what each side can make. It is usually not difficult to visualize the opening and responding hands in combination. The responder's correct action is easily determined by considering the type of hand the opener is likely to have. Thus:

*Opener has either six or seven probable tricks* (depending on the vulnerability). Therefore the responder needs either four or three likely tricks for game in a major suit.

♠ 8 3   ♡ 9 8 2   ◇ A K 7 2   ♣ A 8 5 4

With three sure tricks you can raise a vulnerable bid of 3♡ or 3♠ to game. Not vulnerable, the odds would favour a pass.

---

* A minimum by ordinary standards, that is. Some players favour a pre-empt on extremely weak hands, even six to the jack and a 'bust'.

*Opener is expected to have a seven-card suit.* Therefore two small cards, or a singleton honour, constitute sound normal support for a game contract.

*Opener does not have a secondary major suit.* Responder has no need therefore to explore the other major unless he has a good six-card suit.

*Opener is not to be relied on for any defensive values.* Therefore, in assessing what the opponents can make, responder is guided by the defensive tricks in his own hand.

♠ A 8 7    ♡ J 8 3    ◇ K Q J 8 5    ♣ 10 4

Your partner opens 3♡ and the next player overcalls with 4♠. You cannot expect to take four defensive tricks on your own and should rely on none from partner. You should bid 5♡ in the hope that opponents may go to 5♠. A sacrifice in 5♡ will not be expensive.

Remember that the opener's estimate of six or seven playing tricks does not assume an unfortunate trump situation. If you have a singleton in partner's suit his hand may prove to be worth one trick less than he hoped. Suppose your partner opens 3♠ and you have this hand:

♠ 7    ♡ K 10 4    ◇ A Q 5 3    ♣ A Q 8 4 2

You have three and one-half quick tricks, but your singleton trump is a discouraging feature. If your side is not vulnerable, partner's maximum will be six tricks and therefore you should pass 3♠, though 4♠ may be made if things go favourably. Opposite a vulnerable three-bid you would raise to 4♠ despite the singleton trump.

Note that in neither case should you even dream of bidding 3NT. Do not bid 3NT in response to a three-bid merely because you have the other suits sewn up: either you must have a reasonable hope of nine tricks in your own hand, or your holding in your partner's suit must be such that you expect to bring it in. Suppose your partner opens 3◇, not vulnerable, and you have either of these hands:

(1) ♠ K 10 2    ♡ A Q 3    ◇ 7    ♣ A K Q J 9 2
(2) ♠ K J 3    ♡ K Q 9    ◇ 10 4    ♣ A J 10 6 3

With (1) you could justifiably bid 3NT. With (2) you cannot really expect to come close to nine tricks unless you can bring in partner's diamond suit. As this is unlikely, you should pass.

Although you need a strong hand before you can expect to make game opposite partner's three-opening, there are many hands where it is right to raise defensively. There are also many hands where game is likely to be borderline but where you do not need to consider the prospects in detail because a raise must be tactically right in any case. Not vulnerable, your partner opens with 3♡ and you hold these hands:

(1) ♠ 4 2  ♡ Q 10 6  ◇ J 8 3  ♣ A Q 7 5 2
(2) ♠ K 8 7 4 3  ♡ J 9 4 3  ◇ A 7  ♣ K Q

With (1) you must anticipate that the opponents can make 4♠ at least. Therefore it is a sound move to raise to 4♡, forcing the opponents to take a decision at a high level. Take away the ♣ A and you would expect the opponents to make at least eleven tricks. There is much to be said for an " advance sacrifice " of 5♡! Much of the sting in pre-emptive openings proceeds from this type of action.

With (2) you may or may not be able to make game, but in any event the raise to 4♡ must be sound. The opponents can surely make four of a minor, perhaps five; it is not unknown for opponents to take a dive in 4♠.

## Responding over Intervention

When your partner opens with a three-bid the opponents will be obliged to work largely in the dark. Do not help them by taking premature action, especially in the form of a double. Suppose your partner opens 3♡, the next player overcalls with 3♠, and you hold:

♠ K Q 10 3  ♡ 4  ◇ Q 8 7 4 2  ♣ A K 2

Do not double in this situation. For one thing, you could not safely double a takeout of 4♣ or 3NT. Secondly, if you pass with normal rhythm you may well have the opportunity of doubling 4♠! Under pressure, opponents often misjudge their best action at this level.

Incidentally, if it even occurred to you to double to warn partner against contesting further, you must have been keeping doubtful company. A player who has pre-empted should seldom bid again even when he has been supported. A sequence such as the following would be an atrocity:

| Opener | Opponent | Responder | Opponent |
|--------|----------|-----------|----------|
| 3♠ | 4♡ | Pass | Pass |
| 4♠ | | | |

Almost as bad is this sort of sequence:

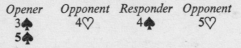

| Opener | Opponent | Responder | Opponent |
|--------|----------|-----------|----------|
| 3♣     | 4♡       | 4♠        | 5♡       |
| 5♣     |          |           |          |

Responder may well have bid 4♠ in the hope of pushing the opponents one higher. Opener may double 5♡ if he has fair defence, but to sacrifice in front of partner is the worst form of back-seat driving.

### Doubles and Overcalls of a Three-bid

Various schemes of defence to three-bids have been tried out. Some players treat 3♢ over 3♣, 4♣ over any other opening, as a takeout request (Lower Minor convention). Some bid the next highest suit to ask for a takeout (Fishbein convention). However, the majority favour a simple scheme whereby an overcall suggest a one-suited hand, a double is primarily for takeout, and notrumps is to play. Because of the general shortage of bidding space, these measures have to be used somewhat more flexibly than over a one-bid.

For a start, action by the second player is seldom justified unless he has at least 15 or 16 points, including distribution. With less, the odds simply do not favour entering the auction at such a high level. The following would be about the minimum for a vulnerable bid of 3♠ over an enemy three-bid:

♠ A J 10 5 3   ♡ A 7   ♢ 9 3 2   ♣ K Q 6

Secondly, a double must contain preparedness for any move by partner, including a pass. With a one-suited hand you always bid the suit rather than double; if the hand is too strong for a simple overcall you jump to game.

With two-suited hands the choice between doubling or overcalling is apt to depend on the rank of the suits. The player on your right opens 3♡ and you hold:

♠ K Q 7 4 3   ♡ 6 5   ♢ K 2   ♣ A K J 4

A bid of 3♠ is best. If you doubled and found partner with a moderate hand, his best suit diamonds, you would be in trouble. Now suppose the opening bid is 3♠ and you hold:

♠ A 2   ♡ K Q 8 3   ♢ A Q 9 4 2   ♣ 10 7

This time the double is preferred as it may be the only way to reach a 4–4 heart fit. If partner responds in clubs you can comfortably bid 4◊.

After a three-bid an overcall in notrumps has to do duty for a wider range of hands than after a one-bid. Suppose that 3♡ is opened on your right and you hold:

♠ 7 4    ♡ K 10 3    ◊ A 8    ♣ A Q J 8 6 2

Shut your eyes and bid 3NT!*

As in all competitive situations, the fourth player may reopen after a three-bid with a weaker hand than the second player; he needs about the equivalent of an opening bid.

## Responding to Doubles and Overcalls

When a three-bid has been doubled for takeout, the partner of the doubler calls the full value of his hand. Remember, though, that the doubler is already assuming some values in his partner's hand. Suppose he has doubled an enemy 3♡ bid with this hand:

♠ A K 4 3    ♡ 8 2    ◊ K Q 10 5    ♣ K 10 8

Clearly he cannot hope to make any contract unless his partner has some values, about 8 or 9 points. It follows that if partner has no more than that he should make a minimum response to the double. For a jump response, 10 points are needed, though the responder may count points for shortages on the assumption that a trump fit exists. Suppose the bidding goes:

| Opponent | Partner | Opponent | You |
|----------|---------|----------|-----|
| 3◊ | Double | Pass | ? |

You have the following hands:

(1) ♠ J 10 6 5 2    ♡ 10 6      ◊ 9 8 4    ♣ A K 7
(2) ♠ Q 9 8 3      ♡ A 10 5 2    ◊ 8 7 4    ♣ K 6

In (1) you have 10 points, counting a point for the fifth spade and another for the heart shortage (on the assumption that a spade fit exists). You are just about worth a jump to 4♠. In (2) also you have

---

* This presupposes, of course, that 3NT is not used conventionally as an enquiry for partner's best suit, a defensive mechanism which has many adherents.

just enough for game, as it is reasonable to think there will be a 4–4 fit in either spades or hearts. To cater for both possibilities you bid 4◇, the opponent's suit.

### Other Pre-emptive Bids

An opening bid of 4♡ or 4♠ should be *at least* one trick stronger than a three-bid because the game bid is much more likely to be doubled. A player with two aces and a K–Q will assume his partner can contribute a trick or two and will not go quietly.

Bids of 4♡ and 4♠ are sometimes made on hands that are strong enough in high cards for a one-opening.

(1) ♠ 7  ♡ A K J 10 6 4 3  ◇ Q 10 4 ♣ 9 6

(2) ♠ A Q J 10 8 3 2 ♡ 7  ◇ 6 2  ♣ K Q 9

The first hand is a typical 4♡ opening, not vulnerable. The second is worth a vulnerable bid of 4♠.

### Pre-emptive Overcalls

Pre-emptive bids may also be made after an opponent has opened the bidding. Weak jump overcalls (a single jump) have been discussed in Chapter 7. A pre-emptive jump overcall (double jump) is justified, not vulnerable, on this sort of hand:

♠ K J 10 8 7 4 2  ♡ 7  ◇ 9  ♣ J 10 5 2

Bid 3♠ over any opening bid of one on your right.

### Pre-emptive Responses

A double-jump response to partner's opening bid, such as 3♡ over 1◇, is pre-emptive. The values are about the same as for a non-vulnerable opening three-bid, such as K–Q–J–10–x–x–x and no other high card.

## PRE-EMPTIVE BIDDING QUIZ

You are the dealer with neither side vulnerable. What is your call with each of the following hands?

(1) ♠ 8  ♡ Q J 10 9 7 6 5 2  ◇ J 3  ♣ 9 4

(2) ♠ A K 10 9 6 3　♡ Q 10 8 2　◇ 9 3　♣ 7
(3) ♠ Q 4　♡ A K J 8 7 3 2　◇ A 10　♣ 9 6
(4) ♠ A Q J 5 3　♡ 8 2　◇ A 7 6 4　♣ 7 5
(5) ♠ A 8　♡ 7 4　◇ K 3　♣ Q J 10 9 4 3 2

(1) 3♡. This hand will take six tricks with hearts as trumps and as it has less than the values for a one-bid it qualifies for a non-vulnerable three-bid. You might make the same bid at game all, reckoning that if you went down 800 you would be saving a slam.

(2) *Pass.* The reason for not opening with a pre-emptive bid of 2♠ or 3♠ is that partner would not expect you to have a secondary heart suit. If the four-card suit were in diamonds or clubs the hand would present an ideal weak two-bid. As it is, an aggressive player might open 1♠.

(3) 4♡. An opening game bid in a major suit may sometimes be made for tactical reasons with a hand that contains the values for a one-bid. Here 4♡ may help to shut out an enemy spade contract. The alternative is 1♡.

(4) 1♠. The alternative is not a weak two-bid but a pass. The objection to 2♠ is twofold: the spades are sub-standard, and the honour strength is ' topweight '.

(5) 1♣. This hand contains too much outside the long suit for 3♣, which might cause you to miss a game.

Neither side vulnerable, your partner opens 3♠ and next hand passes. What is your call with each of the following?

(6) ♠ 7　　♡ K Q 9　　◇ Q J 10 8 4 2　♣ K J 8
(7) ♠ 10　　♡ A K 9 6 3　◇ A 9 7 3　　♣ A J 3
(8) ♠ K 5 2　♡ A Q 3　　◇ Q J 4　　♣ A J 8 5

(6) *Pass.* Opener is expected to have six winners with spades as trumps. By no stretch of the imagination is it likely that your hand will provide four winners at a spade contract, or nine at a notrump contract, so you must pass.

(7) 4♠. Any other call—the thumbscrews. You have four certain winners to add to your partner's six, and although your spade support is not tremendous it should be adequate. To bid 3NT, when there is no likelihood that you will be able to bring in the

opener's spade suit, would be particularly unwise with a good partner, who would assume that you had your reasons and would not revert to 4♠.

(8) *3NT*. Here your spades are good enough for you to be able to assume that you can bring in the suit. Nine tricks in notrumps looks a better proposition than ten in spades.

With neither side vulnerable, the player on your right opens 3♠. What is your call with each of the following?

(9)  ♠ 7          ♡ A J 10 6    ◇ A Q 9 3    ♣ K Q 10 7
(10) ♣ Q J 5 4    ♡ 8 3         ◇ A K J 2    ♣ K 10 3
(11) ♠ A Q 8 3    ♡ J 4         ◇ K Q 9 2    ♣ A Q 10

(9) *Double*. This three-suited hand is the classic type with which to double an opening three-bid. If partner, having strength in spades, passes the double for penalties, the defensive capacity of your hand will not fall below his expectations.

(10) *Pass*. Despite its high-card strength, this hand does not justify any form of action. A double would be a request for takeout and it is a fact of life that if you double with a hand of this pattern your partner will always respond in hearts. To bid 3NT would be a wild gamble. If you are lucky, your partner may have enough to re-open with a double, which you will happily pass.

(11) *3NT*. The use of a double as a takeout request means that with this type of hand you either have to pass or bid 3NT. With 18 points in high cards you should accept the challenge, although clearly 3NT will fail if partner is weak.

With neither side vulnerable, the player on your left opens 3♣, your partner bids 3♡, and next hand passes. What is your call with each of the following?

(12) ♠ A Q 4 3    ♡ 10 8    ◇ A 8 6 2      ♣ 8 6 4
(13) ♠ J 10 8 4   ♡ J 9 6   ◇ A Q         ♣ K J 8 2
(14) ♠ K Q 5      ♡ A Q 3   ◇ K J 10 6 4 2  ♣ 4

(12) *4♡*. Your partner probably has at least 16 points, including distribution. As you have 10 points in high cards there is every reason to suppose that game can be made. A bid of 3♠ would suggest a longer suit, and in any case, if your partner had held spades as well as hearts, he would probably have doubled for takeout.

(13) 3*NT*. Although you have adequate support for hearts, in a heart contract there is a prospect of a club opening lead and ruff. It may be better to bid 3NT, which must be safe.

(14) 4*NT*. As partner is missing two of the top honours in hearts it is reasonable to assume that he has considerable length in the suit. A small slam in hearts will be virtually certain if he has two aces, and this you test by invoking the Blackwood convention (see Chapter 12). There might even be a grand slam. A raise to 5♡ would not be bad.

With your side vulnerable, the player on your left opens 3◇, your partner doubles and next hand passes. What is your call with each of the following?

| | | | |
|---|---|---|---|
| (15) ♠ J 7 2 | ♡ Q 8 4 3 | ◇ Q 10 6 3 | ♣ 5 4 |
| (16) ♠ K 8 7 2 | ♡ 10 9 6 4 | ◇ A 4 | ♣ 10 6 5 |
| (17) ♠ K 9 7 3 | ♡ 8 5 | ◇ 9 8 | ♣ A Q 10 8 4 |

(15) 3♡. This is not the sort of hand with which to convert a takeout double into a penalty double by passing. Your trumps are too weak and you have too much in the major suit, where partner also is likely to have length.

(16) 3♡. To bid 4◇, inviting partner to name his better major, would be over-optimistic here. It is best to bid the lower-valued suit and hope that the doubler can make another move.

(17) 4◇. You have game values but it might be a mistake to plunge into either 4♠ or 5♣. You expect partner to bid 4♡ over 4◇. You plan to remove this to 4♠ and he will judge then that you hold both black suits, probably with better clubs than spades. With ♠ A-x-x ♡ A-K-Q-10 ◇ x-x-x ♣ K-x-x he will transfer to 5♣.

# CHAPTER 10

## Penalty Doubles, Lead-directing Doubles, and Redoubles

*Doubling a low contract – Doubling a high contract – Doubles after competitive bidding – Doubles of slam contracts – Doubles of notrump contracts – Redoubles*

THE CHASTISEMENT of opponents who have over-extended themselves is an important part of bridge. In the long run you cannot be a really big winner unless you double the opponents, not just when they overbid but also when they have reached a reasonable contract that is due for bad breaks.

However, as the economists so rightly say, there is no such thing as a free lunch; there is always danger that declarer may take advantage of the double to save a trick or even make a contract that would otherwise have failed. All the same, the stronger the game, the more frequently the axe is wielded, at any rate against low contracts. The average player tends to wait to double high contracts on the strength of high cards, permitting opponents who come in at a low level on a wing and a prayer to escape unpunished. The expert knows that opponents will not reach a high contract without having a good idea of their expectations, whereas anyone may make a reasonable overcall and run into trouble.

### Doubling a Low Contract

One of the most likely occasions for a penalty double is when your partner opens the bidding, you yourself hold at least moderate values (say 8 points or more), and next hand overcalls in a suit where you have length. At the two level, especially, a double should be your first thought. At the same time, you have to consider what your prospects would be if you were to bid to your own best contract instead of doubling. The more uncertain they seem, the more you should be inclined to take the money and double. On the other hand, when you have support for your partner's suit you should always show that support in preference to doubling.

Doubles of overcalls, especially when they would not give the opponents game if the contract were made, are tentative in nature and partner is not expected to pass with an unsuitable hand. That is why a degree of honour strength is needed; your hand should be of some use to partner if he decides not to stand the double. But the nature of your trump holding, and your holding in partner's suit, are more important than your high-card strength.

*The trump holding.* When you double a two-level overcall your partner must know what to expect. He will assume that you have four trumps, maybe three. The best holding is not necessarily one with top cards, but one that has a sting in it for the overcaller.

| Opener | Opponent | You | Opponent |
|--------|----------|-----|----------|
| 1♠ | 2♢ | ? | |

You hold:

(1) ♠ J 2    ♡ K Q 10 2    ♢ A K 5    ♣ 9 7 4 3

(2) ♠ 10 4    ♡ A 5 3    ♢ J 10 4 2    ♣ K J 8 2

A double of 2♢ is much more clearly marked with the second hand, where the overcaller is certain to make fewer trump tricks than he had hoped. With the first hand you have no real surprise for the overcaller: he knows he hasn't got the A–K! There is another factor that makes the double less attractive with the first hand: with these values you may well be able to make a game in a major suit or in notrumps. In this case the double is not likely to show a great profit. In (2) you not only have good prospects of a penalty, but no guarantee of game your way.

If you should chance to be endowed with five or more cards in your opponent's suit, remember that your partner is likely to be correspondingly short and may remove a double. Of course, if your hand is reasonably strong in high cards, that will not matter, as you will be able to cope with any development.

With neither side vulnerable your partner opens 1♠, there is an overcall of 2♢, and you hold:

(1) ♠ 4    ♡ 6 3    ♢ Q J 9 5 2    ♣ Q 8 7 6 4

(2) ♠ 5    ♡ K 10 3 2    ♢ A J 8 6 3    ♣ Q J 7

With (1) you should pass. No doubt you could defeat 2♢, but as a matter of convention you are expected to hold more general strength when you double at this level. The great danger of doubling is that opponents may remove to 2♡ and your partner may double that. In that case you would be very anxious about the outcome, and equally unhappy about removing it to 2NT or 3♣.

Your best hope of a good score is that partner will reopen with a double, which you will happily pass, or that the opponents will venture further, not being warned of the bad break in diamonds.

With hand (2) the double is automatic. If partner takes it out into 2♠ you will be disappointed but you can proceed with 2NT.

Doubles with three trumps are not made at the one level, but at the two level they are often rewarding when there is a ruff to be had as well as a trump trick.

| Opener | Opponent | You | Opponent |
|--------|----------|-----|----------|
| 1♠ | 2♣ | ? | |

Double 2♣ with this hand:

♠ 2   ♡ Q 8 7 4   ◇ A 8 5 3 2   ♣ K 10 4

As you have a quick entry in trumps you will surely be able to register at least one ruff.

*The holding in opener's suit.* The profitability of a low-level double depends on the relationship between the penalty you obtain and the score you could have made by bidding on. Your holding in partner's suit has a bearing on both.

The more you have in your partner's suit, the more likely it is that your hands belong in attack and that a double will yield inadequate compensation. Either declarer or dummy will be short in the suit and some of your side's high cards will be wasted.

But if you are short in your partner's suit it is possible that the hands are a misfit, so prospects of game are uncertain. At the same time, your partner's high cards are also more likely to win tricks against the doubled contract.

The best doubles, therefore, are based on a shortage in the opener's suit, a singleton or a doubleton. A void, unless you have a sound alternative lead, tends to be frustrating; you may find that you never develop tricks in the suit. Suppose that as responder you hold:

♠ 7 4   ♡ K 10 4 3   ◇ A Q J   ♣ J 8 6 3

If your partner opens 1♠ and the next hand overcalls with either 2♣ or 2◇, you double, as the penalty should be equal to the value of any score you can make. But if your partner opens 1◇ a double of 2♣ is less attractive, as you have so much in diamonds; a bid of 2NT, though not ideal, would be preferable.

### When to Remove a Double

A double of a simple overcall is only a proposition, not a command. Three defensive tricks and two small trumps would be ideal for a pass. Suppose that here you are the opening bidder:

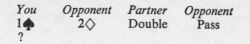

| You | Opponent | Partner | Opponent |
|-----|----------|---------|----------|
| 1♠  | 2◇       | Double  | Pass     |
| ?   |          |         |          |

You hold:

♠ K Q 9 4 2    ♡ J 8 3    ◇ 6 3    ♣ A K 4

With this or any better hand you leave the double in. If you were weaker defensively you would not be entirely happy, though whether you would actually remove the double would depend on just how attractive you judged the escape route to be. When the decision seems close, these are some other factors that may come into the reckoning:

(a) When partner has doubled 2♡—which would give them game if made—you are entitled to assume that he has fairly solid defensive prospects. You will therefore be more disposed to pass the double.

(b) When the doubling side is vulnerable, the opponents not, a double is likely to be based on good trumps and the probability of a misfit. At this score you may trust your partner to hold at least two, probably three, tricks in the trump suit.

(c) Hardly ever should you pass with a void in the suit doubled. Beware of the argument, " As I had none, I thought you would have a long string." More likely, the remainder of the suit will be divided 5–4–4–0 or 6–4–3–0 and your partner's four trumps will be cut up.

(d) Be disinclined to pass when you hold a second suit of five cards. Suppose you open 1♠ on:

♠ A Q J 3    ♡ Q 10 7 5 2    ◇ K 4    ♣ 7 3

There is an overcall of 2♣, which your partner doubles. In a sense you have adequate defensive help, but there is a big danger: partner may hold ♡ A–K–x or even ♡ A–K–x–x, and those expected tricks may go adrift. Worse, there may be an easy 4♡ your way. Take out the double into 2♡, therefore, expecting to find some support.

139

## Doubling a High Contract

There is a difference between doubling a freely bid contract, where opponents bid to their game without opposition, and doubling after a competitive auction. We deal first with freely bid contracts. Doubles of this kind should be based on more than a collection of picture cards and a suspicion that the opponents are overbidding. Apart from the fact that the declarer may save a trick in the play, the odds do not favour close doubles of game contracts. It is silly to risk a redouble and an overtrick, worth an extra 580 (730 instead of 150) for the sake of an extra 50.

How the defenders' cards are divided is at least as important as the cards they hold. S. J. Simon once gave this extreme, but irrefutable, example:

| North | East | South | West |
|-------|------|-------|------|
| 1♣ | Pass | 2NT | Pass |
| | | (limit) | |
| 3NT | Pass | Pass | Double |
| Pass | Pass | Pass | |

West holds: ♠ A 10 9  ♡ K Q 10  ◇ A K J x x  ♣ K x

Simon pointed out that this was actually a very poor double; the contract is going to be made even if North's clubs are no better than A–Q–10–9–x–x (the least he can have, for obviously he has not raised to 3NT on " points "). By the time declarer has run the clubs, West is bound to be in trouble with his discards and may be squeezed or end-played. But suppose instead that West had this hand:

♠ 10 x x  ♡ K Q 10  ◇ A K J x x  ♣ x x

Now the opponents (instead of West) no doubt hold ♠A, but as long as partner has ♣K the contract is likely to be set two tricks. West lays down ◇K, shifts to a heart, and waits for a diamond lead through declarer's queen.

The moral is that the best time to double is not when you have a strong hand but when your two hands in combination will shock the declarer. Two aces against a slam do not qualify under this heading except against opponents who have not heard of the Blackwood convention. In the same way, to double a suit game on A–K and two kings is unduly innocent—we would far rather double with nothing more than Q–J–9–x of trumps over declarer and a singleton of a suit bid by dummy. This last item is an asset because it suggests that partner is a force to be reckoned with.

It is particularly unwise to double when *either* opponent is un-limited. For example, the bidding goes:

| South | West | North | East |
|-------|------|-------|------|
| 1♠ | Pass | 2◇ | Pass |
| 2NT | Pass | 3NT | Pass |
| Pass | Pass | | |

Sitting West, you hold:

♠ K J 8 3  ♡ Q J 8  ◇ 4  ♣ A J 7 5 3

Prospects may seem good, but a double is dangerous because, while South's 2NT was limited, North's raise to three was not. North might have plenty in reserve; then you would walk into a redouble and two overtricks, *very* expensive.

For a double of game to be at all safe, it must be clear that *neither* opponent has undisclosed strength. For example:

| West | East |
|------|------|
| 1♣ | 1♠ |
| 2♣ | 2NT |
| 3NT | Pass |

Here West's 2♣ was limited and so was East's 2NT. In all such auctions declarer expects to make his contract only if the cards lie reasonably well; if they lie badly, he expects to go down. It is your job to see that, as often as possible, he goes down doubled.

### Doubles after Competitive Bidding

When your side has the superior cards, but the opponents have outbid the highest contract you think you can make, it is usually right to double even though you cannot see the necessary defensive tricks in your own hand. In auctions of this type there are many hands where neither partner has the beating of the contract himself, but few where they do not have it between them.

Remember, though, that the more enthusiastically your partner has supported your suit, the less he may have in defensive values. Consider these two auctions:

| (1) | You | Opponent | Partner | Opponent |
|-----|-----|----------|---------|----------|
| | 1♡ | 1♠ | 4♡ | 4♠ |
| | ? | | | |

141

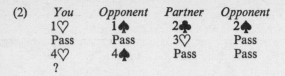

| (2) | *You* | *Opponent* | *Partner* | *Opponent* |
|-----|-------|------------|-----------|------------|
|     | 1♡    | 1♠         | 2♣        | 2♠         |
|     | Pass  | Pass       | 3♡        | Pass       |
|     | 4♡    | 4♠         | Pass      | Pass       |
|     | ?     |            |           |            |

In the first sequence partner has indicated an attacking type of hand. You do not assume him to be worthless defensively, but you should not double unless you can see the first three defensive tricks in your own hand. If partner has fair defence he will double himself on the strength of your opening bid.

In the second auction it is certain that your side has the superior cards. Whenever you bid a game voluntarily and the opponents have taken an obvious sacrifice, they must not be allowed to travel at excursion rates: you must double whenever you think you have reached your limit. In (2) your partner has in fact made a " forcing pass "—one which obliges you either to bid on or double.

The forcing pass is an important weapon in competitive auctions. One obvious case occurs when the sequence would have been forcing but for the intervention. The bidding goes:

| *Partner* | *Opponent* | *You* | *Opponent* |
|-----------|------------|-------|------------|
| 1NT       | Pass       | 3♡    | 3♠         |
| Pass      | Pass       | ?     |            |

Without the 3♠ intervention the partnership would have been committed to game. Opener's pass is forcing, therefore, and suggests that his hand is reasonably well suited both to defence and attack.


### Doubles of Slam Contracts

As there are not many opportunities to double a freely bid slam for penalty, and the profit will be small, a slam double is used to request a specific lead, namely an " unusual " one. This is often called a " Lightner " double.

When you think that a normal lead from partner is likely to be best, or when you think no lead is likely to defeat the slam, you do not double. When you do double, it means you are asking partner not to make his normal lead. Partner decides what he would have led without the double—and then leads something else.

Here is a situation where you would use the slam double. You are East and the bidding goes:

| South | West | North | East |
|-------|------|-------|------|
| 1♡ | Pass | 3♣ | 3♠ |
| 4♣ | Pass | 4♡ | Pass |
| 4NT | Pass | 5♡ | Pass |
| 6♡ | Pass | Pass | ? |

Your hand is:

♠ Q 10 9 8 5 4 3    ♡ 8 5    ◇ A 7 6 4    ♣ –

As a club lead and ruff is likely to beat the contract, you double to warn partner against leading your suit. Partner won't need to be a genius to deduce, from his own hand and the bidding, that a club is required. Note that the double would be just as clearcut without ◇ A: it would still represent your best chance to beat the contract.

There is not often much doubt as to what constitutes an unusual lead. Obviously a suit that has been bid by either defender is barred, and so is a trump. In an uncontested auction the lead of an unbid suit is not " unusual " either; in such a case, a double will call for dummy's suit. When dummy has bid two suits the double refers to the first suit in the absence of any contrary indication; such a double is based on A–K or A–Q more often than on a void.

## Doubles of Notrump Contracts

At any level a double of a notrump contract is for penalties. At game level some doubles have a lead-directing quality. We consider first the double of 1NT and the manoeuvres that may follow.

### Doubles after a 1NT Opening

One cannot expect to get rich on these doubles, but there are two types of hand on which it is customary to attempt punitive action after 1NT on your right:

(1) Hands at least equal to the upper limit of the opening bid. Assuming a strong notrump, you need 17 or 18 points for this type of double. Even then you are gambling on partner's having his share of the outstanding points.

(2) Hands containing a powerful suit and at least one quick entry. Now you may defeat 1NT even without having the balance of points.

With the first type of hand the doubler can hardly count his chickens. His strength is behind the opener, and in theory his finesses will succeed while declarer's will fail, but there may be a danger of giving a trick away every time he leads. That is the determining factor with hands like these:

(1) ♠ A Q 6   ♡ K Q 3   ◇ 9 7 5 4 2   ♣ A Q

(2) ♠ K J 8 3   ♡ A J 8   ◇ K 8 2   ♣ A Q 6

Hand (1) presents a reasonable double of 1NT as you intend to plug away in diamonds and the declarer will have to come to you in the other suits. With hand (2) a pass is at least as good as a double; if you double and find declarer with ♠A-Q-x and the 10 in dummy, life will become very frustrating.

When you double 1NT partner is expected to pass with a balanced hand, no matter how weak. He takes out only with quite a long suit and less than 5 or 6 points.

♠ J 8 3 2   ♡ 9 6 2   ◇ 10 5 3   ♣ 8 7 4

With this hand partner must leave your double of 1NT, the more so as his only four-card suit is high-ranking. He realizes that the contract may be made, but to play at the two level, probably doubled, will be at least as expensive unless the doubler has a long suit; and in that case the doubler may distinguish himself by defeating 1NT all by himself.

## Doubling a Suit Takeout of 1NT

At duplicate, and in some rubber-bridge games where a weak notrump is common, an understanding is needed to cope with the situation where 1NT is doubled and the third player tries to escape by bidding a suit. It is recommended that the fourth player should double freely on balanced hands containing two or more likely defensive tricks. Suppose you are fourth hand in this sequence:

| Opponent | Partner | Opponent | You |
|----------|---------|----------|-----|
| 1NT | Double | 2♣ | ? |

You hold:

♠ J 7 6  ♡ A 9 4 2  ◇ 10 8 3  ♣ Q 9 7

With this hand you should double not just 2♣ but any other rescue by the third player, as your side surely holds the balance of the cards.

Players who employ a weak notrump are of necessity well versed in Houdini-type manoeuvres and may remove 1NT without waiting for the axe to descend. Suppose the dealer opens with a weak 1NT and his partner holds:

♠ J 10 8 4 2  ♡ 7 3  ◇ 10 8 2  ♣ J 6 3

Second hand passes, but the player with this hand judges that 1NT is surely going to be doubled. So he bids 2♠ straight off, hoping that no one will have enough trumps to double. To counter such evasions, a double by the fourth player in such a sequence suggests the sort of values on which he would have doubled 1NT. He may have only two or three cards in the suit doubled. It is still, in principle, a penalty double.

## The Double of 3NT

A double of 3NT always gives rise to inferences that will have a bearing on the opening lead. As the lead can make a difference of several tricks it is sometimes right to double for a lead even when you cannot be sure of beating the contract. The meaning of the double depends on the nature of the bidding. These are general principles:

(1) *The doubler or his partner has bid a suit.* In this case the double asks for that suit to be led. When both partners have bid, the doubler is asking for his own suit.

(2) *The doubling side has not bid but dummy has bid one or more suits.* Here the double is usually prompted by strength in the first suit which has been bid by dummy. This is a typical sequence:

| South | West | North | East |
|-------|------|-------|------|
| 1♣ | Pass | 1♠ | Pass |
| 1NT | Pass | 3NT | Double |

East's double infringes the general principle that it is unsound to double a game contract when one opponent (in this case North) may have plenty in hand. The double is an urgent request for a spade lead. East may not be confident of beating the contract even with a spade lead, but he gauges that it is the only chance.

However, it does not follow that dummy's suit should always be led when the defending side has not bid. Consider this sequence:

| North | East | South | West |
|-------|------|-------|------|
| 1♣ | Pass | 1♠ | Pass |
| 2♣ | Pass | 2NT | Pass |
| 3NT | Double | Pass | Pass |
| Pass | | | |

Obviously North–South, who are both limited, will need to bring in the club suit, so there is no need for East to double to attract a club lead. No doubt East has some strength in clubs, but for West to lead a club would cost a tempo. West should make his normal lead.

(3) *Neither side has bid a suit.* In this case the doubler is saying to his partner: " I have a solid suit or a near-solid suit plus an entry. Please try to find my suit." So the opening leader should put aside his Q–10–x–x–x and lead his shortest suit, especially a major suit, instead.

### Redoubles

Redoubles are of two kinds—business redoubles, designed to chasten the opponents, and SOS redoubles, demanding a takeout by partner.

One point worth making about business redoubles is that it is unwise to redouble when there is any question about the trump suit. A 4–0 trump break is apt to ruin the best of contracts.

After a competitive auction a redouble at game level is often good tactics when you feel your own contract is borderline but are confident of a big penalty if the opponents bid on in their suit. Such a redouble puts the opposition under a considerable strain.

In the part-score area a redouble commonly has the opposite sense to what it appears to say. A player who thinks that his side can make the doubled contract will usually be content to pass, so when the last player to speak redoubles he is asking his partner to try some other denomination. This is an obvious example:

| South | West | North | East |
|-------|------|-------|------|
| 1♡ | Pass | Pass | Double |
| Pass | Pass | Redouble | |

North is probably void in hearts and is asking his partner to bid his next best suit.

The other occasion for an SOS redouble is when the redoubler could in theory hold enough to ensure the contract, but would not for tactical reasons redouble if he had such a hand. This often occurs when partner has been doubled in a simple overcall.

| South | West | North | East |
|-------|------|-------|------|
| 1♠ | 2♣ | Double | Redouble |

If East liked 2♣ doubled he would not paint the lily by redoubling, so this again is a distress signal.

## QUIZ ON PENALTY DOUBLES, LEAD-DIRECTING DOUBLES, AND REDOUBLES

Suppose you are South in the following auctions, with neither side vulnerable. What is your call with the hands shown?

(1)
| North | East | South | West |
|-------|------|-------|------|
| 1♠ | 2♣ | ? | |

♠ K Q 7  ♡ 7 6 4  ◇ 8 6 3  ♣ A J 4 2

(2)
| North | East | South | West |
|-------|------|-------|------|
| 1♠ | 2♡ | ? | |

♠ 10  ♡ K 6 4 2  ◇ A 10 8 2  ♣ A 6 4 3

(3)
| North | East | South | West |
|-------|------|-------|------|
| 1♠ | 2◇ | ? | |

♠ 6 3  ♡ 8 2  ◇ K J 8 6 4 2  ♣ Q 5 2

(4)
| North | East | South | West |
|-------|------|-------|------|
| 1♡ | 2◇ | ? | |

♠ J 6 4 3  ♡ 5 2  ◇ A 10 2  ♣ A J 6 3

(5)
| South | West | North | East |
|-------|------|-------|------|
| 1♠ | 2♣ | Double | Pass |

♠ K J 6 3 2  ♡ K Q 7 5 4  ◇ K 8  ♣ 4

(6)
| South | West | North | East |
|-------|------|-------|------|
| 1◇ | Pass | 2♣ | 2♡ |
| Pass | Pass | Double | Pass |
| ? | | | |

♠ A 8 2  ♡ 9 4 3  ◇ A Q J 6 3 2  ♣ 10

(7)

| North | East | South | West |
|---|---|---|---|
| 1♠ | Pass | 2♣ | 2♦ |
| Double | Pass | | |

♠ K Q 10   ♡ Q 8 4   ♦ 4 3   ♣ A 8 7 4 2

(8)

| North | East | South | West |
|---|---|---|---|
| 1♠ | 2♡ | 3♣ | 3♡ |
| 3♠ | Pass | 3NT | Pass |
| Pass | 4♡ | ? | |

♠ 5 2   ♡ K 6   ♦ K 10 7 5   ♣ A Q 8 5 3

(9)

| East | South | West | North |
|---|---|---|---|
| 1♦ | Double | 1♡ | 1♠ |
| 2♡ | 2♠ | 3♡ | Double |
| Pass | ? | | |

♠ A Q J 4   ♡ Q 7   ♦ 8 3 2   ♣ K Q J 6

(10)

| South | West | North | East |
|---|---|---|---|
| 1♠ | Pass | 2♠ | 3♣ |
| 3NT | 4♣ | Double | Pass |
| ? | | | |

♠ A K Q 9 3 2   ♡ 10 7   ♦ A J 5   ♣ K 2

(11)

| North | East | South | West |
|---|---|---|---|
| 1♡ | Pass | 1♠ | 2♦ |
| 3♠ | 4♦ | 4♠ | 5♦ |
| Pass | Pass | ? | |

♠ K J 8 4 2   ♡ Q 10 6   ♦ 8 5 3   ♣ A 5

(1) 2♠. A double of 2♣ is unlikely to work out well with so much strength in partner's suit.

(2) *Double*. Your trump holding is less than magnificent but the shortness in spades tips the scales. Either your partner's suit will be good for several tricks, or you will be able to obtain one or more ruffs.

(3) *Pass*. There is not much point in doubling 2♦, as partner will probably be unable to stand the double. Also, you are not prepared

for partner to double a rescue if the opponents hie themselves into a more viable contract. With so many trumps one is content to defend, undoubled, with the additional chance that partner may reopen with a takeout double.

(4) *Double.* It can be right to double a two-level overcall in a minor suit on three trumps when no other action stands out. Such doubles often bring in a bigger penalty than when the trumps are massed.

(5) 2♡. Partner is counting on you to hold three defensive tricks. As you have only about two, with no compensation in the form of trump strength, it is right to remove the double, especially as you have length in the unbid major suit.

(6) *Pass.* As you have the great asset of three trumps and a shortage in partner's suit, this double is likely to prove profitable even though you have less than three tricks in high cards.

(7) 3♠. Partner probably has a singleton club, so defensive prospects against 2◇ doubled are quite good. However, it tends to be wrong to accept a double at a low level without having expressed support for partner's suit. Game is likely and a penalty of more than 300 is unlikely.

(8) *Double.* This deal has the appearance of a misfit on which it might not even have been possible to make your previous call of 3NT. Now that the chance to double at a higher level has occurred, you should gladly accept it.

(9) 3♠. Here the takeout is prudent because your previous bidding may have misinformed partner. (The double of 1◇ implied support for the other three suits, and partner may therefore have doubled 3♡ in the hope of finding you with some heart strength.) 3♠ must surely be a playable spot.

(10) 4♠. Your bid of 3NT may have caused partner to expect a more balanced defensive hand than you actually have and may have prompted his double. You cannot be sure of making 4♠, but there is little prospect of gaining much from 4♣ doubled.

(11) 5♠. Partner has left you in charge and you should decide in favour of offence rather than defence. Partner is long in your suit and you are not short in his, which means that your side's high cards may prove ineffectual in defence. You have no wasted values in diamonds, where your partner probably has a singleton or void, so you can reasonably expect to make 5♠.

Suppose you are West in the following hands. Which card do you lead?

(12)

| | South | West | North | East |
|---|---|---|---|---|
| | 1◇ | Pass | 2♡ | Pass |
| | 2♠ | Pass | 4◇ | Pass |
| | 4NT | Pass | 5♡ | Pass |
| | 6◇ | Pass | Pass | Double |
| | Pass | Pass | Pass | |

♠ 8 4 2    ♡ 8 6    ◇ 10 8 5    ♣ Q 10 7 4 2

(13)

| | North | East | South | West |
|---|---|---|---|---|
| | 1♠ | 4◇ | 4♡ | Pass |
| | 4NT | Pass | 5◇ | Pass |
| | 6♡ | Double | Pass | Pass |
| | Pass | | | |

♠ 10 7    ♡ 10 8 3    ◇ J 6    ♣ J 9 6 5 4 2

(14)

| | North | East | South | West |
|---|---|---|---|---|
| | 1♣ | Pass | 1♠ | 2♡ |
| | 3♣ | Pass | 4♣ | Pass |
| | 4◇ | Pass | 6♣ | Pass |
| | Pass | 6♡ | 6♠ | Pass |
| | Pass | Double | Pass | Pass |
| | Pass | | | |

♠ 9 4    ♡ A Q J 10 7 2    ◇ 8    ♣ 10 8 6 3

(15)

| | West | North | East | South |
|---|---|---|---|---|
| | 1♡ | Pass | Pass | 1NT |
| | Pass | 2NT | Pass | 3NT |
| | Pass | Pass | Double | Pass |
| | Pass | Pass | | |

♠ Q J 10    ♡ Q 10 6 4 3    ◇ A K 9 5    ♣ 2

(12) ♠8. The double asks for an unusual lead, which means that a club or a trump is ruled out. As between the other two suits, the odds heavily favour a spade, for partner might have doubled North's 5♡ had he wanted to suggest a lead of that suit. Also, if

South has two heart losers they can hardly run away, but his spades may be discarded on North's hearts if the suit is not led at once.

(13) ♣ 5. Partner cannot want a diamond, for that would be normal. A void in one of the unbid suits is frequently the reason for a lead-directing double.

(14) ♣ 3. You cannot afford the luxury of laying down ♡A first, for it may be ruffed.

(15) ♡4. When either defender has bid a suit, a double asks for that suit to be led against a notrump contract. Partner probably holds a high heart and has doubled to make sure that the confident enemy bidding will not deter you from leading the suit.

You are South in the following auctions. What is your call?

| (16) | North | East | South | West |
|---|---|---|---|---|
| | 1◇ | Double | Pass | Pass |
| | Redouble | Pass | ? | |

♠ 10 9 8 2   ♡ Q 6 2   ◇ J 7 3   ♣ 7 6 4

| (17) | East | South | West | North |
|---|---|---|---|---|
| | 1♠ | 2♡ | Double | Redouble |
| | Pass | ? | | |

♠ 8 2   ♡ A 9 7 5 3 2   ◇ A Q 4   ♣ 7 4

| (18) | South | West | North | East |
|---|---|---|---|---|
| | 1♠ | Pass | 1NT | Pass |
| | Pass | Double | Redouble | Pass |
| | ? | | | |

♠ A K 6 4 2   ♡ J 10 4   ◇ 8 5   ♣ A 9 7

(16) 1♠. The redouble of a part-score contract when the double has been passed by partner is always SOS. Although you are not without support for diamonds you must not embarrass partner by passing.

(17) 3◇. The redouble is for rescue because if partner had been happy about the double of 2♡ he would have passed.

(18) *Pass*. Here the redouble, made before partner has passed the double, is strength-showing. Partner expects the opponents to remove 1NT doubled (or redoubled) and is saying to you, " I am maximum, I think we have them on the run."

# CHAPTER 11

# The Contested Auction

*Responding to an opening after an overcall – Opener's rebid after an overcall – Responding to an opening after a double – Opener's rebid after a double – Part scores – Competitive bidding and sacrifices – Psychic bids*

IT IS TIME to consider how to cope with enemy intervention. The principles of bidding discussed in the early chapters presume no knowledge of how the opponents' cards are distributed and may therefore require modification when the bidding has given some guide as to how the cards lie.

## Responding to an Opening after an Overcall

The principle here is that if you intend to raise your partner's suit and are uncertain as to what level, you should usually choose the higher bid. But if you propose any other form of action, you should tend to be conservative.

The more you have in your partner's suit, the more it will pay your side to play the hand. There is also the consideration that if you have a good fit the opponents may have one also, and by raising to the limit you may present the next player with a problem. Conversely, when your side has no immediate fit, it is less likely that the opponents have one.

In a contested auction courtesy responses are no longer made on a bare 6 points. Suppose you are the responder in this auction:

| Opener | Opponent | Responder | Opponent |
|--------|----------|-----------|----------|
| 1♣ | 1♡ | ? | |

You hold:

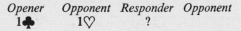

♠ Q 8 5 2 ♡ 8 5 4 ◇ A 10 5 2 ♣ 7 5

Had there been no intervention you would have kept the bidding open with 1♠, in case partner had a big hand. There is no need to do so now, as partner has another chance to bid. In the same way, responder does not make a free bid of 1NT on minimum values; such a bid now suggests 8 to 10 points.

When there is a choice between bidding a new suit and raising opener's suit, it is usually advisable to raise in a contested auction. This is a typical case:

| Opener | Opponent | Responder | Opponent |
|--------|----------|-----------|----------|
| 1♢ | 1♡ | ? | |

Responder holds:

♠ A 9 7 4  ♡ 9 4  ♢ J 10 5 3  ♣ Q 10 4

The responder may feel an urge to make a " cheap " bid of 1♠, but if partner raises with three-card support, as is liable to happen in a contested auction, it may prove false economy. In a competitive situation you go for the known fit. Suppose you bid 1♠, next hand bids 2♡ and your partner passes. Now you cannot show diamond support without overbidding your hand. It is better to limit your hand with 2♢ on the first round. Later you may be able to bid spades without overstating your strength.

### Cue-bidding the Opponent's Suit

This is a useful move when responder holds the values for game but is stuck for a natural bid, as in this sequence:

| Opener | Opponent | Responder | Opponent |
|--------|----------|-----------|----------|
| 1♣ | 1♠ | ? | |

Responder holds:

♠ 9 8 2  ♡ K 9 7 3  ♢ A J 4  ♣ K Q 6

Here 2♠, a general force to game with no relation to responder's holding in spades, is the only satisfactory bid.

The cue-bid may also be used when responder has strong support for opener's suit. Partner opens 1♡, there is a butt-in of 2♣, and you hold:

♠ K Q 8 3  ♡ A J 8 6  ♢ 10 7  ♣ A 5 4

Bid 3♣ and jump to game in hearts on the next round. At first, partner will assume that you are making a general-purpose force, but later he will place you with a hand of this type.

153

## Opener's Rebid after an Overcall

When second hand intervenes, the opener is still under an obligation to bid again if his partner responds in a new suit. But he does not necessarily make the same rebid as he would have made without the intervention. Opener should make adjustments in a sequence like this:

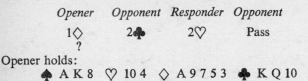

| Opener | Opponent | Responder | Opponent |
|--------|----------|-----------|----------|
| 1◇     | 2♣       | 2♡        | Pass     |
| ?      |          |           |          |

Opener holds:

    ♠ A K 8   ♡ 10 4   ◇ A 9 7 5 3   ♣ K Q 10

The rebid is 3NT, not 2NT. 2NT would suggest no more than 15 points, a hand on which opener would have rebid 1NT had the level been lower. As the responder has shown at least 10 points by bidding a new suit freely, and opener holds 16, he should bid game. Similarly:

| Opener | Opponent | Responder | Opponent |
|--------|----------|-----------|----------|
| 1♣     | 1♡       | 1♠        | Pass     |
| ?      |          |           |          |

Opener holds:

    ♠ K 8 7 6   ♡ 4 2   ◇ A J 5   ♣ A K 8 7

With no butt-in this hand would represent a maximum raise to 2♠. As the bidding has gone, the hand is worth 3♠, as responder would not have made a free bid on a borderline hand.

When fourth hand intervenes the opener is released from the obligation to rebid, but even with a minimum hand he should not fail to show four-card support for partner.

With strong hands a cue-bid in the opponent's suit may be the stand-by, as in this sequence:

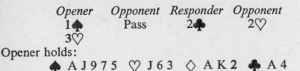

| Opener | Opponent | Responder | Opponent |
|--------|----------|-----------|----------|
| 1♠     | Pass     | 2♣        | 2♡       |
| 3♡     |          |           |          |

Opener holds:

    ♠ A J 9 7 5   ♡ J 6 3   ◇ A K 2   ♣ A 4

With no intervention, opener would have been willing to bid 3NT over 2♣, taking a chance on the hearts.

## Responding to an Opening after a Double

When partner opens and the next player doubles for takeout, the best course, with 10 or more points in high cards, is to redouble. This indicates that the hand " belongs " to the opening side and suggests strength in the other suits rather than opener's suit. The following would be ideal for a redouble by third hand after 1♠ had been doubled for takeout:

♠ 4   ♡ A 10 8 3   ◇ A 9 8 5   ♣ Q J 7 2

It is unlikely that opener will be left to play in 1♠ redoubled; and if he is, the responder's high cards may enable him to make it despite the singleton spade.

Since a redouble is the standard move on hands that contain defensive values, other calls tend to suggest attacking-type hands:

*Direct raises of opener's suit are pre-emptive in character.* Close decisions are resolved by bidding one more than you would have bid without the double.

*A simple bid in a new suit is not forcing.* It suggests a useful suit but too few points for a redouble.

*A jump shift is forcing for one round only.* This shows a type of responding hand on which a redouble would serve no useful purpose. For example:

♠ 4   ♡ J 8 2   ◇ A K 10 9 5 4   ♣ K Q 3

After 1♣ by opener, double from a non-vulnerable opponent, the probable effect of a redouble would be to allow the opponents to confuse the issue by bouncing in spades. It is better to bid 2◇, forcing for one round. (Alternatively, some players treat any jump as weak and pre-emptive.)

*1NT shows about 7 to 10 points.* This is often a good tactical move over a double, preventing the fourth player from responding at the one level.

*A response of 2NT* may be used to show a sound raise to three of opener's suit. This is a useful understanding, provided, of course, that partner shares it. Here 2NT is not needed in a natural sense, as with a strong balanced hand responder would redouble.

A special meaning exists when opener takes action in front of the redoubler in a situation like this:

| Opener | Opponent | Responder | Opponent |
|--------|----------|-----------|----------|
| 1♡ | Double | Redouble | 2♣ |
| 2♡ | | | |

Opener's anticipatory rebid says: " I'm not giving you a chance to double 2♣ as my hand is unsuitable. I have a weakish hand with a long heart suit." The message would be the same if fourth hand had passed over the redouble. Now compare this sequence:

| Opener | Opponent | Responder | Opponent |
|--------|----------|-----------|----------|
| 1♡ | Double | Redouble | 2♣ |
| Pass | Pass | Double | Pass |
| 2♡ | | | |

This time the opener is showing a stronger hand, still unsuited to defence but no longer below standard in terms of high cards.

### Part Scores

Only about one hand in three provides a reasonable chance of game, so it follows that part-score bidding is of great importance. First, it is necessary to understand the value of a part score in relation to game.

#### Value of a Part Score

Nobody can state the value of a part score precisely, because a number of imponderables enter. The obvious advantage of a part score of 40 or more is that it takes you half-way to game. However, it would be wrong to say that a part score was therefore worth " half a game ". For one thing, the opponents may score the next game, annulling your partial. For another, if your side can make just 2♡, but no more, the opponents won't let you buy the contract at that level. Only about once in six, perhaps, will your part score enable you to make a game that would otherwise have been beyond your reach. As the equity value of a game ranges from about 300 to 500, according to vulnerability, the equity value of a part score, as a step to making game, is about 70 points, to which must be added, of course, the points for the part score itself.

However, the assessment does not end there, as a part score may arouse the opponents' combativeness. An old-time British player once wrote: " Game and 90 doesn't always win the rubber, but by the time the opponents have won it they may wish it had done." Not a marvel of clear expression, but the thought is there: a part score is a great provoker of indiscretions. Half the 700s in this world arise from part-score battles. Furthermore, the side that has a part score has a genuine tactical advantage. Take the familiar situation where South opens with one of a suit at 60 up and North responds 1NT. The opponents, not knowing whether North has 4 points or 14, are in a dilemma. If one of them, holding 12 points or so, attempts to contest in any way he may stub his toes badly.

The effect of these considerations is that the concealed value of a part score varies from about 100 when neither side is vulnerable to about 150 when both sides are vulnerable. This means that, when not vulnerable, a player should not abandon a safe part score for a doubtful game unless the game has an even chance of succeeding. Vulnerable, the odds are slightly more in favour of bidding a close game.

Note that we say " a player should not abandon a *safe* part score ". Suppose your partner opens 1♣ and, holding a fairly balanced 10 points, you respond 1♡. Partner rebids 1NT, indicating 13 to 15. Now there is generally a fair play for game when the partnership holds 25 points in high cards, and if you knew you had 25 points you would bid the game. But you will have 25 only if partner is maximum, and if you raise to 2NT you may go down in that. In the long run it will pay to stay in 1NT. There is the further possibility that an opponent may reopen and find that the strength is not as evenly divided as he imagined.

The situation is different when the bidding has reached a higher level and you are only one short of game. For example, if you have already reached 2NT or three of a major, there is a better case for bidding a borderline game.

## Opening the Bidding in a Part-Score Situation

Two points arise here: Is it wise to open light? And in what way, if any, should the choice of opening bid be affected by the part score?

There are three situations to consider—when your side has a part score, when opponents have one, and when both sides have one. All experienced rubber bridge players open light when they have a partial themselves. This is not so much because they hope to snatch a game with moderate values as because the side that opens has a tactical advantage in many ways. Equally, when both sides have a part score, attack is the best defence on a minimum balanced hand. The best action is not so clear when opponents have a part score and you have a borderline hand with no good rebid. Here it may be best to pass unless you hold a suit of spades and can open 1♠.

In all part-score situations it is good tactics to open moderate hands with a comparatively high-ranking bid such as 1♠ or 1NT. At 60 up 1NT has a wide range—from about 14 to 19 when you are playing a strong notrump, from 12 to 18 when you are playing a weak notrump. Opening three-bids, also, vary from very weak to quite strong.

### Effect of a Part Score on Competitive Bidding

The presence of a part score has an important effect on tactics in a competitive auction. When your side has a partial you should be willing to take risks to defend it. To go down 500 to save a game and retain your part score is good business, and even the loss of 700 in the same cause is no disaster. It follows that when opponents have the part score, and the superior cards, it is sensible to go quietly and let them make the game. Many players do precisely the opposite, to their cost.

### Competitive Bidding and Sacrifices

Good judgment in competitive bidding comes only from long experience. The variety of possible situations is so great that to give odd examples would not be very helpful. It is possible, however, to lay down certain guide-rules:

(1) When your side has the balance of the cards and the opponents are defending, take a certain 300 rather than let them stretch you beyond your limit.

(2) When your side is defending, and you are sure that opponents can make their contract, defend with vigour. To concede 700 looks bad, but in real terms the loss is not serious. (The cost, as against par, is less than when you go one down in a part-score contract you ought to have made.) Meanwhile, the opponents will sometimes miscalculate, either by bidding too high, or by failing to double, or by defending badly. Keep them at full stretch.

(3) When it is not so certain that opponents can make their contract, take your chance and don't invite a certain penalty. In

general, you should not sacrifice when you can see the probability of enough defensive tricks to hold opponents to their contract. The odd J–x or its equivalent will often produce an extra trick when partner has a high card in the same suit. A defender who holds a singleton king under an opponent's long trump suit may regard it as a liability rather than as an asset, but sometimes partner turns up with Q–x—an equally gloomy holding from his point of view.

In the part-score zone be satisfied as a rule to push opponents to the three level; in the game zone it is always an achievement to push them into the no-go area of five in a major suit.

(4) When nobody is sure who can make what, always bid one more. This is a matter of simple mathematics. If you go one down in 5♡ and they would have been one down in their contract of 4♠, with both sides vulnerable, you are 200 worse off than you might have been. If they would have made 4♠ and you go one down, you have saved 520 by bidding on. If they would have made their game, and you make yours, you have gained no less than 1270. There is one other favourable possibility: perhaps you would have been one down in 5♡, but they go to 5♠ and don't make it. That is 720 better for you than letting them make 4♠.

We turn next to features of a hand that are favourable or unfavourable for the purpose of a sacrifice.

(1) First, does it look as though there is a good fit with your partner's hand? Obviously, a holding such as x–x–x or x–x–x–x in a suit bid and supported by the opponents is a good feature, as you may expect partner to hold a singleton or void. It is nevertheless wise not to be too much influenced by that factor, as partner's support may be largely based on the same feature.

In general, you should aim to play the hand, rather than to defend, when you and your partner both hold length in the same suits. Sometimes this is apparent from partner's bidding, sometimes it is a matter of inference. Suppose you hold as South:

♠ K Q 10 8 4   ♡ K 5   ◇ 6 3   ♣ A Q J 4

The bidding goes:

| South | West | North | East |
|-------|------|-------|------|
| 1♠ | 2◇ | 2♠ | 3♡ |
| 3♠ | 4♡ | Pass | Pass |
| ? | | | |

Now you may think that as you have some good cards outside your spade suit, including a possible trump trick, you should take

159

your chance on beating 4♡. However, there is a sinister feature in the hand. It seems quite likely that partner will have length in clubs, perhaps four or five to the king. That will kill your defensive chances. Certainly you should go to 4♠ and perhaps even to five.

(2) A satisfactory trump suit is an essential basis for any out-and-out sacrifice. Then at least you have the assurance of making a certain number of tricks; furthermore, the opponents, not possessing a trump trick and not knowing the precise nature of your distribution in the other suits, may be uncertain at what point to double.

On the other side, you will sometimes see a player who holds two suits such as K–x–x–x–x and A–Q–x–x–x–x bidding to the skies after he has obtained delayed support for the K–x–x–x–x suit. When that suit breaks badly, 1100 may follow.

(3) On a slightly different plane, a player must use his ears. For example, when a non-vulnerable opponent jumps to game, having discovered a fit, it is generally safe to give him one more push. Considerations of that sort bring us to the next section.

### Psychic Bids

A psychic bid, in the words of a *Punch* cartoon, is one that makes an opponent think that you hold cards which up to then he thought he held himself. Not a bad description, in its way. If you decide to open 1♠ as dealer on a suit consisting of 10–x–x there is a fair chance that if one opponent holds K–J–x–x–x and the other A–Q–x–x, neither of them will get round to bidding the suit.

However, despite their attractions, these out-and-out psychics have been out of fashion since the earliest days of contract, mainly because partner often has length in the imaginary suit and supports it to the death. Psychic openings are attempted from time to time at duplicate, but at any other form of scoring they are an expensive quirk.

Nevertheless, there is scope for psychic or semi-psychic manoeuvres at other stages of the auction. The essential condition is that there should be some sort of safety umbrella. Here, quite briefly, are some examples of deceptive bids that may save a game and are unlikely to be costly.

(1) Players who use the weak notrump have many opportunities. After two passes you hold:

♠ Q 7   ♡ 8 5 3   ◇ J 4   ♣ A Q J 9 7 3

1NT is more likely to have an inhibiting effect on the opponents than 3♣. As partner passed originally it is unlikely that he will carry you to game; and if he does, the opponents may not be able to double.

(2) Your partner passes and the opponent on your right opens 1◇. Not vulnerable, you hold:

♠ J 9 7 6 3    ♡ A 8 5    ◇ 4    ♣ Q 8 7 2

Your side is certainly outgunned, and the odds are that the opponents can make a game. Their natural contract may be 4♡, and an overcall of 1♡ by you is unlikely to come to great harm. If you are doubled immediately you can retreat to 1♠. If you end up in something like 3♡ doubled, the result may not be calamitous. You will make a few tricks by ruffing before the opponents catch on to the fact that you are ruffing in the short trump hand.

Even an opening bid of 1♡, after two passes, is a fair proposition on this type of hand.

(3) When you hold a really strong suit elsewhere you have more licence for bluff bids in a short suit. Again you are not vulnerable against vulnerable opponents, and in third position you hold:

♠ 7 3    ♡ J 9 4    ◇ A K Q J 8 6 3    ♣ 5

You could open with a pre-empt of 5◇, but it would probably cost you 500 or so, less the honours. As an alternative, try 1♠. The worst that can happen is that, as before, you will end up in 5◇ doubled.

(4) As we noted earlier in this chapter, a solid trump suit provides security in a competitive auction. Here is an example of how this asset can be exploited:

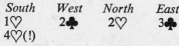

| South | West | North | East |
|-------|------|-------|------|
| 1♡ | 2♣ | 2♡ | 3♣ |
| 4♡(!) | | | |

South holds:

♠ Q J 8    ♡ A K Q J 3    ◇ 10 8 2    ♣ 7 4

The jump to 4♡ is quite unjustified and you would probably go two down if doubled. But the solid trump suit protects you like a suit of armour. The opponents, lacking a trump trick and concluding that you have distributional values, are more likely to go to 5♣ than to double; and 5♣ you will probably be able to defeat.

We look next at deceptive bids which are not at all dangerous and which may cause the opponents to misjudge.

(5) At favourable vulnerability you hold as East:

♠ K J 9 4  ♡ 6  ◇ Q 7 6 4 3  ♣ 10 5 3

The bidding goes:

| South | West | North | East |
|-------|------|-------|------|
| 1♡ | 1♠ | 2◇ | ? |

Your objective is to buy the contract as cheaply as you can in spades. A good move for the moment is to bid 3♣. This carries no risk and, particularly if South is strong in clubs, it may cause the opponents to double you prematurely in 3♠ or 4♠.

(6) Finally, as every poker player knows, there is as much profit in understating good cards as in overstating bad ones. At equal vulnerability you hold as North:

♠ 6  ♡ Q J 7 4 2  ◇ 4  ♣ A 10 7 6 4 2

The bidding goes:

| South | West | North | East |
|-------|------|-------|------|
| 1♡ | 1♠ | ? | |

Be cool! Bid simply 2♡.

## QUIZ ON THE CONTESTED AUCTION

With neither side vulnerable, your partner opens 1♠ and the next player bids 2◇. What is your call with each of the following?

(1) ♠ 9 5          ♡ Q 8 6 2  ◇ A K 3    ♣ Q 10 5 4
(2) ♠ K J 9 7 4 2  ♡ Q J 7 6  ◇ A        ♣ Q 4
(3) ♠ Q 10 9 4     ♡ 10 4     ◇ A J 7 2   ♣ K 7 5

(1) 2NT. 2NT in this sequence indicates about 11 or 12 and thus reflects your hand very well. Your heart suit is not strong enough to introduce in a competitive situation and a double of 2◇ has no appeal. The 2◇ overcall will be based on a long suit headed by the Q–J and the trump tricks you would make against 2◇ doubled would be merely the tricks your opponent expected to lose.

(2) 3◇. In view of your enormous distributional strength, a direct raise to 4♠ would not begin to do justice to your hand. Equally, a Blackwood 4NT would not be bright, for if partner showed two aces you would not know what to do. Best is to cue-bid. 3◇ and then support spades, leaving the next move to partner.

(3) 3♠. If ever a kind of Devil's Island is established for erring bridge players, space should be reserved for the type of player who doubles in this situation. It is never right to double at a low level with four cards in partner's major suit.

You are South and the bidding has gone:

| South | West | North | East |
|-------|------|-------|------|
| 1♣ | 1♠ | 2♡ | Pass |
| ? | | | |

What is your call with each of the following hands?

(4) ♠ 7 2    ♡ K J 4    ◇ A 8 3    ♣ A K 9 8 6

(5) ♠ K    ♡ 5 3    ◇ A Q 8 4    ♣ K Q J 6 5 3

(6) ♠ A Q 5 2    ♡ J 7    ◇ J 8 6    ♣ A J 8 6

(4) 4♡. Partner would not have introduced a four-card suit in this situation, nor would he have entered on a doubtful hand. If you had the same hand with a trick fewer you would still raise partner's heart call to three, so with the actual hand it must be sound to bid four.

(5) 3♣. A cautious rebid is indicated as you can attach no value to ♠K and have no fit in responder's heart suit. To bid 3◇ would be a reverse, suggesting a stronger hand.

(6) 2NT. The intervention has robbed you of your intended rebid, as 2♠ would now be interpreted as a cue-bid. You cannot raise hearts, so 2NT, which does not show extra values in this sequence, is the only solution.

You are South and the bidding has gone:

| South | West | North | East |
|-------|------|-------|------|
| 1◇ | Pass | 1♡ | 1♠ |
| ? | | | |

What is your call with each of the following?

(7) ♠ J 8 3    ♡ 7 4    ◇ A Q 5 4 2    ♣ A Q 9

(8) ♠ 8 6    ♡ 8 7 3 2    ◇ A K J 8 6    ♣ A 4

(9) ♠ A J 9    ♡ 8 3    ◇ A Q 4 2    ♣ Q J 4 2

(7) *Pass.* This is a minimum hand and partner's heart bid has made it no better. As East's overcall has relieved you of the obligation to rebid, you should pass.

(8) 2♡. To pass here would be poor tactics. With four-card support for responder's suit, the principle is to accept the challenge even with the barest opening.

(9) 1NT. Here again it would be tactically unwise to miss the opportunity of showing the nature of your hand. If you passed, your partner might contest with 2◇ or 2♡, either of which might well be inferior to 1NT.

You are South and the bidding has gone:

| South | West | North | East |
|-------|------|-------|------|
| 1♡ | 1♠ | 2◇ | 2♠ |
| ? | | | |

What is your call with each of the following?

(10) ♠ K Q 10  ♡ Q 7 6 5 2  ◇ K J  ♣ A 10 3

(11) ♠ 7 6 4  ♡ A K J 9 2  ◇ K 10 8 5  ♣ A

(12) ♠ 9 3  ♡ K Q J 8 7  ◇ A J 8  ♣ Q 10 4

(10) 2NT. You have a sound opening and an encouraging holding in partner's suit. Since your hearts are not exactly overpowering the best move is 2NT, which defines your values accurately. Partner is likely to have at least 10 points, so with a stronger hand you would have jumped to game.

(11) 4◇. You have 17 points in support of diamonds and should judge your hand to be worth even more as you have no wastage in spades, where partner is likely to be short. 4◇ is forcing but does not necessarily commit the hand to diamonds, as partner may still bid 4♡.

(12) 3◇. If East had not bid 2♠ it would have been reasonable to rebid 2♡. In a contested auction it is preferable, when the choice is close, to raise your partner rather than rebid your own suit. What you must not do is bow the knee to 2♠ just because your hand is a minimum in high cards.

Your partner opens with 1♠ and the next player doubles for takeout. What is your call with each of the following?

(13) ♠ 7     ♡ K 10 8 4     ◇ A Q 8 4 3     ♣ 6 5 2
(14) ♠ 10 4     ♡ J 8 2     ◇ Q J 7 2     ♣ K 8 7 4
(15) ♠ J 8 7 4 2     ♡ 6     ◇ K Q 9 6 2     ♣ 10 7
(16) ♠ Q 10 7 4     ♡ 9 5     ◇ A J 8 6     ♣ K 6 3

(13) *Redouble*. This says that your side holds the balance of strength and that there are prospects of doubling the opponents. The singleton in partner's suit is no disadvantage. The redouble may enable partner to penalize a takeout of 2♣, which you yourself would hardly be entitled to double.

(14) *Pass*. Over an opponent's double of 1♠ there is no point in entering with sketchy values and no fit for partner's suit. If partner had opened 1♡, there would be some point in bidding 1NT to shut out a spade bid.

(15) 4♠. With 11 points in support of spades this hand would normally be worth a raise to three only. In view of the double the raise to four is justified as a pre-emptive manoeuvre.

(16) 2NT. This response, it will be remembered, signifies the values for a sound, as opposed to a pre-emptive, double raise of partner's suit. The opener must bid 4♠ on any hand where he would have gone to game after a normal raise to three.

# PART III

---

*Advanced Bidding*

# CHAPTER 12

## Slam Bidding

*Diagnosis and valuation – The Blackwood convention – Slam tries below game level – Slam sequences after a notrump opening – Trump solidity – Gerber convention*

THE ACID test of good bidding occurs in the slam zone. This is not because the mechanics in themselves present any special difficulty, but because at slam level there is need for much greater accuracy.

A contract of 2◇, for example, may be reasonable whether declarer is due to make ten tricks or only seven, as in this last case the opponents can presumably make something. Similarly, it may be reasonable to bid game in a major suit whether declarer makes nine, ten or eleven tricks. In the slam zone the tolerances are much narrower. If you reach a small slam and have less than an even chance of making it, you are in a poor contract. If you reach a grand slam and the chances are less than about 3 to 1 in your favour, then again you have not distinguished yourself.

There are two stages in slam bidding. First, there is the attempt to diagnose the possibility of slam at an early stage and to estimate the chances at a safe level. Secondly, there are the technical manoeuvres designed to avoid such embarrassing happenings as playing in a small slam with two top losers. We take these two stages in turn.

### Diagnosis and Valuation

The first item on the agenda is not to guard against having two losers but to find twelve winners. If point count were the only test, the magic figure would be 33 or 34. There are certain recurring situations where these values may be present. Thus:

*You open with an above-minimum hand and your partner responds with a jump shift.* A jump shift is usually based on at least 17 points and guarantees a game opposite a minimum (possibly unsuitable) opening. If opener has anything more than a minimum, or has a good fit, slam must be on the horizon.

*Your partner opens, you yourself have opening values and your partner makes a jump rebid.* Opener's jump rebid usually shows 17 to 19 points. If the responder has opening values, the partnership is close to the slam zone.

*Your partner opens 2♣ and you have the values for a positive response.* Since a 2♣ opening is based either on game-going values or on at least 23 high-card points, the values that make up a positive response will be sufficient for slam unless both players are minimum or there is a misfit.

*At any stage of the auction your partner raises to game and you have appreciable undisclosed values.* The concept of undisclosed values is very important in slam bidding. A player must always be aware of how many points he has shown and whether he has any extra. Suppose you are the opening hand in this auction:

| Opener | Responder |
|--------|-----------|
| 1♣ | 1♡ |
| 1♠ | 4♠ |
| ? | |

You have not so far suggested more than 13 points. If you actually have more, these are undisclosed values, and you should consider carefully before passing the raise to game. Partner has shown at least 13 points and may have up to 16. It follows from these figures that a slam may be there if you have 17 points or more.

Many players, when they hold a good hand, fall into the trap of bidding the same cards twice. Remember, it is only the *extra* values that justify a further advance. This is a typical situation:

| Opener | Responder |
|--------|-----------|
| 1♣ | 1♡ |
| 2♣ | 3♡ |
| ? | |

Opener holds:

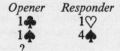

♠ A Q J 2   ♡ A 10 4   ◇ K 6   ♣ A J 9 7

Here the opener may think, after partner has rebid his hearts, that the way to slam is open, but that is quite wrong. He has a fine hand but should do no more than bid 4♡ at this point. He will then have shown all essential features. Any slam effort must come from partner.

Point count, therefore, is useful for diagnosis; but it is not a conclusive method of valuation. In the slam zone, to be a really good bidder one must take into account the " fit "—or lack of it. As the target narrows, the hand should be subjected to increasing criticism.

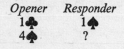

Responder holds:

♠ K J 10 7 5   ♡ Q J 8   ◇ K Q   ♣ 7 5 4

Responder has 13 points and so far has promised only 6. Opener's raise to game suggests 19 or 20 points, and if he is maximum the combined count will be 33. On this basis some players would launch into Blackwood with the responding hand, but they would arrive at a poor contract more often than not. Responder should say to himself: " As partner is long in both black suits he will be short in the red suits, so some of my points are certain to be wasted. My ◇K–Q are not worth anything like 5 points. Furthermore, as I have three small clubs, partner's club suit will need to be exceptionally strong if we are to avoid losing a club trick." Note that when slam in a suit is under consideration, three low cards in partner's side suit are a most unattractive holding.

With the three hands below, how would the reader rate the chances of slam after the bidding has gone:

| Opener | Responder |
|--------|-----------|
| 1♠ | 2♣ |
| 2♡ | 4♡ |
| ? | |

Opener holds:

(1) ♠ A Q J 6 3   ♡ A Q J 2   ◇ 10 3   ♣ K 4
(2) ♠ A K J 4 2   ♡ K Q 10 3   ◇ 6   ♣ K Q 2
(3) ♠ K Q J 8   ♡ A Q 7 3   ◇ A 8   ♣ J 8 4

With (1) slam is not certain but prospects are bright. Opener can count on at least 31 points and his holding in partner's club suit is very advantageous. As he cannot be sure of the diamond situation he should bid 5♣, an exploratory manoeuvre discussed later.

In (2) opener's hand is so suitable in every way that valuation hardly comes into it. Opener assumes that both black suits can be developed if necessary and inquires immediately for aces (via Blackwood; below). If partner has three aces he intends to bid 7♡.

Hand (3) contains 17 high-card points, but their disposition is poor; there is danger of losing a club or a diamond or both. As there will be 33 points only if the responder is maximum, opener should pass.

We pass now from valuation to methods of locating " controls ". It is convenient to begin with the standard form of ace-inquiry.

### The Blackwood Convention

This is one of the best known conventions in bridge. To find out how many aces his partner holds, a player bids 4NT. In reply, the responder bids 5♣ to show no aces (or all four); 5◇ to show one ace; 5♡ to show two aces, and 5♠ to show three aces. If the Blackwooder subsequently bids 5NT he is saying that no aces are missing and is asking his partner to show kings in the same way.

Before using Blackwood a player should be sure:

(1) That twelve tricks can be brought in provided the desired *number* of aces is held. (It is, for example, unsound for a player who holds one ace to use Blackwood when a slam will be on only if partner has the two *right* aces.)

(2) That five-odd will be safe even if two aces are missing.

(3) That he will know precisely what to do next after partner's Blackwood response.

It is generally wrong to use Blackwood with a void, or when the response may not clarify whether there are two losers in a particular suit. For example:

| Opener | Responder |
|--------|-----------|
| 1♣ | 1♡ |
| 1♠ | 4♠ |
| ? | |

Opener holds:

(1) ♠ A Q 10 3 2    ♡ K 4    ◇ –    ♣ K J 9 7 4 3
(2) ♠ A J 10 3    ♡ K 6    ◇ 8 5    ♣ A K Q 6 3

In both cases opener has the values for slam, but in neither case is Blackwood the solution. If there is an ace missing, opener will need to know which one it is and the response won't tell him. With the first hand opener should bid 5◇; with the second, 5♡. (5♣ would be a little ambiguous, arousing suspicions about the nature of your spades.)

The situation is different in this example:

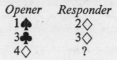

| Opener | Responder |
|--------|-----------|
| 1♠ | 2♦ |
| 3♣ | 3♦ |
| 4♦ | ? |

Responder holds:

♠ K    ♡ 10 8 3    ◇ A Q 10 7 3 2    ♣ K J 5

The 3♦ bid is forcing, as both players have bid constructively. It is almost impossible, in view of the sequence followed by the opener and the good cards held by the responder, that opener should have two losers in hearts. It is quite safe, therefore, to introduce a Blackwood 4NT.

It is particularly unwise to use Blackwood when a disappointing response to 4NT might carry the bidding beyond a safe level, as in this auction:

| Opener | Responder |
|--------|-----------|
| 1♡ | 2♦ |
| 4♦ | ? |

Responder holds:

♠ Q 9    ♡ 8    ◇ K Q J 7 4 2    ♣ K Q 10 5

Responder may think that there will be a slam if partner has three aces, but it would be futile to bid 4NT to find out. If opener were to respond 5♡ the partnership would be overboard. The best move is to bid 5♣; opener may place his partner with the ace, but as he is missing K–Q–J of trumps he is unlikely to bid 6◇ with only two aces, or even with three aces and two losing spades. Responder's failure to bid 4♠, as a slam try, is highly significant.

Use Blackwood not as a stepping stone to good slams, but as a means of avoiding bad ones. There is a genuine distinction there. The time to go a-Blackwooding is when you can say to yourself, " As long as we are not missing two aces I want to be in six." That is *not* the same as saying, " If we have enough aces I am prepared to take a chance on six."

Not every 4NT is Blackwood; in some sequences it is simply a natural bid. It is indispensable in this sense when one partner wants to suggest a slam in notrumps but lacks the strength to go all the way himself. As a misunderstanding in this area may be very costly, it is wise to avoid ambiguous sequences with a strange partner. With a regular partner, two principles apply:

1. *A bid of 4NT is always natural if neither player has at any time made a natural (as opposed to conventional) bid in a suit.* For example:

| (1) | Opener | Responder | (2) | Opener | Responder |
|-----|--------|-----------|-----|--------|-----------|
|     | 2NT    | <u>4NT</u> |     | 1NT    | 2♣        |
|     |        |           |     | 2NT    | <u>4NT</u> |

In each case 4NT is a slam try in notrumps.

2. *A bid of 4NT is also natural when, although suits have been called, it is clear that no suit has been agreed as the trump suit,* as in this case:

| Opener | Responder |
|--------|-----------|
| 1♠     | 2♡        |
| 3NT    | <u>4NT</u> |

Here 4NT is natural because neither spades nor hearts have been agreed as trumps. If responder wants to inquire for aces in this kind of situation he must manufacture a bid in a new suit. For example, over 3NT responder might bid 4♣ and opener 4♡. At that point 4NT by responder would be conventional.

There are, however, two occasions when 4NT is treated as conventional, even though no suit has been ostensibly agreed. The first is when the player jumps, as here:

| Opener | Responder |
|--------|-----------|
| 1♠     | 2♡        |
| 3♣     | <u>4NT</u> |

The jump to 4NT is Blackwood, though only the responder knows where he intends to play.

Secondly, 4NT is conventional when it follows a jump shift:

| Opener | Responder |
|--------|-----------|
| 1♡     | 3♢        |
| 3NT    | <u>4NT</u> |

Responder is in charge and his bid of 4NT is Blackwood.

*Stopping at 5NT.* There is a device for stopping at 5NT when partner's response to Blackwood has demonstrated that two aces are missing. The Blackwood bidder, over the disappointing response, introduces a completely new suit at the five level. The message is, "We can't make six of anything. Try 5NT."

| Opener | Responder |
|--------|-----------|
| 1♠ | 2♣ |
| 4♣ | 4NT |
| 5◇ | 5♡ |
| 5NT | Pass |

Responder cannot bid 5NT himself, of course, as that would be Blackwood for kings.

*Responding to Blackwood with a void.* Void suits are not counted as aces when responding to Blackwood, but if the responder to 4NT has a strong enough hand he may indicate a void by responding at the six level in the denomination that at the five level would have indicated the number of aces held.

| Opener | Responder |
|--------|-----------|
| 1◇ | 2♣ |
| 3♣ | 3♠ |
| 4♠ | 4NT |
| 6◇ | |

Here the opener is showing one ace and a void, which obviously must be in hearts.

*Responding to Blackwood over intervention.* Occasionally an opponent will interfere with the Blackwood machinery by bidding a suit over 4NT. In this case the responder may indicate aces by the usual " step " system. For example:

| South | West | North | East |
|-------|------|-------|------|
| 1♠ | 2♡ | 3♠ | 4♡ |
| 4NT | 5♡ | ? | |

At this point 5♠ by North would show one ace, 5NT would show two, and so on. Double would be for penalties and would imply that North was not interested in a slam. A pass would suggest no ace, but North might deem it advisable to pass even if he held an ace.

### Slam Tries below Game Level

The Blackwood convention may keep you out of a slam when the opponents have two aces, but it nevertheless carries the bidding to a high level. To play a hand in 5♡ or 5♠ represents failure, as you are taking an extra risk for no reward.

It is certainly far more satisfactory to be able to weigh the slam possibilities without going beyond the game level. Cue-bids enable you to do this. They may also help you in ways that Blackwood cannot—by telling you *which* ace is held, or whether there are extra values.

When a trump suit has been agreed and the partnership is committed to game, any bid in a new suit is a cue-bid. It shows control in that suit, usually the ace or void, sometimes a king or singleton. It is largely because of the usefulness of cue-bids that it is such a great advantage to agree a trump suit at the lowest level.

A cue-bid can be made only when (a) a trump suit has been agreed, and (b) the partnership is by this time committed to game.

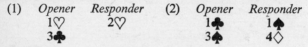

In (1) 3♣ is not a cue-bid, for although a trump suit has been agreed the partnership is not yet committed to game.

In (2) 4◇ is a cue-bid, showing interest in a slam with spades as trumps. The responder may have something like this:

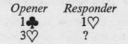

After his partner's 3♠ bid the responder can count on 33 points if his partner is maximum, and he has an excellent fit in clubs. At this point 4NT would be a crude move; for one thing, if opener showed two aces, responder would have no idea whether the heart position was secure.

A cue-bid of 4◇ is clearly much more intelligent. If opener happened to have a void in diamonds he would be warned immediately of the duplication. Over 4♡ by opener, showing a hand suitable for slam with a heart control, responder could bid 6♠ straight off. If opener were to bid 4♠ over 4◇, indicating no heart control or a minimum hand or both, responder would have to decide whether his values justified a further effort of 5♣.

With a weaker hand the player who initiates a cue-bidding sequence may elicit an encouraging response but be unable to make any further advance, as in this example:

|  | Opener | Responder |
|---|---|---|
|  | 1♣ | 1♡ |
|  | 3♡ | ? |

The responder's hand is:

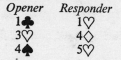

As the Q–10 of partner's suit may be useful cards, responder can make one slam try with 4◇; but then he must leave any further action to his partner. The bidding may continue:

| Opener | Responder |
| --- | --- |
| 1♣ | 1♡ |
| 3♡ | 4◇ |
| 4♠ | 5♡ |

Opener can now place his partner with a hand of this general strength and is free either to bid the slam or pass.

### Cue-bidding a Second-round Control

Cue-bidding is not confined to aces and voids. Often it is very helpful to show a king or singleton, and sometimes this is the only constructive move available.

There are also times when a player may make a repeat cue-bid in the same suit, as here:

| Opener | Responder |
| --- | --- |
| 1NT | 3♠ |
| 4♠ | 5◇ |
| 5♡ | 6◇ |

Responder may have this hand:

The second cue-bid in diamonds is obviously an attempt to reach a grand slam. By proceeding in this fashion, instead of merely using Blackwood for aces and kings, responder indicates that he is interested in such features as third-round control of diamonds and trump solidity, as well as aces.

The cue-bid of a second-round control usually denies the presence of a first-round control in another suit that might have been shown instead. Thus 6◇ in the last example denies ♣A.

It may, however, be good tactics to cue-bid a second-round

177

control in preference to a first-round control when the former keeps the bidding below game. The bidding goes:

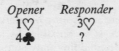

Responder holds:

♠ A 7 4    ♡ Q 9 8 5    ◇ 3    ♣ Q 8 6 4 2

At this point 4◇ would be more prudent than 4♠.

## Advance Cue-bids

Occasionally it will be found that there is no space to agree a trump suit and then make a cue-bid. Consider the responder's predicament in this sequence:

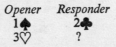

The responder holds:

♠ 4    ♡ K 10 7 3    ◇ A 10 4    ♣ Q J 10 8 3

A simple raise to 4♡ would be unenterprising, while a jump to 5♡ would leave opener in the dark as to the diamond situation. Responder's best move, therefore, is a cue-bid of 4◇. It is not necessary for opener to know what is intended at this stage. Whether opener now bids 4♠, 4♡ or 5♣, responder continues with 5♡ and the scales fall from opener's eyes.

## Slam Sequences after a Notrump Opening

It is possible to investigate slam prospects with considerable accuracy after an opening bid of 1NT. The principles we describe apply to a notrump opening of any strength.

The simplest slam exploration after an opening bid of 1NT or 2NT is a direct raise to 4NT by the responder. This is a natural raise and invites opener to bid 6NT with a maximum and pass with a minimum.

More often, responder will begin with a jump in a suit over 1NT. There is then much scope for what solo players call " prop and cop ". A player who has opened 1NT and has ambitions after his partner's forcing response must not fail to make an advance cue-bid, showing interest in a slam. Suppose you open with a strong notrump and your partner forces with 3♡. You hold:

♠ K Q 7    ♡ A J 9 3    ◇ K 2    ♣ A 10 5 4

The objection to a simple bid of 4♡ is that your hand is much more suitable for a heart contract than it might have been; responder could easily have enough for slam and yet be unable to take any safe action over 4♡. At the same time, responder's hand may not be in the slam range at all, and therefore you cannot safely go beyond the level of 4♡.

The solution is to bid 4♣, indicating ♣A and interest in a heart slam. The advance cue-bid always has this sense; it would be quite wrong to bid 4♣ simply to show something like ♣ A–K–Q–x.

Observe the value of the negative inference that the responder can draw in a sequence such as this:

| Opener | Responder |
|--------|-----------|
| 1NT | 3♡ |
| 4♡ | ? |

Responder holds:

♠ A K J 7    ♡ A J 10 8 3    ◇ J 2    ♣ 8 3

As the opener has not made an advance cue-bid of 4♣ or 4◇, it may be assumed that he has no more than one ace and is missing one of the trump honours.

### Trump Solidity

Sometimes the only doubt about a grand slam is the trump situation. The traditional method of ascertaining whether there is a gap in the trump suit is the grand slam force, which utilizes a direct bid of 5NT, an otherwise idle bid.

There is no problem in recognizing the grand slam force. In the Blackwood convention, as we have seen, you cannot bid 5NT, asking for kings, without first bidding 4NT to ask for aces. This is so even when you hold all the aces yourself. A bid of 5NT which is not preceded by 4NT is therefore not Blackwood, but the grand slam force, asking partner about his holding in the trump suit.

When bid in this direct fashion 5NT requires partner to bid seven in the agreed suit if he holds two of the top three trump honours. For example:

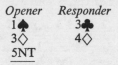

| Opener | Responder |
|--------|-----------|
| 1♠ | 3♣ |
| 3◇ | 4◇ |
| 5NT | |

Opener holds:

♠ A K J 8 5 2    ♡ –    ◇ Q 7 4 3 2    ♣ A 4

He bids 5NT to determine whether his partner holds ◇ A–K.

This is the standard form of the convention, but a more accurate scale of responses can be devised. In *Bridge for Tournament Players* the present authors recommended the following system:

The responder to 5NT bids

| | |
|---|---|
| 6♣ | No top honour (A, K or Q) |
| 6◇ | One top honour |
| 6♡ | Two top honours |
| 6♠ | Three top honours |

The convention will now serve a player who holds, say, A–Q–x–x of the trump suit and needs to find partner with the king; or a player holding J–x–x–x–x who wants to be in seven only if partner holds A–K–Q. Regular partnerships may employ still more sophisticated systems where responder distinguishes between a trump suit headed by the queen and one headed by the king or ace.

### Gerber Convention

There can be a problem in asking for aces over an opening 1NT or 2NT, because a raise to 4NT may be needed in a natural sense. The popular solution is to use 4♣ to ask for aces. The responses are by the usual steps:

4◇ shows no aces or four aces.
4♡ shows one ace.
4♠ shows two aces.
4NT shows three aces.

After the ace-showing response, the 4♣ bidder may continue with 5♣ to ask for kings.

## SLAM BIDDING QUIZ

You are South and the bidding has proceeded:

| South | West | North | East |
|-------|------|-------|------|
| 1♡ | Pass | 1♠ | Pass |
| 2♣ | Pass | 3NT | Pass |
| ? | | | |

What is your call with each of the following hands?

(1) ♠ Q 8    ♡ A K Q 6    ◇ J 5 3    ♣ A Q J 9

(2) ♠ 9    ♡ A K 10 7 2    ◇ K J    ♣ A J 9 8 3

(3) ♠ –    ♡ K Q 10 3 2    ◇ A J 8 7    ♣ A Q 10 8

(1) 4NT. Partner has indicated at least 13 points in high cards, with a probable upper limit of about 16. As the combined hands may contain 33 or 34 points you bid 4NT, a natural raise. If North has only 13 or 14 points, he passes; if he has 16, or a healthy-looking 15, he bids six.

(2) 4♣. A slam may be there if a suitable 5–3 trump suit can be located. The best move is to indicate 5–5 in hearts and clubs by bidding 4♣. If partner raises to 5♣ it will be reasonable to bid 6♣. If he bids 4♡ you bid 5♡, leaving partner with the final decision.

(3) 4◇. Partner is marked with strength in the unbid diamond suit, and if he happens to have four of them a slam may be possible.

You are South and the bidding has proceeded:

| North | South |
|-------|-------|
| 1♠ | 2♣ |
| 4♣ | ? |

What is your call with each of the following hands?

(4) ♠ K 9    ♡ 10 7 3    ◇ A 10 8    ♣ A Q 10 3 2

(5) ♠ 7    ♡ J 9 6 3    ◇ Q 9 2    ♣ K Q J 5 3

(6) ♠ A 6 4    ♡ K 8    ◇ K 4    ♣ A 10 7 5 4 3

(4) 4◇. If you took away ♠K you would still have a sound 2♣ bid, on which you would expect to make game in view of partner's strong bidding. The king of partner's suit is a key card

and entitles you to set your sights on a slam. The best advance is to cue-bid ◇A, which is both informative and safe. A Blackwood 4NT would be folly, because a response of 5◇ would land you in a slam, possibly with no play for it.

(5) 5♣. This is a moderate hand, with which it might have been more discreet to respond 1NT rather than 2♣. But one mustn't get cold feet now; the jump raise in a minor suit is forcing and commits the partnership to game in one suit or the other.

(6) 4NT. Partner's raise to 4♣ is forcing and indicates a game even if you have no more than 10 points, a minimum, for your two-level response. As you have appreciably more, and good controls, you expect to make a slam if partner has an ace.

You are South and the bidding has gone:

| South | North |
|-------|-------|
| 1◇ | 2♠ |
| 3◇ | 4◇ |
| ? | |

What would you bid next with each of the following hands?

(7) ♠ K 5    ♡ A 8 3    ◇ K Q J 8 4 2    ♣ J 7
(8) ♠ A J 2    ♡ 4    ◇ Q J 10 6 3 2    ♣ A K 6
(9) ♠ J 8 6    ♡ 10 4    ◇ A Q J 6 4    ♣ K J 2

(7) 4♡. In view of partner's jump shift, it is safe to assume that the values for slam are present. However, you are not really in a position to take charge by bidding 4NT, for if partner responded 5♡ you would not know whether there were two club losers. Therefore you cue-bid ♡A, leaving partner to judge.

(8) 5♣. With such a commanding hand you can vow here and now not to stop short of 6◇. The only real question is whether you can reach seven.

First you bid 5♣, indicating the ace. Let's assume that partner now bids either 5◇ or 5♡. In either case you bid 5♠. Partner now knows that (a) you have both the black aces and (b) you are interested in a grand slam.

If he happens to hold ◇A–K, together with ♡A and a suitable spade holding, your manoeuvres will embolden him to bid 7◇.

(9) 4♠. With a moderate hand, you are mainly concerned to select the safest game contract. By returning to partner's major

suit you imply that it may be easier to make ten tricks in spades than eleven in diamonds.

Suppose you are South in the following auctions. What do you call?

(10)

| North | South |
| --- | --- |
| 1◇ | 1♠ |
| 4♣ | ? |

South holds: ♠ K Q 10 3 2   ♡ 9 7 4   ◇ Q 10 6   ♣ A 5

(11)

| North | South |
| --- | --- |
| 1♡ | 1♠ |
| 3♡ | ? |

South holds: ♠ A 10 9 3 2   ♡ A 7   ◇ A 8 3   ♣ A 10 9

(12)

| North | South |
| --- | --- |
| 1♠ | 2◇ |
| 3♣ | 3◇ |
| 4◇ | ? |

South holds: ♠ K Q   ♡ 10 6 4 2   ◇ A J 10 8 7 5   ♣ 9

(13)

| South | North |
| --- | --- |
| 1♠ | 2♡ |
| 3♡ | 4◇ |
| ? | |

South holds: ♠ Q 8 7 3 2   ♡ A J 8 3   ◇ Q 6   ♣ A 9

(14)

| North | South |
| --- | --- |
| 1◇ | 1♡ |
| 2♠ | 3♡ |
| 4♡ | ? |

South holds: ♠ Q 4   ♡ K J 10 6 4 2   ◇ A 7   ♣ 9 6 3

(15)

| South | North |
| --- | --- |
| 1♠ | 2♣ |
| 3♡ | 4♡ |
| ? | |

South holds: ♠ A K Q 5 2   ♡ A Q 10 4   ◇ Q 7   ♣ K 4

(10) 5♣. If partner holds only two aces a Blackwood investigation won't help, as you will not be able to gauge the heart situation. The ace-showing cue-bid of 5♣ is best.

(11) *4NT.* This is an occasion where the Blackwood convention is employed to *tell* partner about aces. Over the 5♣ response you bid 5NT, guaranteeing four aces. If partner holds something like ♠K–x ♡K–Q–J–x–x–x–x ♢K–J–x ♣Q he can arise in his might and bid the grand slam.

(12) *4NT.* This is an ideal Blackwood situation, for the bidding suggests that partner holds a singleton heart and thus you can still bid the diamond slam even if he has only two aces.

(13) *4♡.* The fact that you have bid your hand to the full need not preclude you from showing a control below game level; but to advance to 5♣ would be unsound.

(14) *5♢.* You would have bid this way without ♢A, which is a key card. The diamond cue-bid conveys accurate and important information; in contrast, a Blackwood 4NT would be fuzzy.

(15) *Pass.* You have already given a picture of your hand by jumping to 3♡. You are not entitled to progress any further, as partner may have strained himself to bid 4♡ on a minimum hand. If he had the cards you need—♣A, ♢K, ♡K–x–x–x—he would take stronger action.

# CHAPTER 13

# Conventions in Constructive Bidding

*Flint convention – Transfer bids – Multicoloured 2◇ – Blackwood variations – Swiss convention*

AS SOCIAL creatures pursuing an intellectual pastime, many bridge players would agree that a case could be made for limiting the use of conventions. But as competitors, few are willing to deny themselves a gadget that takes their fancy and offers a genuine gain in efficiency.

The conventions that follow enjoy a wide popularity among tournament players. There are, of course, many others. We have restricted our list to those that (a) are likely to prove of lasting popularity and (b) help to solve problems left untouched by standard methods.

## The Flint Convention

In standard bidding any response to an opening bid of 2NT is forcing to game. It is frustrating, therefore, when your partner opens 2NT, to have a hand on which you think 3♡ or 3♠ will be the only makable contract; you know you cannot play there. The Flint convention meets such situations very neatly. It comes into operation when partner opens 2NT and you have this type of hand:

(1) ♠ 9 5 3      ♡ J 9 7 5 4 2    ◇ 9 8 4    ♣ 7

(2) ♠ 10 8 7 6 4 3    ♡ 5 3          ◇ J 2    ♣ 10 4 3

With either hand you respond 3◇ and your partner is requested to bid 3♡. Then, with the first hand you pass, while with the second you bid 3♠, which your partner passes.

In its original form the convention was as simple as that. But the 2NT bidder, in turn, began to feel thwarted, as sometimes his strength seemed to demand a game. In consequence, ' Extended Flint ' was devised to allow the opener to speak again.

*Extended Flint*

You open 2NT and your partner responds 3◇, requesting you to bid 3♡. Now suppose that you happen to hold a particularly suitable hand, such as this:

♠ A 8   ♡ A Q 8 3   ◇ A J 10   ♣ A K 9 4

You assume that partner, if his suit is hearts, has at least six. In that case you are willing to take a flyer at 4♡. However, your partner will pass a response of 3♡—and you dare not jump straight to four in case his suit should be spades. The solution is to follow this scheme:

*With an ordinary 2NT hand* (no special strength in hearts) bid 3♡, as at present.

*With exceptionally good support for hearts* bid 3♠! This shows a hand like the one above. If your partner's suit happens to be spades he passes, but if his suit is hearts he bids game.

*With strong support for spades* bid 3♡, as at present. If your partner has spades he will convert and you can raise to four.

*With strong support for both major suits* bid 3NT, inviting partner to name the suit.

The Flint convention does not prevent a response of 3◇ from being used in a natural sense. Suppose your partner opens 2NT and you hold:

♠ 7   ♡ A 10 4   ◇ Q 9 8 4 3 2   ♣ Q 10 6

With this hand there may be a slam in diamonds if partner has a diamond fit and good controls. You bid 3◇ and then, over his expected 3♡ (Flint convention), you revert to 3NT. This tells him that you hold a diamond suit and have ambitions beyond 3NT.

It is also possible for the responder to show a two-suited hand.

| Opener | Responder |
|--------|-----------|
| 2NT    | 3◇        |
| 3♡     | 4♡        |

The rule is that if on the second round responder makes any bid inconsistent with the Flint convention he has diamonds and is bidding naturally. In this auction, therefore, he has hearts and diamonds; with only a heart suit he would have bid 3♡ over 2NT.

## Transfer Bids

We have not shortened our account of the Flint convention, but this has in fact lost ground because it conflicts with certain sequences that occur when transfers are played; and there is no doubt that transfer bids are here to stay.

The first example of a transfer was the so-called Texas convention. In response to an opening 1NT or 2NT, a response of 4♣ requested opener to bid 4♡, and 4◇ invited 4♠. With better than normal slam prospects, opener was free to bid the intermediate suit, 4◇ over 4♣, 4♡ over 4◇.

These Texas bids in turn became unnecessary when transfers over 1NT and 2NT, known originally as Jacoby transfers, became popular. Over an opening bid of 1NT:

2◇ shows hearts and requires opener to bid 2♡.
2♡ shows spades and requires opener to bid 2♠.

This device enables responder to show his suit and make a game suggestion without carrying the auction beyond 2NT. Your partner opens 1NT and you hold:

♠ K 9 7 6 3    ♡ Q 10 4    ◇ Q 8 2    ♣ 10 3

With this hand you respond 2♡. Your partner rebids 2♠ and now you bid 2NT, having shown spades on the way. Or suppose you were stronger—with ◇A instead of ◇Q: then you would bid 2♡ and follow with 3NT, showing the values for a raise to game, including a spade suit.

It is usual to play 1NT–2◇–2♡–3♡ as forcing and promising a six-card suit. This gives the opener a chance to make an encouraging move below the game level.

A change of suit by responder in a sequence such as 1NT–2♡–2♠–3♣, is treated initially as a two-suiter; but it may be simply a trial bid to test whether the opener can do more than sign off in 3♠.

After a sequence such as 1NT–2◇ the opener is not obliged to bid simply 2♡. If a maximum for 1NT, with at least K–x–x in hearts (the indicated suit) he may bid 2NT; and with four hearts he may bid 3♡.

It is usual to treat 2♠ over 1NT as equal to a raise to 2NT. In this case 2NT over 1NT asks the opener to bid 3♣; opener may pass this or transfer to 3◇ (weak).

A similar style of responses is used over an opening 2NT. 3◇ and

187

3♡ are transfers to 3♡ and 3♠ respectively; again, the opener, if maximum, may make a stronger rebid, taking the partnership beyond the minimum level. A response of 3♣ to 2NT will show interest in the minor suits.

A response of 2♠, when transfers are in use, can be put to various uses. A sound system is to treat 2♠ as equal to a raise to 2NT; then 2NT requests a transfer to 3♣ which responder may pass or remove to 3◇ (weak).

### Multicoloured 2◇

The "multi", as it is called, represents the most important technical advance since the first edition of this book. An opening bid of 2◇ is made on a variety of hands. The principal use is to describe weak two bids in the major suits. For the rest, it is possible to use the bid to introduce powerful hands in the minors or a strong balanced hand. At one time powerful 4-4-4-1 types were included in the schedule, but these hands are rare and most players confine the bid to two types:

(1) a weak two-bid in hearts or spades, or

(2) an opening 2NT, usually in the 21–22 range.

There are three standard responses to the 2◇ opening:

2♡     "If you have the weak two in hearts, this is where we play."

2♠     "If you have the weak two in spades, this is where we play." If the opener in fact has hearts, then (in most variations) he will bid 3♣, which leaves responder room for various actions.

2NT     "Tell me your suit." Opener may now bid 3♡ or 3♣, to show lower or upper range with hearts, 3♠ or 3◇, to show lower or upper range with spades.

In all cases the opener rebids in notrumps when he has the strong notrump type. Note that the range for 2◇–2♡–2NT is 21–22; hands that are slightly weaker may be opened with a direct 2NT.

There are various schemes of defence against the multi. For example, in second position a defender may bid 2♡ when he has a take-out double of spades, 2♠ natural, 2NT with all-round strength, and may double when he has a takeout double of hearts.

For a fuller (and slightly different) account of the convention, see *Bridge the Modern Game*, by Terence Reese and David Bird, published by Faber.

## Blackwood variations

There are many variations, and extensions, of ordinary Blackwood, as described in Chapter 12. For one thing, most tournament players respond 5♣ with 0 or 3 aces, 5◇ with 1 or 4. They trust their partners to distinguish, despite the fact that calamitous misunderstandings have occurred at the very highest level. The first convention we describe, Roman Blackwood, is not so popular as it used to be, perhaps because it does not deal particularly well with voids.

*Roman Blackwood*

After a bid of 4NT the responses are:

| | |
|---|---|
| 5♣ | 0 or 3 aces |
| 5◇ | 1 or 4 aces |
| 5♡ | 2 aces of the same colour |
| 5♠ | 2 aces of the same rank (major or minor) |
| 5NT | 2 " odd " aces (hearts–clubs or diamonds–spades) |

Now a player holding one ace can always identify the two aces shown by his partner. The word " CRO ", standing for Colour, Rank, Odd, serves as a mnemonic for the order in which two aces are shown.

The 5♠ and 5NT responses to Roman Blackwood take the bidding a step or two higher than normal Blackwood, but this is not serious provided an economical method of asking for kings is adopted. Say that the response to 4NT is 5◇: then the next suit, provided it is not the intended trump suit, is an inquiry for kings, with responses on the same principle as above (one step, 0 or 3; two steps, 1 or 4, and so on). If the " next " suit is a possible trump suit and so not available for conventional use, then 5NT asks for kings.

*Five-ace Blackwood*

This is another variation favoured by tournament players. Over 4NT the responder bids 5♡ with two aces, 5♠ with two aces and the king of an important suit bid by the partnership, 5NT with two aces and two such kings. This convention is often valuable in its negative aspects: it may establish that a critical king is missing.

*When there is intervention over the Blackwood 4NT*

Opponents who are on the sacrifice trail will sometimes overcall a

Blackwood 4NT, preventing the normal system of responses. Responder may then need to use a different method to show the number of aces he holds. The inelegantly named DOPI is one of the methods used. Suppose that over North's 4NT East bids 5◇. South now Doubles with 0 aces, Passes with 1. With two or more aces he may proceed by steps—5♡ with two, and so on.

## Swiss Convention

Bridge theorists abhor a vacuum and it was inevitable that a constructive use would be found for the virtually idle bids of 4♣ and 4◇ in response to a major-suit opening. The Swiss convention employs these bids to show hands of about 13 to 16 points, including trump support, but lacking a strong side suit. Your partner opens 1♠ and you hold:

(1) ♠ A 9 8 4    ♡ K 6    ◇ Q 10 8 3    ♣ A J 5
(2) ♠ A K J 7    ♡ A 8 7 3    ◇ 4    ♣ J 7 6 2

Playing limit raises, it is difficult to describe these hands. They are too strong in high cards for a direct bid of game, and a preliminary bid in a moderate side suit would not help to paint the picture.

Playing the Swiss convention, you bid 4♣ with (1), showing 13 to 16 points in support of spades. With (2) you bid 4◇, showing the same values with exceptionally strong trump support.

Various meanings have been attached to the responses of 4♣ and 4◇ besides those we have described. In one popular form of the convention 4♣ shows good controls, usually defined as two aces and a singleton, while 4◇ shows similar values but not so many controls.

### Rebid by Opening Hand

With no interest in a slam, opener simply rebids his own suit over the Swiss response. An intermediate bid, such as 4◇ over 4♣, serves as a generalized slam invitation without reference to the suit named.

### Overall Plan for the Responding Hand

With the aid of the Swiss convention the responder can delineate very accurately the different types of hand that are worth a raise to game in opener's major suit. This is the scheme:

(1) *Powerful trump support, less than 10 points in high cards.*

(1) ♠ K Q 9 7 3  ♡ 8  ◇ J 6  ♣ J 9 7 4 3

(2) ♠ A Q J 7  ♡ 10 3  ◇ 10 8 6 5 4 3  ♣ 9

With this type of hand you give a direct raise to game.

(2) *13 to 15 points in support of partner's suit, with a fair side suit.*

(1) ♠ K J 8 7  ♡ 3  ◇ Q J 7  ♣ A 10 9 5 4

(2) ♠ A 10 9 2  ♡ 10 5  ◇ K Q 10 7 4 3  ♣ 9

The first hand is worth 14 points in support of spades, the second 13 points. In each case you respond with a minimum bid in the side suit and, over any natural rebid by opener, jump to 4♠ on the next round. This sequence, known as a delayed game raise, shows that your two main features are trump support and a side suit.

(3) *13 to 16 points, but no side suit.*

(1) ♠ Q 9 8 4  ♡ A J 7 3  ◇ 5  ♣ A 10 4 2

(2) ♠ K J 10 8 6  ♡ K Q 10  ◇ 7  ♣ Q 8 4 3

Over 1♠ from partner you employ one of the Swiss variations described above, 4♣ with the first hand, 4◇ with the second.

(4) *16 points or more, including a fair side suit.*

(1) ♠ A J 6 2  ♡ K Q 6 5 3  ◇ 4  ♣ A 10 7

With this hand you bid 3♡, a normal jump shift, and support spades on the next round.

Some of these procedures are standard, but the comprehensive coverage would not be possible without the Swiss convention, which takes care of the comparatively balanced hands that are otherwise difficult to express. It is also possible to bid a Swiss 4♣ or 4◇ and proceed with a slam try over a sign-off.

## Swiss for Minor Suits

Players have been heard to complain that it is actually more difficult to portray a strong supporting hand after an opening bid of 1♣ or 1◇ than after an opening bid in a major suit. It is possible to use artificial responses at the three level to express such hands, and in previous editions we have developed this notion. However, the idea has never caught on, so it must be abandoned.

There are, to be sure, many other conventions of merit, but it is easy to become cluttered up with them. As Oliver Wendell Holmes observed, science is an excellent piece of furniture for a man to have in his upper storey if he has commonsense on the ground floor.

# CHAPTER 14

## Conventions in the Contested Auction

*The unusual notrump – The negative double – Michaels cue-bid*


THE THEORY that attack is the best means of defence appears to commend itself very warmly to the modern bridge player, especially the tournament player, who in competitive situations is willing to take action with the most slender values in an attempt to harry the opening side. Most of the fashionable conventions in defensive bidding are directed towards this end.

### The Unusual Notrump

Bridge players are like the Athenians of whom Pericles said: " They were born neither to have rest themselves nor to allow others to have it." The Unusual Notrump caters for this propensity very well, as it enables the defending side to make life uncomfortable for the opponents on many hands where they were previously allowed an easy ride.

When an overcall in notrumps cannot logically be genuine it is termed " Unusual " and indicates a desire to contest the bidding in one of the minor suits. This is a typical sequence:

| South | West | North | East |
|-------|------|-------|------|
| 1♡ | Pass | 2♡ | Pass |
| Pass | 2NT | | |

As he did not bid on the first round West can hardly have a strong balanced hand and his bid of 2NT cannot be genuine. Therefore he is showing length in both minor suits and inviting partner to compete. West may have no more than 9 or 10 points and 5–4 or 5–5 in the minors.

The use of the Unusual Notrump is not limited to cases where the opponents have shown willingness to pass the hand out at a low level. It can also be used in an attempt to find an economical sacrifice when the opponents have clearly the superior hands.

| South | West | North | East |
|-------|------|-------|------|
| 1♡ | Pass | 1♠ | Pass |
| 2♠ | 2NT | | |

Here South has opened and his partner, too, may be strong, but the North–South fit in spades increases the probability of an East–West fit in a minor suit. East–West may well be able to contest the part score or even to sacrifice over 4♠.

When the player has passed originally, an overcall of 1NT may be unusual.

| South | West | North | East |
|-------|------|-------|------|
| Pass | Pass | Pass | 1♡ |
| 1NT | | | |

Obviously South is showing the minor suits, for it would be very poor tactics to come in with 1NT on a balanced hand not good enough for an opening bid. With a really freakish two-suiter, 6–6 or 6–5, South could bid 2NT!

This is not quite the same:

| South | West | North | East |
|-------|------|-------|------|
| Pass | 1♠ | Pass | Pass |
| 1NT | | | |

Here South's 1NT is normal protection.

An " unusual " overcall in notrumps always shows the minor suits when no minor suit has been bid. When the opening side has bid one of the minors the Unusual Notrump shows the two lowest-ranking unbid suits. In the following sequence South is showing hearts and clubs.

| South | West | North | East |
|-------|------|-------|------|
| Pass | Pass | Pass | 1♢ |
| 2NT | | | |

When the opponents have bid two suits the Unusual Notrump suggests fewer high cards but a more distributional type of hand than a takeout double, which also would indicate length in the unbid suits.

When the opponents have followed a strength-showing sequence, 2NT may be construed as unusual even when the player has not passed.

| South | West | North | East |
|-------|------|-------|------|
| 1♠ | Pass | 2♡ | 2NT |

2NT is " unusual " here as it is most unlikely that East can have the values for a genuine bid; and if he had such values he would probably pass, as the opponents are in a forcing situation. Again, 2NT is more suggestive of distribution than a takeout double.

An immediate overcall of 2NT even by a player who has not passed is generally played as " unusual ". With a big hand there is always the alternative of a takeout double.

Some of the most effective uses of the Unusual Notrump are by the opening side. Here North, lacking space, bids notrumps to indicate an option between the suit he has bid and the suit partner has opened. North holds:

♠ 8　♡ Q 7 3　◇ K Q J 8 6 2　♣ A J 10

With North–South vulnerable, the bidding goes:

| South | West | North | East |
|-------|------|-------|------|
| 1♡ | 1♣ | 2◇ | 3♣ |
| Pass | 4♣ | 4NT | |

At duplicate, especially, North must bid one more rather than double 4♣. As no suit has been agreed, 4NT can hardly be Blackwood. Partner may interpet it at first as offering a choice between diamonds and clubs; but when North bids 5◇ over 5♣ it will be apparent that the alternative is between diamonds and hearts.

In the next sequence a defender conveys that he has a second string to his bow:

| South | West | North | East |
|-------|------|-------|------|
| 1♡ | 2◇ | 4♡ | Pass |
| Pass | 4NT | | |

West is indicating that he wants to sacrifice and has values in clubs as well as diamonds. He has a hand of this sort:

♠ 7 3　♡ 4　◇ A Q J 9 7 5　♣ K Q 10 2

Partner will appreciate that the diamonds are much better than the clubs, as with 5–5 or 6–5 West would bid clubs himself.

### The Negative Double (also called " Sputnik ")

This convention is popular with the *avant garde* of tournament players. It is used when responding to an opening bid in competition, as in this sequence:

| Opener | Opponent | Responder | Opponent |
|--------|----------|-----------|----------|
| 1◇ | 1♠ | ? | |

In this situation a responder who has only modest values may find himself with no good bid to make. Suppose his hand is:

♠ 9 6 2    ♡ A 7 5 3    ◇ 10 6    ♣ K J 8 2

A bid of 2♣ or 2♡ would suggest a better suit, while 1NT would be wrong with no guard in spades. A pass would merely allow the overcaller to achieve his object of interrupting the flow of information.

Playing the negative double, the responder has a means of expressing a hand of this kind. The double suggests:

*Less than opening values* (since the double is not needed on hands with 13 points or more, strong enough to cue-bid the opponent's suit).

*No attractive biddable suit* (since a natural bid in a suit is always preferred to a double).

*Preparedness for any normal rebid by opener* (which implies at least 7 points in high cards for a double at the one level).

In response to the double, the opener bids naturally. A simple rebid in any suit is not forcing; a cue-bid in the overcaller's suit is the only absolute force. With strength in the overcaller's suit opener may make a penalty pass.

Suppose you are the opener in this auction:

| Opener | Opponent | Partner | Opponent |
|--------|----------|---------|----------|
| 1♡ | 2♣ | Double | Pass |

You hold:    ?

(1) ♠ 10 4    ♡ A K 10 5 3    ◇ K Q 8    ♣ Q J 4

(2) ♠ K 10 8    ♡ A Q 10 7 6    ◇ A K J 2    ♣ 8

With (1) you should make the forward-going bid of 2NT rather than 2♡, as a player who makes a negative double will often have a doubleton in opener's suit. You may expect partner to have some strength in spades as there is nowhere else for his points to be, but you cannot quite bid 3NT all by yourself.

With (2) you force with 3♣. There must be at least 26 points in the combined hands and partner must have a fit for spades or diamonds, if not for hearts.

Playing the negative double, the responder sometimes has to pass with a hand suitable for a normal penalty double. The bidding goes:

| Opener | Opponent | Responder | Opponent |
|--------|----------|-----------|----------|
| 1♠ | 2◇ | ? | |

Responder holds:

(1) ♠ 10 4   ♡ 7 5   ◇ Q J 9 4 3   ♣ A 7 6 3

(2) ♠ Q 7 2   ♡ J 3   ◇ A Q 9 2   ♣ K J 8 2

With (1) responder should pass, hoping his partner can reopen with a double. An immediate double would achieve nothing, as partner would surely remove it. Responder might be embarrassed later. With (2) responder is too strong to pass. He may double for the moment, as he can take care of any developments. Note that the double is more economical than a bid of 2NT or 3NT.

The negative double has its greatest value as a counter to a ' nuisance ' overcall of 1♠, which is so liable to shut out a heart fit. As it is seldom good tactics to double for penalties at the one level, the use of the negative double here is undoubtedly an advantage and many partnerships use it in this situation only. Others take the view that its use can profitably be extended to doubles of all overcalls at the two level and to doubles of weak jump overcalls at the three level. With good partnership co-operation the opportunities for penalizing the opponents are not lessened.

### Michaels Cue-bid

An immediate overcall in an opponent's suit signifies, by tradition, a ' giant ' on which you hope to make game even if partner is very weak. Such hands occur rarely, and when they do they can be introduced with a takeout double. The Michaels cue-bid puts the overcall to much more frequent and effective use.

The idea is to portray two-suited hands which are difficult to express by either a normal overcall, a takeout double or an Unusual Notrump. The strength may vary considerably, according to the vulnerability. The type of hand shown depends on whether the opponents have opened a minor or a major suit.

*Over a minor suit:* an immediate cue-bid shows the major suits (at least nine cards). The high-card strength is in the range of 6 to 11 points.

*Over a major suit:* the cue-bid shows the unbid major suit and an unspecified minor suit. The high-card strength is unlimited.

Both the following hands qualify for the Michaels cue-bid over an opponent's minor-suit opening:

(1) ♠ J 8 7 5 3    ♡ K J 9 2    ◇ 9 3   ♣ A 2

(2) ♠ A J 10 7 3    ♡ J 10 8 6 5    ◇ 6 2   ♣ 8

In response, 2NT is natural; the only force (asking the cue-bidder to name his longer or better major) is a further cue-bid—3◇ over 2◇. The next two hands would qualify for a cue-bid of 2♡ over an opening 1♡:

(1) ♠ Q J 8 7 3    ♡ 10   ◇ K Q 9 7 3 2   ♣ 6

(2) ♠ J 9 8 6 3    ♡ –   ◇ A 5 2      ♣ A Q J 9 4

If the responder has no support for the unbid major he can bid notrumps as a request to the cue-bidder to show his minor suit.

*In fourth position.* The cue-bid conveys at first the same distributional message.

| South | West | North | East |
|-------|------|-------|------|
| 1♡ | Pass | Pass | 2♡ |

West will assume that his partner has spades and a strong minor, e.g. K–x–x–x–x and A–K–J–x–x–x.

Despite this arrangement, East may still use the cue-bid on the traditional type where he wants to ensure a response from his partner. Though partner will at first misunderstand, whatever he bids will be indicative.

*In competitive sequences.* The cue-bid can be used to advantage when both opponents have bid, as in these sequences:

| | South | West | North | East |
|---|-------|------|-------|------|
| (1) | 1♠ | Pass | 1NT | 2♠ |

| | South | West | North | East |
|---|-------|------|-------|------|
| (2) | 1♡ | Pass | 2♣ | 2♡ |

In each case East indicates five of the other major and a good minor. In the second sequence the minor suit is presumably diamonds. An unusual 2NT would convey the same sort of message, but the cue-bid is more precise and more economical as partner need go no higher than 2♠.

# CHAPTER 15

## One-club Systems

*The Precision system – Strong One-Club Systems – The Blue Team Club*

THERE have always been two main streams in bidding: on the one side, the more or less natural systems which use 2♣ or the forcing two as their strong bid; on the other, systems which use 1♣ as their big bid and put opening two-bids to other uses. In the 1970s, tournament players, influenced no doubt by the successes of Italian teams in world championship events, began to show an increasing disposition to try out 1♣ systems. Three such systems are described in this chapter, beginning with the most recent, and perhaps the most popular, the Precision system.

It should be mentioned that these systems are not fixed and unchanging entities. There are almost as many versions of Precision, for example, as there are partnerships who play it. We present here what might be called the classical version.

### The Precision System

This system combines a strong 1♣ with another modern fashion—five-card majors, to which a response of 1NT is forcing. These are the main opening sequences:

**Opening bid**

| | |
|---|---|
| 1♣ | Standard opening on almost all hands of 16 points or more. The negative response on 0–7 is 1◇. Other suit responses are positive, showing 8 points and at least a five-card suit. |
| 1◇ | 12–15, often a three-card suit. A raise to 2◇ is stronger than a raise to 3◇, which is pre-emptive. |
| 1♡, 1♠ | 12–15, a five-card suit in principle. A response of 1NT is forcing for one round. |

| | |
|---|---|
| 1NT | 13–15 in all positions. Any system of responses can be played. In the Precision scheme a response of 2♣ is non-forcing Stayman, a response of 2◇ is conventional and game-forcing. |
| 2♣ | Either a one-suited hand with six clubs, or a semi-two-suiter with five clubs or six clubs and a four-card major, range 12–15. (Hands with four diamonds and five clubs are opened with 1◇.) In response, 2◇ is a relay, forcing as far as 2NT; 2♡ and 2♠ are invitational, suggesting 8–10 points and a five-card suit; 2NT is natural, and 3♣ a constructive raise. |
| 2◇ | 12–15 with a singleton diamond, either 4–4–1–4 or 4–4–0–5 or 3–4–1–5 or 4–3–1–5. The only forcing response is 2NT. Opener rebids as follows: when 3–4–1–5, 3♣ or 3♡ (upper range); when 4–3–1–5, 3◇ or 3♠ (upper range): when 4–4–1–4, 3NT with singleton ◇A or ◇K, otherwise 4♣ (lower range) or 4♡ (upper range); when 4–4–0–5, 4◇. |
| 2♡, 2♠ | Weak two-bid, about 7–10 with a good six-card suit. In response, a new suit is forcing; 2NT asks the opener to name any suit in which he holds a singleton or void. |
| 2NT | Natural, 22–23. In response, 3♣ is Stayman, 3◇ and 3♡ are transfers to 3♡ and 3♠ respectively. |
| 3♣ | May be played as a pre-empt or (fitting better into the scheme of any 1♣ system) a strong suit with at least one trick outside. |
| 3◇, 3♡, 3♠ | Normal pre-empts. |
| 3NT | Solid minor suit, no outside strength, as in Acol. |
| 4♣, 4◇ | Can be played either as natural bids or as transfers to 4♡ and 4♠. |
| 4♡, 4♠ | Normal pre-empts. |

The two standard-bearers of the Precision system are the opening 1♣ and the five-card majors in conjunction with a forcing 1NT response. Both of these call for further discussion.

## Opening 1♣ and Responses

Except for strong balanced hands that are opened with 2NT, all hands of 16 points and upwards (allowing for the usual adjustments in the case of singleton honours) are opened with 1♣. Hands of

14 or 15 points may be opened with 1♣ if exceptionally strong in both playing tricks and controls. Assuming for the moment no interference, this is the schedule of responses:

*Responses to 1♣*

| | |
|---|---|
| 1◇ | 0–7, except for one sequence, the " impossible negative ", described below. |
| 1♡, 1♠, 2♣, 2◇ | Positive responses, promising upwards of 8 points and at least a five-card suit. The bidding cannot die below 2NT. |
| 1NT | 8–10, either 4–4–3–2 or 4–3–3–3 distribution. A rebid of 2♣ by the opener is Stayman. |
| 2♡, 2♠ | These are semi-positive, denoting a six-card major with little or no outside strength. Respond 2♠ on:<br>♠ K J 10 7 6 4  ♡ 5 3  ◇ J 7 2  ♣ 8 5<br>Opener may pass this response. A rebid of 2NT or a change of suit is forcing. |
| 2NT | 11–13 balanced, or 16 upwards. A rebid of 3♣ by the opener is Baron. |
| 3♣, 3◇ | Pre-emptive; alternatively, they may be used to denote a seven-card minor suit headed by the A–Q or K–Q. |
| 3♡, 3♠ | Seven-card suit, about 3–6 points. |
| 3NT | 14–15, 4–3–3–3 distribution. |

*Developments after 1♣–1◇*

A non-jump rebid in a suit by opener is not forcing. A jump rebid is forcing as far as the three level.

With a balanced hand the opener rebids 1NT with 18–20, 2NT with 19–21, 3NT with 24–26 (the vacant space being occupied by an opening 2NT).

*The Impossible Negative*

Suppose that the responder to 1♣ holds:

♠ 5  ♡ K 10 7 4  ◇ Q 8 5 3  ♣ A 9 6 2

He has ample strength for a positive response but has no five-card suit, and to respond 1NT would be unreasonable with this distribution. The solution is to respond 1◇ and on the next round make a jump that is inconsistent with an original negative. These are the sequences that denote the impossible negative:

| 1♣ | 1◇ | |
|----|----|----|
| 1♡ | 2♠ | (jump in the singleton suit) |
| 1♣ | 1◇ | |
| 1♠ | 2NT | (jump in notrumps when opener bids the singleton suit) |
| 1♣ | 1◇ | |
| 1NT | 3♡ | (after a rebid in notrumps, a jump in *the suit below* the singleton) |

### When there is Intervention over 1♣

The general scheme when opponents overcall at a low level is to pass with bad hands, double (negative) on 5–8, and lower the requirements for a suit response to 5–8. With stronger hands responder may cue-bid or bid notrumps.

We pass now to the other main feature of the system, five-card majors and the response of 1NT.

### Five-card Majors and the Forcing Notrump

Over 1♡ or 1♠ a response of 1NT is forcing for one round but not necessarily strong. Before considering the different types on which the response may be given, it will help to examine the opener's rebids.

When the opener has a second suit of four cards or more he normally bids it. With two strong suits he may make a jump rebid. With a maximum 5–3–3–2 he may raise to 2NT. He may rebid a six-card suit, possibly with a jump. Lacking any of these features, he will rebid in his lowest three-card suit. Thus:

    (1) ♠ K J 8 5 3  ♡ K J 8  ◇ A 5  ♣ 7 6 2

Rebid 2♣—never 2♡ with only three.

    (2) ♠ 4  ♡ A J 8 7 5 2  ◇ Q 7 6 3  ♣ A Q

Rebid 2◇; partner will pass this only with a minimum of four diamonds and a singleton heart.

Now we look at the types on which responder will bid 1NT over 1♡:

(1) ♠ Q 5 3   ♡ J 4   ◇ Q 7 6 2   ♣ K 8 5 2

A standard player would make the same response on this hand. If opener, over 1NT, bids two of a minor, responder will put him back to 2♡, as the hearts are assumed to be a five-card suit and the minor suit may be of only three cards.

(2) ♠ K 8   ♡ 5   ◇ K J 7 6 4 3 2   ♣ 7 5 3

This hand lacks the values for a response at the two level, so responder begins with 1NT. If opener rebids 2♡, 3◇ would again be a sign-off, though it might be wiser on this occasion to let partner play in his six-card suit.

(3) ♠ J 8 4   ♡ 7   ◇ K 10 7 5 3   ♣ A 6 4 2

After 1♡–1NT–2♣, responder should pass. This may prove the best spot. Responder may raise a rebid of 2◇ to 3◇, but no more.

(4) ♠ K J 5   ♡ 6 4 3   ◇ A 10 4   ♣ Q 9 7 6

This type of hand is a little awkward for standard systems as it is strong for a response of 1NT but rather weak for any other treatment. Here the responder, playing Precision, bids 1NT, intending to follow with 2NT over a rebid in a new suit.

It will be readily seen from these examples that the use of 1NT as a forcing relay considerably extends the responder's range of expression. It is possible to devise many other conventional sequences.


## A Developing System

Before leaving Precision, it is fair to say that this system has not the solid background of, say, the Italian systems, which have been tested for very many years at international level. Precision, by comparison, is still a developing system. Various asking bids have been devised, which can be played in conjunction with the 1♣ opening. Readers who wish to make a study of these and other refinements are referred to Terence Reese's *Precision Bidding and Precision Play*.

## Strong One-Club Systems

Strong one-club systems have been with us since the game began. Old-timers will recall the Vanderbilt Club and the Barton Club (an egregious style in which the responder showed his tally of aces immediately in response to the 1♣ opening). Taking distributional points into account, these are the main opening sequences in the Schenken Big Club system:

## Opening bid

| | |
|---|---|
| 1♣ | From 19 points (or 18 h.c.p.) upwards; 1♢ is the negative response. |
| 1♢ | 12–16 h.c.p., may be a three-card suit. |
| 1♡, 1♠ | 12–16 h.c.p., four cards or more. A response of 3♣ is conventional, showing good trump support and 16–17 points. The opener is asked to name a singleton or void. |
| 1NT | Balanced 16–18. In response, 2♣ is non-forcing Stayman; 2♢ is a game force, over which opener's first duty is to show major-suit stoppers (not length). |
| 2♣ | Good club suit, with possibly a four-card major, 11–16 h.c.p. As in Precision, 2♢ is an artificial response, asking initially for a four-card major; other suit responses are invitational. |
| 2♢ | Big hand, conventional responses. |
| 2♡, 2♠ | Weak two-bid, 7–11, with 2NT the only forcing response. Opener who is better than minimum shows a feature in a side suit. |
| 2NT | This may be played as a tactical opening, about 17–20 h.c.p. with a good minor suit, or as a minor two-suiter (similar to the Unusual Notrump overcall). The range for this is 10–12 non-vulnerable, 13–16 vulnerable. A takeout into 3♡ or 3♠ signifies a desire to play at that level. |
| 3♣ | Solid club suit (minimum A–K–Q–10–x–x), 11–16 h.c.p. |

The Schenken system is well equipped for dealing with big hands. We take a closer look now at the 1♣ and 2♢ openings.

### Opening 1♣ and Responses

The requirements for a balanced hand are 18–22 h.c.p. (stronger hands being opened with 2♢). A one-suited hand will generally contain 17 h.c.p. and at least 2 points for distribution. With a strong six-card spade suit, or a major two-suiter, 14 h.c.p. is the minimum.

### Responses to 1♣

| | |
|---|---|
| 1♢ | Negative, 0–6 h.c.p. |
| 2♣ | This is a novel feature, showing 7–8 points without reference to clubs. Responder is pledged to make at least one further bid. |
| 1♡, 1♠, 2♢ | Positive, at least 9 h.c.p., including 1½ high-card tricks. |
| 1NT | 9–11 balanced; 2♣ by opener is now Stayman. |
| 2NT | 12–13 balanced; 3♣ by opener is Stayman. |
| 3♣ | Positive, a good club suit (remember that 2♣ is artificial). |
| 2♡, 2♠, 3♢ | Positive, solid or near-solid suit. |

### *Developments after 1♣–1♢*

A non-jump rebid by opener is not forcing. A single jump rebid is forcing for one round. A rebid of 1NT suggests 19–20, of 2NT 21–22; after these rebids 2♣ and 3♣ respectively are Stayman.

### *When there is Intervention over 1♣*

Whereas most 1♣ systems use the double of an overcall as a tentative move on a moderate hand, Schenken uses a double of an overcall up to 3♢ to indicate positive values. A cue-bid shows positive values and a control in the opponent's suit. All other bids are natural and limited.

### *Opening 2♢ and Responses*

This is a specialized bid, used on strong balanced hands from 23 upwards, or on any powerful hand where the opener's interest lies in finding his partner with particular cards. It follows that the main suit must be playable without support. In reply, partner's first duty is to announce his aces.

**Responses to 2◇**

| | |
|---|---|
| 2♡ | Negative, no ace. |
| 2NT | Shows ♡A (as the response of 2♡ has been pre-empted). |
| 2♠, 3♣, 3◇ | Ace of the suit named. |
| Suit jump | Ace of the suit named and the ace immediately below it (e.g. 4♣ shows ♣A and ♠A). |
| 3NT | Two non-touching aces—spades and diamonds or hearts and clubs. |
| 4NT | Three aces and happy days! |

*Developments after the First Response to 2◇*

When the opener has the balanced type he rebids in notrumps. Then 3♣ by responder is Stayman.

When opener holds the unbalanced type he may either introduce his suit or, if interested in specific cards, inquire for kings by bidding the next suit. Thus 2◇–2♡–2♠ is an inquiry for kings, and so is 2◇–3♣–3◇. After 2◇–2♠, 2NT would be natural, so now 3♣ asks for kings.

Over this relay, responder shows his kings according to the same scale as over the opening 2◇. Even then, the party is not necessarily over. Opener may employ a further relay to ask for queens. Here is the sort of hand that suits the method:

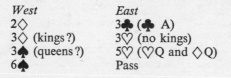

| West | East |
|---|---|
| ♠ A K Q J 10 x x | ♠ x x |
| ♡ A J x x x | ♡ Q x x |
| ◇ – | ◇ Q 10 x x |
| ♣ x | ♣ A J x x |

The bidding goes:

| West | East |
|---|---|
| 2◇ | 3♣ (♣ A) |
| 3◇ (kings?) | 3♡ (no kings) |
| 3♠ (queens?) | 5♡ (♡Q and ◇Q) |
| 6♠ | Pass |

West sets off wanting to know about three cards, ♣A and ♡ K–Q, and the system enables him to find out.

205

## The Blue Team Club

The *Blue Team Club** is a descendant of the *Neapolitan Club*, which was employed with great success by some members of the Italian team during the late 1950s and 1960s. At first sight it is similar to the Schenken system, but when we come to developments after the opening bid we are in a different country. Here, first, are the main opening sequences:

### Opening bid

| | |
|---|---|
| 1♣ | From 18 upwards on balanced hands (omitting 21–22), from 17 upwards on unbalanced hands. Responses are in terms of controls. |
| 1◇ | 12–16, may be a three-card suit. |
| 1♡, 1♠ | 12–16, may be a very weak four-card suit. Within this range there is a distinction between "strong" and "weak" hands, which affects the opening bid. |
| 1NT | Either 16–17 balanced or 13–15 with clubs the only four-card suit. |
| 2♣ | 12–16 with long clubs, or a good two-suiter, 15–16 with very fair clubs. |
| 2◇ | 4–4–4–1 distribution, 17–24 points. |
| 2NT | Balanced 21–22. A response of 3♣ is "weak transfer", 3◇ is Stayman. |
| 3♣ | Powerful suit, at least one outside guard, about 12–15. A response of 3◇ is a "notrump probe", asking for guards. |

It is necessary to add a word of explanation about most of these sequences.

*Opening 1♣ and Responses*

The minimum for balanced hands is 18, and for unbalanced hands (unless exceptionally powerful) 17. The first response is on the step system and is tied to controls, an ace counting as two controls, a king as one control.

---

* The version described here is based on *The Blue Club* by Benito Garozzo and Leon Yallouze, adapted for British readers by Terence Reese.

### Responses to 1♣

| | |
|---|---|
| 1◇ | Negative, 0–5 points. |
| 1♡ | Upwards of 6 points, but fewer than three controls. Forcing as far as 2NT. |
| 1♠ | Three controls—an ace and a king or three kings. Forcing to game. |
| 1NT | Four controls. |
| 2♣ | Five controls. |
| 2◇ | Six controls. |
| 2NT | Seven or more controls. |
| 2♡, 2♠ | Natural and weak—a six-card suit and about 2–5 points. |

### *Developments after* 1♣–1◇

With a balanced hand the opener rebids 1NT on 18–20, 2NT on 23–24, 3NT on 25–26. After the rebid of 1NT, 2♣ by responder is " weak transfer ", the opener being required to bid 2◇; then a continuation of 2♡ or 2♠ is a sign-off, 2NT means a weak hand with long clubs. Still over the rebid of 1NT, 2◇ is " constructive Stayman ", 2♡ and 2♠ are encouraging, 2NT signifies precisely K–Q–x–x–x in one of the minor suits.

When the opener rebids 2NT or 3NT a bid of clubs is similarly a weak transfer, and 3◇ is Stayman.

When the opener is unbalanced he may prefer to rebid in a four-card major at the one level rather than in a five-card minor. A jump rebid is forcing for one round.

### *When there is a Positive Response to* 1♣

When there is a positive response to 1♣ (including the limited 1♡ response), opener with a balanced 18–20 will rebid in notrumps. With 23 upwards he may rebid at minimum level, to gain bidding space.

The bidding after a positive response is on natural lines. A jump rebid over a positive sets the suit and asks the responder to show controls.

### *When there is Intervention over* 1♣

The system of showing controls is maintained, with some necessary adjustments. Following a suit overcall at the range of one, the responder passes when in the zone of 1◇ (0–5) and doubles when in the zone of 1♡ (6 upwards with less than three controls); from then on, a bid at the lowest level means three controls, the next bid four controls, and so on, excluding the bids of 2♡ and 2♠, which retain their usual meaning of a long weak suit.

When there is an overcall of two in a suit, responder passes with fewer than three controls, doubles for penalties, bids 2NT with three or four controls, cue-bids with five or more. Any new suit is natural and forcing.

When 1♣ is doubled, responder passes on 0–3, redoubles with 3–5 and good clubs, bids 1◇ on 4–5. Responses from 1♡ onwards are unchanged.

## Opening Suit Bids of One and Responses

Here we come up against a style of bidding unfamiliar to players of standard systems. Hands below the range for 1♣ are classified as " weak " or " strong ". To be classified as strong, the hand must be two-suited, with at least one good suit, and must be in the upper range of points, 15–16. When strong, the opener prepares either to reverse or bid at the three level on the next round. A further principle is that the second suit to be named is always at least as long as the first suit. Omitting for the moment hands where one of the suits is clubs, these examples will illustrate how the two principles are combined:

(1) ♠ A Q 5　♡ 10 8 6 3　◇ K J 4　♣ K Q 2

Open 1♡. The hand is a point short for 1NT and there are no inhibitions about bidding a weak four-card major.

(2) ♠ 7 4　♡ K J 7 5　◇ A K 8 5　♣ Q 7 3

A weak hand, so the suits are bid in descending order. Open 1♡ and over 2♣ bid 2◇, as in standard bidding.

(3) ♠ A J 6 3　♡ 6 5　◇ K J 10 7 3　♣ K 2

With 4–5 the tendency is to open the higher suit when practical. Here 1♠ is correct, as over 2♡ the opener can rebid 2NT, which always shows a minimum opening. If the hearts and clubs were reversed it would be better to open 1◇ and rebid 2◇ over 2♣.

(4) ♠ A 4　♡ A Q J 8 5　◇ K Q 10 7 6　♣ 3

A " strong " type; open 1♢ and follow with 2♡ on the next round.

    (5) ♠ A K J 10 7 6   ♡ J 7 6 2   ♢ A Q   ♣ 3

Open 1♡ and follow with 2♠. When a reverse is planned, the first suit may be very weak.

    (6) ♠ K 7 5 3   ♡ A K   ♢ K Q J 8 7 3   ♣ 5

Open 1♠ and bid 3♢ over a response of either 2♡ or 2♣.
Occasionally the responder will bid the suit in which opener was intending to reverse. When that happens, the opener may either give a jump raise in this suit (very strong) or show a control in a minor by jumping to 4♣ or 4♢.

    (7) ♠ A Q 10 7 4   ♡ K Q 8 5 2   ♢ A 3   ♣ 6

Over 1♡ partner bids 1♠. Opener jumps to 4♢, which shows a superfit in spades and first-round control of diamonds.

When one of the opener's suits is clubs it is not always possible to respect the two principles.

    (8) ♠ 6 3   ♡ A Q 7 4   ♢ K 5   ♣ K J 10 6 4

The only possible opening is 1♡. Over 2♢ it is in order to bid 3♣, for had the hand been " strong " the player would have opened 2♣.

When the hand is strong and the higher suit is longer or the same length, it is necessary to reverse the normal procedure by jumping in the shorter suit (clubs) on the next round.

    (9) ♠ 6   ♡ A K 9 8 6 4   ♢ A 3   ♣ K Q 6 3

Open 1♡ and over 1♠ jump to 3♣. Over 2♢ the solution is to bid simply 2♡ for the moment, since the response at the level of two is forcing as far as 2NT.

This style of bidding the shorter suit first (known as *canapé*) applies to the responding hand in all strong sequences. Two examples will illustrate:

    (1) ♠ A J 7 4   ♡ 9   ♢ K Q 9 7 5 2   ♣ K 3

Over 1♡ bid 1♠ and follow with 3♢.

    (2) ♠ 8 7   ♡ A Q 9 8 5 2   ♢ A 3   ♣ K 7 4

Over 1◇ (or 1♠) respond 2♣. On the next round bid the hearts, a " responder's reverse ", forcing to game.

A response at the level of two, as we have noted, is forcing as far as 2NT. A jump shift is used to emphasize a strong suit. The requirements in other respects are less than in standard bidding; A–K–Q–x–x–x and a side ace would qualify.

## Opening 1NT and Responses

An opening 1NT may be either a balanced 16–17 or a comparatively weak hand in which the only long suit is clubs. The responses are complicated by the fact that opener may have one or other of two distinct types. Players feeling their way into the *Blue Club* usually decide against this ambiguity and play the strong notrump throughout.

## Opening 2♣ and Responses

The opening may be either a one-suited hand with good clubs, 12–16, or a good two-suiter, 15–16 with very fair clubs. In response, 2◇ is a relay, 2♡ and 2♠ are non-forcing, 2NT is natural, and raises are defensive.

Over the 2◇ relay the opener with a one-suiter and two outside guards rebids 2NT; with only one outside guard, 3♣. Responder may then proceed with 3◇, asking for guards, or with three of a major, a strong sequence. In either case developments can be complicated.

## Opening 2◇ and Responses

The opening 2◇ shows a 4–4–4–1 hand in the range of 17–24. In this area, also, there are signs of the midnight oil, with conventional sequences sometimes lasting for five or six rounds. Newcomers to the system may prefer to use the traditional Roman 2◇ opening, with a range of 17–20 only. Then 2NT is the only forcing response; over this, the opener rebids in his short suit.

## Opening 2♡ and 2♠

The requirements for the Mini-two opening are: range 7–11, with 7–9 counting as " lower range "; suit from K–Q–x–x–x–x or better (described as " maximum ") down to Q–10–9–8–x–x (" minimum "). The only forcing response over 2♠ is a relay of 2NT; over 2♡ either 2♠ or 2NT is a relay.

Over the relay response the opener advances one step with minimum points and suit, two steps with minimum points and maximum suit, three steps with maximum points and minimum suit, four steps with maximum in each, five steps with a suit consisting of A–K–Q–x–x–x.

## Slam Bidding in the Blue Club

Italian teams have always been renowned for their accurate slam bidding. Apart from questions of judgment, this is partly due to the style of the early bidding. The showing of controls in response to 1♣, and the sequences that establish the trump suit at a low level, leave them plenty of space to identify controls.

Their use of 4NT is a distinctive feature. This is conventional Blackwood only when bid with a jump or on the first or second round of the auction. For the rest, it is sometimes natural, sometimes a retreat, but more often it is a " general slam try ". Over this the responder may sign off in the likely trump suit or may show an additional feature, such as a control not yet established, or an extra high card in a suit bid by the partnership. To be free from the toils of conventional Blackwood is on many occasions a glorious liberation!

# CHAPTER 16

## Bidding Tactics at Duplicate

*Match-point scoring – Part-score bidding – The game zone – The slam zone – Competitive auctions – Sacrifices – Doubles of freely bid contracts – Competitive Manoeuvres over 1NT*

ALL SERIOUS bridge competitions are conducted on what is called the duplicate principle. Hands dealt and played at one table are played again at one or more other tables, and a direct comparison is then made. This has been mainly responsible for the advances in bidding technique over the years.

Many players who give duplicate a trial prefer it to rubber bridge. In this chapter, and in Chapter 31 which deals with play, we describe the adjustments a rubber-bridge player needs to make to succeed at duplicate. But first we give a brief account of the mechanics of duplicate for those readers who have never played it.

The cards are not played into the centre of the table. Each player places his cards face downwards on his side of the table and, when play is finished, puts them into a container, called a " duplicate board ". The vulnerability and the position of the dealer are shown on the board. In a straight match between two teams of four the board is then passed to the second table, where the North player takes the cards that were held by North at the other table, and so on. When the hand has been replayed it is possible to compare the results gained by players who held the same cards under the same conditions.

In a pairs event the same boards are played at every competing table. Seven is a convenient number of tables for a small duplicate, but there may be hundreds. (The term " duplicate ", used by itself, means a pairs event with match-point scoring.)

In both team and pair events each hand is scored as a separate entity. There is no carrying forward of part scores or games. Scoring for odd tricks and slams is the same as in rubber bridge; there is a 50-point bonus for bidding and making a part score; 300 for bidding and making a non-vulnerable game; and 500 for a vulnerable game.

The score thus reckoned is then converted to match points. In a team event the conversion is to International Match Points, IMPs as they are known, on a scale ranging from 1 to 24. In this chapter we are concerned with match-point scoring at duplicate.

## Match-point scoring

In a pairs event every deal carries the same maximum and minimum score as every other deal. No matter if the best score in the room is no more than, say, 140, the pair that reaches this score (called a " top ") gains as big an advantage as if it had been a grand slam.

Suppose there are seven competing tables. The North–South pair with the worst score receives no match points, the next pair 1 match point, and so on, the pair with the top score receiving 6 match points (one less than the number of competing tables). The East–West score complements, at every table, the North–South score. When two or more pairs have the same score the points are shared. In Britain and some other countries it is customary to double the number of match points to avoid halves.

The fact that each board carries the same number of points, with part-score hands enjoying the same importance as slam hands, means that bidding and play are extremely keen, each pair striving for the slightest advantage. Players will open in third or fourth position on hands that would be thrown in at rubber bridge and may risk big penalties for the sake of contesting part-score hands. Borderline doubles are frequent, and risks are taken to play in notrumps because of the extra 10 points.

On many hands the winning tactics are the same for duplicate as for rubber bridge, but it is impossible to do well at duplicate unless one adjusts one's methods on the remaining hands.

## Part-score Bidding

In competitive auctions, which we deal with later, part-score bidding at duplicate is an altogether different affair from rubber bridge. In an uncontested auction the tactics are mostly the same. The security of the contract is paramount; a safe minor-suit contract is preferred to a risky partial in notrumps. This is because some pairs will usually be too high, in which case any plus score may be worth an average or better score. Here are some situations where duplicate players sometimes adopt mistaken tactics, aiming at a high value instead of a safe contract.

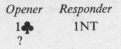

Opener holds:

♠ K Q   ♡ K J 2   ◇ Q 4   ♣ Q J 9 8 6 2

A declarer with an aceless hand opposite at notrumps often has difficulty in establishing the long suit. Therefore, at any form of scoring, it is sensible to rebid 2♣ with this hand, rather than pass 1NT.

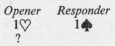

Opener holds:

♠ K 3   ♡ A Q J 8 6   ◇ 10 8   ♣ A 10 7 4

Here the correct rebid is 2♣, the normal exploratory move. It is foolish to bid 2♡ simply because it is duplicate, for partner is also aware that hearts are higher valued than clubs.

The next example shows one of the situations in the part-score area where it is correct to bid differently at duplicate.

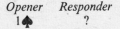

Responder holds:

♠ 5 2   ♡ A 8 5 2    ◇ K 10 8 7   ♣ Q J 3

At rubber bridge the responder would bid 2◇, judging the hand to be outside the range of 1NT. At duplicate it will pay to bid 1NT, not because of the extra 10 points but because the primary object is to record a plus score rather than to make a game. If you end up with nine tricks, scoring 150, you won't do badly, and 120 may be close to a " top " if game is not on.

A difference of another kind arises in third or fourth position. Consider these two hands:

(1) ♠ K 8 6 4 2   ♡ 5   ◇ K 9 3    ♣ A J 5 3
(2) ♠ A Q 10 2   ♡ J 9   ◇ 10 8 7 4   ♣ K J 6

With (1) many rubber-bridge players would open 1♠, even vulnerable, for despite partner's pass game might still be there. At duplicate the possibility of a game counts for no more than the possibility of a part score; it is better to pass, for if partner responds in hearts or notrumps a minus score is likely.

With (2) a rubber-bridge player would be less inclined to open, for he could not hope to score more than a partial. A duplicate player might well open, for there would be a fair chance of a plus score after any response.

### The Game Zone

At duplicate you do not want to be in a game unless you have more than a 50 per cent chance of making it. Imagine that you are the only pair to reach game; in this case you cannot gain in terms of match points unless you make it more often than not. Indeed, assuming that some pairs may go down through being in the *wrong* game, you can afford to stop in a partial unless game appears distinctly odds-on.

Therefore you simply do not try for game on borderline hands. If partner opens with 1NT you do not raise to 2NT with a scrappy 8 points, and so on.

When the values for game are clearly present there may be a choice of contracts. There is very little scope for the minor suits; you don't want to play in 5♣ or 5◇ unless 3NT is clearly hopeless. It is true that a sound trump contract will usually produce at least one more trick than a notrump contract, but there are too many hands where a reasonable chance of 430 or 630 in notrumps is preferable to a safe eleven tricks in the minor suit.

A pair that, looking for a possible slam, has gone beyond what is obviously a lay-down game in notrumps is practically committed to bidding 6♣ or 6◇: it can scarcely be profitable to play in five.

On the other hand, it is a mistake to aim at game in notrumps rather than a major suit where there is a 4–4 fit. After all, 450 beats 430. Suppose your partner opens a strong 1NT and you have this hand:

♠ 7 4    ♡ K 10 9 2    ◇ Q 9 8 3    ♣ A K 2

At duplicate you should initiate a Stayman sequence. Game in notrumps will surely be safe, but if partner has four hearts the odds are that you will make an extra trick at the heart contract. Playing rubber bridge you might reasonably bid 3NT, taking the view that this could hardly fail, whereas 4♡ might be upset by bad distribution.

But when game itself may be borderline, the notrump contract is preferred. The precise score for tricks does not matter so much now; making the contract is what counts.

## The Slam Zone

In a perfect world the criterion for slam bidding at duplicate would be very simple: you would always go for the more ambitious contract if you had at least an even chance of making it. Thus, a 51 per cent grand slam would be preferred to a certain small slam, and so on. In fact, to follow such a strategy would be very unsound indeed. This is because, almost invariably, some pairs will arrive at the wrong contract. Clearly it is not a good idea to bid a grand slam which you think will be only slightly odds-on when some pairs may not progress beyond game; you stand to gain a better than average score, say 60 per cent or 70 per cent, merely by bidding a lay-down small slam; to bid seven would give you 90 per cent or 10 per cent— not a good bargain. In the same way, you should prefer a sound slam in any suit to a shaky 6NT; in particular, when the only sound slam is in a minor suit you should seldom go beyond six, as you can be almost certain that some pairs will be in 3NT.

When you are fairly certain that the field will be in a slam it is reasonable to bid a grand slam depending on a queen finesse at worst. It is correct, at duplicate, to bid a grand slam depending on a 3–2 break; but this again assumes that other pairs will all be in six at least, and such an assumption is rarely justified. There is always some pair accepting a penalty worth less than a slam. Only in the highest company is it right to press for grand slams that may be justified by the theoretical odds.

## Competitive Auctions

So far the main theme has been that, at match points, it pays to take a cautious line in the uncontested auction. In competitive auctions the situation is quite different. You must not allow your opponents to play at a low part score unless you are sure they are a lot stronger than you are. This is because small differences are just as important as big ones; you can well afford an occasional 500 or 800 penalty if, rather more often, you succeed in pushing the opponents one too high and collect 50 instead of losing 110.

Suppose that, with neither side vulnerable, the player on your right opens 1♠, his partner raises to 2♠, and this comes back to you. With the following hands it would be right to pass at rubber bridge, while at duplicate it will pay to contest:

| | | | | |
|---|---|---|---|---|
| (1) | ♠ A 7 3 | ♡ 8 | ◇ Q 9 8 6 4 | ♣ K Q 9 2 |
| (2) | ♠ 3 | ♡ K 10 4 2 | ◇ Q 10 3 | ♣ A 9 8 6 2 |
| (3) | ♠ K 9 8 2 | ♡ Q J 6 | ◇ K Q J 9 | ♣ 8 2 |

With (1) you would offer an Unusual 2NT; with (2) a takeout double. With (3) it might be safer to push with 3◇ rather than with a double; any form of action would seem highly dubious to a rubber-bridge player, but in a keen game of duplicate the odds favour trying to push the opponents to 3♠, where you will have fair prospects of defeating them. So 3◇ is not as foolhardy as it may look, (a) because an opponent is not likely to have a strong trump holding, and (b) because partner must be short in spades, so probably has some support for diamonds.

In the examples above there was no reason to think that your side was badly outgunned. When you are fairly sure that the opponents have the cards you should usually take competitive action only when you are not vulnerable. The opponents' part score will be worth more than 100 points, so the question is whether you have a good chance of losing no more than that. Note that when the hand belongs to the opponents and you have pushed them, you do not double the final contract. If you get them down one undoubled, you will do well enough. (Also, be firm with partners who, when you have risked your life to compete, bid one more themselves on inadequate values.)

In the same way, when the deal belongs to your side you must be unwilling to accept 100 in lieu of a part score; you must either bid one more, or you must double if you think you may get 300. Suppose you are South in this situation:

| South | West | North | East |
|---|---|---|---|
| 1NT | 2♡ | 2♠ | 3♡ |
| ? | | | |

With neither side vulnerable, you hold:

♠ A K 10    ♡ Q 5 2    ◇ K J 8 6 2    ♣ K 7

217

As partner did not double 2♡, and you have a poor hand defensively, you cannot expect 3♡ to be more than one down, if that. Therefore you must bid 3♠, even though you cannot be sure of making it. To let the opponents play in 3♡ undoubled must be bad, and to double and take 100 would not be good enough if other pairs were scoring 110 or 140.

When both sides have game values and the problem is whether to double or bid one more, the rule for rubber bridge is well known: when in doubt, bid on. In a pairs, to lose 790 when you yourself could have made 650 is just a bad board, no worse than making 110 when everyone else has made 140. If you think the odds are against their making 4♠ and against your making 5♡, you must double.

When the two sides seem to be evenly matched and you have pushed the opponents one higher than they would have gone under their own steam, you do not double the final contract. A double invites a " bottom " if the opponents make the contract and gains little when they do not. If the contract is due to go down you don't *need* to double.

But you do need to double when you think you could have made 3♡ and your opponents have defended in 3♠. You must now assume that if they make it you are due for a bad board anyway; you won't make it much worse if you double them into game.

### Sacrifices

At rubber bridge it is usually regarded as a fair deal to save a game for 500. At duplicate it never is! It is either a triumph (if the opponents are vulnerable) or a disaster (if they are not).

In a field of even quality you try to judge matters by that criterion. In a more mixed game the tendency is towards caution; it is unrewarding to sacrifice against a game contract that may not be reached at some tables, or may be misplayed at others.

Sacrifices against slam contracts at a cost of 700 or more are overdone by many players, who seem to forget that the slam may not be bid at some tables. In that case your only hope of a superior score is to take your chance on beating the slam. Slam sacrifices are advisable only when the bidding suggests that the slam will be universal or when you judge that the sacrifice will cost less than the value of a game.

## Doubles of Freely Bid Contracts

As one can afford to incur occasional big losses in exchange for frequent small gains, it might seem that penalty doubles of freely bid contracts would be a somewhat more common manoeuvre at duplicate. After all, a certain proportion of fairly normal contracts, perhaps one in four or five, are due to fail through natural causes, and if you can double some of them you should do well.

In fact such doubles are no more attractive at duplicate than at rubber bridge. Take the case where opponents bid to 3NT in tentative fashion and you judge that the cards lie poorly for them. Perhaps you can double and pick up 300, but on the other hand if you get them two down you can expect to score well without doubling, for some pairs will not be in game. If you double, an experienced declarer will draw the right conclusions about how things are breaking and will usually save a trick, so you will be no better off. If you have misjudged, the doubled contract may be made.

In the same way, it is not necessarily wise to double a borderline game in hearts or spades when you hold four trumps or place your partner with four. Declarer will know the trumps are not breaking and will play accordingly.

However, when a double *looks* good, and will not give declarer any advantage in the play, the odds are less unfavourable at duplicate than at other forms of scoring. A redouble and an overtrick won't compel you to write home for more money!

## Competitive Manoeuvres over 1NT

Especially against a weak 1NT of 12–14 points, most duplicate players use overcalls of 2♣ and, in some cases, 2♢ in a conventional sense.

In the *Landy* convention an overcall of 2♣ indicates at least nine cards in the majors, divided 5–4. In *Astro* 2♢ indicates spades and another suit, 2♣ indicates hearts and a minor. In the *Sharples* and *Ripstra* conventions 2♣ and 2♢ suggest length in the major suits and in the suit named. The most flexible method is *Cansino*, where 2♣ denotes clubs and two other suits, 2♢ a major two-suiter. These conventional overcalls may be used in both second and fourth position.

219

# PART IV

*The Declarer's Play*

# CHAPTER 17

## Finesses, Suit Establishment and Safety Plays

*Leading towards high cards – Simple and combination finesses –*
*The two-way finesse – Refusing a finesse – Percentage plays –*
*Safety plays – Table of probabilities*

IN MOST hands the declarer does not start life with all the tricks he needs to make his contract—if he did, it would mean that he was an excessively cautious bidder. More often than not, therefore, declarer has a certain amount of work to do before he can hope to make the desired entry in the " We " column.

The first stage in the play of any hand is to count the tricks that are already available and to consider the best means of creating additional tricks. This, of course, requires a grasp of how many tricks each suit is capable of producing. In this chapter we consider the standard ways of building tricks in a single suit.

There are hundreds of card combinations and clearly it is impossible to study them all. We will look at the most frequent, drawing attention to some general principles that will enable the reader to make a swift assessment of the best form of play.

### Leading Towards High Cards

The first principle of card play is that in general it pays to lead towards high cards rather than away from them. In this way declarer benefits from the disposition of the opponents' cards if they are favourably placed. In the examples that follow we assume that South can lead from either hand, according to choice.

(1)       K Q 5 3     (2)        Q 7
   A J 8        10 9 6    K J 6 5      10 9 4
       7 4 2              A 8 3 2

In (1) South can make three tricks by taking advantage of the fact that the opponents' cards are favourably placed. He leads up to, and not away from, dummy's high cards. The only trick the opponents make is the ace. Similarly, in (2), South can make the ace and queen separately so long as the first play is a low card from the South hand towards the Q–7. To lead the queen from dummy could never gain against correct defence, for if East held the king he would play it.

| (3) | J 7 | (4) | K J 7 4 | |
|---|---|---|---|---|
| Q 10 8 3 | | 9 5 | A 8 | 10 9 5 2 |
| | A K 6 4 2 | | Q 6 3 | |

Figure (3) illustrates a situation where the best chance for four tricks is to lead up to the J–7. This is much better than simply playing the A–K and another. Leading towards the jack saves a trick whenever West holds Q–10–x–x or Q–x, and the only time it costs is when East holds the singleton queen, in which case four tricks are impossible anyway.

With (4) it seems that players are often tempted to lead low to the king and then back to the queen. The disadvantage of this method of play is that it produces only two tricks when West has the doubleton ace. If entries allow, it is better to lead twice from the South hand. West then has to play the ace on the second round, giving declarer three tricks.

| (5) | K 6 | (6) | J 7 4 3 | |
|---|---|---|---|---|
| A J 4 | | 10 9 7 3 | K 10 8 5 | A 9 2 |
| | Q 8 5 2 | | Q 6 | |

These two examples illustrate a further principle: when the honours are divided it is usually better to play first towards the *shorter* hand. In (5) only one trick can be scored if the first lead is made from the North hand, but if South leads first up to the K–6 he can make two tricks. The king wins (it will not avail West to play the ace) and on the next round South plays low from his own hand. He leads low again on the third round and is rewarded with a second trick when West has to play the ace on the eight.

Similarly, in (6), declarer should begin with a low card towards the Q–6. West wins and declarer, as before, plays low from the dummy on the second and third rounds. Eventually he makes a trick with the jack.

### Simple and Combination Finesses

The following are examples of the simple finesse. In the first, declarer is missing the king, and the object is to take advantage if West has it.

(1)       A Q 7 5 3     (2)       K 10 7 4 3

    K 8         10 9 2     Q 8         A 9 6

      J 6 4                J 5 2

There is an important rule for simple finesses: unless a strong sequence is held, the lead of a high card should be avoided.

Thus in (1) it would be a fatal error to begin by leading the jack. West would cover with the king and declarer would then be bound to lose a trick in the suit. The only chance of making five tricks is to lead low and finesse the queen, hoping the king will fall under the ace on the next round.

In (2) South can make four tricks if he begins with a low card, but not if he leads the jack and West covers.

(3)                 A J 10 4

        K 8 5 3       7 6

             Q 9 2

With this holding it is safe to start the suit by leading a high card, because South has a strong sequence of intermediate cards. It is worth noting, however, that the correct card to lead is the nine rather than the queen, as this allows four tricks to be run without interruption. Suppose the queen is led and West does not cover: declarer cannot afford to unblock with dummy's ten, so must play the four; the next round will leave the lead in dummy and South will need another entry to his hand before he can finesse again.

When two or more honour cards are missing it is usually right to begin with a deep finesse.

(4)      A Q 10 4     (5)  K J 9 3

      7 5 2            8 7 4

In (4) the only chance to trap both the king and the jack is to finesse the ten on the first round. The best way of gaining three tricks in (5) is not so plain. If West has A–Q–x, the winning play is to finesse the jack on the first round; if he has Q–10–x, a finesse of the nine is better. The deep finesse actually gives the best chance because it also wins when West holds Q–10–x–x or A–Q–10–x.

(6)     A Q 9 5 3     (7)  K 10 8 2

      6 4              6 5 3

In (6) players tend to overlook the advantage of a first-round finesse of the nine. This is a 'free shot', for it gains a trick whenever West holds J–10–x or J–10–x–x. If the nine loses to the jack or ten South can still finesse the queen on the next round. In (7) the best play is to finesse the eight on the first round. This gains when West holds Q–9–x, J–9–x, A–Q–9–x or A–J–9–x.

(8)    A J 9 6          (9)    K 10 9 4
       7 5 4                6 3 2

The combination shown in (8) frequently occurs. The best play is to finesse the nine, playing West for Q–10–x or K–10–x. It may be noted that an experienced opponent, with one of those holdings, may well decide to play the king or queen on the first round, as though he had the K–Q–x. Declarer should nevertheless stick to his first intention by winning with the ace and finessing the nine on the next round.

Figure (9) illustrates a position where South has to make his main decision on the second round. He begins with a finesse of the nine, which, we will say, loses to the jack or queen. When South leads to the next round West plays low and the choice lies between going up with the king (playing West for A–x–x) or finessing the ten. In such situations the odds favour the finesse of the lower card. (See " Principle of Restricted Choice " in Chapter 26.)

### The Two-way Finesse

When the declarer is well endowed with intermediate cards he may be able to finesse for a queen or jack in either direction. Sometimes it is possible to tempt an opponent into an injudicious cover.

(1)    K 10 7 3         (2)    K 9 7 3
      A J 9 8              Q 10 8 6

In (1) declarer can play East or West for the missing queen. Whatever he intends, it is good play to start by leading the jack from the closed hand. In some cases it would be right for West, with Q–x or Q–x–x, to cover the jack, and he may save the declarer a guess here. Figure (2) shows a similar position. The first play should be the ten from hand, hoping that West may be tempted to cover with the jack.

When declarer does not have such strong intermediate cards, a study of the situation may reveal that there is advantage in finessing one way rather than the other.

(3)    A 6 4               (4)  K J 5 4 3
        K J 10 5 2              A 10

In (3) South can make five tricks by means of a successful finesse against either opponent holding Q–x or Q–x–x. However, there is a sound reason for playing the ace first and then finessing the jack. This way, declarer can pick up Q–9–x–x in East's hand. If the king were played first he would not be able to pick up Q–9–x–x in either hand. (4) shows a different aspect of the same sort of problem. South might make five tricks by playing either opponent for Q–x–x, but a better percentage play is to lead from the North hand and finesse the ten. This brings in five tricks when East holds Q–x as well as when he has Q–x–x. There is no way of making five tricks when West has the doubleton queen.

(5)          Q 9 7 4    (6)       K J 9 3
  A J 8 5         6    10 7 2       Q 8 5
      K 10 3 2          A 6 4

In many cases the spot cards determine the first finesse. In (5) the question is whether to lead first towards the king or the queen. Leading up to the king is superior because South can then pick up A–J–8–x in West's hand, losing only one trick. After the king has lost to the ace declarer leads the ten, and East's void will show up. Declarer must always lose two tricks when East holds A–J–8–x.

Figure (6) illustrates a different aspect of the two-way finesse. The normal play is to cash the ace and finesse the jack, but if East is marked with the queen, or if he must be kept out of the lead, declarer may attempt a " backward finesse ". In this case he leads the jack from dummy, wins East's queen with the ace, and then leads back towards the K–9–3, finessing against West's tenspot.

### Refusing a Finesse

It is often said that learning how to take a finesse is not as difficult as learning when not to take one. There are certain situations, all involving the king, where a finesse cannot gain a trick in any circumstances.

(1)  Q J 7 5           (2)      Q 4
      A 4 3                A J 7 5 3 2

In (1) it may be expedient to finesse by leading the queen if declarer wants to make two tricks without losing the lead. But when the aim is to make as many tricks as possible the right play is to refuse the finesse and lead twice towards the Q–J–x–x. To lead an honour from dummy will cost a trick if West has K–x or K–10–x–x.

In (2) there is no distribution that will enable declarer to make six tricks. He can make five tricks whenever the opponents' cards are 3–2, and also when the king is bare—so long as he begins by leading the ace. To lead the four and finesse the jack would cost a trick when West held the singleton king

(3)  A Q 6 3               (4)     7 4 2
        J 4                         A Q 8 5 3

To make the maximum in (3) declarer should refuse the finesse and lead low towards the J–4. If East has the king and plays it, declarer has three tricks. If he ducks, South wins with the jack, returns to the ace and leads the six. In this way he makes three tricks whenever East holds K–x or K–x–x. Similarly, with A–J–x–x–x opposite Q–x, the best chance for four tricks is to lead low towards the Q–x. This gains when the player in front of the queen holds K–x.

Finally, with the common holding shown in (4), a first-round finesse of the queen cannot gain a trick and will cost when West holds a singleton king. This is only a small chance, of course, but when time and entries allow, it is better to lay down the ace and later lead up to the queen.

## Percentage Plays

It is often convenient to express the comparison between one line of play and another in percentage terms. A finesse, for example, is normally a 50 per cent chance, while a 3–2 break is a 68 per cent chance. By an extension of meaning, the term ' percentage play ' is widely used to denote the play that presents the best chance. We look first at some common holdings where the choice is close.

(1)  K 5 4 3               (2)       7 5
       A J 8 6 2                    A K J 10 6 3

The declarer in (1) leads low to the king and returns a low card, to which East follows. There is an old saying, ' eight ever, nine never ', meaning that with nine cards it is better to refuse the finesse and play for the drop of the queen. Mathematically, that is right, but by only a small margin. If there is any indication to suggest that East is more likely to be long in the suit than West, then declarer should take the finesse.

In (2) the finesse stands out and the only question is whether to finesse on the first round or to play off the ace and then enter dummy for a second-round finesse. It is better to finesse on the first round, for this gains against any low singleton in the West hand, assuming that the finesse can be repeated. Playing off the ace gains only when West has a singleton queen.

(3)   A Q 10 5          (4)  A K 10 9 3
        K 7 4                    6 2

In (3) South plays off the ace and king, then leads low towards the Q–10. Suppose West follows suit and the jack has not appeared. The odds slightly favour playing for the drop, but here again declarer should be influenced by any knowledge he may possess of the adverse distribution.

Suppose that in (4) the declarer requires four tricks. He may play off the A–K, hoping for the drop of a doubleton honour, he may finesse the ten and then play for the drop, or he may finesse twice—first the nine, then the ten. Playing off the top cards loses when either defender holds a low doubleton; taking two finesses goes wrong when East holds Q–J alone or Q–J–x. As in most similar situations, the best line is to take two finesses.

(5)  A J 10 7 4 2      (6)  A J 9 6 3
       8 5 3                  Q 4 2

There are three ways of tackling (5); declarer may play off the ace first, he may take two finesses, or he may take one finesse and then play off the ace. Again the best line is to take two finesses.

With (6) many players favour a finesse of the jack. If it holds they continue either by laying down the ace, playing West for K–x, or leading the queen from hand, playing East for 10–x. It is actually a little better to begin with the queen. If this is covered by the king and ace declarer should later finesse the nine, playing West for K–10–x.

(7)  Q 10 6 3        (8)  Q 10 6 3
     A 9 5 4               A 9 5 4 2

Figure (7) is a tricky situation where faces alter cases, as the saying goes: declarer has to take into account what West might do if he held such-and-such. Probably the best line is to lead low from the closed hand and put in the ten if there is no reaction. If this loses to the jack, the nine should be finessed on the next round. With a slightly stronger holding, Q–10–8–x opposite A–9–x–x, it is simpler to take two finesses, leading first the queen and then the ten.

In (8), where nine cards are held, the best mathematical chance for four tricks is to play the ace followed by the two, losing only when East holds K–J–x (or K–J–x–x). There is much to be said, however, for leading low away from the ace. West, holding K–x, may solve declarer's problem by going up with the king or by hesitating before playing low. (To make five tricks with this holding, South may either lead the queen from dummy, striving to pin a singleton jack, or the ace from hand, playing East for a singleton king.)

(9)  A 10 5
    K 9 6 3

(10)  A J 4 3
     10 7 5 2

Figure (9) is a combination which can be handled in various ways. To play off the ace and king is as good a way as any of making three tricks; it succeeds against a doubleton honour or against any 3–3 break. This form of play, however, has the disadvantage of surrendering control of the suit and declarer may prefer to lead low to the ten. If this loses to the jack or queen he may have to decide later whether to play for a 3–3 break or for East to hold Q–J–x–x.

With (10), which in one form or another occurs very often, South can make three tricks by playing either opponent for a doubleton honour: if West, then low to the jack is best; if East, then low from dummy, or the ten from hand. Lacking any indication, it is normal to play towards the jack, as this takes care, without any guessing, of K–Q–x in West's hand.

Finally, there are some situations where only one division of the opponents' cards will enable declarer to achieve his objective.

(11)          J 3
 K 10             Q 8 6
     A 9 7 5 4 2

(12)      A 10 8 4
 K 9 5           J
     Q 7 6 3 2

Suppose that in (11) the declarer requires five tricks. The only chance is to lead low from the closed hand. If West rises with the king, his ten is pinned when the jack is led from dummy on the next round. In effect, declarer is playing West for precisely K–10 or Q–10. This is also the best way to set about A–9–x–x–x opposite

J–x–x, though here there is the alternative chance of finding an opponent with a doubleton K–Q.

With (12) the only chance to make all the tricks is to lead the queen, hoping to pin the singleton jack. A singleton king on either side would not help the declarer.

In some cases the bidding may indicate the necessity for an unusual form of play.

| (13) | A 4 2 | (14) | A 7 3 |
|------|-------|------|-------|
| K Q 7 | 10 | K J 6 | 10 8 |
| J 9 8 6 5 3 | | Q 9 5 4 2 | |

In (13), suppose that West has bid notrumps and is thought to hold a fairly strong three-card combination. The most likely way to hold him to one trick is by means of the unorthodox lead of the jack, hoping to pin a singleton ten.

In (14), suppose West has doubled the final contract and is likely to hold at least K–J–x of this trump suit. There is still a chance to hold him to one trick. A low card is led from dummy and East's eight is covered by the nine and jack. On the next round the lead of the queen pins East's ten.

## Safety Plays

Bombproof safety plays, where nothing can go wrong if the suit is played correctly, are not very common. The stock example is A–Q–10–x–x opposite K–9–x–x, where declarer needs only to lay down the ace or queen, rather than the king, to be sure of picking up J–x–x–x on either side.

Much more often, the safety play simply takes care of a particular adverse distribution.

| (1) | K 7 4 2 | (2) | A Q 9 6 4 3 |
|-----|---------|-----|-------------|
| – | J 10 6 3 | K 10 8 | – |
| A Q 9 8 5 | | J 7 5 2 | |

In (1), missing the ten as well as the jack, it is correct to play the king first, as this enables J–10–x–x to be picked up in East's hand. If West holds J–10–x–x nothing can be done about it. A combination such as Q–7–4–2 opposite K–J–8–6–5 presents the same principle. Declarer can pick up A–10–9–x on one side only. He must therefore play the queen first.

Figure (2) is a case where it is correct to lead an unsupported honour. South intends to finesse for the king, of course, and there-fore it costs nothing to lead the jack first. If he were to lead low and finesse the queen, West would later get a trick with the K–10.

(3)    K 7 3               (4)    J 6 4 2
       A 10 6 4 2                    A 10 8 7 5 3

Figure (3) illustrates a common holding. Declarer plays the king from dummy and continues with the three, on which East plays low. Barring special considerations, such as the fear of a ruff, it must be right to put in the ten. One trick must be lost in any event and the ten saves a trick when East holds Q–J–x–x.

It is worth remarking that with a similar combination, but only seven cards, K–x–x opposite A–10–x–x, the best play for three tricks is not the king, to be followed by a finesse of the ten, but ace, king, and low towards the 10–x. This takes care of Q–x or J–x in the West hand, which is more likely than a low doubleton.

In (4) there is no advantage in laying down the ace. If the lead is in the declarer's own hand he should begin with a low card towards the jack, so that he can pick up K–Q–9 in the East hand.

The safety plays described so far are in the nature of " extra chance " plays. They guard against a particular distribution and cannot cost a trick. Here are two more of the same kind:

(5)    K 9                (6)    K J 6 3
       A 10 6 4 3                     A 9 5 2

Needing four tricks from (5), South should lead low and put in dummy's nine. This takes care of J–x or Q–x in West's hand.

The safety play in (6) is a comparatively rare bird. Needing four tricks, and intending in principle to finesse the jack, declarer may be tempted to lay down the ace with the idea of guarding against a singleton queen. That, however, would not help him to win four tricks, no matter who held the singleton queen. The right play is to lead low from the closed hand. Declarer can then win all the tricks when West holds the singleton queen as well as when he holds Q–x or Q–x–x.

The majority of safety plays occur when the declarer, for tactical reasons, is aiming to make, not the maximum, but a particular number of tricks in the suit. Here are four very common examples:

(7)    J 7 3              (8)    K J 6 3
       A K 6 4 2                   A 7 2

In (7), if four tricks will be enough for the contract, declarer should play the ace and then lead low towards the J–x. This saves the situation when West began with Q–10–x–x, though of course it costs an overtrick when either defender has Q–x.

In the same way, with (8), when the object is to make precisely three tricks the best play is king, ace, and low towards the J–x. This avoids calamity when West holds 10–9–x–x and East Q–x.

(9)  A Q 7 5 4 3          (10)  A Q J 6 4
     9 6 2                             7 5 3

It has already been noted that with A–Q–x–x–x opposite x–x–x a first-round finesse of the queen cannot gain and is less safe than cashing the ace and leading towards the queen. With nine cards, as in (9), the finesse is necessary if declarer needs all six tricks; but when he can afford to lose a trick he should lay down the ace, as a precaution against a singleton king.

In (10) it is normal to finesse the queen, hoping for five tricks; but the safety play for four tricks, assuming that South has sufficient entries, is to lay down the ace first, taking care of a singleton king in the East hand.

Because so many hands are played at a trump contract with eight or nine trumps in the combined hands, special consideration has been given to plays designed to take care of a 4–0 or 4–1 break. Here are some examples:

(11)    A 9 3          (12)    K 10 8 4
     Q J 7 6 4 2                       A 9 7 5 3

Suppose that in (11) South can afford to lose one trick, but not two. The first move should be a low card away from the ace, guarding against K–10–8–x in either hand. To lead the queen costs a trick when West is void, and to lead the ace costs when East is void. Similarly, with A–10–x–x–x–x opposite Q–x–x–x, declarer should avoid the trap of laying down the ace.

Figure (12) illustrates a combination that often occurs in a slam. To avoid losing two tricks declarer leads low from either hand and simply covers the card played by the next opponent. This method is proof against Q–J–x–x in either hand.

(13)    A J 5          (14)    A 9 3
     K 9 7 4 2                         K J 6 5 4

With these two combinations four tricks can be ensured against any 4–1 break. With the first, declarer cashes the ace and later leads up to the J–5. With the second he cashes the king, then leads low and puts in the nine if West follows with a low card.

Players tend to be less familiar with those safety plays that are designed to keep the losers to two tricks.

(15)    A 10 6 4 2        (16)       10 6 2
        J 5 3                       A Q 5 4 3

We saw earlier that the best play for four tricks in (15) is to lead low and finesse the ten. However, if this lost to a singleton king or queen declarer would have three losers. When declarer can afford to lose two tricks he should cash the ace and then lead up to the J–5. In (16) the safety play for three tricks is to cash the ace and lead low towards the 10–6. With A–10–x opposite Q–x–x–x–x the play for three tricks is similar: ace first, then up to the 10–x.

(17)       10 4        (18)       10 5
      K Q 7 5 3 2         A Q 8 6 4 3 2

In (17) there is no sure way to make four tricks, but the safest line is low towards the 10–4, saving a trick when West holds A–J–9–x. In Figure 18 a low card from hand ensures five tricks against K–J–9–x in either hand.

Some special situations occur when the declarer has a singleton and can take only one finesse.

(19)        7         (20)       5
    A Q 10 9 5 3        A J 10 7 4 2

(19) shows a position where the best play for five tricks is to finesse the queen rather than the ten. If the opponents' cards are 3–3 the queen has the same chance as the ten, but the queen also wins four tricks when West has J–x. In the corresponding situation where West has K–x, a finesse of the ten does not help declarer.

The play in (20) requires clear thinking. If the object is to make five tricks declarer must finesse the jack, playing East for K–Q–x; but when he needs only four tricks he should play the ace, followed by a low card. This is because, while both methods of play succeed against a 3–3 break, ace and another wins also when either opponent holds a doubleton honour. It is true that to finesse the ten would gain if West held a low doubleton, but the doubleton honour, K–x or Q–x, is a more likely combination. The same principle arises when declarer has a holding such as A–x opposite

J–10–x–x–x. He plays the ace and on the next round should duck in both hands, saving a trick when the fourth player holds K–x or Q–x. This play is based on the supposition that not many defenders, holding K–Q–9–x in front of dummy's J–10–x–x–x, would have the hardihood to play low on the second round.

### Table of Probabilities

To know the most likely division of the defenders' cards is of great assistance to declarer in planning the play. At the start of the hand the probabilities, in the absence of any other indication, are as follows:

| *When the defenders have between them:* | *These are likely to be divided:* | |
|---|---|---|
| 7 cards | 4–3 | 62 per cent |
| | 5–2 | 31 per cent |
| | 6–1 | 7 per cent |
| 6 cards | 4–2 | 48 per cent |
| | 3–3 | 36 per cent |
| | 5–1 | 15 per cent |
| 5 cards | 3–2 | 68 per cent |
| | 4–1 | 28 per cent |
| | 5–0 | 4 per cent |
| 4 cards | 3–1 | 50 per cent |
| | 2–2 | 40 per cent |
| | 4–0 | 10 per cent |
| 3 cards | 2–1 | 78 per cent |
| | 3–0 | 22 per cent |
| 2 cards | 1–1 | 52 per cent |
| | 2–0 | 48 per cent |

It will be seen that when the defenders have an odd number of cards in a suit the more even distributions (4–3, 3–2, 2–1) are by far the most likely, and are indeed odds-on in each case. But when the defenders have an even number of cards, the even distributions 3–3 and 2–2 are odds-against.

Needless to say, the expectancies may be greatly affected by the bidding or by developments in the play. This aspect is discussed at some length in Chapter 26.

235

# CHAPTER 18

## The Play in Notrumps

*Counting the winners – The hold-up – When not to hold up – Which suit to develop – Ducking*

IN THE MAJORITY of cases the defenders will not be able to take enough tricks straight off to defeat the contract and the declarer will not have enough ready-made winners to make the contract. Each side will struggle to make extra tricks, and the declarer's first concern is to form a plan of campaign.

When the opening lead is made, therefore, and declarer's partner puts down his hand, there is usually an interval before the first card is played from dummy. This may be so even when the play from dummy requires no consideration.

The essential stages of planning are: (1) Note the contract; (2) Count the sure winners; (3) Observe how many more are needed; (4) Decide where they will come from; (5) Decide what are the dangers; (6) Decide what is the safest way to develop the extra tricks.

### Counting the Winners

The selection of the correct method of play depends first and foremost on how many extra tricks the declarer needs. The careful declarer, therefore, never fails to count his winners before playing to the first trick.

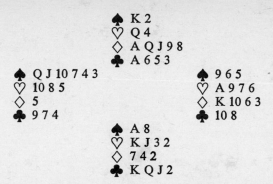

The contract is 3NT and West leads ♠Q. A declarer who neglected to count his winners might be tempted to win in his own hand and finesse ◇Q, especially as it is frequently good tactics at a notrump contract to tackle first the longest and strongest suit. In this case East would return a spade and declarer would make only eight tricks.

Admittedly this would be unlucky, but a more careful declarer would note a cast-iron way of making the contract. There are seven winners at the outset: two spades, one diamond and four clubs. Needing two more for the contract, declarer should first dislodge ♡A. Now there are nine certain tricks.

## The Hold-up

Frequently at notrumps neither side has enough ready-made winners and the hand develops into a race between the opposing sides to set up their long suits. The hold-up is a weapon that looms large in this struggle. It consists of holding back a winning card in order to run one of the opponents out of the suit. This is a standard example:

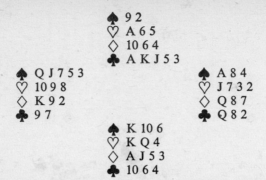

The contract is 3NT and West leads ♠5, on which East plays the ace. East returns ♠8 and declarer's correct play is to hold up the king. He wins the next spade and attacks clubs. As the cards lie he must lose a club trick, but the contract is safe because East has no more spades and declarer has control of the other suits.

It is clear that if declarer failed to hold up ♠K until the third round he would be defeated, for when East came in with ♣Q he would return a spade, enabling West to clear the suit. Sometimes the advantage of the hold-up is not quite so obvious.

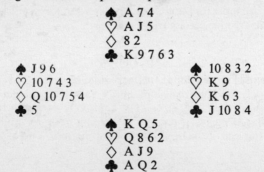

South is in 3NT and West leads ◇5, on which East plays the king. Declarer appears to have ample tricks, including the possibility of a double guard in diamonds, and he may be tempted to win with ◇A and lay down ♣A–Q. With West showing out, declarer has only eight winning tricks. His best chance now is to take the heart finesse, but this loses and the defenders, with ◇Q–10 over the J–9, take four tricks in diamonds to defeat the contract.

238

South can hardly fail in 3NT if he holds up ◇A until the third round. He should note that he starts life with eight winners and can establish a ninth in hearts if the clubs do not break. He therefore does not need the possibility of a second stopper in diamonds, providing he takes care to run East out of the suit by holding up the ace. It is true that East might have four diamonds, in which case the hold-up would be ineffective, but the contract would then be safe in any event.

Occasionally the same sort of tactical point arises in a different guise:

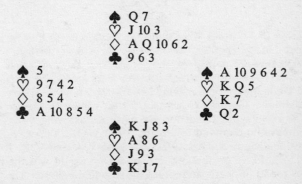

♠ Q 7
♡ J 10 3
◇ A Q 10 6 2
♣ 9 6 3

♠ 5                    ♠ A 10 9 6 4 2
♡ 9 7 4 2              ♡ K Q 5
◇ 8 5 4               ◇ K 7
♣ A 10 8 5 4          ♣ Q 2

♠ K J 8 3
♡ A 8 6
◇ J 9 3
♣ K J 7

South plays in 2NT after East has opened the bidding with 1♠. Holding a singleton spade, West decides to play for his own suit and leads ♣5, on which East plays the queen. If South captures this trick and takes the diamond finesse, the defence will eventually make four clubs, ◇K and ♠A. As no switch looks dangerous, South should hold up on the first round of clubs. East will probably return a club, but now West's suit is shut out and the defenders will make no more than five tricks.

A hold-up is especially effective when it leaves a defender with a minor tenace. (A tenace is any broken combination such as A–Q or K–x.) The commonest example is when a defender leads the king from K–Q–10–x and declarer, holding A–J–x (or A–x–x in dummy, J–x–x in hand), plays low. The leader cannot now continue the suit without giving up a trick. The play by declarer is known as a "Bath coup", having first been executed in that city.

Even when declarer has two sure tricks in the suit led, it is often necessary to hold up. This hand is a typical example.

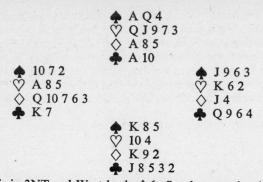

♠ A Q 4
♡ Q J 9 7 3
◇ A 8 5
♣ A 10

♠ 10 7 2          ♠ J 9 6 3
♡ A 8 5           ♡ K 6 2
◇ Q 10 7 6 3      ◇ J 4
♣ K 7             ♣ Q 9 6 4

♠ K 8 5
♡ 10 4
◇ K 9 2
♣ J 8 5 3 2

South is in 3NT and West leads ◇6. South notes that he has six winners and, given time, can develop three more in hearts. The danger is that the defenders may set up their diamonds first. Since there is no other suit in which declarer fears attack, he should hold up on the first diamond, playing low from both hands. He wins the next diamond and attacks hearts. If West wins with the ace he will have no re-entry for the diamonds, while if East wins with the king he will have no diamond to return. By playing in this way declarer ensures the contract unless West has both ♡A and ♡K. If South failed to hold up on the first diamond East would win the first or second round of hearts and return his second diamond. This would establish three diamond winners for West while he still had ♡A.

## When Not to Hold up

Bridge is a contrary sort of game, and there is an art in not holding up just as much as in holding up. One time when the hold-up is likely to be wrong is when declarer can be sure of a second stopper by taking the first trick.

(1)                    10 2        (2)                    9 4
     Q 9 7 5 3    K 8 4        A J 8 6 3    Q 7
               A J 6                     K 10 5 2

In (1) West leads the five. With this combination of honours South can make sure of a second trick by playing low from dummy and winning with the ace if East plays the king or queen.

In (2) West leads the six, dummy plays the four and East the queen. Here, again, it would be a mistake to hold off. By winning the queen with the king South ensures a double guard whenever the suit is divided 5–2.

Such situations are familiar and are easy to work out at the table. More often, the decision whether or not to hold up depends on tactical considerations. Declarer must ask himself, first, whether the suit led represents a serious threat; if it does not, he should not hold up. Secondly, he must consider whether a switch to another suit would be more dangerous. In the next deal the hold-up should be avoided on both grounds.

South is in 3NT and West leads ♠3. When leading low from a long suit most players lead fourth-best, and declarer should therefore note straightaway that West appears to have only a four-card spade suit. South can afford to lose two spades and two diamonds, so he should take the first spade and run ◇9. Now nothing can defeat him.

The danger of holding up is that East, with a trick in the bag, may switch to hearts. In this case, whether declarer ducks or not, he will wind up losing two hearts, two diamonds and one spade.

Finally, a somewhat striking example where declarer should refuse even to take a ' free ' finesse in the opponents' suit:

The contract is 3NT and West leads ♡6. If the queen is played, East will win and shift to a spade, after which the declarer will wind up with no more than seven tricks.

Declarer should appreciate that with this heart combination the defenders can never take more than three heart tricks, for if West has five of them East will not have a third one to play through declarer's ten. Therefore the safest play is to win the first trick with the ace and tackle clubs, making game for the loss of a club and three spades.

## Which Suit to Develop

On many hands the declarer sees that he will need to develop more than one suit. The question then arises, which suit should he attack first? Sometimes the deciding factor will be that he cannot afford to let a particular opponent win the first defensive trick.

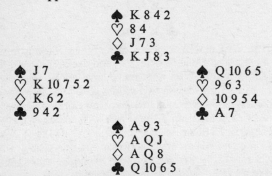

```
                    ♠ K 8 4 2
                    ♡ 8 4
                    ◇ J 7 3
                    ♣ K J 8 3
  ♠ J 7                              ♠ Q 10 6 5
  ♡ K 10 7 5 2                       ♡ 9 6 3
  ◇ K 6 2                            ◇ 10 9 5 4
  ♣ 9 4 2                            ♣ A 7
                    ♠ A 9 3
                    ♡ A Q J
                    ◇ A Q 8
                    ♣ Q 10 6 5
```

The contract is 3NT and West leads ♡5, on which East plays the nine and South the queen. Declarer can count four winners in the major suits, and the clubs will produce three tricks after the ace has been dislodged. He will still need two tricks in diamonds.

It may seem natural to tackle clubs first, but declarer should consider what the consequences may be. If East has the ace he will win the first or second round and lead a heart through the A–J. This will set up three heart tricks for the defence and when the diamond finesse loses the contract will fail.

Now suppose that the diamonds are tackled before the clubs. Declarer crosses to ♠K at trick two and leads a diamond to the queen. If the finesse succeeds, declarer shifts to clubs and makes

242

the contract. If the finesse fails, West will be unable to attack hearts to advantage and again South will make the contract, as he will have time to force out ♣A.

The choice of suits to attack on the last hand was dictated by the need to protect declarer's holding in a third suit. The next hand illustrates a different principle: *when there are two entry cards to force out, attack the entry held by the danger hand first.*

```
                    ♠ Q 10
                    ♡ 9 7 5 3
                    ◇ K J 10
                    ♣ Q 9 6 4
     ♠ J 6                          ♠ A 8 7 5 4 2
     ♡ Q 6 2                        ♡ K J 4
     ◇ 8 7 4 3 2                    ◇ A 9 6
     ♣ K 7 5                        ♣ 2
                    ♠ K 9 3
                    ♡ A 10 8
                    ◇ Q 5
                    ♣ A J 10 8 3
```

The contract is 2NT, East having opened the bidding with 1♠. West leads ♠J, the queen is played from dummy, and East ducks; that is to say, he holds up the ace, his object being to leave West with a spade to play when he gains the lead.

Declarer should reason that if the club finesse succeeds the contract will be in no danger, but if it loses he will want one trick from diamonds. Meanwhile there is the threat of East's spade suit. From ♠J–x–x West would have led a low card, so East presumably has a six-card suit. Declarer must avoid losing four spades, ◇A and ♣K.

East's only potential entry card is ◇A and therefore, following the principle stated above, South must attack the danger hand by leading a diamond at trick two. East may win and clear the spades, but then he has no quick entry. More likely, East will play low on the diamond lead. South can then afford to play clubs. This will provide him with seven tricks and an eighth must come from whatever suit the opponents play next.

If South fails to attack East's entry first, he goes down. A club finesse is won by West and the spades are cleared. Declarer can run only seven tricks before letting East in with ◇A.

Sometimes the choice of suit depends on considerations of

timing; by going for the correct suit declarer can give himself chances in both suits.

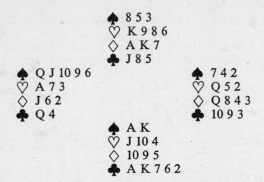

Playing at 3NT, South wins the spade opening lead and must decide whether to tackle hearts or clubs. If he leads ♡J he has a 50 per cent chance of finding West with the queen, which would give him nine tricks; if he cashes ♣A–K he has a more slender chance of catching a doubleton queen. Nevertheless, the club suit is the one to attack. This is because South can combine the chances in both suits; if the doubleton queen does not appear he has time to lead ♡J. Declarer cannot reverse the procedure by tackling hearts before clubs, because if the heart finesse fails East will return a spade, removing declarer's only entry. It will not then be possible to profit from the fall of ♣Q.

On many hands there are several possible ways of making the necessary tricks and the problem is to select the safest.

♠ A 8 5 3
♡ 7 6 3
◇ A Q J 4
♣ K 5

♠ J 9 4
♡ K J 8 5 4
◇ 7
♣ 10 8 6 3

♠ 10 7 6
♡ 10 9 2
◇ K 10 8 3
♣ A 7 2

♠ K Q 2
♡ A Q
◇ 9 6 5 2
♣ Q J 9 4

South is the declarer at 3NT. West leads his fourth best heart and South sees that his ready winners are three spades, two hearts and ◇A. Three more tricks are wanted. Where will they come from? There are possibilities in three suits. If the opponents' spades are 3–3, dummy's long spades will provide a trick. In clubs, two tricks can surely be won by forcing out the ace, and if the ten falls in three rounds the nine will be a winner as well. To assess the diamond situation is more difficult; declarer might make either one, two or three extra tricks, according to how the opponents' cards are divided.

Mathematically, there is a better chance of developing three extra tricks in clubs than in diamonds, but that is not the only reason why South should attack clubs first. A valuable principle applies. It is usually right to attack a suit where one or more top cards are bound to be lost in any event. In line with this, South should determine that his first move will be to drive out ♣A.

Suppose, therefore, that South wins the heart opening lead with the queen and leads a low club to the king. East will probably win this and return ♡10.

Declarer now has eight tricks, but it would be dangerous to lose the lead again because West probably has three more hearts to cash. South plays off ♣Q–J, but the ten does not fall. Now the following cards are left:

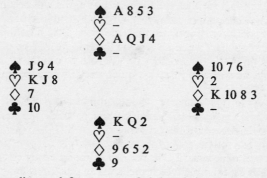

```
                ♠ A 8 5 3
                ♡ –
                ◇ A Q J 4
                ♣ –
   ♠ J 9 4                    ♠ 10 7 6
   ♡ K J 8                    ♡ 2
   ◇ 7                        ◇ K 10 8 3
   ♣ 10                       ♣ –
                ♠ K Q 2
                ♡ –
                ◇ 9 6 5 2
                ♣ 9
```

Either a diamond finesse or a 3–3 break in spades would yield the ninth trick. Clearly, it is a better idea to try the spades first, because if this goes wrong the diamond finesse will still be available.

Declarer must have a clear idea of what he is trying to achieve at this time, otherwise he may muddle the entries. With K–Q–x

245

opposite A–x–x–x it is normal to play the K–Q first so that four tricks can be run without interruption. That would be a mistake here because after taking the K–Q–A, in that order, South would be in dummy and unable to take the diamond finesse if he needed it. The best play is to lead a spade to the ace, then back to the king. When all follow to the next spade, the queen, the contract is assured and South does not need the diamond finesse. He returns to ◇A, cashes the last spade, and makes game with four spades, two hearts, one diamond and two clubs.

## Ducking

The reader may have been struck by the effectiveness of East's play in an earlier hand when, holding ♠A–8–7–x–x–x, he ducked his partner's opening lead, a manoeuvre that certainly made declarer's task more difficult. However, the same form of play can very frequently be used by the declarer as well. Suppose South is playing a notrump contract and has to develop any one of these combinations:

   (1)  K 7 4 3    (2)  A 10 7 5 3    (3)  A Q 7 4 2
        A 8 5             8 4 2            9 5 3

In each case the intention is to give up the trick or tricks that have to be lost, in the hope that the long card or cards will become good. In any such situation it is usually right to give up an early trick. With (1), where declarer hopes to find the suit 3–3, he should duck the very first round; when he regains the lead he will be in control. If he plays off A–K and another he will lose communication within the suit and he will also lose two quick tricks when the opponents' cards are 4–2.

Similarly, in (2) declarer should duck twice before playing the ace, while in (3) it will often be best to duck the first round, deferring the finesse until the next round.

Declarer will often duck for safety; that is to say, give up a trick, perhaps unnecessarily, to be sure of maintaining communication. Here is an example which incidentally illustrates an important principle of play (to be developed further in Chapter 26): when the contract would be endangered only by a certain lie of the cards, declarer should assume that the cards do lie in that way.

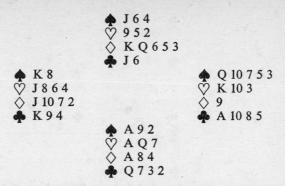

♠ J 6 4
♡ 9 5 2
◇ K Q 6 5 3
♣ J 6

♠ K 8                    ♠ Q 10 7 5 3
♡ J 8 6 4                ♡ K 10 3
◇ J 10 7 2               ◇ 9
♣ K 9 4                  ♣ A 10 8 5

♠ A 9 2
♡ A Q 7
◇ A 8 4
♣ Q 7 3 2

South plays at 1NT and West leads ♡4, on which East plays the king. South should not hold up at this stage, for the hearts present no great danger and a switch to spades would be unwelcome. At trick two he cashes ◇A and continues with a low diamond. We will suppose at this point that West, who knows that the J–10–7 are all " equals ", elects to play the jack.

If the contract were 2NT South would play the queen from dummy, hoping for a 3–2 break, but at 1NT the safety play is to duck, ensuring four diamond tricks. In the actual case, if declarer failed to duck he could go down at 1NT, as the only tricks he would make in diamonds would be the A–K–Q.

Ducking may also be effective when declarer does not hold the ace of the suit, as in these combinations:

(1)          K 8 6 4 2          (2)          K Q 6 5 4
      A J 5            Q 10 7          J 9 7            A 10 2
              9 3                              8 3

In (1) declarer could lead low and play the king, but in that case he would need two side entries to bring in the long cards. If there is only one side entry he must duck the first round; it makes no difference whether he leads the two from dummy or the three from his own hand. In (2), if South starts with a low card to the king, East may duck; now again two side entries will be needed before the long cards can be brought in. If declarer plays low from each hand on the first round, and plays an honour on the second round, he will need only one side entry.

The same sort of play is required on the following deal, which is a test for the defending side also.

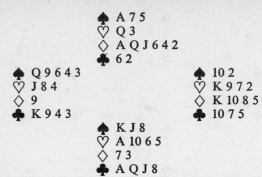

&spades; A 7 5
&hearts; Q 3
&diams; A Q J 6 4 2
&clubs; 6 2

&spades; Q 9 6 4 3
&hearts; J 8 4
&diams; 9
&clubs; K 9 4 3

&spades; 10 2
&hearts; K 9 7 2
&diams; K 10 8 5
&clubs; 10 7 5

&spades; K J 8
&hearts; A 10 6 5
&diams; 7 3
&clubs; A Q J 8

The contract is 3NT and West leads &spades;4, which is won by declarer's jack. Suppose that South leads a diamond to the queen. If East wins and returns his partner's suit the declarer will go up with &spades;K, lead a diamond to the ace and play two more rounds to establish the suit. This will give him ample tricks for the contract. However, it would be a good move for East to duck the first round of diamonds, allowing dummy's queen to hold. Declarer would then be short of an entry to the table and would be unable to establish and run the diamonds.

The correct play for South, as he can afford to lose two diamond tricks, is to duck the first round completely. The opponents will probably continue spades. South wins with the king and, as he still has a second diamond and dummy has A–Q–J, he can force out &diams; K while there is still &spades;A for entry.

In the examples so far, the object of ducking has been to maintain a lifeline to a long suit. On this final hand the declarer concedes an early trick because to lose it later would be dangerous.

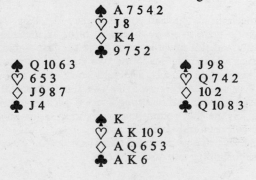

&spades; A 7 5 4 2
&hearts; J 8
&diams; K 4
&clubs; 9 7 5 2

&spades; Q 10 6 3
&hearts; 6 5 3
&diams; J 9 8 7
&clubs; J 4

&spades; J 9 8
&hearts; Q 7 4 2
&diams; 10 2
&clubs; Q 10 8 3

&spades; K
&hearts; A K 10 9
&diams; A Q 6 5 3
&clubs; A K 6

The contract is 6NT and West hits on the lead of ♡6. Declarer plays the jack from dummy and East plays low, as he reads declarer for the top hearts. In dummy with ♡J, South leads a second heart and finesses the ten, which holds.

Declarer can count eleven top tricks now, and barring a 5–1 break a twelfth trick can be set up in diamonds. There is an entry problem, however, because of the blocked position in spades. Suppose South plays off ♠K, then crosses to ◇K and cashes ♠A, discarding a club. He may continue by clearing the diamonds, but when West wins the fourth round he will defeat the contract by cashing a spade winner.

The solution is to cash ♠K at trick three, then duck the first round of diamonds. When the next diamond is won by the king, ♠A can be cashed and the rest of the tricks taken without interruption.

There are, to be sure, many other problems in the field of communication and these will be examined in Chapter 20.

# CHAPTER 19

## The Play in Trump Contracts

*Counting losers – When not to draw trumps – The crossruff –
Establishing a suit by ruffing – Dummy reversal*

A CONSIDERABLE difference arises between the play of a
hand at a trump contract and the play at notrumps. At notrumps
a winner is always a winner. At a trump contract a winner may
suffer the fate of being ruffed by the opposing side. The possibility
of this happening leads to all kinds of tactical moves and counter-
moves that do not exist at notrumps. Indeed, the difference in
approach is seen before the declarer even plays a card from dummy.
This is because at a trump contract the declarer starts counting his
losers, a task which is not as simple as it sounds but on many hands
is the key to successful play.

### Counting Losers

When the dummy goes down the declarer should go through each
suit in turn and count how many immediate losers he has in the
suit; that is, tricks that the defenders can take immediately they get
the lead. If his total losers are more than he can afford, he clearly
must attempt to do something about it before he loses the lead.
For example:

```
                    ♠ Q 10 5 2
                    ♡ K 7
                    ◇ A 8 4
                    ♣ K 7 6 4
    ♠ 8 7                              ♠ A 4
    ♡ J 6 5 2                          ♡ 10 9 8 4
    ◇ Q J 10 7                         ◇ K 5 3
    ♣ J 9 5                            ♣ A 10 3 2
                    ♠ K J 9 6 3
                    ♡ A Q 3
                    ◇ 9 6 2
                    ♣ Q 8
```

The contract is 4♠ and West leads ◇Q. After ◇A has been driven out the declarer will have four potential losers—two diamonds, the ace of trumps and ♣A. The obvious play is to take three rounds of hearts immediately, discarding a diamond from dummy. Four losers are now reduced to three and declarer can proceed to draw trumps.

Although counting losers is the first and most important task, the next step is to ensure that there are enough winners. The golden rule is that you should always draw your opponents' trumps if you will be left with enough winners for your contract.

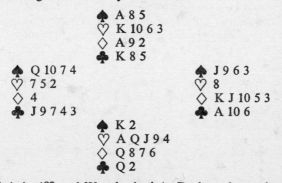

South is in 4♡ and West leads ◇4. Declarer has only one immediate loser in the shape of ♣A. He next counts his certain winners: five trumps, the two top spades, ◇A, and a sure trick in clubs after driving out the ace. That is nine tricks. It may well be possible to make a tenth trick with ◇Q, but South should see that he does not need to rely on that possibility, for he can be sure of a trick by ruffing his fourth diamond in dummy.

It seems, therefore, that declarer is in the happy position of being able to draw the opponents' trumps while still leaving himself with enough winners for his contract. There is one possible snag: if the trumps were 4–0, and he drew them all, he would not be able to ruff a diamond. This can be put to the test by taking a round of trumps. If a defender shows out, declarer can go for a diamond ruff before drawing any more trumps; in the actual case, there will be no problems.

If declarer works all this out before he plays from dummy he will avoid the temptation of allowing the diamond opening to run round to the queen. It is not difficult to see what would happen if he followed this plan. East would win with ◇K and return a diamond for his partner to ruff. West would then switch to a club and a second ruff would follow, putting the contract one down. If the play went like that, South would have some explaining to do to his partner. He should, at least, avoid using the word " unlucky "!

One small question may have occurred to the reader: suppose ◇A is ruffed? That would indeed be a disaster, but is it likely? A 5–1 break is no less than fifteen times more common than a 6–0 break, so it is clear that precautions should be taken against the possibility of a singleton diamond rather than a void. Furthermore, the four would be a very odd lead from K–J–10–5–4–3!

In the next hand the count of losers and winners suggests two possible lines of play and the problem is to select the safer.

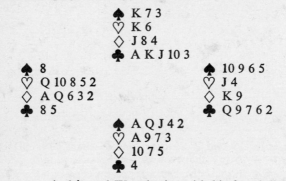

```
                    ♠ K 7 3
                    ♡ K 6
                    ◇ J 8 4
                    ♣ A K J 10 3
 ♠ 8                                  ♠ 10 9 6 5
 ♡ Q 10 8 5 2                         ♡ J 4
 ◇ A Q 6 3 2                          ◇ K 9
 ♣ 8 5                                ♣ Q 9 7 6 2
                    ♠ A Q J 4 2
                    ♡ A 9 7 3
                    ◇ 10 7 5
                    ♣ 4
```

The contract is 4♠ and West begins with his fourth-best heart. Declarer has only three immediate losers, all in diamonds. As to the count of winners, nine tricks are easy to see: five in trumps, barring a 5–0 break, two in hearts and two in clubs. Declarer could aim to develop a tenth trick either by ruffing a losing heart in dummy or by establishing an extra trick in clubs.

There are certain dangers in ruffing a heart. If declarer ruffs low in dummy he may be overruffed, and if he ruffs with the king he may set up a trump trick for the opposition.

Playing on clubs is safer because this can be done after the enemy trumps have been drawn. As ♡K will be needed later as an entry, the first heart is taken with the ace and four rounds of trumps are drawn. Now it would be wrong to finesse in clubs, because that would create the possibility of four losers: if the finesse lost, the defenders would take three diamonds as well. Declarer plays a club to the ace, therefore, discards a diamond on ♣K, then leads the ♣J. It does not matter who has the queen, because the worst that can happen is that declarer loses a club trick and two diamonds. He still has a trump with which to hold up a diamond attack and there is still ♡K in dummy as an entry for ♣10, declarer's tenth trick.

There was one other pitfall that had to be avoided. Suppose declarer had hastened to discard a diamond on ♣K before drawing trumps. He would then have had only one entry left to the table and might never get the extra club trick going.

There is an ancient saying in chess, " *Primum roquari, deinde philosophari* ", (" First castle, then start philosophizing "). An equivalent injunction in bridge would be " First draw trumps, then take a look round ", which would be the wrong order of priority; but the fact remains that you should always draw trumps if you can see the way to your contract after this has been done.

## When Not to Draw Trumps

Despite the counsel given up to now, there is very often a tactical reason why declarer should postpone drawing trumps even when he could easily do so. The trump suit may be needed to obtain necessary entries for going to and fro. Declarer may want to organize a discard before letting the opponents win a possible trump trick. Or he may need to take one or more ruffs in the short trump hand. An example follows of each of these situations:

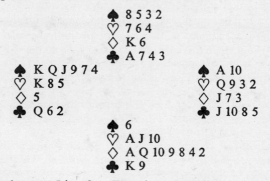

```
              ♠ 8 5 3 2
              ♡ 7 6 4
              ◇ K 6
              ♣ A 7 4 3
♠ K Q J 9 7 4              ♠ A 10
♡ K 8 5                   ♡ Q 9 3 2
◇ 5                       ◇ J 7 3
♣ Q 6 2                   ♣ J 10 8 5
              ♠ 6
              ♡ A J 10
              ◇ A Q 10 9 8 4 2
              ♣ K 9
```

South plays at 5◇ after West has overcalled in spades. The defenders begin with two rounds of spades and South ruffs. Now it would be easy to draw the opponents' trumps, but it wouldn't be very bright because thereafter South would be an entry short for the double finesse in hearts. The heart holding is of a familiar type where the best chance to lose only one trick lies in taking two finesses. Accordingly, when in dummy with ◇K declarer should lead a heart to the ten and king. He wins any return in his own hand, draws the outstanding trumps, and in due course enters dummy with ♣A to take a second finesse in hearts.

We have already seen a simple case where declarer's count of losers indicated the necessity of taking a discard before touching the trump suit. Here is an example where the danger is much less obvious.

```
                    ♠ J 10 6 3
                    ♡ Q 10 5
                    ◇ Q 8 5
                    ♣ K 7 2
    ♠ A                             ♠ 8 5
    ♡ K 9 6 2                       ♡ 8 7 4 3
    ◇ 10 9 7                        ◇ K J 4 2
    ♣ Q J 10 6 3                    ♣ 9 5 4
                    ♠ K Q 9 7 4 2
                    ♡ A J
                    ◇ A 6 3
                    ♣ A 8
```

The contract is 4♠ and West leads ♣Q, which South wins with the ace. Suppose he plays a spade: in this case West will win and shift to ◇10. The contract is suddenly in danger. Whether or not the declarer plays dummy's ◇Q on the first round, the defenders will set up two winners in this suit and will eventually make ♡K as well.

Clearly it is more important to reduce four losers to three than to start on the trumps. The safe play is to establish ♡Q before ◇A can be knocked out. Declarer wins the first trick with ♣A and lays down ♡A-J. If West wins and attacks diamonds, South wins with the ace, enters dummy with ♣K, and discards a diamond on ♡Q. Then he can afford to attack spades.

The commonest reason of all for not drawing trumps is that the declarer needs to take one or more ruffs in dummy. This is always a possibility to be considered when declarer has a plain suit which is longer in his hand than in dummy. Here is a case where it is easy to see that ruffs are needed, but declarer must be careful with his entries.

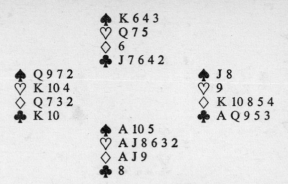

```
                    ♠ K 6 4 3
                    ♡ Q 7 5
                    ◇ 6
                    ♣ J 7 6 4 2
     ♠ Q 9 7 2                    ♠ J 8
     ♡ K 10 4                     ♡ 9
     ◇ Q 7 3 2                    ◇ K 10 8 5 4
     ♣ K 10                       ♣ A Q 9 5 3
                    ♠ A 10 5
                    ♡ A J 8 6 3 2
                    ◇ A J 9
                    ♣ 8
```

South is in 4♡ and West leads ♣2. Allowing for a possible loser in the trump suit, declarer has only eight tricks—five hearts, two spades and one diamond. The obvious plan is to ruff two diamonds, but if declarer simply wins the spade lead with the ace, takes ◇A and ruffs a diamond, he will be in trouble. If he comes back to hand with ♡A and ruffs the next diamond with ♡Q he will lose two trump tricks. The best line is to win the opening spade lead in dummy. Then, after a diamond to the ace and a diamond ruff, he can return to hand with ♠A for another diamond ruff. ♡Q runs to the king and the defenders make a trick in clubs, but that is all.

## The Crossruff

On some hands it is imprudent to lead trumps at all. Declarer's object is to make as many trumps as possible by the process known as crossruffing. This type of strategy may be followed when declarer has a short suit in both hands. If the trump suit itself is not robust, so that there is no guarantee of being able to draw trumps successfully, that may be a further pointer in favour of the crossruff.

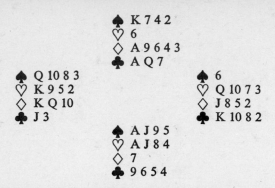

The contract is 4♠ and West leads ◇Q. Declarer sees at once that even if he were successful in drawing trumps he would still be looking round for tricks, so instead he plans a crossruff.

As he is aiming to take three heart ruffs on the table, the first move after winning with ◇A is to lead a heart to the ace and ruff a heart. Then he ruffs a diamond, ruffs a heart, and successfully ruffs a fourth heart with a low trump, leaving this position:

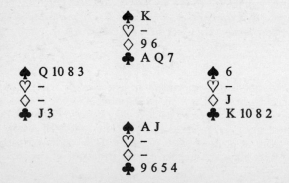

Declarer has taken the first seven tricks and prospects are good so long as he commits no folly at this stage. Another diamond is played from the dummy. If East showed out it would be safe to ruff with the jack, cross to ♣A, and ruff the last diamond with the ace, making five-odd. In the actual case, when East follows to the fourth diamond it is unsafe to ruff with the jack, because of the danger that West may overruff and return a trump, bringing down the A–K together. Declarer ruffs high, therefore, and still makes

♣A and ♠K. Note that the crossruff has proceeded smoothly despite West's strong trump holding, which became unimportant as the play progressed.

There is a technique in crossruffing and certain precautions to be observed. One of the most important is for declarer to cash his side winners before embarking on a crossruff; otherwise he may never make them.

```
                    ♠ A 8 5 4 2
                    ♡ K 7 6 3
                    ◇ K 10 4
                    ♣ Q
    ♠ J 10                          ♠ K Q 9 6 3
    ♡ Q 9 5 4 2                     ♡ J 8
    ◇ 3                             ◇ J 7 6 2
    ♣ K J 9 5 2                     ♣ 10 4
                    ♠ 7
                    ♡ A 10
                    ◇ A Q 9 8 5
                    ♣ A 8 7 6 3
```

The contract is 5◇ and ♠J is led. Declarer might count on making five trumps in his own hand, ♡A–K and two aces, in which case two club ruffs in dummy would give him the contract. However, this assumes a favourable trump break and no accident from overruffing. Playing on crossruff lines, the declarer is less dependent on good breaks.

After winning with ♠A South leads a club to the ace, ruffs a club and ruffs a spade. The next move is important; before continuing the crossruff declarer must cash the other two side winners, ♡A–K. If he does not, East will discard a heart when the next club is ruffed with dummy's king. After two rounds of hearts, therefore, these cards are left:

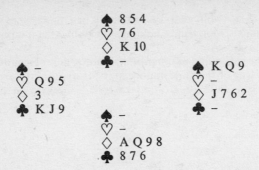

Declarer is on the table and might lead either a heart or a spade. If he selects a spade, East will follow suit; declarer must then ruff with the queen for safety. Next he ruffs a club with the king, making sure that East will not overruff, and in that way cannot fail to make two more tricks. He leads a heart and ruffs low, knowing that West has to follow, and then ruffs a club with ◇10. East overruffs, but declarer is left with two good trumps.

Apart from cashing the side winners before crossruffing, another useful principle was seen in this example. If declarer can afford to ruff with a master trump and still have enough tricks for his contract, he should not ruff low, running the risk of being overruffed and nailed to the ground by a trump return.

### Establishing a Suit by Ruffing

One of the most useful functions of the trump suit is to assist in the establishment of other long suits. It may be a second suit in the declarer's hand or, more often, a long suit in dummy.

```
                    ♠ K 7 4
                    ♡ 9 5
                    ◇ A K 8 5 2
                    ♣ 7 5 2
    ♠ Q 10 8 2                    ♠ 9 6 5
    ♡ J 7 4                       ♡ 8 6 3
    ◇ 10 3                        ◇ Q J 9 6
    ♣ Q J 9 6                     ♣ 10 8 4
                    ♠ A J 3
                    ♡ A K Q 10 2
                    ◇ 7 4
                    ♣ A K 3
```

258

South is in 6♡ and West leads ♣Q, which is taken by the ace. There is no reason to delay tackling trumps and South is relieved when they fall in three rounds. He has eleven winners now and two obvious chances of increasing the total. If the opponents' diamonds are 3–3 he can ruff the third round, then return to ♠K for two discards, making seven-odd. If the diamonds don't break there is still the chance of the spade finesse.

However, there is a better plan, requiring only a 4–2 break in diamonds. Suits are invariably easier to establish if declarer can afford to duck a trick and South should do so now, ducking a round of diamonds. East's best return is a spade, but South goes right up with the ace, leads a diamond to the ace and ruffs a diamond. By this time ◇K–8 are good for two discards.

Notwithstanding a widespread impression to the contrary, the trump suit can be expected to break reasonably well part of the time, and when it does it can serve many different functions. In the next deal it provides entry to dummy as well as the means of establishing a long suit.

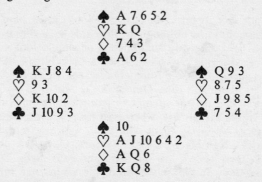

♠ A 7 6 5 2
♡ K Q
◇ 7 4 3
♣ A 6 2

♠ K J 8 4        ♠ Q 9 3
♡ 9 3           ♡ 8 7 5
◇ K 10 2       ◇ J 9 8 5
♣ J 10 9 3      ♣ 7 5 4

♠ 10
♡ A J 10 6 4 2
◇ A Q 6
♣ K Q 8

Playing in 6♡ against a club opening lead, South has on the surface only eleven tricks in the shape of six trumps, one spade, one diamond and three clubs. To avoid risking the diamond finesse, he aims to set up dummy's fifth spade.

Declarer wins the club in his own hand, plays a spade to the ace and ruffs a spade. He enters dummy with a trump, ruffs another spade and re-enters with another trump. If either opponent showed out at this time, indicating a 4–1 trump break, declarer would be obliged to abandon the spade suit, draw trumps and trust to the diamond finesse. When in fact both defenders follow to the second trump, declarer continues with a third spade ruff. With the opponents' spades 4–3, the fifth card has been established and South has twelve tricks safely tucked away.

In the next example the establishment of dummy's side suit is accomplished by the important manoeuvre known as the " ruffing finesse ".

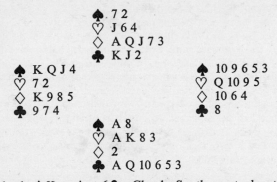

&#9824; 7 2
&#9825; J 6 4
&#9826; A Q J 7 3
&#9827; K J 2

&#9824; K Q J 4        &#9824; 10 9 6 5 3
&#9825; 7 2            &#9825; Q 10 9 5
&#9826; K 9 8 5        &#9826; 10 6 4
&#9827; 9 7 4          &#9827; 8

&#9824; A 8
&#9825; A K 8 3
&#9826; 2
&#9827; A Q 10 6 5 3

West leads &#9824;K against 6&#9827;. Clearly South must plan to make tricks in diamonds and although, as the cards lie, a simple finesse of &#9826;Q would be a successful initial step, he should look for a safer play. Before drawing trumps he leads a diamond to the ace and returns the queen. This is a ruffing finesse, for if East holds the king and plays it, South will ruff. Dummy's &#9826;J will then be declarer's eleventh trick and he will attempt to set up a long diamond for the contract. In the actual case, when East plays low on the diamond, South discards his losing spade and is still secure even though West wins the trick. He ruffs West's spade return, plays &#9827;A and a club to the jack, then leads a low diamond and ruffs high. When both opponents follow, dummy's last two diamonds become winners and there is still &#9827;K for entry

Sometimes declarer has to choose between trying to establish dummy's long suit and trying to score ruffs in dummy. In such a case, the entry situation will be a key factor in reaching a decision. With plenty of entries in your own hand you go for ruffs in dummy; with plenty of entries in dummy you play to establish dummy's side suit.

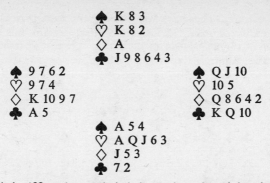

South is in 4♡ and a spade is led. Declarer has eight tricks in the shape of five trumps, ♠A–K and ♢A. Suppose he aims to make two more by ruffing diamonds. He wins the spade lead with dummy's king to preserve entries to his own hand, cashes ♢A, enters his hand with ♠A, and ruffs a diamond. After returning to hand with a trump he ruffs another diamond with the king of trumps.

So far everything has gone smoothly, but declarer has no good way to enter his hand to draw the opponents' last trump. Whatever he leads from dummy, the opponents take two clubs and one spade and then lead a black suit to promote a trump trick.

Since the ruffing plan evidently will not work, declarer should try establishing the club suit. He wins the spade opening, concedes a club, wins the spade return and concedes another club. The opponents cash a spade and then lead a diamond to remove dummy's side entry. However, declarer proceeds to ruff a club with the ace of trumps, then takes three rounds of trumps, ending in dummy with the king. Provided the clubs are 3–2, which is normal, he can cash his club winners and make the contract.

## Dummy Reversal

As a general principle, the declarer does not seek ruffs in his own hand except in the course of establishing a side suit or playing a crossruff. In many cases it is positively dangerous to allow the strong trump hand to become shortened. However, an interesting and invaluable form of play occurs when declarer, reversing the usual procedure, gains tricks by ruffing in the hand that is long in trumps. Suppose declarer has Q–J–x of trumps in dummy, A–K–10–x–x in his own hand, and is able to take three ruffs in the hand with the long trumps. There are still three more trump tricks to take with the aid of dummy's Q–J–x, so in effect declarer has extended the power of the trump suit to six tricks. That is what he does in the following hand:

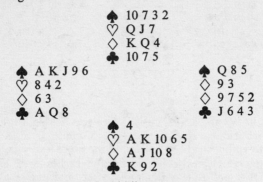

♠ 10 7 3 2
♡ Q J 7
◇ K Q 4
♣ 10 7 5

♠ A K J 9 6          ♠ Q 8 5
♡ 8 4 2              ◇ 9 3
◇ 6 3                ◇ 9 7 5 2
♣ A Q 8              ♣ J 6 4 3

♠ 4
♡ A K 10 6 5
◇ A J 10 8
♣ K 9 2

West is the dealer and the bidding goes:

| South | West | North | East |
|-------|------|-------|------|
|       | 1♠   | Pass  | Pass |
| Dble  | Pass | 1NT   | Pass |
| 2♡    | Pass | 3♡    | Pass |
| 4♡    | Pass | Pass  | Pass |

West opens the bidding with 1♠ but South becomes declarer in 4♡. West leads ♠K and, ill-advisedly as it turns out, continues with a second spade, which South ruffs. South has nine ready winners and has a much better way of developing a tenth than by looking for a trick in clubs. He should aim to ruff three times in his own hand. For this he will need to enter dummy twice in diamonds and it will be good technique to utilize these entries first, before the opponents can take discards. He plays a diamond to the king, therefore, ruffs a spade, leads a diamond to the queen, and ruffs the fourth spade with ♡K. The position is:

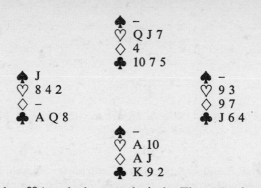

South plays ♡A and a heart to the jack. The queen draws the last trump from West, while South discards a club. The two diamond winners now make up ten tricks. When the declarer uses dummy's trumps in this way to draw the opponents' trumps, he is said to " reverse the dummy ", and in this case the dummy reversal brings matters to a satisfactory conclusion.

# CHAPTER 20

## Entries

*Unblocking plays – Overtaking – Use of entries – Blocking plays – Entry-killing and Avoidance plays*

THE CARE and organization of entries is a highly important subject. There are relatively few hands where the declarer is so well endowed with high cards that he need pay no heed at all to problems of communication. More often than not, the presence or absence of entries in one hand or the other will influence the declarer's thinking as he deliberates on the strategy to be followed, the suits to be developed, and so on.

At the same time, when short of entries, there is much the declarer can do to create them. For example, the winners in an established suit may be cashed in a particular way, with the object of enabling tricks to be won in one hand rather than the other. Entry play may also involve the attempt to interrupt the communications of the opponents, often a very effective stratagem.

### Unblocking Plays

One of the most attractive ways of creating entries is by the process known as unblocking. In effect, declarer plays an unnecessarily high card in order to improve his communications.

| (1) | A 10 4 | (2) | A 9 4 | (3) | J 10 4 |
| | K Q 9 6 3 | | K Q 8 3 | | A K 9 5 2 |

In each case South has the lead and hopes to run all the tricks with the minimum use of side entries. In (1) he leads the king and unblocks with the ten in dummy. He continues with a low card to the ace. If West shows out on this trick declarer is poised to finesse the nine on the next round, picking up East's J–x–x–x. Had declarer not taken the precaution of unblocking, East would refuse to cover the ten when it was led and declarer would need a side entry to his hand before he could run the suit.

Similarly, in (2), it is advisable to lead the king and drop the nine under it. Suppose that on the next round, when declarer plays the three to the ace, West plays either the jack or ten. Now it may be that West began with J–10–x, but declarer may think it more likely that he began with a doubleton honour, the J–x or 10–x; in that case the unblock has prepared the ground for a finesse of the eight on the third round. In (3) the declarer begins by laying down the ace in case West holds the singleton queen. If West follows small, however, declarer unblocks with the ten, as he intends to cross to dummy for a finesse. If he were to keep the J–10 the run of the suit might be obstructed.

| (4) J 10 5 | (5) J 8 3 | (6) Q J 4 |
|------------|-----------|-----------|
| K 7        | Q 6 2     | A 8 6     |

These are examples of unblocking plays that are often made on the opening lead. Suppose, in (4), that at a notrump contract West leads low to his partner's ace. If declarer wants an extra entry to dummy he should drop the king under the ace, so that when opponents continue the suit they will have to let dummy into the lead. In (5) declarer is playing a suit contract and West leads the king, presumably from a suit headed by the A–K. It may well be good policy to unblock with the queen so that dummy can be entered later with the jack (barring a ruff, which declarer cannot avoid anyway). In (6) West leads a low card against a notrump contract. Suppose that the declarer wants to be sure of having an entry to dummy later in the hand: in that case he should play low from the table and win with the ace, after which either the queen or the jack will be an entry.

Here are more cases where it may suit declarer's purpose to unblock when his left-hand opponent leads a low card in the suit.

| (7) K J 4 | (8) A 10 2 | (9) A 10 6 3 |
|-----------|------------|--------------|
| A 9       | J 4        | Q 5          |

In (7), when West leads low, it may be tempting to take a " free " finesse by putting in the jack, but declarer should note that even if the jack wins it will not be possible to take three tricks straight off. If that is the objective, it is better to play low in dummy and unblock with the ace, even if East contributes a low card. Then the jack can be finessed and three tricks taken. In (8) West leads low, declarer plays low from dummy, and East plays the king or queen. Declarer must be ready to unblock with the jack so that he can finesse the ten later. (9) is an example of the same type of play, more hazardous because it involves the possible sacrifice of a winning card. When West leads low and East plays the king, declarer unblocks with the queen so that, hopefully, he can run three quick tricks by taking a successful finesse against West's jack.

Unblocking plays may very well be needed even when declarer has complete control of a suit. For example, with K–Q–9–7–4 of trumps in one hand and A–J–10–6 in the other it is proper to begin by leading the ten to the king, so keeping the entry position fluid. With a long trump suit such as A–Q–9–8–7–5, opposite the K–6–3 in dummy, a declarer who has to ruff an early trick should ruff with the seven as a matter of course; now dummy will have two entries if trumps are 2–2.

Here are some situations where the correct method of unblocking is not by any means obvious:

$$\text{(10)} \quad \text{K Q 5 2} \qquad \text{(11)} \quad \text{A Q 10 4} \qquad \text{(12)} \quad \text{A J 8}$$
$$\text{10 8 6 3} \qquad\qquad\qquad \text{J 9 5} \qquad\qquad\qquad \text{Q 10 9 7}$$

In tackling the combination (10), the six is led towards the K–Q. Suppose the queen holds the trick. Declarer returns to hand for the next lead and should now play the eight. Suppose that West goes up with the ace. Declarer is left with the K–5 opposite the 10–3 and is in the comfortable position of being able to win the next two rounds of the suit in dummy if he wants to, or the next round in dummy and the last one in his own hand. (11) shows a position which we have already encountered in a slightly different form. Declarer must start by playing the nine, not the jack. This is the only way to take four straight tricks when West holds the K–x–x–x. In (12) it may seem that it hardly matters which card declarer leads, but if entries to the closed hand are precious the queen is the only correct play. If West plays low, declarer unblocks with the jack and can then continue with the ten. In that way declarer can take two finesses against the king and still keep the lead in his own hand in case he wants to play another suit next.

### Overtaking

Often the remedy for lack of communication lies in overtaking an honour card. Assume that in the following examples the declarer is playing a notrump contract and is short of entries to dummy.

(1)  K 10 9 8 6 3      (2)  A J 10 8 4      (3)  A 10 8 5 2
         Q                       K                    K Q

In (1), if declarer leads the queen, the defenders will duck and declarer will probably need three entries in all to get the suit going. An entry can be saved by overtaking the queen and giving up two tricks to the ace and jack. In (2) declarer overtakes the king with the ace and leads the jack. If the suit is divided 4–3 and the nine falls in three rounds, it will be possible to develop four tricks. In (3), if declarer has only one side entry to the table, the proper method of play depends on how many tricks he needs from the suit. If he requires four tricks it is best to overtake the queen on the second round and play a third round. By this method of play declarer makes four tricks whenever the suit is 3–3 or the jack is a doubleton, and he has the extra chance of bringing down the nine in two rounds, leaving the 10–8 as equals against the jack. A similar play occurs when declarer has the A–Q opposite the K–9–8–5–3. Declarer plays the ace and overtakes the queen with the king, making four tricks not only when the suit is 3–3, but also when either defender holds J–x or 10–x.

## Use of Entries

When entries are in short supply they must be used economically. The prodigal use of entries frequently leads to defeat in contracts that with more careful planning could have been made quite easily. Consider this hand:

```
                    ♠ 3 2
                    ♡ A Q 5 2
                    ◇ 9 6 4
                    ♣ K Q 7 3
  ♠ 8 7 6                         ♠ 9 5
  ♡ 10 6 4                        ♡ K J 9 3
  ◇ K Q J 3                       ◇ 8 7 5
  ♣ A 10 8                        ♣ J 9 5 2
                    ♠ A K Q J 10 4
                    ♡ 8 7
                    ◇ A 10 2
                    ♣ 6 4
```

The contract is 4♠ and West leads ◇K. Let us suppose that declarer draws trumps and then leads a club to the king, which

267

holds. He exits from the table with a diamond, hoping that the opponents will pursue this suit, allowing him to ruff the fourth round and lead another club. But West is not so co-operative and after cashing two diamonds he shifts to a heart. South now has to finesse, with the result that he goes down. What has happened is that South has wasted a precious entry to his own hand. Instead of hastening to draw trumps he should lead a club at trick two. Then the trump suit provides an entry back to his hand. After drawing trumps he plays another club and in that way sets up ♣Q for a heart discard.

In the next deal the declarer's problem is to ensure that he will have an entry to dummy.

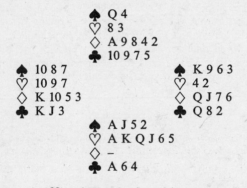

♠ Q 4
♡ 8 3
◊ A 9 8 4 2
♣ 10 9 7 5

♠ 10 8 7          ♠ K 9 6 3
♡ 10 9 7          ♡ 4 2
◊ K 10 5 3        ◊ Q J 7 6
♣ K J 3           ♣ Q 8 2

♠ A J 5 2
♡ A K Q J 6 5
◊ –
♣ A 6 4

The contract is 4♡ and West begins with a trump. South appears to have ten sure tricks, but if he is artless enough to return a low spade to the queen East will win with the king and make the obvious return of a second trump. Dummy's ◊ A will then waste its sweetness on the desert air, and South will eventually lose two spades and two clubs.

The correct play is to lead ♠J at trick two. If the opponents win and play a trump, ♠Q will be an entry to the table, enabling ◊A to be cashed. If East holds off when ♠J is led, South continues with ♠A and a spade ruff, making an overtrick.

The stratagem of surrendering a trick to gain an entry is very common. On the deal that follows, South, with one jack in his hand, was resigning himself to the loss of the rubber when suddenly he found himself in 6◇ doubled, a contract that depended on the careful use of entries.

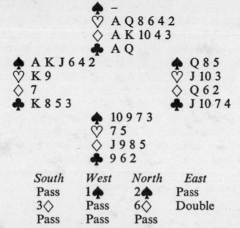

|        | ♠ —           |        |         |
|--------|---------------|--------|---------|
|        | ♡ A Q 8 6 4 2 |        |         |
|        | ◇ A K 10 4 3  |        |         |
|        | ♣ A Q         |        |         |

| ♠ A K J 6 4 2 |  | ♠ Q 8 5    |
|---------------|--|------------|
| ♡ K 9         |  | ♡ J 10 3   |
| ◇ 7           |  | ◇ Q 6 2    |
| ♣ K 8 5 3     |  | ♣ J 10 7 4 |

|        | ♠ 10 9 7 3  |
|        | ♡ 7 5       |
|        | ◇ J 9 8 5   |
|        | ♣ 9 6 2     |

| South | West | North | East   |
|-------|------|-------|--------|
| Pass  | 1♠   | 2♠    | Pass   |
| 3◇    | Pass | 6◇    | Double |
| Pass  | Pass | Pass  |        |

East doubled because he felt sure his ◇Q would be a winner and hoped his side would be able to find another trick somewhere.

West led ♠K and South realized that to ruff low and cash the top diamonds would leave him awkwardly placed if ◇Q were still out. He therefore decided to concede a trump trick in order to create an additional entry to his own hand. In line with this, he ruffed with the king of trumps and led a low trump from the table. When East won and played another spade South ruffed with the ace, entered his hand with ◇8, and finessed ♡Q. The rest of the story hardly needs telling. After ruffing the third round of hearts declarer was able to draw the outstanding trump with the jack and finesse ♣Q, leaving the dummy high.

### Blocking Plays

We began this chapter with a description of unblocking plays aimed at facilitating the run of a suit. Plays that are designed to block the run of an opponent's suit are almost equally important, especially at notrumps.

| (1)    | A 9 4      | (2)   | A 4        |
|--------|------------|-------|------------|
| K 10 7 5 2 | Q 6    | K J 8 5 3 | Q 7     |
|        | J 8 3      |       | 10 9 6 2   |

In (1) West leads the five. If declarer expects to lose the first lead to West, he should go up with the ace to block the suit. It is true that West may have led from K–Q–x–x–x, in which case South could have won the trick with the jack, but the lead will more often be from either the K–10–x–x–x or the Q–10–x–x–x, and in that case the play of the ace will be best. East may unblock by throwing the queen, but this will not help him unless he can gain the lead. (2) shows a similar situation, although this time declarer can be sure that it is right to go up with the ace on the first round, as West would not have led low from the K–Q–J. Note that on this occasion it would not help East to unblock with the queen, as declarer has the 10–9. A similar situation arises when declarer holds the A–J opposite 9–x–x–x; again the play of the ace is the most likely way to prevent the enemy from taking four rapid tricks.

In the next two examples the declarer makes a blocking play to obstruct the run of a suit bid on his right.

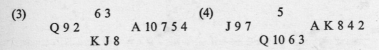

| (3) | 6 3 | | (4) | 5 | |
|---|---|---|---|---|---|
| Q 9 2 | | A 10 7 5 4 | J 9 7 | | A K 8 4 2 |
| | K J 8 | | | Q 10 6 3 | |

In (3) West leads the two of a suit bid by his partner. East wins with the ace and returns his original fourth-best, the five, in approved fashion. The declarer has to take a position; the jack would hold the trick if East held the A–Q and West had led from 10–x–x, but most players in East's position, holding A–Q–x–x–x, would play the queen on the opening lead. Therefore South may well decide to go in with the king on the second round, leaving the suit blocked until West has cashed the queen and given his partner the lead. In (4) the seven is led to the king and East, who has bid this suit, returns the four. It may seem natural to finesse the ten, hoping East has A–K–J–x–x. However, the spot cards tend to betray the position. If declarer can read West for the J–x–x he can block the suit by going in with the queen. Declarer will still have a stopper if it turns out that West has led from A–x–x.

| (5) | Q 9 5 3 | | (6) | K Q 4 | |
|---|---|---|---|---|---|
| 10 8 6 2 | | 7 | 9 8 5 3 | | J 7 2 |
| | A K J 4 | | | A 10 6 | |

Figure (5) is an example of a different form of blocking, seen from the West position. South plays off the A–K, then leads the four. West must not fail to note that, if he plays the eight, he gives the declarer a chance to gain two entries to dummy by finessing the nine. West may therefore have good cause to put in the ten. Here the play is simple because the lie of the cards is known and the ten cannot cost, but sometimes this type of play calls for considerable alertness. For example, in (6) the declarer, needing two entries to his hand, may cash dummy's king and then lead the four, intending to finesse the ten. East spoils the plan only if he is wide-awake and goes in with the jack.

### Entry-killing and Avoidance Plays

It is sometimes possible to achieve remarkable results by playing a high card earlier than would be considered normal. Assume, in these two examples, that the declarer has no outside entry to dummy.

(1)        A J 9 6 2     (2)       A J 10 7 4
   K 10 5         Q 8 4     Q 5         K 8 3
         7 3                9 6 2

In (1) declarer leads low and finesses the nine. If East wins with the queen declarer can make four tricks in the suit when he regains the lead. Even if East ducks, declarer has two tricks. But if West goes in with the king on the first round South makes only one trick! In (2), also, West should go in with the queen to prevent declarer from finessing. If declarer ducks in dummy he will lose two tricks, while if he wins with the ace and continues with the jack, East can shut out the suit completely by holding up his king.

Note that both these plays, though usually made by the defence, are also available to the declarer, as can readily be seen by switching the cards:

(3)        K 10 5     (4)       Q 5
   7 3         A J 9 6 2   9 6 2      A J 10 7 4
         Q 8 4               K 8 3

In each case declarer, if he can judge the position, should play high from dummy when West leads the suit.

Manoeuvres of a similar kind may be necessary when declarer wants to establish a suit without allowing a certain defender to gain the lead. In these examples West is the player who is to be kept out.

(5)      653     (6)      10 6

   J 7 2      K 10     J 9 3      Q 7 2

      A Q 9 8 4        A K 8 5 4

In (5) declarer leads the suit from dummy. If East plays the king South plays low! If East plays the ten South finesses the queen and then crosses to dummy in another suit for the next lead; this time, when East's king appears, it is allowed to hold the trick. In (6) declarer, to deny West an entry, must lead twice from dummy towards the A–K–x–x–x. If East plays the queen on the first or second round it is allowed to hold the trick.

Because they are designed to avoid losing the lead to a particular defender, such manoeuvres are called avoidance plays. A defender can sometimes thwart them by jettisoning a vital card before the suit is played. Thus if East, in (5), had discarded the king before declarer touched the suit, declarer would be unable to establish the long cards without allowing West into the lead.

There are other ways in which the sacrifice of a high card may shut out a long suit. Here is an example of the play known as the Merrimac Coup:

        ♠ A 4
        ♡ 6 5 3
        ◇ K J 10 7 4
        ♣ J 6 5

♠ 10 8 5 3           ♠ K 9 7 2
♡ J 10 9 7          ♡ A 4 2
◇ A 6 3           ◇ Q 5
♣ 8 2            ♣ Q 10 9 7

        ♠ Q J 6
        ♡ K Q 8
        ◇ 9 8 2
        ♣ A K 4 3

The contract is 3NT and West leads ♡J, which East wins with the ace. Declarer wins the next heart with the king and returns ◇9, which loses to East's queen.

East places his partner with ◇A but notes also that West can have had no more than four hearts originally (as the queen is held by South). A heart continuation, therefore, would lead to no more than four defensive tricks, and meanwhile declarer would doubtless take nine. A better plan is to drive out the entry for dummy's diamonds, and accordingly East shifts to ♠K. This gives South an extra trick in spades, but it kills the diamond suit, for West can hold off the next round of diamonds.*

Another type of shut-out play is actually commoner than the Merrimac Coup but has not so far been dignified by any special title. It consists of killing the entry to a suit by playing that suit until declarer loses communication with his dummy.

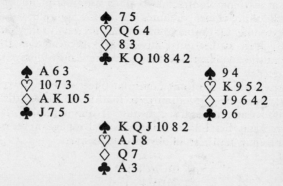

```
              ♠ 7 5
              ♡ Q 6 4
              ◇ 8 3
              ♣ K Q 10 8 4 2
♠ A 6 3                        ♠ 9 4
♡ 10 7 3                       ♡ K 9 5 2
◇ A K 10 5                     ◇ J 9 6 4 2
♣ J 7 5                        ♣ 9 6
              ♠ K Q J 10 8 2
              ♡ A J 8
              ◇ Q 7
              ♣ A 3
```

The contract is 4♠ and West cashes ◇A–K. He may think that the best chance of a setting trick is to shift to hearts, banking on East to have the K–J, but small prayers are more readily answered than big ones and a different form of defence succeeds even if East has only ♡K. At trick three, West shifts to a club. South wins with the ace and returns a trump, but West fastens on the first trump and plays another club. Dummy's clubs are now useless, as East still has a trump; however South plays, he must lose a heart trick eventually.

It may be added that this type of play is often effective even at notrumps. Suppose the dummy has a set-up suit, such as A–K–Q–x–x, with no side entry. If the defenders can lead this suit enough times they may force the declarer to cash it before he is really ready to do so, and this may break up his hand. This type of play is

---

* Similar to the Merrimac is the Deschapelles Coup. In both cases a defender leads an unsupported honour, usually the king or queen to drive out the ace. But whereas the purpose of the Merrimac Coup is to force out an opponent's entry, the object of the Deschapelles is to create an entry for partner. For example, West holds K–x–x of a suit, dummy A–x and East Q–x–x–x. By leading the queen East establishes an entry to West's hand.

especially likely to succeed when declarer's hand consists of combinations that need to be developed rather than of ready-made winners.

Another manoeuvre connected with entries is the hold-up. The advantages of holding up at notrumps to prevent the defenders from running a long suit have been described in an earlier chapter. Players sometimes overlook the possibility that a hold-up may be advantageous at a trump contract also. For example, if an opponent leads a side suit of which you hold, say, x–x–x opposite A–x–x, it is advisable to hold up for one round unless the way to the contract is absolutely clear. If the suit is divided 5–2, then there is at least a chance that the opponent who first gains the lead will have none of this suit to play.

Similarly, with A–x in one hand and three or four low cards in the other, it may be a good move to hold up to prevent the opponents from using this suit as a means of communication later on. In the two hands that follow, there is great advantage in the hold-up, though this may not be at all obvious at the start.

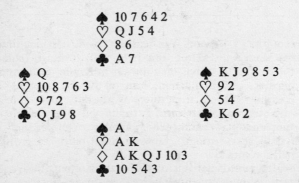

The contract is 6◇ and West leads ♣Q. Without the club lead declarer would have had twelve easy tricks; as it is, he calculates that he has a good chance to dispose of his club losers by ruffing the third one and discarding the fourth on ♡Q. Suppose, therefore, that he wins with ♣A, plays off ♡A–K, and leads a second club. In this case East will win and play a trump. South goes up with the ace and successfully takes a club ruff with dummy's last trump, but is defeated because East is able to ruff the third round of hearts. South can overruff but is left with a losing club.

In effect, the declarer has lost his contract because he allowed the defenders to make two damaging plays: to dislodge ♣A and to lead a round of trumps. If declarer holds up at trick one the defenders cannot do both and are placed in a dilemma. They would like to lead a trump to stop club ruffs, but if they do so ♣A remains as an entry to the table after trumps have been drawn, allowing South to enjoy four heart tricks. Therefore the best that West can do is play a second club. Now South cashes ♡A–K as before, ruffs a club, and leads ♡Q. East ruffs but South has a further resource: he overruffs and leads the fourth club, making his contract as East is unable to overruff dummy's ◇8.

The next hand affords another example of the same general principle:

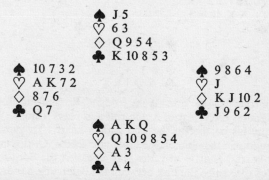

```
                    ♠ J 5
                    ♡ 6 3
                    ◇ Q 9 5 4
                    ♣ K 10 8 5 3
  ♠ 10 7 3 2                        ♠ 9 8 6 4
  ♡ A K 7 2                         ♡ J
  ◇ 8 7 6                           ◇ K J 10 2
  ♣ Q 7                             ♣ J 9 6 2
                    ♠ A K Q
                    ♡ Q 10 9 8 5 4
                    ◇ A 3
                    ♣ A 4
```

The contract is 4♡ and West leads a diamond. Declarer hopefully plays the queen from dummy but East covers with the king. Suppose the declarer takes the position that the contract now depends simply on finding East with ♡J. In this case he may decide to win the diamond with the ace, enter dummy with ♣K, and lead a low heart, which would bring forth the jack, queen and king. This would no doubt appear very satisfactory, but danger would now threaten from another quarter. West would exit with his second club, win the next round of trumps and put his partner in with a diamond. Declarer would now face defeat, as East would return a club and West, with ♡7–2 behind South's 9–8–5–4, would be bound to score the setting trick.

This can be avoided if South holds up on the first round of diamonds, preventing the opponents from going to and fro in this suit later in the play. Many hands are like that. It is true that occasionally the declarer will encounter a humiliating ruff when the suit led breaks very badly for no good reason, but nevertheless the hold-up is in general the right play. After all, if the gremlins are around, virtually no contract is invulnerable.

Finally, there is an attractive play called the Scissors Coup, where the declarer leads a suit with the object of destroying the defenders' communications in another suit.

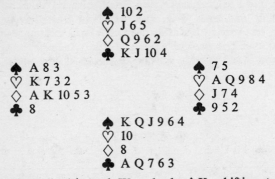

The contract is 4♠ and West leads ◇K, shifting to ♣8. If declarer ignores the threat of a club ruff and plays trumps, West will win and put his partner in the lead with a heart. To prevent this, South should win the club on the table and lead ◇Q, discarding his singleton heart. That is why the play is called the Scissors Coup. The lead of ◇Q snips the link between the defending hands.

_____

# CHAPTER 21

## Further Plays in the Trump Suit

*Trump control – Developing a side suit – The ruffing game –
Trump promotion*

THE PRECEDING chapters have described some of the cardinal
principles of play at trump contracts, in so far as they differ from the
play at notrumps. The special properties of the trump suit give rise
to a number of finer points which are the subject of the present
chapter. Perhaps the most critical area is that of control. The
defenders will often try to shorten the declarer's trump holding to a
point where he cannot draw the trumps against him. In this connec-
tion it is most important to grasp the meaning of the expression
" trump control ". What does it involve?

### Trump Control

When studying the play at trump contracts the reader will often
come across the expression " losing control ". That is a very bad
thing to happen, as will be seen in this example:

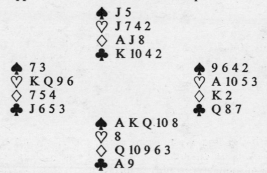

♠ J 5
♡ J 7 4 2
◇ A J 8
♣ K 10 4 2

♠ 7 3
♡ K Q 9 6
◇ 7 5 4
♣ J 6 5 3

♠ 9 6 4 2
♡ A 10 5 3
◇ K 2
♣ Q 8 7

♠ A K Q 10 8
♡ 8
◇ Q 10 9 6 3
♣ A 9

As the cards lie, 5◇ would be an easier contract, but South finishes
in 4♠. West leads ♡K and continues with a low heart. Reading
his partner for the queen, East finesses the ten.

277

Declarer sees that he can afford to lose three tricks outside the trump suit and that the main danger to his contract lies in being forced to ruff too often. Accordingly, it would be good play for South to hold off the second heart, discarding a diamond. East continues with ♡A and now the declarer is obliged to ruff.

Unfortunately for him, South has to play off all his remaining trumps to draw East's trumps. Having done this, he finesses ◇10. East wins with the king and plays a fourth heart, which beats the contract as South has no more trumps left. The combination of the heart lead, the 4–2 break in spades, and the losing finesse in diamonds, has caused him to lose control. The defenders have successfully " played a forcing game ", as the expression is.

On the hand above, when South refused to ruff the second heart, he was in effect using a form of hold-up play in an attempt to exhaust East of hearts. He would have succeeded had East not held a fourth heart. We look now at various other stratagems which have the same objective of enabling the declarer to keep control.

### Refusing to Draw the Master Trump

When control is in the balance it is usually wrong to draw the master trump—or trumps. To do so would merely give the defenders an extra opportunity to " force " declarer.

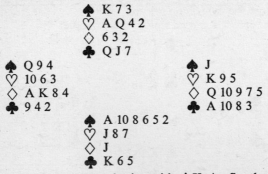

South is in 3♠ and West begins with ◇K–A. South ruffs and takes ♠K–A, East discarding a heart on the second round. It would be a mistake now to play a third trump to remove the queen, for West would play a third diamond, reducing South to one trump. When East came in with ♣A he would play a fourth diamond, forcing South to ruff once again. Somewhere along the line declarer would have to take the heart finesse, and when it lost East would have a diamond to cash.

The hand presents no problem if declarer ignores the master trump against him. After two rounds of trumps he goes about the business of establishing his side tricks and makes the contract for the loss of one trick in each suit.

When the declarer has two good trumps against him he may, in the interest of keeping control, allow them to make separately. It depends on how many tricks he can afford to lose.

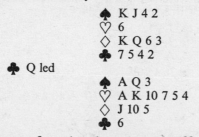

♠ K J 4 2
♡ 6
♢ K Q 6 3
♣ 7 5 4 2

♣ Q led

♠ A Q 3
♡ A K 10 7 5 4
♢ J 10 5
♣ 6

Suppose, first, that the contract is 4♡. South ruffs the second round of clubs and plays off ♡A–K, to which all follow. As he has two losers outside the trumps he has no option but to play a third round of hearts, hoping for a 3–3 break.

But suppose the contract were only 3♡. It would then be a mistake to draw a third round of trumps, for if they were to break 4–2 South would lose control. He has already ruffed once; four rounds of trumps are played, and then a club return forces his last trump, with ♢A still against him. In 3♡, therefore, South should leave the two trumps outstanding and force out ♢A, ensuring the contract.

This is another hand where the declarer can afford to lose trump tricks but not to lose control:

♠ A 5
♡ A J 8
♢ 7 5 3
♣ K Q 9 4 2

♢ K led

♠ K J 10 9 3
♡ K 5 2
♢ 4
♣ A 10 6 3

279

South is in 4♠ and the defenders begin with two rounds of diamonds. The safe play is to ruff, play off ♠A–K, then set about the clubs. South can afford to lose two trumps and a diamond but must not risk a losing finesse in spades which, combined with the repeated diamond force, would be fatal if the trumps were 4–2.

## Enlisting Dummy's Trumps

In many hands the declarer's best ally, in the struggle to keep control, is the dummy. This is a typical example:

```
              ♠ J 8 4
              ♡ 7 5 2
              ◇ A J 4 3
              ♣ A J 6
♠ 9 5 3 2                    ♠ 7 6
♡ K Q J 4                    ♡ A 10 8 6 3
◇ 9 6 2                      ◇ K 7 5
♣ 8 3                        ♣ 9 5 4
              ♠ A K Q 10
              ♡ 9
              ◇ Q 10 8
              ♣ K Q 10 7 2
```

The contract is 4♠ and the defence begins with two rounds of hearts. If South plays the hand wide open, ruffing the second heart and playing off three rounds of trumps, he will lose one spade and four hearts. Instead, he must refuse to ruff until dummy can take care of heart leads. On the second and third hearts he discards two diamonds. Then a fourth heart can be ruffed by dummy's ♠J and South has no difficulty in making the remainder.

It is often good play to surrender a trump trick at a stage when dummy can cope with a forcing continuation. This occurs particularly when dummy or declarer has a strong side suit.

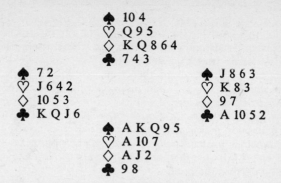

&spades; 10 4
&hearts; Q 9 5
&diams; K Q 8 6 4
&clubs; 7 4 3

&spades; 7 2          &spades; J 8 6 3
&hearts; J 6 4 2      &hearts; K 8 3
&diams; 10 5 3      &diams; 9 7
&clubs; K Q J 6     &clubs; A 10 5 2

&spades; A K Q 9 5
&hearts; A 10 7
&diams; A J 2
&clubs; 9 8

The contract is 4&spades; and the defenders begin with three rounds of clubs. If South ruffs and tries to draw trumps the hand will go out of control. His best play, after ruffing the third club, is to lead &spades;9. East wins but can do no damage because dummy's &spades;10 will arrest any further club.

## Developing a Side Suit

We turn now to another aspect of control, where the declarer's worry is not the trump suit but a side suit which has to be developed. When the side suit is not solid it is usually right to attempt to develop it before drawing trumps. This is a typical situation:

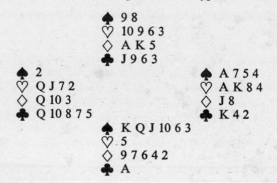

&spades; 9 8
&hearts; 10 9 6 3
&diams; A K 5
&clubs; J 9 6 3

&spades; 2           &spades; A 7 5 4
&hearts; Q J 7 2     &hearts; A K 8 4
&diams; Q 10 3      &diams; J 8
&clubs; Q 10 8 7 5   &clubs; K 4 2

&spades; K Q J 10 6 3
&hearts; 5
&diams; 9 7 6 4 2
&clubs; A

Playing in 4&spades; after the opponents have competed in hearts, South receives a heart lead and ruffs the second round. Suppose he forces out the ace of trumps, ruffs the heart return and draws a second trump. In this case he soon finds himself out of business. He cannot prevent the defenders from winning a heart trick if he draws trumps or a trump trick if he does not.

Let's return to the scene of the crime. South has little chance unless the diamonds are 3–2, and therefore, after ruffing the second round of hearts, he should play off $\diamondsuit$A–K–x. If the opponents return anything but a trump, South wins and proceeds to ruff two winning diamonds, making the contract regardless of how the trumps break or whether East overruffs or not. If the opponents return a trump when in with their diamond trick, South can draw trumps and cash the established diamonds.

In the next case declarer combines the principle of attacking the side suit with a loser-on-loser play.

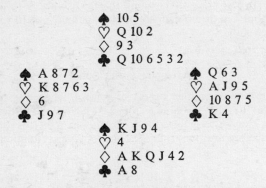

The contract is 3$\diamondsuit$ and West leads $\heartsuit$6. East covers the ten with the jack and leads a second round, which South ruffs.

If the declarer plays off two rounds of trumps now, the " tempo " will be against him. Say that he leads a spade to the ten and queen. East will play a third heart, on which South may discard his losing club. He must ruff the next heart, however, and when West comes in with $\spadesuit$A the fifth heart will force declarer to ruff for the third time. East will then have the long trump.

After ruffing the second heart South should lead a spade. When the defenders win and force again in hearts, declarer discards his losing club. Dummy can deal with any further hearts, and South remains in control.

## The Ruffing Game

One of the advantages of playing at a trump contract is that it may be possible to score extra tricks by ruffing. When that offers the best chance, declarer should fix his sights firmly on it and not be diverted by other possibilities.

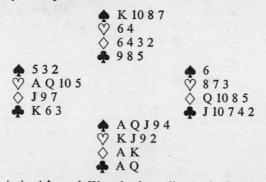

```
              ♠ K 10 8 7
              ♡ 6 4
              ◇ 6 4 3 2
              ♣ 9 8 5
  ♠ 5 3 2                  ♠ 6
  ♡ A Q 10 5               ♡ 8 7 3
  ◇ J 9 7                  ◇ Q 10 8 5
  ♣ K 6 3                  ♣ J 10 7 4 2
              ♠ A Q J 9 4
              ♡ K J 9 2
              ◇ A K
              ♣ A Q
```

South is in 4♠ and West leads a diamond. Suppose declarer crosses to dummy with a trump in order to lead a heart. The jack loses to the queen and a trump comes back. Declarer plays a second heart from dummy, this time finessing the nine, but he is fighting an uphill battle, for West wins and returns his last trump. Declarer is left with only one trump in dummy to take care of two losing hearts. When the club finesse later fails, so does the contract.

South can make the hand by scoring two heart ruffs in dummy. He does this by leading a heart from his hand at trick two, permitting the opponents to take two heart tricks. The defenders can return a trump each time they are in but South is firmly in the saddle and the club finesse no longer matters.

When preparing for a ruff, it will often be to declarer's advantage to lose the lead to one opponent rather than the other, as in this deal:

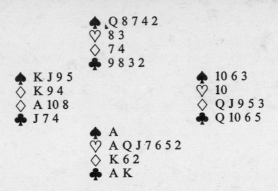

The contract is 4♡ and a club is led. Suppose that declarer returns a low diamond to pave the way for a ruff. East will overtake his partner's eight and return a trump, and South will wind up losing a trump trick and three diamonds.

Declarer's best chance of making the contract is to return ◇K at trick two. As the cards lie, West wins with the ace but cannot do very much. If he returns a trump declarer simply plays another diamond. If East wins this he has no more trumps to play, while if West wins it he can return a trump only at the cost of a trick.

The next example illustrates a well-known form of safety play.

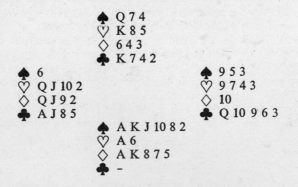

Playing in 6♠, South wins the heart lead with the ace and sees that if he draws three rounds of trumps he may later lose two diamonds. On general principles, it is right to attend to the side suit before drawing all the trumps. Declarer may draw one round of trumps with the ace. Then he lays down ♢A, crosses to ♡K, and leads a second diamond from dummy.

As the cards lie, East has an unenviable choice. If he plays a trump he is ruffing a loser; South will later draw East's outstanding trump and will have a spade in dummy to take care of the fourth round of diamonds. If, instead, East discards on the diamond lead, South will win and play a third round. West will take this trick, but the next diamond will be ruffed by dummy's ♠Q.

The sequence of play was very important on this hand. By cashing one high diamond, then making the next lead from the table, South protected ♢K from being ruffed. When there is a possibility of a ruff it is essential to protect master cards by leading towards them.

On the next hand the stress is slightly different: declarer tests the side suit before drawing all the trumps because he hopes to find a special distribution that will enable him to ruff a possible loser.

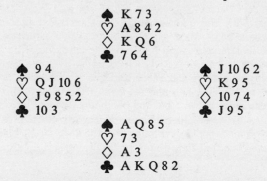

The contract is 7♣ and West leads ♡Q. Declarer wins in dummy and is relieved when all follow to two rounds of trumps. However, he is not home yet; he can discard his heart loser on the third round of diamonds, but the fourth spade in his own hand is not accounted for.

The best play is to take ♠A–K–Q before drawing the last trump. If spades are 3–3, no problem. As it happens, the spades are 4–2, but the player with the long spades also holds the outstanding trump and therefore the fourth round of spades can safely be ruffed.

It may seem that to play off the top spades before drawing the trump is somewhat risky. That is an illusion, because if the spades are not breaking, and the player who is short has the long trump, the contract cannot be made whether the trump is drawn or not.

285

The same principle appears on the next hand, but in less obvious form:

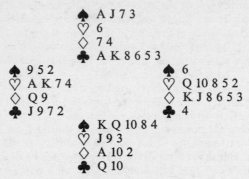

♠ A J 7 3
♡ 6
◇ 7 4
♣ A K 8 6 5 3

♠ 9 5 2
♡ A K 7 4
◇ Q 9
♣ J 9 7 2

♠ 6
♡ Q 10 8 5 2
◇ K J 8 6 5 3
♣ 4

♠ K Q 10 8 4
♡ J 9 3
◇ A 10 2
♣ Q 10

South reaches the creditable contract of 6♠ and West leads ♡K. East signals with the eight and West shows good judgment by playing a second heart, his object being to weaken the dummy. South ruffs on the table and plays ♠A–K. As the cards lie, if he draws a third round he will never get the clubs going. It costs nothing to test the clubs by playing the queen and ace. If the clubs break the outstanding trump is drawn and the rest of the hand is easy. As it turns out, the clubs are 4–1 but the defenders cannot ruff. South is able to ruff a club, return to ♠J and make the rest of the tricks.

When the defenders play a ruffing game the declarer may be able to arrange matters so that they do not profit.

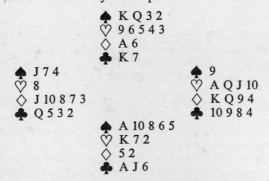

♠ K Q 3 2
♡ 9 6 5 4 3
◇ A 6
♣ K 7

♠ J 7 4
♡ 8
◇ J 10 8 7 3
♣ Q 5 3 2

♠ 9
♡ A Q J 10
◇ K Q 9 4
♣ 10 9 8 4

♠ A 10 8 6 5
♡ K 7 2
◇ 5 2
♣ A J 6

South plays in 4♠ after East has opened the bidding with 1♡. West leads ♡8 to his partner's ace and East returns the queen. South sees that a ruff is certain and the danger is that West will return a diamond. Declarer therefore ducks the second heart to leave himself in better control. West ruffs the next heart and plays a diamond, but declarer goes in with the ace and has the tempo to establish dummy's fifth heart for a diamond discard.

In the final example declarer nullifies a threatened ruff by the use of avoidance play:

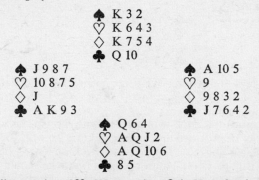

Defending against 3♡, West cashes ♣A–K and exits with ◇J. Declarer plays the A–Q of trumps and, finding West with four of them, is in difficulties. He needs to establish a spade trick for his contract, but if he draws trumps before tackling spades he will be wide open in clubs. On the other hand, if he leads a spade at this point the king will lose to the ace, West will ruff the diamond return, and eventually declarer will lose another spade trick.

The solution is to cross to dummy's king of trumps and lead a spade from the table. If East goes up with the ace to give his partner a diamond ruff, declarer makes two spade tricks instead of one. If East ducks the spade, or if West has the ace, declarer plays the queen and can now afford to draw trumps.

## Trump Promotion

To sustain a ruff is bad enough, but to suffer an overruff can be especially damaging. One of the most effective weapons of the defenders is to lead a side suit in which a defender can overruff the declarer; if declarer ruffs high it will cost him a trump trick. This is the manoeuvre known as "trump promotion". Sometimes the declarer can counter by discarding a loser from another suit.

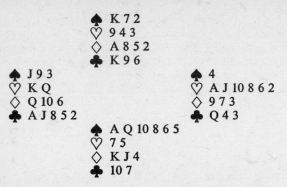

```
                    ♠ K 7 2
                    ♡ 9 4 3
                    ◇ A 8 5 2
                    ♣ K 9 6
  ♠ J 9 3                           ♠ 4
  ♡ K Q                             ♡ A J 10 8 6 2
  ◇ Q 10 6                          ◇ 9 7 3
  ♣ A J 8 5 2                       ♣ Q 4 3
                    ♠ A Q 10 8 6 5
                    ♡ 7 5
                    ◇ K J 4
                    ♣ 10 7
```

South plays in 3♠ after West has opened 1♣ and East has bid hearts. West opens ♡K and follows with ♡Q; East overtakes and plays a third round.

If South ruffs this trick with ♠Q, or with the ten, he will lose a trump trick. He will also lose to ♣A and ◇Q, so will go down one.

Declarer has nine more or less certain tricks so long as he does not concede a trump. On the third round of hearts he should discard a diamond—a potential loser. Then he ends up with six spade tricks, two diamonds and a club.

A declarer who has been forced to ruff high may employ a form of avoidance play to bolster his trump holding. In this example South must appreciate that his trump suit may not be as robust as it seems.

```
                    ♠ A K 8 4
                    ♡ 10 5
                    ◇ Q 10 2
                    ♣ 9 6 4 2
  ♠ 10 7 6 5                       ♠ Q J 2
  ♡ 8 6 4 3                        ♡ A
  ◇ 8 4 3                          ◇ 9 7 6 5
  ♣ 8 3                            ♣ A K Q J 5
                    ♠ 9 3
                    ♡ K Q J 9 7 2
                    ◇ A K J
                    ♣ 10 7
```

South plays in 4♡ after East has opened the bidding with 1♣. Clubs are led and continued and South is obliged to ruff the third one with a high trump. Suppose he now leads a trump to dummy's ten. East will return a fourth club and West's eight will become promoted to winning rank. To prevent this, declarer should cross to dummy's ♠A after ruffing the third club. ♡5 is led from the table and when the ace comes up declarer can afford to ruff the next club high. He then leads the seven of trumps to dummy's ten, enters his hand with a diamond, and draws the remaining trumps.

On the next hand the defenders employ the manoeuvre known as the uppercut. The declarer must refuse the temptation to overruff.

```
              ♠ Q 7 5 2
              ♡ A 5 4
              ◇ 8 6 5 3
              ♣ K 2
 ♠ J 9                         ♠ K 10 8 6 3
 ♡ K 8 6                       ♡ 9
 ◇ A K J 9 2                   ◇ 10 7
 ♣ 9 6 4                       ♣ J 8 7 5 3
              ♠ A 4
              ♡ Q J 10 7 3 2
              ◇ Q 4
              ♣ A Q 10
```

The contract is 4♡ and West begins with ◇K–A–J. Although ◇J is a master it is good play for East to contribute his nine of trumps. If South makes the mistake of overruffing he will lose a heart and a spade in addition to the two diamonds already conceded. As his second spade is an almost certain loser he should discard it on the third diamond, keeping his trumps intact. Then he can pick up West's ♡K and make the rest of the tricks.

The ever-useful " loser on loser " play may save the ship when declarer plans to ruff in dummy but has reason to fear an overruff.

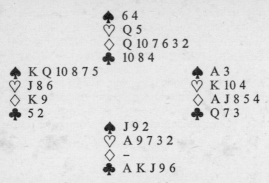

The contract is 3♣ and West leads ♠K. East overtakes with the ace and returns the three. West wins and plays a third spade.

Suppose declarer tries ♣8 from dummy. East will overruff and return a trump. When South tackles hearts the defenders will play another round of trumps, and South will lose two hearts in addition to two spades and a club.

On the third spade South should discard a heart from dummy, transferring the loser from one suit to another. No doubt East will also discard a heart, but declarer is in control. If West plays a fourth spade, dummy again discards a heart and South ruffs. A heart is ruffed in dummy, the closed hand is entered with ♣A, and another heart is ruffed. East may overruff, but it will be the last trick for the defence.

One other way to avoid a damaging overruff is to trump high at the right moment. Even experienced players have been known to miss their way on this type of hand:

West leads ♡J against 5◇.  The obvious line for declarer is to ruff two spades;  he is prepared to lose a diamond and a heart.  He wins with ♡A, therefore, and plays three rounds of spades.  It may seem natural to ruff with the nine, saving the ace for the next round, but as the cards lie East will overruff and return a trump, leaving South with two more losers.

The best play, in view of the strong intermediates in diamonds, is to ruff the third spade with ◇A and the fourth spade with ◇9. East will overruff this time, but all he will make after that is a heart.

# PART V

---

*Defensive Play*

# CHAPTER 22

## Opening Leads

*The card to lead – Leads in notrumps – Leads in trump contracts – Leads against slam contracts – Special lead conventions*

THE SELECTION of a sound opening lead is a task that calls for at least as much judgment and experience as any other phase of the game. There are two general objectives: to get at the defenders' tricks as quickly as possible and to avoid giving declarer a trick that he could not have won by his own efforts. To reconcile these aims can be difficult and may involve a larger number of uncertain factors than any other decision in bridge.

The selection of the actual card to lead is logically the last step in the process, but nevertheless we start with it in order to simplify the later discussion of tactics for leading against notrumps, trump contracts and slams.

### The Card to Lead

To co-operate effectively the defenders must speak the same language. Thus, once the suit to lead has been determined, the choice of card will nearly always be guided by convention; that is to say, you lead a certain card because your partner will expect you to lead that card from that combination. The following are the leads your partner will expect from various combinations in the plain suits:

#### With a Four-card or Longer Suit

(1) *When the suit is headed by three honours in sequence,* lead the highest card in order to prevent declarer from winning with a low card.

K Q J x    Q J 10 x x    J 10 9 x x

A special case is a suit headed by the A–K–Q. Against a notrump contract the defender may lead the ace, requesting partner to drop his highest card, a procedure which will often indicate the best

295

continuation. However, it is not unknown to lead the fourth-best card from A–K–Q–x–x if the bidding has suggested that declarer has a stopper in the suit. Against a trump contract it is usual to lead the king and continue with the ace.

(2) *From a suit headed by a " broken sequence "*, lead the top card; but from a suit containing an " interior sequence ", lead the middle honour:

$$\underline{K} Q \, 10 \, x \qquad \underline{Q} J \, 9 \, x \, x \qquad \underline{J} \, 10 \, 8 \, x$$

The holding A–K–J–x–x again provides an exception; now the king is the conventional card.

$$A \underline{Q} J \, x \, x \qquad K \underline{J} \, 10 \, x \qquad Q \, \underline{10} \, 9 \, x$$

From these interior sequences lead the card that is underlined. With a five-card suit, however, and especially the holding K–10–9–x–x, the conventional card may not turn out well. For example:

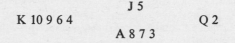

The lead of the ten gives declarer a second stopper, whereas the lead of the fourth best, the six, will quickly establish the suit.

There is only one other combination of three honours, the A–Q–10. An opening lead from a four-card suit headed by this combination would be unattractive, even against a notrump contract; it must be better to retain the honours over declarer. From a five-card suit the choice is not easy; with no side entry the fourth-best card would be normal, but with a sure side entry the ace is a better choice. After the play to the first trick it will usually be possible to judge whether to continue with a low card or with the queen, to pin a doubleton jack.

(3) *From a suit headed by two honours in sequence*, lead the fourth-best card against notrumps but the highest card against a trump contract.

$$K Q \underline{x} \, x \, x \qquad Q J \, x \, \underline{x} \qquad J \, 10 \, x \, \underline{x}$$

In each case the lead of the card underlined will afford the best chance of establishing the suit against a notrump contract. At a trump contract, where the defender is less willing to concede an early trick for the sake of a long-term advantage, the top card is led.

Note that with A–K–x–x the king, rather than the ace, is the standard lead against a trump contract.

(4) *From a suit containing only one honour, or two honours not in sequence*, lead, as a rule, the fourth-best card; but lead the ace against a trump contract. It is not usually a sound idea to underlead an ace at a suit contract, except with deceptive intent.

A minor exception is that the ten is led from 10–9–8–x, and usually from 10–9–7–x.

(5) *From four or more small cards*, it is usual to lead fourth best in order to give partner a count of the suit. But with a holding such as 9–8–7–x or 8–7–5–x it is better to lead the top card against a trump contract in order to warn partner that the suit is not headed by an honour.

### With a Three-card Suit

(1) *With two or more honours in sequence*, lead the highest card, both against suit contracts and notrumps. (*Exception:* lead the king from A–K–x.)

(2) *With only one honour card, or two not in sequence*, lead third best. (*Exceptions:* lead the ace at a trump contract, the queen from A–Q–x against notrumps.)

(3) *From three small cards, such as* 7–5–3, the top card is generally regarded as the standard lead. The disadvantage of leading the bottom card is that partner will not be able to tell whether or not the suit is headed by an honour. An alternative method is discussed later.

### With a Doubleton Suit

*Always lead the top card.* This applies also to A–K bare. When the king is led on the next round partner will know, from the failure to lead K–A, that the lead is a doubleton.

We turn now to the more difficult problem of which suit to lead.

## Leads in Notrumps

The general aim of the defence is to establish its long suits before the declarer has established his; hence the maxim, " lead your longest and strongest suit ". But that is not much more than half right, for the real objective on most hands is to lead the longest and strongest suit held by the *partnership*. In other words, the leader should often play for his partner's hand rather than his own. Nevertheless the leading of the longest suit is a sound principle and affords a convenient means of narrowing the problem. Thus we consider:

(*a*) When is it right to lead a suit other than the longest and strongest?

(*b*) What governs the choice between one short suit and another?

(*c*) When partner has bid a suit, how strong is the obligation to lead it?

(*d*) How is the choice of lead affected when partner has doubled?

## (a) When is it right to lead a suit other than the longest and strongest?

There are certain obvious cases. The opponents may have bid the leader's best suit. A lead from a strong sequence such as Q–J–10–8 is more attractive than fourth best from J–x–x–x–x–x. Some four-card combinations, such as A–Q–x–x, A–J–x–x, K–Q–x–x, are costly to lead from and it must be better to keep the honours in storage. This is a difficult type of hand:

♠ J 5    ♡ J 10 4    ◇ K 7 6 4 3    ♣ 9 5 2

The reasons why the lead of a low diamond does not exactly stand out are that the spot cards are very poor and that the hand contains no side entry; partner will need to have quite a favourable holding to get the suit going. The alternative lead, assuming the suit has not been bid, is ♡J, and this would be a clear first choice with ♡9 instead of ♡4. In the actual case the deciding factor is whether the opponents appear to be *limited*. If the contract is only 1NT or 2NT, or the opponents have reached 3NT by slow stages, it will be reasonable to conclude that partner has fair values and to make the relatively safe, and possibly constructive, lead of ♡J. But if the opponents appear to have strength in reserve, or if they are marked with long suits which they will quickly develop, then the more risky, but more dynamic, lead of the fourth-best diamond is indicated.

This is a similar example. South holds:

♠ A 7 5 2    ♡ Q 4    ◇ K J 7 3    ♣ 7 5 2

East opens 1NT and is raised to 3NT. The neutral lead of ♣7 is as attractive as either a low diamond or a low spade and would be still more so if 1NT had been passed out. But suppose the bidding has been:

| West | East |
|------|------|
| 1♡ | 1♠ |
| 2♡ | 2NT |
| 3NT | Pass |

Now the choice is between ♢3 and ♣7, and for various reasons the diamond is better. As West probably has a six-card heart suit the defence must play an attacking rather than a waiting game; it would be pessimistic to assume that East had a double guard in diamonds; and as South has fair strength himself it is unlikely that North will hold enough in clubs to make that lead worthwhile.

#### (b) What governs the choice between one short suit and another?

Remember that the object is to try to strike partner's best suit. The opponents' bidding will usually provide a clue.

Suppose South is on lead in these two cases:

| (1) | West | East | | (2) | West | East |
|-----|------|------|--|-----|------|------|
| | | 1♢ | | | 1♡ | 2♣ |
| | 1♡ | 1NT | | | 2♡ | 2NT |
| | 3NT | Pass | | | 3NT | Pass |

In (1), as between the two unbid suits, South is more likely to find his partner at home in spades than in clubs, since declarer would probably have shown a biddable spade suit at the one level. In (2), if North is marked with a fair hand he is unlikely to hold a five-card spade suit, which he could have shown over 1♡. Thus a diamond may appear the better choice.

When the bidding affords no guide it is better to lead from a three-card holding than from a doubleton, as less will be required from partner to make the lead effective. It is natural, also, to prefer a sequence such as 9–8–6 to a more flimsy trio.

#### (c) When partner has bid a suit, how strong is the obligation to lead it?

Since it is usual to lead partner's suit, this question becomes relevant only when the opening leader is short of it and has a promising alternative of his own. These are the factors to be considered:

Is there a strong inference that opponents have a sound guard, very possibly a double guard, in partner's suit? Clearly, if an opponent has jumped to 2NT or 3NT over partner's intervention it is fair to assume that he has the suit well protected. But if they settle in notrumps only on the last round, then the odds are that they hold only a single guard.

How strong is partner's suit likely to be? If all he has done is open with one of a minor suit he may have a nugatory holding such as K–x–x–x. If he was third in hand his suit is entitled to more respect, as he may have opened specifically to indicate a lead. If he has made a vulnerable overcall, or has bid at the two level, he surely has a sound suit.

### (d) How is the choice of lead affected when partner has doubled?

We have already noted, in Chapter 14, that doubles of a notrump contract are often lead-directing. These are the proposals they make:

(*i*) When both defenders have bid a suit the double requests the leader's suit.

(*ii*) When the defending side has bid only one suit, the double requests that suit.

(*iii*) When no suit has been bid by the defending side the double requests the lead of a suit bid by dummy—usually the first suit.

(*iv*) When no one has bid a suit, the double says: " Don't lead your long suit: try to find mine." After such a double a player who holds, say, ♠ Q–x–x ♡ x ♢ Q–10–x–x–x ♣ 10 x x x, will reach for the singleton heart, expecting to find his partner with A–K–Q–J–x or, perhaps, K–Q–J–10–x and a side ace.

Commonsense will distinguish these lead-directing doubles from a normal penalty double. If South plays in 3NT after North has opened 1♡ and rebid 2♡ or 3♡, a double by East will no doubt be fortified by at least one trick in hearts, but he is not asking West to lead a heart. That would simply lose a tempo.

There are two special situations. One occurs when the opponents have given evidence of relying on a long minor suit—notably when the declarer has opened 3NT (see Chapter 5). The declarer in this case may be wide open somewhere and the opening leader should lay down an ace if he has one, so that there will be time to switch if necessary.

The other special situation occurs when the player on lead is so strong that a conventional opening, aimed at maintaining communications, would be pointless. For example, South is declarer in 3NT and West, who has opened 1♡, holds:

♠ Q 7   ♡ K J 10 9 6 4   ◇ A J 2   ♣ K 6

West has no hope of finding his partner with ♡A, so nothing can be gained by the normal lead of ♡J. The opening salvo should be ♡K, in the hope of pinning a singleton queen. The same tactics may be followed on occasions with other broken sequences, such as A–J–10–8–x–x or Q–10–9–8–x–x. The ace may bring down the singleton queen or king, and the queen may pin a singleton jack.


### Leads in Trump Contracts

A player who is leading against a trump contract has many additional tactical possibilities to consider. We examine in turn safe leads, attacking leads, short-suit leads, forcing leads, and trump leads.

*Safe leads.* Safety is a much more important consideration when leading against a suit contract than against notrumps. Against notrumps, a lead from K–J–x–x–x will quite possibly give up a trick, but the defenders hope in time to establish the suit and get the trick back with interest. In a suit contract a trick given up by the lead will not as a rule come back. In this respect an ace is not a safe lead, for although it will usually win the trick it forfeits the chance of capturing an enemy king or queen, which is what aces were created for. In most cases an innocuous lead from an assortment of low cards is preferable to a lead away from an honour card, especially when no side suit has been mentioned by the opponents, and especially against a part-score contract. Of course, some leads, such as the king from K–Q–J–x, are ideal because they combine safety with attack. When no safe lead presents itself, a lead from a king or queen is less likely to cost than a lead from an ace or jack; and the longer the suit the less dangerous the lead.

*Attacking leads.* When there is evidence that the opponents have length and strength in a side suit, the defenders cannot usually afford to play a safe game: they must aim to set up quick tricks in the remaining suits. In suitable cases there should be a willingness to lead from " dangerous " holdings such as J–x–x or K–x–x or K–J–x or even A–Q–x. The fact that opponents have not settled in notrumps is after all an indication that they have gaps in at least one suit; and if the lead does cost a trick, it may not be a vital one.

*Short-suit leads.* The lead from a singleton or doubleton of an unbid suit is an excellent opening because it is relatively safe and may lead to a ruff. Obviously, the player's trump holding is relevant: if a trump trick is held, the defender will have a second chance to put partner in the lead.

Three warnings may not be out of place. First, to lead a singleton into the declarer's second suit is usually a very bad mistake: it is a complete give-away and may cause declarer to take a deep finesse later through partner's strength. Secondly, it is not brilliant to lead a singleton when there is no possibility that partner will have enough strength to gain the lead. Finally, players who lead a singleton against a small slam when holding a certain trick in their own hand should be studied carefully but not imitated. Obviously, if partner holds the ace of this suit (most unlikely) the contract will be defeated anyway. The most likely effect of the lead will be to kill a promising holding such as K–10–x–x.

"*Forcing*" *leads.* When the right conditions exist, a forcing lead, aimed at weakening the declarer's trump control, is the defenders' strongest weapon. Suppose that North and South have bid as follows:

| South | North |
|-------|-------|
| 1♠    | 2♦    |
| 2NT   | 3♠    |
| 4♠    | Pass  |

West holds:

♠ 10 7 5 2   ♡ K J 8 5 3   ◇ 7 4   ♣ A 5

It is highly probable that the spades are 5–3, and if the declarer can be forced to ruff he will be in danger of losing control. West should nail his colours to a heart lead.

*Trump leads.* Some players habitually lead a trump because nothing else appeals to them. That is a negative and rather dubious policy; it often solves a guess for the declarer and, still more often, gives him a tempo, enabling him to draw trumps and set about establishing tricks in a side suit.

The time to lead trumps is when the bidding suggests either that the opponents have found a good fit and are proposing to crossruff if given the chance, or that the declarer has a two-suiter and will be

302

attempting to set up the second suit by ruffing.  Suppose the bidding goes:

| South | North |
|-------|-------|
| 1♡    | 1♠    |
| 2◇    | 2NT   |
| 3◇    | 4♡    |
| Pass  |       |

West holds either:

    (1) ♠ Q 7 4  ♡ 6 2  ◇ K J 9 5  ♣ Q J 8 3

or

    (2) ♠ Q 7 4 2  ♡ 6 2  ◇ K 5  ♣ Q J 8 5 3

Most players would lead a trump with hand (1) but would be somewhat less inclined to do so with (2).  Actually, a trump lead is more to the point in (2).  When South, in the first example, tries to ruff diamonds he may be overruffed by East.  In the second case East will have long diamonds and dummy will be able to ruff safely in front of him.

There is a certain prejudice against leading a singleton trump because of the danger of killing partner's possible Q–x–x or J–x–x–x. However, the risk of disclosing partner's queen is also present when the leader has two or even three small trumps.  When there is a positive reason for a trump attack, the risk should be accepted. Even a player who holds Q–x–x himself must be prepared to lead a trump to stop a certain crossruff, and a trump is often good play from Q–x–x–x or K–x–x.

A trump lead is clearly marked when partner is known to have a strong holding and the game is to prevent the declarer from making low trumps by ruffing.  The standard example is when there has been a penalty pass, as in this sequence:

| South | West   | North | East |
|-------|--------|-------|------|
| 1♡    | Double | Pass  | Pass |
| Pass  |        |       |      |

To pass a double at the one level, sitting under the bidder, East must hold a strong sequence of trumps.  It is almost a convention that West should lead a trump, whatever his holding.  A trump is also a good lead when the opponents are doubled after partner has opened at notrumps.

A less certain inference can be drawn when the player in fourth position, though marked with fair values, passes out an opening bid at the one level. With both sides vulnerable the bidding goes:

| South | West | North | East |
|-------|------|-------|------|
| 1◇ | Pass | Pass | Pass |

West holds:

♠ J 9 5   ♡ A 8 6 3   ◇ 7 2   ♣ Q 8 3 2

Here South has opened with a one-bid, North must be very weak, and West hasn't got much himself. Yet East has not contested at the one level. Probably East likes the diamonds, and as West has no very brilliant lead elsewhere he should begin with a trump. There is a chance that East holds something like K–J–10–9–x.

Finally, there is a rule concerning trump leads to which there are very few exceptions: *when the trumps are not in sequence, lead the lowest.* To lead the nine from 9–8–x can never gain; sometimes it will allow declarer an extra entry to dummy by finessing against the eight on the second round. Similarly the eight should be led from J–10–8 in a trump suit which has been bid and supported. The lead of the jack may be cataclysmic if dummy plays low with Q–9–x–x and partner's singleton king comes up.

## Leads against Slam Contracts

Since the defenders are now looking for only two tricks (or one), they obviously do not follow the same principles that govern the choice of lead against lesser contracts. Assuming that the hands are not freakish, and that the opponents' bidding is thought to be sound, it is usual to look for a safe lead against a grand slam, an attacking lead against a small slam.

A critical question is whether an ace should be led against a small slam. Such a lead may lose a vital tempo in the race to set up a second trick, but on the other hand it may be essential to take two tricks in the suit quickly. Clearly an ace should be led if the defender has another probable trick elsewhere, such as a trump trick, and also when the bidding offers no particular likelihood that the opponents have second-round control of the suit. Equally clearly, one should not lead an ace in a suit that has been bid by the opponents if there is a reasonable prospect of establishing a second trick elsewhere. For

304

the rest, our experience suggests that more slams are made because an ace was not led than the other way round!

## Special Lead Conventions

There are perfectionists in every field and it has to be frankly admitted that, from the point of view of conveying accurate information, standard leads are not the best that can be devised. By partnership arrangement it is possible to effect a noticeable improvement in certain areas. The following special conventions are widely played and can be thoroughly recommended.

### Ace from A–K

To lead the king equally from K–Q–x and from A–K–x, which is the standard procedure, creates problems for the partner of the leader, notably when he holds J–x–x. By arranging to lead the ace from a combination headed by the A–K, this particular ambiguity can be avoided; a lead of the king will now always be from K–Q. It is true that in theory one ambiguity is substituted for another; an ace lead may be either unsupported or from A–K–x. But in practice unsupported aces are not often led, and when they are the king will often be visible.

A consequence of arranging to lead the ace from a combination headed by the A–K is that the lead of the king followed by the ace indicates A–K bare.

### "Mud"

This convention aims to solve the longstanding problem of the lead from three low cards, such as 8–5–2. The disadvantage of leading the top card, which is the most common form of standard practice, is that partner may not know, even after a second round, whether the lead was from two cards or three; at a trump contract, especially, this may be critical. The disadvantage of leading the bottom card is that partner will not be able to tell whether the suit is headed by an honour. This may be the best method, nevertheless.

Playing " Mud " (Middle, Up, Down), the opening lead from three small is the middle card. In principle the player intends to play the top card on the next round, whereupon partner will know the position.

## Rusinow and Roman Leads

It has been noted that if the king is led equally from combinations headed by the A–K and the K–Q, a partner who holds J–x–x is uncertain whether to encourage. To lead the ace from A–K solves this problem but creates the difficulty (at a trump contract) that the lead of an ace may be from A–K–x–x or from a holding such as A–x–x–x.

Rusinow leads are the logical extension of the lead of the ace from A–K. They apply only to the lead of an unbid suit (not the suit bid by partner). With three or more cards, the procedure is to lead the *lower* of two touching honours. With any doubleton, the top card is led. Thus when an ace is led, the king is known to be missing; when the queen is led, the king is known to be behind it, and so on. A defender with A–x–x–x knows, when his partner leads the king and continues with the queen, that he has K–Q bare.

Roman leads employ the same principle and extend it to use against notrump contracts, with this refinement: against notrump contracts only, the ten is a " strong card ", always from an interior sequence. Thus the ten is led from K–J–10 or K–10–9, but from J–10–9–x–x the lead is the jack. Partner may not know at first whether the jack is from Q–J or J–10, but this will not as a rule matter. When standard leads are played, partner can never tell whether the ten is from 10–9–8–x or from a much stronger holding, and this uncertainty often causes the defence to go off the rails. When Roman leads are in use, the lead from 10–9–8–x is the nine.

# CHAPTER 23

## Defending Against Notrump Contracts

*The play by third hand – The right card to lead or to play on partner's lead – When to cover an honour – Preserving the entry of the key defender – Nullifying the declarer's long suits – When to shift to another suit*

MOST notrump contracts cannot be beaten simply by cashing high cards and therefore the defenders must usually attempt to establish a long suit in one hand or the other. Sometimes it is difficult to select the right suit because, unlike the declarer, each defender sees only his own portion of the partnership assets. In order to be able to use their combined resources effectively, the defenders must exchange information by means of conventional leads and plays. We have seen how this process begins in the previous chapter.

There are also other ways of deciding how the missing cards are distributed. The leads and plays made by a defender contain a message not only about the suit he has played, but often about other suits as well. For example, when your partner leads a low card against a notrump contract you usually assume that he has led from his longest and strongest suit, and you thereby acquire negative information about his holdings in the other suits.

Some of the most significant indications, as the play progresses, are gained by studying the declarer's own approach to his contract. Declarer is presumably doing his best according to his lights; in the process he must inevitably reveal a lot about his hand.

However, this type of indication is usually not present in the early stages. Sometimes declarer's play from dummy at trick one will be indicative, but more often he will simply be following suit. Thus the third player, like the opening leader, has to rely to a large extent on general rules. Our first task is to examine the principles that guide the play by third hand after the declarer has played from dummy to the opening lead.

## The Play by Third Hand

The easiest decision for the third player occurs when partner appears to have led fourth best from his own long suit and dummy has only small cards of this suit. The correct procedure now, with very few exceptions, is to play the highest card.

(1)          7        (2)      6 5 2

A J 8 5 4    K 9 6 3    K 9 7 4       Q 10 3

       Q 10 2          A J 8

In (1) West leads the five and the seven is played from dummy. East should play the king, of course, but players have been known to duck on the grounds that the declarer might have A–Q–J. Similarly, in (2), when partner leads the four, third hand should put on the queen; players have been observed to contribute the ten, explaining that they hoped this would drive out the king or ace. Mistakes like this are never made by defenders who appreciate that it is not the fate of individual high cards that matters, but the promotion of the combined assets.

There *are* one or two situations where third hand does not put up his highest card, but they have nothing in common with the two previous examples. Instead, the object is to coax out declarer's stopper in the suit. This is the commonest case:

          10 2

J 9 8 4 3          A Q 6

         K 7 5

West leads the four and the two is played from dummy. If East plays the ace and continues with the queen, declarer will probably hold up his king, and unless West has an outside entry the long cards may be wasted. East does better to play the queen on the opening lead. It will then seem dangerous for the declarer to hold up, as he might lose his trick altogether. Once declarer has parted with the king the defenders can immediately run four tricks, whether West or East gains the lead.

The same type of play will usually work out best in this more advanced situation:

          3

Q 9 7 4 2         A J 6

        K 10 8 5

Suppose, first, that West leads the four and East plays the ace, continuing with the jack. Declarer may take this with the king and play to keep East out of the lead, retaining a second guard with the 10–8. Now suppose that East plays the jack, rather than the ace, on the opening lead; then if declarer parts with the king the defenders can run four tricks whoever gains the lead.

Playing the jack may cost a trick if declarer has the queen and not the king, but this may be an acceptable risk. On this occasion East can be fairly certain that South has a fair holding; West, if he has led fourth best, cannot have more than five cards in the suit, so South is marked with four.

We have been considering cases where dummy has no significant high card in the suit led. It is quite another matter when dummy does have a high card. Observe this very common situation:

$$Q\ 7\ 4$$
$$K\ 9\ 6\ 5 \qquad\qquad A\ J\ 3$$
$$10\ 8\ 2$$

West leads the five and dummy plays low. (Declarer's best chance is that West has led from the jack rather than from the A–K.) Now it is apparent that East must put in the jack, finessing against the dummy. In general, against a notrump contract, it is right for the third player to retain a card that will beat an isolated king, queen or jack in dummy. These are some further examples:

(3)         J 7 4        (4)         K 8 4
   Q 8 6 5 2      K 10 3     J 10 7 5      A 9 3
       A 9                    Q 6 2

When West leads the five in (3) and dummy plays low, East inserts the ten, not the king. It is true that the ten may lose to the queen, but in this case the declarer is sure to make one trick however East plays. In (4) West leads the five and the four is played from dummy. East must put in the nine, keeping the ace over dummy's king. This manoeuvre cannot possibly cost a trick in the long run. If partner has led from the J–10, as here, finessing the nine will save a trick.

The same type of play is often correct with much lower cards. These situations are instructive:

(5)         K 10 5        (6)         Q 9 5
   J 9 6 4 2      Q 8 3     J 8 6 4 2      A 10 7
       A 7                    K 3

In (5) West leads the four, declarer plays the five from dummy, and East finesses the eight. Of course, if West had led from A-8-6-4-2 the queen would be best; but if East can place South with the ace he must not allow the queen to be beheaded, for then dummy's K-10 would be good for two more tricks. Similarly, when in (6) West leads the four and dummy plays the five, East must play the seven to hold declarer to one trick.

A feature of the last example is that East can be certain that declarer has only one card higher than the four! This assurance derives from the celebrated " Rule of Eleven ". The third player observes the rank of the card led, subtracts it from eleven, and in that way learns the number of higher cards held in the other three hands. Subtracting four (West's lead) from eleven, East concludes that there are seven higher cards in the other three hands; he can already see six, so can be sure that declarer has only one.

In case you are wondering " why eleven? ", the explanation is quite simple. The cards in bridge range, in effect, from two to fourteen (the ace being fourteen). So, if the four is led you know there are altogether ten higher cards. Three of these are held by the opening leader, and therefore, to discover how many are held by the other hands, you subtract, not from fourteen, but from eleven.

Sometimes (though not so often as some writers have suggested) the Rule of Eleven is a pointer to the best play by third hand. Consider these situations:

(7)                J 4          (8)                    J 7
     K Q 8 6 2      A 9 7          A 10 8 6 4 2      K 9 5
                10 5 3                                Q 3

In each case West leads the six and dummy plays low. East may be tempted to finesse against the jack, lest declarer hold K-Q-x-x (in 7) or A-Q-x (in 8). Application of the Rule of Eleven avoids such a disaster, for in each case East can calculate that declarer has only one card to beat the card led. That being so, it cannot cost for East to go up with his high card.

So far we have been considering situations where the opening lead has been a low card. When the lead is an honour card the third player must consider whether there is a danger of the suit being blocked.

The guiding principle here is that a defender should be very reluctant to allow himself to be left with an isolated high card in a suit which his partner is trying to establish:

(9)        8 4 3     (10)        9 5 3

Q J 10 7 6     K 5     J 10 8 6 2     K Q 4

        A 9 2                A 7

In (9) West leads the queen from his sequence. It is essential for East to unblock by playing the king. Suppose he ducks; South will probably hold up for two rounds and East will be left on lead, unable to clear the suit.

In (10) West leads the jack and the unblock is equally important. East must play the queen and continue with the king.

It is often necessary to unblock at the possible cost of a trick, as here:

(11)        K 7 4     (12)        A 9 3

Q J 9 6 3     A 5     Q 10 7 5 4     K 8

        10 8 2                J 6 2

West leads the queen in (11) and declarer plays low from dummy. East should unblock by going up with the ace and returning the five to clear the suit. In (12) West leads the five and declarer goes up with the ace in an attempt to obstruct the run of the suit. If East plays low, declarer's plan will succeed; East should drop the king so that when he gains the lead he can play the eight through the declarer's J-6.

When partner leads a short suit the third player has different problems, which we deal with later when considering the general subject of protecting the entry of the key defender. First it is necessary to say a word about the conventions the defenders use to exchange the maximum information.

### The Right Card to Lead or to Play on Partner's Lead

A defender leading to a trick normally plays the top card from a sequence; but in all other positions it is conventional to play the lowest card. Here are two examples where the play by third hand shows the logic of that arrangement:

(1)        7 4 2     (2)        8 7 4

K 9 6 5 3     Q J 8     K 9 6 5     Q 10 3

        A 10                A J 2

In (1) West leads the five, East plays the jack, and South wins with the ace. Now unless South is playing an unusually cunning game (winning with the ace when holding A–Q), West may assume that his partner holds the queen. If East had played the queen on the first round no such inference would have been available concerning the jack.

In (2) East's queen is headed by the declarer's ace. Because East would play the jack with Q–J, West places South with the jack and knows it would be dangerous to lay down the king.

No less important is the right card to play to indicate length. Note, first, that the convention of leading fourth best is not limited to the first time a suit is led: it applies also on the second round when a defender is returning his partner's lead. The usefulness of this arrangement can be seen in these examples:

(3)                6                (4)                10 6
    K J 8 5 2        A 9 7 3        K J 9 7 2        A 3
            Q 10 4                          Q 8 5 4

West leads the five to his partner's ace and East returns the three, his original fourth best. South's ten loses to the jack. It is not difficult for West to read his partner's card as fourth best, for if East had the A–3 only it would mean that declarer held Q–10–9–7–4. West, therefore, lays down the king, and now East must take care to unblock the suit by dropping the nine. This leaves West in command to cash two more winners.

In (4) West leads the seven to his partner's ace and East returns the three, which again tells West the whole story. Suppose South puts in the eight, seeking to create the impression that he has Q–8–x only; West can tell that South still has the guarded queen, for with A–5–3 East would return the five, not the three.

It must be added that all is not always sweetness and light between two defenders who are trying to read each other's signals; sometimes a defender must break away from convention to avoid a possible block. This is an example:

(5)                8                (6)                4
    K J 6 4 3        A 9 7 5        K 8 5 3 2        A J 10 7
            Q 10 2                          Q 9 6

In (5) West leads the four to East's ace. Now if East returns the five the suit will be irretrievably blocked after West has made the jack and king. East, with his high intermediates, should foresee this danger, and if it is vital to run five tricks quickly he should return the nine. Partner may fail to read the situation, but that cannot be helped. In (6), of course, East must return the jack to trap the queen as well as to unblock the suit.

Whenever a defender opens up a new suit from a holding of three cards, he follows the same scheme as he would on the opening lead. In general the lead of a high card signifies that no honour is behind it; the lead of a low card means that an honour is held. Observe the value of that understanding in these two examples, where East is on lead in the middle game:

(7)             7 4 3              (8)              8 5 2
     A J 9 5          8 6 2            K J 6 3           Q 7 4
             K Q 10                           A 10 9

In (7) East leads the eight and declarer plays the king or queen. West knows the declarer has the outstanding honours and that it is safe to duck, enabling three tricks to be taken when East regains the lead.

In (8) East leads the four and South puts in the ten. After winning with the jack West can safely lead back the three. His partner would have led a higher card from 9–7–4, so there is no danger of finding the declarer with A–Q–10.

### When to Cover an Honour

A particularly critical decision in play is whether or not to cover an opponent's honour. The general rule, which is subject to a number of ifs and buts, is to " cover an honour with an honour ", the reason being evident from these two simple situations:

(1)             Q 5               (2)              Q 5
     J 10 7 6          K 9 3 2          10 7 3           K 4
             A 8 4                            A J 9 8 6 2

Occasionally the declarer will attempt to steal a trick by leading the queen from the table in an example like (1). Obviously East must cover. In (2) South's normal play is to lead the queen from dummy; here, again, East must cover to establish his partner's ten.

A mastery of this department of the game can best be achieved by studying three general rules and noting the exceptions to them:

(a) *When following the dummy, cover any single honour that is led.*
This of course is the principle that East followed in the examples above. When might this be wrong? One case is where the defender's

honour cannot be caught so long as he does not cover; another is when there is no chance that covering will establish a lower card for either defender.

(3)            J 7        (4)        J 8 5 2

     8 5 3           K 6 4 2     Q               K 4 3

          A Q 10 9              A 10 9 7 6

In (3) declarer leads the jack from dummy but East, as his king is so well guarded, plays low. With only K–x–x, East would cover.

In (4) South again leads the jack from dummy. If declarer is marked with length East must not cover, as there is nothing he can hope to establish. So that you may be warned, here is another combination where declarer may set the same kind of trap:

(5)                    Q 7 3

              A             K 9 8

               J 10 6 5 4 2

The declarer, who is marked with some length, leads the queen from dummy. Defenders have been known to cover, with dire results, remarking to partner afterwards, " But you might have had the singleton ten." This is not really a good excuse because well-trained declarers, with Q–x–x opposite A–J–x–x–x–x, lead *low* from dummy, not the queen.

Continuing the list of general rules:

(*b*) *When dummy has a sequence of honours, never cover the first one if you can leave yourself with the choice of covering later.*

As the sole reason for covering an honour is that you hope to promote something for your side when the opponents' honours are all gone, there is obviously no need to cover until the *last* honour is led. To cover earlier may cost a trick in situations like this:

(6)       Q J 10 7 3    (7)    J 10 9 2

    8             K 6 4 2    Q 6          K 7 4 3

        A 9 5              A 8 5

In either case it would be very poor play for East to cover the first lead from dummy. The principle emerges in a less obvious way in the next two examples:

(8)       Q J 8 3    (9)    J 10 5

   10 6 2        K 7 4    Q 8 4        K 9 6

        A 9 5            A 7 3 2

If in (8) East covers the queen with the king he will expose his partner to a second-round finesse through the 10–x and his side will emerge with no tricks at all. Similarly, in (9), it would be a mistake to cover the jack; so long as East delays the cover his side must win two tricks.

It may, however, be right to cover the first honour of a sequence when the defender has a doubleton:

| (10) | Q J 9 4 | | (11) | | J 10 3 | |
|---|---|---|---|---|---|---|
| 6 3 2 | | K 10 | | Q 8 7 5 | | K 2 |
| | A 8 7 5 | | | | A 9 6 4 | |

In (10) the defender's only chance of a trick is to cover the queen. In (11), also, failure to cover will cost a trick; if the jack is allowed to run to West's queen the declarer will lead low from dummy on the next round and make the rest of the tricks.

So far we have considered situations where an honour is led from the exposed hand. When declarer leads from his own hand a different rule applies:

(*c*) *When the declarer leads an honour from his own hand, cover if dummy has two honours but duck if dummy has only one.*

Here is a common example of each of these two situations, with South on lead:

| (12) | A J 8 4 3 | | (13) | | A 7 5 2 | |
|---|---|---|---|---|---|---|
| Q 6 2 | | K 9 5 | | K 8 4 | | Q 9 3 |
| | 10 7 | | | | J 10 6 | |

In (12) West covers the ten because there are two honours in dummy. In (13) he ducks the jack (or ten) because there is only one honour in dummy.

Of course, with a stronger holding, a defender may cover regardless. (Occasionally you may have the K–J–10, or K–10–x, when declarer tries to slip through an unsupported queen.)

It has to be admitted that by covering an honour a defender will sometimes save the declarer a guess. Observe these combinations:

| (14) | A 10 7 5 | | (15) | | A J 8 5 | |
|---|---|---|---|---|---|---|
| Q 6 | | 8 4 3 | | Q 7 4 | | 3 2 |
| | K J 9 2 | | | | K 10 9 6 | |

South leads the jack in (14), the ten in (15), to trap West into a

315

cover. If this is the trump suit, West may be able to judge that declarer's holding is strong and that it would be pointless to cover. In the case of a plain suit there may be no sure answer.

It should be noted in conclusion that it tends to be right for a player with two honours to cover a card from the nine upwards in situations like this:

| (16) | A Q 6 4 | (17) | A 9 5 2 |
|------|---------|------|---------|
| K J 5 | 8 3 2 | K Q 8 6 | 4 3 |
| | 10 9 7 | | J 10 7 |

West must not allow South to slip through the nine in (16) or the ten in (17).

We have dwelt at some length on the subject of covering honours, because it constantly recurs. We move now to the wider tactical measures involved in defending against a notrump contract.

## Preserving the Entry of the Key Defender

The defenders, like the declarer, generally set out to establish long cards in their best suit. Therefore it is fundamental that they, like the declarer, should endeavour to ensure entry to the hand that contains those cards. In so doing they may have recourse to one of two tactical strokes: the first, and most common, is that old stand-by, the ducking play to maintain communications within the suit they are trying to establish; the second involves the management of entry cards in other suits.

*Ducking*. When the defenders' long suit is in the hand of the third player, it may be right for him to duck the opening lead. Suppose that East has overcalled in spades and the distribution of the suit is:

| | 6 5 4 | |
|------|---------|------|
| 9 2 | | A K 10 7 3 |
| | Q J 8 | |

West leads the nine against South's notrump contract. Placing South with Q–J–x at least, East ducks the first round. Then if West wins the first defensive trick he will have a second card to play and East will be able to run four tricks.

This type of ducking play is still more common when the opener has led from a long suit and partner has returned the suit. This is a typical situation:

```
                        ♠ J 8
                        ♡ Q 10 8 4
                        ◇ A 9 4
                        ♣ K Q 6 3
    ♠ K 10 7 6 3                            ♠ A 5 2
    ♡ K 7                                   ♡ J 6 3 2
    ◇ J 6 3                                 ◇ Q 8
    ♣ 5 4 2                                 ♣ J 10 8 7
                        ♠ Q 9 4
                        ♡ A 9 5
                        ◇ K 10 7 5 2
                        ♣ A 9
```

| South | West | North | East |
|-------|------|-------|------|
| 1◇    | Pass | 1♡    | Pass |
| 1NT   | Pass | 3NT   | Pass |
| Pass  |      |       |      |

West leads ♣6, Dummy's ♣8 is played and East wins with ♠A. It is normally right to return partner's suit, and certainly East should do so here. He returns ♠5 and South plays ♠9. Now it is essential for West to duck, as he has no sure entry card outside the spade suit. Declarer cannot establish the diamonds without losing one trick, and as soon as they come in the defenders cash three more spade tricks, defeating the contract.

If West makes the mistake of playing ♠K and clearing the suit, South will follow the simple expedient of leading a low diamond and finessing the nine. East will win with ◇Q and return a heart, but now the declarer can see his way to nine tricks (four diamonds, three clubs and one in each of the majors) and will hop up with ♡A.

*Management of entry cards.* When the defender who holds a long suit has no entry card in the suit itself, it may be necessary to conserve his entry card in another suit. This may require a high level of awareness on the part of his partner. Here is a standard situation:

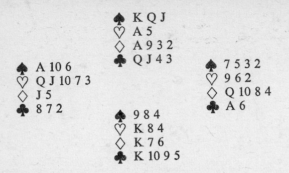

```
                    ♠ K Q J
                    ♡ A 5
                    ◇ A 9 3 2
                    ♣ Q J 4 3
     ♠ A 10 6                      ♠ 7 5 3 2
     ♡ Q J 10 7 3                  ♡ 9 6 2
     ◇ J 5                         ◇ Q 10 8 4
     ♣ 8 7 2                       ♣ A 6
                    ♠ 9 8 4
                    ♡ K 8 4
                    ◇ K 7 6
                    ♣ K 10 9 5
```

South is in 3NT and West leads ♡Q. To make his contract, declarer must force out two aces and hope the defenders cannot cash three heart tricks. The defenders, for their part, must follow the principle of conserving West's entry for the long hearts.

Declarer will probably duck the first heart and, on winning the second one, lead a low club from dummy. If he is allowed to win the trick, and forms the opinion that East has the ace, he will shift to spades and continue this suit until West releases the ace. Then he will lose, at most, two spades, one heart and one club. To prevent this, East should rise with ♣A when the first club is led, protecting his partner's entry. The heart return then spells defeat for South.

The next example presents the same problem in a more difficult guise:

```
                    ♠ K 10 7 4
                    ♡ J 7
                    ◇ 9 5
                    ♣ A K 9 5 3
     ♠ J 5 2                       ♠ Q 8 6 3
     ♡ 10 9 5 3 2                  ♡ A 6 4
     ◇ A 3                         ◇ K 8 2
     ♣ 10 8 6                      ♣ Q 7 4
                    ♠ A 9
                    ♡ K Q 8
                    ◇ Q J 10 7 6 4
                    ♣ J 2
```

| South | West | North | East |
|-------|------|-------|------|
| 1◇ | Pass | 2♣ | Pass |
| 2◇ | Pass | 2♠ | Pass |
| 2NT | Pass | 3NT | All Pass |

318

West leads ♡3 to East's ♡A. As it would suit him to be in dummy at trick two, South unblocks with ♡Q, wins the heart return with dummy's ♡J, and leads ◇5 from the table.

There is some subtlety in the declarer's play. He is doing his best to attack the entry of the danger hand, West. If East plays low on the first round of diamonds, this plan succeeds. It is not easy for East, and might in some circumstances be wrong, but his best hope is to go up with ◇K, playing his partner for A–x. Then the hearts are cleared and South cannot get near to nine tricks without letting West into the lead to make two more hearts. The principle is the same as before: a defender must aim to protect the entries in the hand of a partner who is trying to establish a suit.

## Nullifying the Declarer's Long Suits

The first preoccupation of the defenders in notrumps is to establish their long suits, the second to prevent the declarer from establishing and running his own long suits. The standard weapon is the hold-up. The mechanics of this are no different from ducking, but the purpose is different. A defender ducks with a winner to conserve his own entry, but he holds up to destroy the entry in declarer's (or dummy's) long suit. In the following examples we assume that dummy has no outside entry:

(1)         K Q 10 8 3      (2)         Q 10 9 5 3
      9 4          A 7 5     K 7 2          A 8 4
         J 6 2                    J 6

Figure (1) is a standard position. However the declarer tackles this suit, East holds up the ace on the first round and notes his partner's nine, the beginning of an echo. Declarer being marked with three cards in the suit, East holds up again on the next round and the long cards are useless to declarer unless dummy has an independent entry.

In (2) suppose that dummy has one, and only one, outside entry. Provided both defenders hold up on the first round, the long cards are still shut out, as dummy's side entry will be needed to clear the suit.

Another effective form of hold-up occurs here:

(3)             A Q J 8 3
         9 6 2                 K 7 5
             10 4

319

Declarer leads the ten and plays low in dummy. East holds up and now declarer needs an outside entry to bring the suit in.

A different method of shutting out the long suit in an entry-less hand occurs when second hand plays a high card to prevent declarer from taking a combination finesse. We saw some examples in Chapter 20.

(4)         A J 10 4      (5)        A J 9 5 2
    K 7 6          Q 9 5     Q 10 8         K 6 3
        8 3 2                7 4

In each case South leads low towards the dummy. Assume West plays low. In the first example declarer finesses the ten and can make three tricks whether East ducks or not. In the second example declarer finesses the nine, after which the best East can do is to duck, holding declarer to two tricks. In each case the defenders do better if West goes in with his high card on the first round.

## When to Shift to Another Suit

It is generally sound play to return partner's suit when defending against a notrump contract, but this applies only as long as there is a chance, by playing this suit, to beat the contract. When a defender can see that the possibilities of the first suit are limited, or exhausted, it may be time to look elsewhere. No rule can be formulated that will cover this phase of the defence, but a defender will meet the test if he continually asks himself where he expects his side's tricks to come from. This deal will show the type of thinking required:

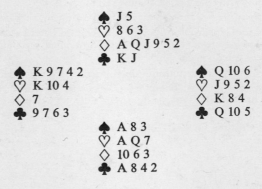

```
              ♠ J 5
              ♡ 8 6 3
              ◇ A Q J 9 5 2
              ♣ K J
   ♠ K 9 7 4 2              ♠ Q 10 6
   ♡ K 10 4                 ♡ J 9 5 2
   ◇ 7                      ◇ K 8 4
   ♣ 9 7 6 3                ♣ Q 10 5
              ♠ A 8 3
              ♡ A Q 7
              ◇ 10 6 3
              ♣ A 8 4 2
```

320

South is in 3NT and West leads ♣4, on which declarer plays dummy's ♣J. East covers with ♣Q and South holds off. When East continues with ♣10 South, although he fears a shift to hearts, dare not release ♣A, as he can see the suit is breaking 5–3. Accordingly he holds up, hoping that East will injudiciously play a third spade. However, East should realize that a spade continuation would be futile, as it is unlikely that West can have an entry in the form of ♡A or ♣A. (With a really good partner, East can be certain of that, for if West had had an entry he would have overtaken ♣10 and cleared the suit himself!)

East therefore should look for tricks in hearts. He must lead ♡9—not a low heart, which would allow South to ensure the contract by ducking. Now, whether South finesses ♡Q or goes in with ♡A, he is bound to go down at least one trick.

As well as asking himself where his side's tricks are to come from, a defender should consider the source of the declarer's tricks. That line of enquiry suggests a quite startling shift by West in this deal:

```
              ♠ K 4
              ♡ 10 7 4 3
              ◇ A Q 10 8 5 2
              ♣ 7
♠ A J 9                        ♠ 8 7 5 3
♡ K 9 2                        ♡ A J 8 5
◇ 4                            ◇ J 7 6
♣ J 10 9 8 3 2                 ♣ Q 6
              ♠ Q 10 6 2
              ♡ Q 6
              ◇ K 9 3
              ♣ A K 5 4
```

| South | West | North | East |
|-------|------|-------|------|
| 1♣    | Pass | 1◇    | Pass |
| 1NT   | Pass | 3◇    | Pass |
| 3♣    | Pass | 3NT   | Pass |
| Pass  | Pass |       |      |

West leads ♣J and East overtakes with ♣Q to avoid blocking the suit. South wins with ♣A and, with eight tricks already in sight, seeks to establish a ninth by leading a low spade at trick two. It may seem normal for West, holding A–J–x in front of the king, to play low, thus ensuring two tricks, but here there are special considerations. West should begin to wonder why South is playing

321

for tricks in spades when there is a good six-card diamond suit on the table. West should conclude that South holds $\diamond$K, for otherwise he would be developing that suit first.

Declarer probably has six diamond tricks, therefore, and no doubt his clubs are headed by the A–K. (If he had only the ace, he would have held it up.) That makes eight tricks and ♠K would be nine. West should therefore see the urgency of going up with ♠A and looking for the setting tricks in hearts. At this stage, technique will help. Allowing for the declarer to hold Q–x, West must prepare an unblock by leading the nine! East goes up with the ace and returns a low heart to the king; then he has the J–8 over dummy's 10–x.

Superhuman defence, you may think; but it is not so; the long diamond suit in dummy is a flashing light which should put the defender immediately on the alert.

# CHAPTER 24

---

# Defending Against Trump Contracts

*Active and passive defence – Preventing ruffs by the declarer –
Tricks from the trump suit – Gaining control*

THERE is more to think about when playing against a trump
contract than against a notrump contract. The trump element
means that declarer has more ways to play the hand, and the defenders in consequence must employ more ways of countering.
At notrumps the defenders try to establish long cards. At a
trump contract this strategy is useful on only a small number of
hands; most of the time the declarer will have enough trumps to
prevent the opposition from ever cashing an established suit. At a
trump contract the defence tends to fall into one of two patterns.
The defenders either try to grab tricks where they can in an effort
to beat the contract before declarer can fulfil his plans, or they follow
the opposite policy of sitting back and seeking merely to do nothing
that might give away a trick. As we have seen, the process of
choosing which policy to follow begins with the opening lead. But
the defenders must be ever ready to switch their tactics as fresh
information becomes available through a sight of dummy, defensive
signals and declarer's method of playing the hand.
This last consideration is often the first tangible indication of
what the defenders should do. Is the declarer trying to score ruffs
in dummy? Then probably it will be right to lead trumps. Has he a
long suit in dummy which he will want to establish? Then it may be
possible to attack the entry cards in dummy, perhaps by forcing the
dummy to ruff. Does it look as though the declarer is not too well
endowed with trumps? Then it may be possible to weaken him by
forcing him to ruff in his own hand. Is the declarer going after the
trump suit in single-minded fashion? Then you may assume that
he can see his way to using a side suit, and you should look for
rapid tricks. When these possibilities are kept in mind, then—
sooner, rather than later—a line of defence will suggest itself that
can be pursued with reasonable confidence.

We conclude this preamble with two injunctions that can be followed through thick and thin. First, always assume that the contract can be defeated somehow or other: thus, if the contract cannot be beaten unless your partner has a certain card, or the declarer has a certain hand pattern, you should arrange your plays on that assumption. Secondly, always try to count the declarer's winners. You will easily see the value of this precept in the next item on our agenda, the choice between active and passive defence.

## Active and Passive Defence

Defenders often find at the end of the play that they could have defeated a contract if they had performed a particular feat of arms, which may have looked risky. If they had counted the declarer's tricks they might have found that the danger was more apparent than real.

<pre>
                    ♠ K 8 7 3
                    ♡ Q 8 5
                    ◇ A Q 7 3
                    ♣ 6 2
     ♠ J 6                         ♠ 5
     ♡ A 7 4 2                     ♡ K J 10 6
     ◇ 8 6 4                       ◇ K 10 9 2
     ♣ Q 9 5 3                     ♣ A 8 7 4
                    ♠ A Q 10 9 4 2
                    ♡ 9 3
                    ◇ J 5
                    ♣ K J 10
</pre>

South is in 4♠ and West leads ♣3 to East's ♣A. As no other return is attractive, East plays back a club, choosing his fourth best in approved fashion.

Declarer wins with ♣K and draws two trumps with ♠A–Q, East discarding a club. Declarer then leads ◇5 and finesses ◇Q in dummy. This is quite a crafty effort, for East, not realizing that South has ◇J, may think it safe to adopt a passive defence by returning ◇10 or a club. In either case, South will then make his contract by discarding a heart on ◇A.

It is easy to imagine the post-mortem:

East: " I couldn't lead away from my ♡K–J–10, partner."

West: " I think you ought to have tried it."

South (smugly): " I had only eleven points, partner."

Let us examine East's plea that he " couldn't lead away from
♡K–J–10 ". The first task, in all such situations, is to count declarer's
known winners. East could be sure that South held six trumps; he
had taken one trick with ♣K, and ◇A was plainly in view. Not
quite so obvious, perhaps, was that South was sure to have a third
club, which he could ruff in dummy for his ninth trick. How does
East know this? Because West has led ♣3, presumably his fourth
best, and ♣2 was in dummy; so West is marked with a four-card
suit. It follows that if South has ♡A, nothing will beat 4♠. As
the object is to beat the contract rather than save possible overtricks,
East certainly should have shifted to a heart.

Here is a case where a count of declarer's winners will indicate a
passive defence:

```
                    ♠ J 7 3
                    ♡ J 8 5
                    ◇ 10 7 6
                    ♣ K Q J 9
 ♠ A 8 5                           ♠ 6 4
 ♡ A K 6 3                         ♡ Q 10 7 4 2
 ◇ Q 9 5 2                         ◇ K 8 4
 ♣ A 10                            ♣ 8 6 4
                    ♠ K Q 10 9 2
                    ♡ 9
                    ◇ A J 3
                    ♣ 7 5 3 2
```

| West | North | East | South |
|------|-------|------|-------|
| 1NT  | Pass  | 2♡   | 2♠    |
| 3♡   | 3♠    | Pass | Pass  |
| Pass |       |      |       |

West begins with two rounds of hearts. South ruffs and plays
trumps, West holding up on the first round and capturing the
second.

West may think first of playing a third heart, forcing South to
ruff again and reducing him to one trump. However, this clearly
will not inconvenience the declarer to any serious degree: South
will not play a third trump immediately but will force out ♣A
while he has a master trump in each hand.

West rejects the heart continuation, therefore, and in view of the
menace of the clubs in dummy hastens perhaps to attack diamonds,

assuring himself that the only chance is to find partner with the K–J.

But opening up the diamonds is a fatal move, for it gives the declarer two diamond tricks. Left to his own devices, he would have been forced to lose two tricks in the suit.

Again, a simple count of winners provides West with the right answer. South has three tricks coming in clubs and four in trumps. If he has ◇A–K he is home, and if he has only ◇A there is no need to attack the suit. There is no hand on which dummy's clubs could furnish a valuable discard and a passive defence is indicated. Accordingly, West should exit with a trump.

### Preventing Ruffs by the Declarer

We turn now to one of the commonest moves in defensive play— preventing the declarer from obtaining ruffs in dummy. This policy is often initiated with the opening lead, but the first opportunity is not always the last one.

It is easy for the defenders to play trumps when they see a menacing singleton in dummy. It is more difficult to find the right defence when the threat of a ruff is not so clear and to lead trumps may cost a trump trick. This hand is typical of many:

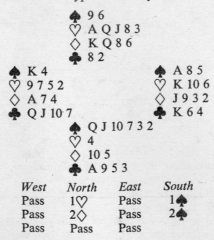

```
              ♠ 9 6
              ♡ A Q J 8 3
              ◇ K Q 8 6
              ♣ 8 2
♠ K 4                        ♠ A 8 5
♡ 9 7 5 2                    ♡ K 10 6
◇ A 7 4                      ◇ J 9 3 2
♣ Q J 10 7                   ♣ K 6 4
              ♠ Q J 10 7 3 2
              ♡ 4
              ◇ 10 5
              ♣ A 9 5 3
```

| West | North | East | South |
|------|-------|------|-------|
| Pass | 1♡ | Pass | 1♠ |
| Pass | 2◇ | Pass | 2♠ |
| Pass | Pass | Pass | |

West leads ♣Q and South, hoping for a continuation, holds off. If West fails to lead a trump at this point, South will make a lot of tricks. Suppose that West plays a heart at trick two: South wins, plays a club to the ace, and ruffs a club. He returns to hand with a heart ruff and trumps the fourth club with ♠9. The defenders make only ♠A–K, a club and ◇A.

This outcome is avoided if West asks himself what he needs to find in partner's hand to beat the contract. It is hard to see a satisfactory result unless East has the ace of trumps, and therefore West must place him with it. Accordingly, West switches to ♠K and continues with a spade to ♠A. East then reverts to ♣K. If South, in an attempt to make the contract, finesses ♡Q he will finish two down, losing two spades, three clubs and one trick in each red suit.

When a trump lead may cost a trick, there may be ways of ensuring that the trick will come back. Imagine that you hold the East cards on the following deal:

```
                    ♠ A 10 7 5 3
                    ♡ Q 5
                    ◇ 9
                    ♣ K 8 7 4 3
    ♠ J 4                            ♠ Q 9 6 2
    ♡ 6 4                            ♡ K J 9
    ◇ K J 7 5 3                      ◇ Q 10 8
    ♣ J 10 9 5                       ♣ A 6 2
                    ♠ K 8
                    ♡ A 10 8 7 3 2
                    ◇ A 6 4 2
                    ♣ Q
```

| South | West | North | East |
|-------|------|-------|------|
| 1♡ | Pass | 1♠ | Pass |
| 2♡ | Pass | 3♡ | Pass |
| 4♡ | Pass | Pass | Pass |

In view of the bidding a trump is a possible lead, but as West has a good sequence in clubs we will suppose that he prefers this. It would often be right for East, holding A–x–x over dummy's king, to let the jack run, but on this occasion East does not want to let South win with the queen and set about ruffing diamonds. East goes up with ♣A, therefore, and returns—♡K!

Study the effect of this card. South may win, cash ◇A, and ruff a diamond; he can take one discard on ♣K, but he must lose two trump tricks to the J–9 and has no parking-place for the fourth diamond.

The reader will observe that a low heart from East, which declarer will run to the queen, is not so efficacious. One diamond is ruffed as before and one diamond is lost, but declarer still has ♡A and loses only one heart trick. Finally, if East does not return a trump at all, South ruffs two diamonds and loses only one club and two trumps. The point of this defence, which turns up in many guises, is that when the declarer is forced to ruff with a high trump he may be obliged to give the trick back in another way.

### Tricks from the Trump Suit

The defenders have numerous ways of gaining tricks in the trump suit itself. One obvious way is ruffing. There are two essentials in this field: diagnosis and communication. The leader's partner often has a communication problem when a plain suit is distributed in this way:

K 10 6 5

8 led                                A 9 4 3

In a case like this, diagnosis will usually not be difficult. When West leads the eight and dummy plays low, East will probably be able to tell from the general situation whether his partner has simply made a passive lead or whether he is trying for a ruff. Communication is more of a problem; assuming that he has no other quick entry, East has to decide whether to play his partner for a singleton or for a doubleton, in which case it may be essential to duck. Doubletons are more common than singletons, and when there is no clear indication it is usually wise to assume that partner has a doubleton.

One of the neatest moves in defence, which depends on accurate diagnosis, is to prepare a ruff for partner by leading a low card away from a holding such as A–x–x–x. The plan is to find partner with a doubleton in the suit and a trump entry, so that when he wins his trump trick he can return his second card to the ace and obtain a ruff.

Sometimes the defenders achieve ruffs that way, but at other times they have ruffs more or less thrust upon them as the declarer is obliged to tackle a side suit before drawing trumps. Here accurate signalling is the key.

```
                    ♠ A Q 8
                    ♡ A 7 6
                    ◇ J 4 3
                    ♣ K J 10 3
  ♠ 6 5 2                          ♠ 9 4
  ♡ Q J 10 3 2                     ♡ K 8 5
  ◇ K 9 7                          ◇ Q 8 5 2
  ♣ 8 5                            ♣ A 9 6 2
                    ♠ K J 10 7 3
                    ♡ 9 4
                    ◇ A 10 6
                    ♣ Q 7 4
```

| West | North | East | South |
|------|-------|------|-------|
| Pass | 1♣ | Pass | 1♠ |
| Pass | 2♠ | Pass | 3♠ |
| Pass | 4♠ | Pass | Pass |
| Pass | | | |

West leads ♡Q and continues the suit when declarer ducks. South has a problem, for if he draws three rounds of trumps there may be no entry to dummy for the fourth club. In an effort to prise out ♣A declarer may try entering his hand with a trump at trick three and leading a low club to the king. In this case West must start an echo with the eight and East, reading the position, must duck. Now if declarer continues clubs a ruff will defeat him, and if he draws trumps East can hold up ♣A.

There are a number of tactical situations around the trump suit where mistakes are often made. We give brief examples, with suitable injunctions.

(1) *Don't force partner to ruff one of declarer's losers.*

It is usually unwise to lead a suit for partner to ruff when declarer will be able to discard a loser. If partner ruffs with a valueless trump, nothing is gained; if he ruffs with what would have been a winning trump, your side loses a trick in the exchange. This is a typical case:

```
              ♠ K 8 4
              ♡ Q 7 6 3
              ◇ K 8 5 2
              ♣ A 4
♠ Q 10 6                      ♠ 5
♡ 9 2                         ♡ A K J 8 5
◇ Q 10                        ◇ J 9 7 4
♣ K J 9 7 5 2                 ♣ Q 10 3
              ♠ A J 9 7 3 2
              ♡ 10 4
              ◇ A 6 3
              ♣ 8 6
```

| West | North | East | South |
|------|-------|------|-------|
| Pass | Pass | 1♡ | 1♠ |
| 2♣ | 2◇ | 3♣ | Pass |
| Pass | 3♠ | Pass | Pass |
| Pass | | | |

West leads ♡9 and it seems that North–South are due to lose five tricks. However, such contracts are often made because of a misjudgment by the defence. East wins with ♡J and cashes ♡K. He should lead a club now, but suppose he plays a low heart, hoping for an overruff. South discards one of his losers, either a diamond or a club, and makes his contract whether West ruffs or not.

It is no better for East to play ♡A at trick three. South will ruff low and West will overruff. Later, a loser will go on ♡Q.

(2) *Be wary of ruffing a loser when declarer (or dummy) leads a suit.*

Defenders are often impelled to nip in with a low trump that otherwise, they feel, would waste its sweetness on the desert air. Yet it often helps declarer if you ruff in front of him or dummy when in effect you will be ruffing one of his losers. This is an example:

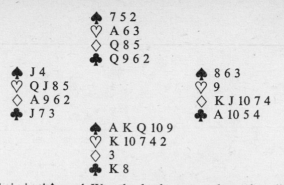

          ♠ 7 5 2
          ♡ A 6 3
          ♢ Q 8 5
          ♣ Q 9 6 2

♠ J 4                    ♠ 8 6 3
♡ Q J 8 5          ♡ 9
♢ A 9 6 2         ♢ K J 10 7 4
♣ J 7 3           ♣ A 10 5 4

          ♠ A K Q 10 9
          ♡ K 10 7 4 2
          ♢ 3
          ♣ K 8

South is in 4♠ and West leads the ace and another diamond. South ruffs and, after taking only one round of trumps, addresses himself to the heart suit. This is good play, for if the hearts are 3–2 it will do no harm to play off the A–K, and if they are 4–1 it may help to discover this while there are still trumps in dummy.

At trick four, therefore, South leads a heart to the ace and returns a heart. If East inserts a trump at this point he gives away the contract. The declarer will ruff a diamond return, draw the defenders' remaining trumps, and play king and another heart, ruffing in dummy. Then his hand will be all winners apart from ♣A.

Note the difference if East discards on the second round of hearts. South may huff and puff as much as he likes, but he cannot avoid losing two heart tricks (or one heart and an overruff) in addition to the minor-suit aces.

(3) *Decline to overruff whenever there may be a chance to set up an extra trump trick for your side.*

Extra tricks can accrue in almost magical fashion when " promotion " occurs. The simplest illustration of this principle appears in the following diagram:

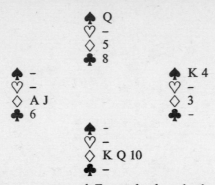

Diamonds are trumps and East, who has the lead, plays ♠K, which South ruffs with ◇Q. Now it is apparent that if West overruffs he makes no more tricks, but if he discards he makes both ◇A and ◇J.

Here are two more trump combinations where it is not difficult to see that the overruff would be a mistake:

| (1) | *Dummy* | | (2) | *Dummy* | |
|---|---|---|---|---|---|
| *West* | | *East* | *West* | | *East* |
| K 10 5 | | | Q 9 5 3 | | |
| | *Declarer* | | | *Declarer* | |
| | A Q J 7 3 | | | A K J 10 6 4 | |

In (1) South ruffs a plain suit with the queen. West makes sure of two tricks by declining to overruff. In (2) South ruffs with the jack; again West ensures two tricks by refusing to overruff.

In these cases not much imagination is required to visualize that refusing to overruff will gain a trick. In the next example the cards held by partner and dummy come into the calculation:

| (3) | 9 5 | | (4) | Q 5 | |
|---|---|---|---|---|---|
| K 7 3 | | J 8 | 9 | | K 8 4 2 |
| | A Q 10 6 4 2 | | | A J 10 7 6 3 | |

In (3) South ruffs with the ten. So long as West does not overruff he comes to two tricks when his partner turns up with the J–8. (4) shows a case where a defender refuses to overruff the short trump hand. When South ruffs a side suit with dummy's queen, East, so long as he keeps his powder dry, ends up with two tricks.

Extra trump tricks can be promoted by reason of length also. A defender with, say, K–4–3–2 of trumps should not overruff a declarer who has A–Q–J–10, for by simply discarding he will eventually come to a long trump as well as the king.

The principle is quite clear, then: when you have a potential winner in any case, don't overruff. Sometimes this defence can be played twice on the same hand, with shattering effect on the declarer.

(4) *Watch for the chance to " uppercut " with a useless trump.*

We turn now to another form of trump promotion, known as the " uppercut ". Every player is familiar with this type of position:

```
(5)                        6 4 3
        10 7 5                           J 8
                        A K Q 9 2
```

This is the trump suit and East has a chance to ruff a plain suit. He must not fail to put in the jack, promoting his partner's ten. The same principle has many variations:

```
(6)         6 5 3        (7)         8 5 2
    Q 10          K 8          J 7 4          A 3
          A J 9 7 4 2               K Q 10 9 6
```

In (6) a ruff with the king promotes two tricks for West's Q–10, and in (7) a ruff with the ace brings partner's jack into the reckoning.

Three mistakes are possible in this area. First, the defender may fail to ruff because partner has played a winner. Secondly, he may fail to contribute his *highest* trump. Thirdly, when a defender is playing to promote a trump trick he may fail to cash all available side winners to prevent the declarer from neutralizing the uppercut by discarding a loser. This defence sometimes calls for keen co-operation between the partners:

```
                      ♠ K 7
                      ♡ K 8 5
                      ◇ Q J 7 4
                      ♣ J 10 3 2
    ♠ 10 8 6                        ♠ 9 5 4 3
    ♡ Q 9                           ♡ J 4
    ◇ 10 8 3                        ◇ A 9 6 5 2
    ♣ A K 9 6 4                     ♣ 8 5
                      ♠ A Q J 2
                      ♡ A 10 7 6 3 2
                      ◇ K
                      ♣ Q 7
```

| South | West | North | East |
|-------|------|-------|------|
| 1♡ | Pass | 2◇ | Pass |
| 2♠ | Pass | 2NT | Pass |
| 3♡ | Pass | 4♡ | Pass |
| Pass | Pass | | |

West leads ♣K and East plays ♣8, beginning an echo. West places the declarer with six hearts from the bidding but sees a chance of a trump trick if his partner holds ♣J and can ruff the third round of clubs. However, to continue with ♣A and another club will not avail if South knows his business, for on the third club he will simply discard his diamond loser. It is essential to cash the diamond winner before attempting the uppercut, and West must therefore lead a diamond at trick two. East wins and plays back his second club; a third club is ruffed with ♡J and South is forced to bow the knee.

We conclude this section with a nice example of an uppercut with small trumps:

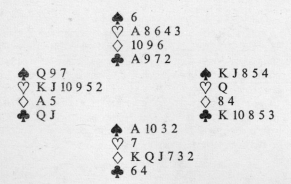

South is in 5◇ and West leads ♣Q. Relieved to have escaped a trump lead, which would have put him out of business, South goes up with ♣A and sets about a crossruff. He leads a spade to the ace, ruffs a spade, then plays ace and another heart. From the way the play has gone, East can be sure that South is going to ruff this trick, but he must not fail to put in ◇8. South overruffs, trumps another spade, and leads a third heart from the table. Now the lowly four of trumps from East is a shrewd blow. South is forced to overruff with the seven, leaving this position:

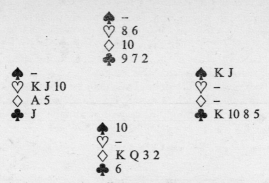

When the last spade is ruffed, West discards a heart and dummy ruffs. Say that declarer returns to hand with a heart ruff and leads ◇K. West wins and leads a club to his partner's ♣K. Now either black card promotes West's ◇5.

## Gaining Control

As we noted in an earlier chapter when studying the declarer's play, almost the worst that can happen to a declarer is to become shortened in trumps. As it is difficult for the defenders to bring this about when dummy can take the strain by ruffing the dangerous suit, it is a common manœuvre to hold up a trump winner until dummy is exhausted. This is the usual setting:

```
              ♠ K 10 3
              ♡ 10 6 5
              ◇ J 8 4
              ♣ Q 9 6 2
♠ 7                          ♠ A 9 6 4
♡ A K 8 4                    ♡ Q J 7 2
◇ 10 7 5                     ◇ 9 2
♣ K 10 8 5 4                 ♣ J 7 3
              ♠ Q J 8 5 2
              ♡ 9 3
              ◇ A K Q 6 3
              ♣ A
```

South is in 4♠ and West begins with three rounds of hearts. South is obliged to ruff the third round and at trick four he leads a spade to ♠K. If East takes this trick he has no effective defence, because dummy can take care of the next round of hearts. East must hold up ♠A, therefore, and when declarer leads another trump East holds up again. Now declarer has lost control. If he turns to diamonds, East will score a ruff, and if he plays a third spade a heart return will be fatal, as East has the " tempo ".

Many effective moves are open to the defence when the declarer is seeking to establish a side suit and his trump control is uneasy. One is to allow him a ruff-and-discard at a moment when he would prefer to use his trumps for establishing a long suit.

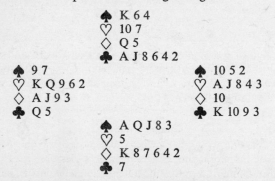

```
              ♠ K 6 4
              ♡ 10 7
              ◇ Q 5
              ♣ A J 8 6 4 2
♠ 9 7                        ♠ 10 5 2
♡ K Q 9 6 2                  ♡ A J 8 4 3
◇ A J 9 3                    ◇ 10
♣ Q 5                        ♣ K 10 9 3
              ♠ A Q J 8 3
              ♡ 5
              ◇ K 8 7 6 4 2
              ♣ 7
```

South is in 4♠ and West leads ♡K. South ruffs the second heart, leads a diamond to the queen, and returns a diamond, on which East discards a heart. It may seem natural for West to lead a trump at this point, but that would not embarrass the declarer. He would win in hand, ruff a third diamond with ♠K, draw trumps, and concede a diamond, losing just two diamonds and a heart.

Let us look again at the position when West was in with ◇9:

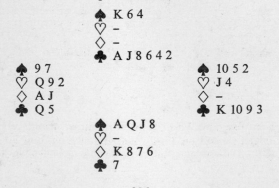

```
              ♠ K 6 4
              ♡ –
              ◇ –
              ♣ A J 8 6 4 2
♠ 9 7                        ♠ 10 5 2
♡ Q 9 2                      ♡ J 4
◇ A J                        ◇ –
♣ Q 5                        ♣ K 10 9 3
              ♠ A Q J 8
              ♡ –
              ◇ K 8 7 6
              ♣ 7
```

336

Now a ruff-and-discard, usually the villain of the piece, is the killing defence. West knows that declarer needs to ruff diamonds in dummy, so it must be sound policy to let him ruff a heart instead, which will not help him to get his diamonds going. Declarer can ruff the heart in either hand. Suppose, first, that he ruffs in dummy. He may come to hand by ruffing a club, trump a diamond with ♠K, and draw trumps; but there is still a top diamond against him and he has no more trumps.

South does better to ruff the heart in his own hand. Then he leads a diamond and ruffs low in dummy. Now we encounter another principle of the defence against a two-suiter; East, whose three trumps have become an embarrassment to the declarer, must not part with one by overruffing. South is now at the end of his tether. He may try the ♣A and a club ruff, followed by another diamond; if he ruffs low again, East will overruff and play a club. However it goes, the declarer will be one trick short.

So two principles arise from this example: when there is a fight for control, play cards which force the declarer to ruff; and when you have a chance to ruff or overruff, consider carefully whether it may be better to retain your trump length.

# CHAPTER 25

# Signalling

*Signalling when partner leads – Signalling when the declarer leads – The trump echo – Suit-preference signals – Special signalling systems*

A FAMOUS lady international player is accustomed to address her partners in these terms: " Don't give me any signals. After a few tricks I will know what you've got better than you know yourself." In the case of that particular player the remark is not so exaggerated as it may sound, but nevertheless bridge is a partnership game and most defenders do best when they systematically exchange information needed to conduct a successful defence.

Many signals have become so well established as to seem part of the natural order of things, rather than the conventions that they are. We gave an example of this sort in an earlier chapter:

10 8 7

K 5 4 2             Q J 9

A 6 3

West leads the two, dummy plays the seven and East the nine. When declarer wins with the ace, West knows that his partner has the Q–J, for otherwise declarer would have won with a lower card. If East had played the queen instead of the nine West would not have been able to draw the same conclusion.

A signal is a play made by a defender who is *following* to a trick. The method of signalling differs according to whether he is following to his partner's lead or to the declarer's (or dummy's).

## Signalling when Partner Leads

The general principle is that the third-hand player, when following to a trick (as opposed to trying to win it), should play a high card to encourage a continuation, a low one to discourage. This applies whether or not his partner has led a high card.

(1)    A 4 3   (2)    10 7 5
  5 led   K 8 7 2  Q led    K 4 3 2

In (1) West leads the five and dummy plays the ace. If East wants his partner to continue when he regains the lead, he drops the eight. Note that when playing an encouraging card from two or more cards in sequence, the highest is played. If East were to play the seven in this example, and West read it as encouraging, he would be entitled to assume that declarer had the eight.

In (2) the most encouraging card East can play when the queen is led is the four. West may or may not be able to read the signal at this time, but if East later has a chance to complete a "high-low" by discarding the two, that will be confirmation that he wants a continuation.

It is important to note that encouraging cards are played, not just to indicate possession of a high card, but to invite a continuation.

At a suit contract, especially, a defender may play low to advise a switch, even though he is strong in the suit led. This is a typical situation:

     ♠ K 7
     ♡ J 10 4
     ◇ 7 6 2
     ♣ A Q J 8 5

♠ 9 4         ♠ 10 6 2
♡ A K 8 7 5 2     ♡ Q 9 3
◇ A J 5       ◇ K 9 4 3
♣ 10 7       ♣ 9 3 2

     ♠ A Q J 8 5 3
     ♡ 6
     ◇ Q 10 8
     ♣ K 6 4

With both sides vulnerable the bidding goes:

| South | West | North | East |
|-------|------|-------|------|
| 1♠ | 2♡ | 3♣ | Pass |
| 3♠ | Pass | 4♠ | Pass |
| Pass | Pass | | |

When West leads ♡K against 4♠ East knows that a heart continuation is safe so far as this suit alone is concerned. But in another sense a second heart would be disastrous: South would ruff and run off eleven tricks in the black suits.

339

As it is very likely that South will be ruffing the next lead of hearts, East should play his lowest heart to request a shift. West must then steel himself to lead a low diamond away from the A–J–x, enabling the defence to take three diamond tricks.

Now suppose that East had held ♣K instead of ♢K. It would then be right to encourage the safe continuation in hearts. East would expect to gain the lead in clubs and would then lead a diamond, hoping to find his partner with A–Q.

In the same way, it can be right to play a mildly encouraging card from, say, three small, to prevent partner from taking a potentially costly shift.

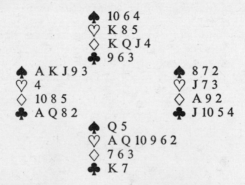

West is the dealer at love all and the bidding goes:

| West | North | East | South |
|------|-------|------|-------|
| 1♠ | Pass | 1NT | 2♡ |
| 2♣ | 3♡ | Pass | Pass |
| Pass | | | |

West leads ♠K and it may seem natural for East, holding 8–7–2, to play the two. The danger of playing that card is that West may look for a switch and may try a club, presenting South with his contract. As he knows that he will come in with ♢A, East should play ♠7, encouraging partner to continue. In due course the defenders take ♢A and two club tricks.

At notrumps the third-hand player may have sufficient length to justify an encouraging signal even when no high card is held. With four or more cards of partner's suit an encouraging signal is more or less automatic.

This brings us to situations where a player may signal to show length without reference to encouragement or discouragement. At a suit contract it is usually more helpful for the third-hand player to indicate the length of his holding in the suit than to indicate strength. This is mainly because of the ruffing factor: it is very important to know whether, and when, partner will be able to ruff the suit led. At a suit contract, therefore, it is usual to play high-low, known as an " echo ", whenever an even number of cards is held. Most players stick to this principle in a situation like the following:

                    Q 7 5 3
        A K 10 9 6 2           8 4
                    J

West, who has bid this suit twice, leads the king against a suit contract. It is plain to East that a continuation of the ace will be ruffed by the declarer. Nevertheless, it is his duty to play the eight. Partner may not be sure who has the outstanding card, but he will allow for the possibility that East has begun an echo. If East were to play the four, the lowest outstanding card, West would be entitled to assume that this was a singleton.

It is normally right to echo with J–x, but not with Q–x. The play of the queen under partner's lead of the king conventionally denotes that the player holds (if not the queen alone) the Q–J. It may well suit the leader to lead small on the next round.

Here are some situations where the advantage of suit-length signals is apparent:

                    Q 7 5
        A K J 9 2             8 6 4 3
                    10

When West leads the king of a side suit it is unhelpful for East to play the three, simply because he has no useful card. Partner can see that! East must play the six, so that West can read him for an even number. True, West still has to judge whether the six is from two cards or four, but that sort of decision is usually quite easy in the light of the bidding and the rest of the dummy. The next diagram shows the other side of the coin:

                    Q 7 5
        A K 10 9 2            8 6 3
                    J 4

West leads the king, East plays the three, and South attempts a small bluff, dropping the jack. West is not deceived. Should it suit the defence to cash a second trick, he will know that the ace will stand up.

This is a common position:

J 8 4 2

A K 10 3            Q 7 5

9 6

When the king is led, East plays the five. He does not want to encourage West to continue with ace and another, setting up dummy's jack.

## Signalling when the Declarer Leads

The defenders do not signal to express encouragement when the declarer (or dummy) leads a suit. They either signal to show suit length, or they do not signal at all. Thus, while a defender who plays high-low to the declarer's lead is indicating an even number of cards (unless deliberately false-carding), a defender who does not play high-low may either have an odd number of cards or may have decided not to signal with an even number. It is usually not difficult to sort matters out at the table; whatever his holding, a defender sitting under dummy's A–10–x–x is clearly not going to signal (except as a bluff) when declarer cashes the king from K–Q–x.

A common situation where signals are obligatory occurs when declarer has a long suit in dummy and the problem for the defenders is how long to hold off:

(1)      K Q 10 8 5      (2)      K Q J 9

7 2          A 9 3      7 6 2          A 8 4 3

J 6 4                 10 5

In (1) when South leads the four West must not fail to indicate an even number of cards by putting in the seven. This tells East that he must hold up his ace until the third round. In (2) South leads the five and West plays the two. East knows at once that he can take his ace on the second round.

When the declarer is playing off a long suit, either at notrumps or at a suit contract, each defender should signal his length in the suit as a matter of course. Such signals will not assist declarer and will help the defenders to count the hand. In particular, they will enable the player who discards first to know how many discards he has got to find. Suit-length signals may also be made in the suit discarded, and it is sometimes possible to convey a wealth of information with a single card. For example, defending against a notrump contract, no suit having been bid, a player sitting over dummy's K–Q–8–4 has to discard from J–10–9–7–x; the discard of the jack provides a clue to the length as well as to the high cards, as the discard would probably not have been safe with only four cards.

## *Summary*

It may be helpful to sum up the general tendencies—they are no more—of signalling in different situations:

(1) When partner leads, a high-low signal encourages him to continue. The signal may be based on either strength or length.

(2) In a suit contract, when no cards of value are held, it is normal to issue a suit-length signal; that is, to play high-low with an even number of cards, low-high with an odd number.

(3) When declarer leads, either at a suit or notrumps, a suit-length signal should be issued when this will be more helpful to partner than to declarer.

All signals, it must be stressed, should be made with discretion. The defender must consider whether the information is already available to partner, or whether there is any value in giving it. This applies also to signals showing length in the trump suit, which is our next subject.

## The Trump Echo

When signalling in the trump suit the standard practice is to echo with three or more cards. This is because the middle card of three can more readily be spared than the top card from 10–x or 9–x. Sometimes the echo directs partner's attention to the possibility of a ruff, as in this type of hand:

                        ♠ A 7 5
                        ♡ A 9 6 3
                        ◇ K Q 10 6
                        ♣ 8 5

        ♠ 9 4 2                         ♠ K J
        ♡ 7 4                           ♡ K J 8 2
        ◇ 8 7 5                         ◇ 9 3
        ♣ A 10 7 4 2                    ♣ Q J 9 6 3

                        ♠ Q 10 8 6 3
                        ♡ Q 10 5
                        ◇ A J 4 2
                        ♣ K

| South | West | North | East |
|-------|------|-------|------|
| Pass | Pass | 1◇ | Pass |
| 1♠ | Pass | 2♠ | Pass |
| 4♠ | Pass | Pass | Pass |

West leads ♡7, dummy plays low and East wins with the king. Declarer wins the heart return with the ten and plays a spade to the ace. The next spade is won by East's king. On these two tricks West echoes with the four and two of trumps, informing East that he has a third trump and can ruff a heart. Without this indication East might well decide to lead ♣Q, in which case declarer would make the contract.

The trump echo is also employed when a defender with three trumps is ruffing a trick before trumps have actually been led. With 10–4–2, for example, the defender ruffs with the four. If his partner can win the first round of trumps, the appearance of the two will indicate that another ruff can be obtained.

The trump echo is no less valuable in assisting partner to count the trumps held by declarer. This may be important information for a defender who has to plan his discards. The echo may also be useful in a negative sense, for when a player fails to echo with three trumps, his partner can infer that there is no possibility of a ruff.

In an earlier work, *Bridge for Tournament Players*, we suggested that a player with four negligible trumps, such as 7–5–4–2, should indicate the length by beginning with the two and then echoing with the five and four, while a player with a sure trick, such as J–10–4–2, should discard upwards. The suggestion made no great impact, so we try again!

Finally, there is a way of signalling in one suit to guide partner's play in another suit. This is the famous and many-sided suit-preference signal.

## Suit-preference Signals

H. W. B. Joseph, Professor of Philosophy at Oxford during the student days of one of the present authors, was wont to say that only two inventions during his long lifetime had brought unmixed benefit —electric light and the bicycle. A personal view is that if he had lived a few years longer he would surely have included the suit-preference signal. The great virtue of this device is that it operates in an area where the cards played would not otherwise have any significance.

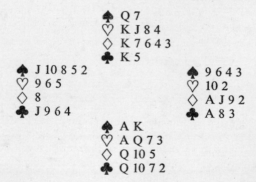

The contract is 4♥ and West leads his singleton diamond. East wins with the ace and returns the two for his partner to ruff. Now, according to the suit-preference convention, the two of diamonds is a highly significant card. By choosing his lowest diamond East indicates that his entry card is in the lower ranking of the alternative suits, a club rather than a spade in this instance. So, although South may have bid clubs, West returns a club and obtains a ruff to defeat a contract that might otherwise have slipped through. Had East held ♠A instead of ♣A he would, of course, have returned a high diamond, the jack or nine, to request a spade lead from his partner.

Though that is the pristine use of the suit-preference signal, many others have been developed. Indeed, almost any card that normally has no significance may be interpreted as a suit-preference signal. These are examples:

(1) *In leading*.

South is in 4♠ after West has overcalled in hearts and has been supported by his partner. West holds:

♠ 8 5
♡ K J 9 7 5 3
◇ 6 3
♣ K J 10

West intends to lead a heart and should choose the three. It will be obvious to East that this is West's lowest card, not a normal fourth best. It says to partner, " If you win this trick, return a club, the lowest suit." If West's diamond and club holdings were reversed he might lead ♡9, which again could hardly be fourth best and so would point to a return in diamonds

Quite often, especially against a slam contract, a player has to make a daring lead. Suppose that North–South have bid confidently to 6♡ and West holds:

♠ –
♡ 7 6 4 3
◇ 9 6 5 2
♣ A K 9 6 3

Assuming that the opponents' bidding commands enough respect to preclude the possibility of winning two tricks in clubs, the best chance may well be to open ♣9, hoping that partner will be able to win with the queen and return a spade. Of course, this kind of shot is not for the faint-hearted, but it may be added that it has been known to succeed even when partner does not hold the required card. In this example, dummy may hold Q–x–x–x and declarer, holding a singleton, may fail to go in with the queen.

(2) *When following suit to partner's lead*.

Suppose that South is in 5◇, East–West having bid up to 4♡. West leads ♡A and East sees:

♠ K 10 6 3
♡ 8
◇ K J 5 2
♣ K J 5 3

    ♠ A Q 9
    ♡ K Q 9 7 5 2
    ◇ 10 4
    ♣ 8 2

East wants a spade switch and the clearest card to play is ♡Q. If East had wanted a club switch he would have dropped ♡2, and had he been satisfied with a heart continuation he would have played a middle heart, such as the seven.

It is necessary to add a word of caution about suit-preference signals at the first trick. They apply only when the leader's partner holds considerable length, so that he is known to be able to choose between three messages, as in the example above. In other circumstances a high card has the normal sense of inviting a continuation and a low card suggests a switch.

(3) *When following suit to a later lead.*

Suppose that East–West are defending against a spade contract and this is the layout of the diamond suit:

     10 6 4

A K J 9 3        7 5 2

     Q 8

West leads the king and East plays the two, a normal suit-length signal. Knowing it is safe to continue diamonds, West lays down the ace. At this trick East has a free shot, in the sense that he can play either the five or the seven. (The seven will not mislead because with 7–2 he would have begun an echo on the opening lead.) In a good partnership, therefore, the seven would be a suit-preference signal, indicating values in the higher ranking of the alternative suits. The five would not necessarily be a request for a club—for East has to play something—but there would be a negative inference that he was not especially anxious for a heart.

Suit-preference signals were originally devised for use at trump contracts, where there are only two plain suits to consider (other than the suit being played). They can often be extended to notrump contracts because there will generally be a suit which, it is apparent, the defenders cannot want to attack. Here is a common situation where a player who has made the opening lead against a notrump contract has the opportunity to signal on a later round.

7 4

Q 10 8 5 3                K J 6

A 9 2

West leads the five against 3NT and South holds up his ace until the third round. Assuming that one suit can be excluded, West, on the third round, can either play the queen as a suit-preference signal for the higher remaining suit, or his lowest remaining card for the lowest suit, or his middle card to express no preference.

(4) *When following to a suit led by the declarer.*
There are many opportunities to indicate preference when declarer plays a suit. Suppose that the declarer at a trump contract is cashing out a side suit distributed as follows:

A K Q 10 3

8 4               J 9 7 5 2

6

East knows that his partner is going to ruff the third round. By adopting a sequence such as 2–9–5 he can suggest that West return the higher-ranking suit.

More simply, when declarer plays off a long suit, a defender who holds, say, 7–4–2, has the opportunity to convey a message by discarding in an unorthodox way. Defenders should not wait for great wealth in a side suit before being willing to convey this type of message; the signal may mean only that one of the alternative suits can be guarded more effectively than the others. Many a slam contract can be saved by minute indications of that sort, for the partner will then know which suit he must take care of.

It is even possible for the signal to propose a lead in the trump suit itself. The best defence would otherwise be almost impossible to find on this deal:

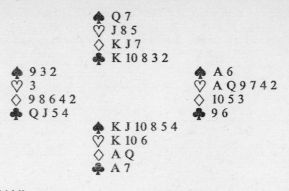

```
              ♠ Q 7
              ♡ J 8 5
              ◇ K J 7
              ♣ K 10 8 3 2
♠ 9 3 2                        ♠ A 6
♡ 3                            ♡ A Q 9 7 4 2
◇ 9 8 6 4 2                    ◇ 10 5 3
♣ Q J 5 4                      ♣ 9 6
              ♠ K J 10 8 5 4
              ♡ K 10 6
              ◇ A Q
              ♣ A 7
```

The bidding goes:

| South | West | North | East |
|-------|------|-------|------|
| 1♠ | Pass | 2♣ | 2♡ |
| 3♠ | Pass | 4♣ | Pass |
| Pass | Pass | | |

West leads ♡3, East wins with the ace and returns the *seven*. South puts in the ten and West ruffs with ♠3.

West may well ask himself, couldn't partner have been a bit more helpful? He must hold a lower card than the seven and he must have been able to afford a higher card. Which suit *does* he want?

At this stage it may occur to West that perhaps his partner doesn't want either a diamond or a club, but a trump. And note that a trump to the ace, followed by another heart ruff, is the only effective defence. If West makes a neutral lead, such as a diamond, South, knowing that another ruff is threatened, will hastily play three rounds of diamonds to dispose of the treacherous heart.

## Special Signalling Systems

It should be mentioned that some tournament players use specialized signalling systems. For example, both at a trump contract and at notrumps, many concentrate always on showing length, irrespective of their high-card holding; they will play high-low with an even number, the bottom card from an odd number. Another method is always to play the second card from the top to encourage. In the Roman system the basic method is to play an odd card to encourage, an even card to discourage. These are known as " odd-even " signals. Finally, some players use what are known as " reverse " signals, otherwise known as upside-down signals. A relatively high card, such as the 8 from 8–6–2, is discouraging, while a low card promises strength.

# PART VI

---

*Advanced Play*

# CHAPTER 26

## Placing the Cards

*Making a necessary assumption – Second-degree assumption – Assessing the probabilities – Discovery play – Inferences from the bidding – Inferences from the opening lead – Inferences from the play*

THE PURPOSE of this chapter is to show how much can be learned about the unseen cards as the play progresses. If the reader proposed to single out any part of the book for special study, we would like it to be this, for an insight into the types of reasoning described will stand a player in better stead than any amount of learning by rote.

Most bridge hands would be quite easy to play or defend if all fifty-two cards were visible. It follows that in any difficult situation it must be worthwhile to attempt to reconstruct the unseen hands. This process is accomplished mainly by the use of inference and assumption; the player reasons that because his opponent has done this or that, he is likely to have such and such, and so on.

There are many facets to inference and assumption. It may help the reader if we summarize in advance how we propose to break up the subject.

(1) *Making a necessary assumption.* If there is any chance that the contract can be made, declarer must assume that the necessary distribution exists. If there is any chance that it can be defeated, the defenders must assume that the cards lie in the required way.

(2) *Second-degree assumption.* Declarer will sometimes make an assumption, favourable or unfavourable, concerning one suit, and as a consequence he will be led to a further assumption concerning another suit.

(3) *Assessing the probabilities.* When there is a choice between two lines of play, such as finessing for a queen or playing for the drop, declarer must understand the mathematical probabilities, and how they vary as the play progresses.

353

(4) *Discovery play.* Sometimes the declarer can improve his estimate of the lie of one suit by testing the lie of another suit.

(5) *Inferences from the bidding.* When the opponents have entered the bidding the normal mathematical expectations concerning the unseen cards are changed. The question then is not " What is the normal percentage play with this combination? " but " In view of the bidding, what is the most likely distribution of the opponents' cards? "

(6) *Inferences from the opening lead.* Many opportunities for deduction arise from the simple fact that the player on lead has made what appears to him the best lead. Against a slam, he probably has not underled an ace, and so on.

(7) *Inferences from the play.* Here the player tries to deduce why his opponent has done what he has done.

Maybe it sounds more like solving a crime novel than playing a bridge hand, and indeed the type of thinking required is precisely that on which the reputation of the fictional sleuth, Sherlock Holmes, was founded. But the reader should not doubt his own ability to draw the appropriate inferences if he addresses his mind correctly.

## Making a Necessary Assumption

Whenever a contract seems difficult but not entirely beyond the bounds of possibility, the declarer should ask himself what distribution he needs to give him a chance of making the contract. He must then assume that the cards do lie as required, and play accordingly. This, of course, is a familiar process which every player employs to some extent. Where the expert scores over the average player is that he pursues it more rigorously. There are three stages in his planning which you may like to think of as the three A's: Appreciation, Assumption, Action. This first example shows a position that arises quite often:

♠ K 5
♡ A K 7
♢ K J 10 6 3
♣ Q 5 2

♠ 7 4
♡ 10 8 6 4 3
♢ A 5 2
♣ A J 6

354

South plays in 4♡ and West leads ♠Q, which is covered by ♠K. East wins with ♠A, holds the next trick with ♠9, and shifts to ♣10.

Prospects are not too good. Two spade tricks have already been lost, there is almost certainly a loser in trumps, and in all probability ♣K is on the wrong side.

Most players would go up with ♣A, draw two rounds of trumps, then return to ♢A and finesse ♢J. Yet the fact is that even if West held ♢Q–x or ♢Q–x–x, either he or his partner would be able to ruff the fourth round of the suit and cash ♣K; and if West held ♢Q–x–x–x South would have no entry for a second finesse.

How would an expert view the situation when East returned ♣10 at trick three? First, he would agree that ♣K was surely wrong. It is not that East would be incapable of a deceptive lead away from the king, but if he had held ♣K–10 he would have made sure that his partner won the second spade, so as to return a club through dummy's ♣Q.

It is correct, therefore, to refuse the club finesse. A good player would realize next that a diamond finesse would not win the contract even if the same player held three diamonds and three trumps. The only chance is to find the diamonds 4–1 and the long trump in the same hand as the long diamond.

Thus the right sequence, after ♣A, is a low diamond to the ten, accepting the risk of a singleton queen. Then come ♡A–K, a diamond to the ace, and another diamond finesse. This play succeeds when West began with ♢Q–x–x–x and three trumps. It is not a very likely distribution, of course, but there is nothing else to play for.

On the next hand the declarer's play is a little more spectacular:

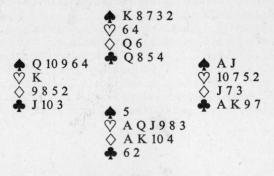

East opens a weak notrump after two passes and the full sequence is:

| West | North | East | South |
|------|-------|------|-------|
| Pass | Pass | 1NT | Double |
| 2♠ | Double | Pass | 3♡ |
| Pass | 4♡ | Pass | Pass |
| Pass | | | |

West leads ♣J and the defenders begin with three rounds of clubs, South ruffing. How should he continue?

The " easy " line is to enter dummy with ◇Q and finesse ♡Q. But this will win the contract only when East has K–x precisely and West x–x–x or 10–x–x.

A little reflection will show that this distribution is not at all likely. In view of the bidding, West must hold five spades, which marks East with a doubleton. Can East hold a doubleton in hearts as well? That is most unlikely, as players who are 5–4 or 6–3 in the minors do not normally open 1NT.

Having reached this point in his *appreciation*, South makes the only possible *assumption* that will save him from losing a trump trick: as there is only one entry to dummy for a trump finesse, he must place West with the singleton ♡K and East with 10–x–x–x. Then the appropriate *action* is to play off ♡A, dropping ♡K, enter dummy with ◇Q, and finesse ♡9. Later, ◇J comes down in three rounds and South makes his contract.

The principle is clear. When the going is hard the declarer must make certain favourable assumptions. Similarly, when prospects are good he may make an unfavourable assumption, as a precautionary measure. When making a favourable assumption, declarer should not ask for the moon. He should make the least favourable assumption that will enable him to make the contract, modest wishes being more readily granted than big ones.

The same attitude of mind is required of the defenders, who all the time should be asking themselves such questions as, " Can we beat it unless partner has ♣K? Is there any chance unless he has a trump trick? Or four trumps? Or a particular singleton? " In short, defenders must assume a lie of the cards that will enable them to beat the contract, again asking for as little as possible. In the next hand East is constrained to assume that his partner holds a particular jack!

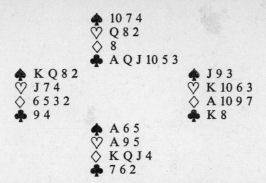

South opens 1◇ and lands in 3NT, against which West leads ♠2. Declarer wins the third round and leads a club to the queen and king.

It is obvious to East that declarer has ♡A and ◇K–Q as part of his opening bid. West may hold ◇J or ♡J, but that is all. If West holds ◇J and declarer has ♡A–J there will be no way of defeating the contract, for South can make nine tricks by establishing a diamond trick and then taking the heart finesse.

If West has ♡J, however, the contract can be defeated by the sparkling return of ♡K. Declarer cannot afford to duck, for if he does, ◇A is the defenders' fifth trick. After taking ♡K with ♡A, declarer cannot make a single diamond trick, for East can win the first round of the suit and return a heart.

When a player has made an assumption about one suit he should go on to consider the consequences of that assumption. Some interesting conclusions may follow. That is the subject of the next section.

## Second-degree Assumption

No man is an island, as the poet said, and in the same way all the elements of a bridge hand are interrelated. Thus one line of thought may lead to another. Observe the declarer's reasoning on the following deal:

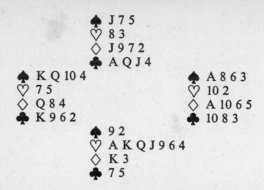

♠ J 7 5
♡ 8 3
◇ J 9 7 2
♣ A Q J 4

♠ K Q 10 4        ♠ A 8 6 3
♡ 7 5            ♡ 10 2
◇ Q 8 4          ◇ A 10 6 5
♣ K 9 6 2        ♣ 10 8 3

♠ 9 2
♡ A K Q J 9 6 4
◇ K 3
♣ 7 5

South opens 4♡ in fourth position. West leads ♠K, which holds the trick, and continues with a low spade to his partner's ace. East gauges that there are no more tricks to be taken in spades and he therefore gives declarer a guess by underleading ◇A.

In the absence of any special indications, it is usual for a declarer to play for two aces to be divided. However, there is another factor to be considered. South is not going to make this contract unless the club finesse succeeds, so he must assume that it *will* succeed. Now he must consider what follows from that.

West is already marked with ♠K–Q and is assumed to hold ♣K. As he passed initially, he is unlikely to hold ◇A as well, and the correct play is to go up with the king.

On the last hand the declarer made a favourable assumption— that the ♣K would be well placed. On hands where he makes an unfavourable assumption, this too may determine his play in another suit.

♠ A Q 9
♡ 6 3
◇ K 7 4 2
♣ A 8 6 4

♠ K J 10 8 6 4
♡ K J 7 2
◇ 8 5
♣ 7

South plays in 4♠ after East has dealt and passed. ♣Q is led and after winning in dummy South makes the obvious play of a heart, on which East plays low. Should he finesse the jack or go up with the king? Having studied what he needs elsewhere in the hand, he finds that he can afford to make an unfavourable assumption about the diamond situation. Whatever South does in hearts, the contract is unlikely to fail unless East has ◇A; declarer should therefore assume that East *has* ◇A. East is already marked with ♣K (remember that West has led ♣Q) and so West is more likely to hold ♡A. Accordingly, declarer finesses ♡J.

By now the reasoning on hands of this next type will be familiar.

```
                    ♠ K 10
                    ♡ Q J 9 4
                    ◇ A Q J
                    ♣ A K 8 6
      ♠ J 9 7 4 2              ♠ A Q 8 5
      ♡ K                      ♡ 6 5
      ◇ 10 7 4                 ◇ K 8 3
      ♣ Q 5 3 2                ♣ J 10 9 7
                    ♠ 6 3
                    ♡ A 10 8 7 3 2
                    ◇ 9 6 5 2
                    ♣ 4
```

South plays in 4♡ after East has dealt and passed. West leads ♠4. After taking ♠A–Q East switches to ♣J. Dummy wins and leads ♡Q, on which East plays low. This is the critical moment. The mathematical odds favour a finesse with ten cards, but South takes into account that he has yet to tackle the diamonds and should reflect on these lines:

" If ◇K is with West I am going to make the contract whatever I do in trumps. So I will credit East with ◇K. That gives him ♠A–Q, ◇K and ♣J–10. With the guarded ♡K as well he would have opened the bidding. It looks as though I can afford to play ♡A. If it turns out that the finesse would have won, then ◇K must be well placed."

So South goes up with ♡A and makes his contract. After the play he can listen attentively when his opponents explain to him the odds against dropping singleton kings.

### Assessing the Probabilities

Bridge is first and foremost a game of deduction. Mathematical knowledge as such is of limited value and, one must say, easy to misapply. We venture to suggest that many readers may be somewhat surprised by the analysis of the following hand:

♠ J 6 4
♡ 7 5
◇ K J 6 4 2
♣ 8 5 3

♠ A K 9 7 5 3
♡ A Q J
◇ A 5
♣ A 9

South is in 6♠ and ♣Q is led. South wins and draws the opponents' trumps, which are 2–2. He then plays off ◇A–K. All follow, but ◇Q does not appear. Declarer is in dummy and can use the entry either to take a heart finesse or to ruff a diamond, hoping to set up two diamond winners for heart discards.

A player imbued with the notion that a 3–3 break was only a 36 per cent chance might take the heart finesse now; but this would be wrong, for it has become better than an even chance that the diamonds will break!

The reason why the odds have changed is not very difficult to follow. We examined in Chapter 17 the simple probabilities relating to suit distribution. The reader may remember, for example, that with six cards outstanding the initial expectancy is that they will be divided 4–2 forty-eight times in 100, 3–3 thirty-six times, 5–1 fifteen times, 6–0 once.

The important word there is " initial ", for these expectancies change constantly as the play progresses. To give an extreme example, suppose the declarer starts out with seven hearts in the two hands and that after ten tricks neither opponent has played a heart. Then they *must* be divided 3–3. From that it is easy to see that the chances of a 3–3 break have increased sharply as play progressed with no hearts appearing.

From this example we extract a general proposition: *as the play advances, the more even divisions become more likely*. This may happen while a single suit is being developed. Observe these two combinations:

(1)    A K 6 4 3
          5 2

(2)    K J 6 5 3
          A 4

The chance of a 3–3 break in (1) is initially 36 per cent. If the A–K are played off, and all follow, the chance of the two remaining cards breaking 1–1 is better than 42 per cent. (This is because the 5–1 and 6–0 distributions have been eliminated.) In practical play the odds will be nearer to 50 per cent. The further the play has advanced the more likely an even break, as we have noted, and other considerations (relating to the natural order of play by the defenders) tend in the same direction.

In (2) the change is still more dramatic. If all follow to the A–K, and the queen has not appeared, the mathematical chance of a 3–3 break is 52 per cent (again it will be more if the play of the whole hand is well advanced). The difference arises because the queen is a *significant* card; that is to say, one which an opponent would not play unless he had to. Thus not only are the 5–1 and 6–0 divisions eliminated, but also those where the queen was doubleton. Of the *a priori* possibilities, all that remain " live " are Q–x–x–x opposite x–x and Q–x–x opposite x–x–x. The second of these, Q–x–x opposite x–x–x, is mathematically more likely.

This sort of calculation is often relevant in notrumps when the declarer has the choice between a finesse for his ninth trick or playing for a 3–3 break with a holding such as A–K–6 opposite 8–7–4–2. If he plays off the A–K and all follow, leaving the queen and jack outstanding, the chance that they will be divided is about as good as the finesse.

The point here is that the queen and jack may not be strictly " significant " cards, but they may seem so to the defender who holds one of them. Players holding such a combination as Q–x–x are usually averse to dropping the queen on the first or second round!

Before leaving this subject, we will look at two very familiar combinations:

(3)     A K 7 6 4 2          (4)     A 10 8 6 4 2
         9 5 3                                K J 9

In (3) the initial expectancy of a 2–2 division is 40 per cent. If all follow to the first round it rises to 45 per cent (at least), as the 4–0 possibility is excluded.

In (4) both opponents follow to the king, but the queen does not appear. Strange as it may seem, the chance of a 2–2 break is now 52 per cent; not only the 4–0 break, but the 3–1 break where the queen was single, has been excluded. This, perhaps, will not surprise the reader who knows that it is better to play for the drop of the queen with nine cards. Yet, since a 3–1 break is initially more likely than 2–2, this example is a confirmation of the theory we have been discussing.

Even more important in the assessment of probabilities is the well-known Principle of Restricted Choice—first so called by Terence Reese in *The Expert Game*. Compare these two holdings:

(5)    A 10 7 3              (6)    A 9 7 3
        K Q 2                      K Q 2

In (5) the declarer plays off the K–Q and continues with the two. Both opponents have followed with low cards and now South has to decide whether to finesse or not. The odds slightly favour playing for the drop of the jack.

In (6) declarer plays off the K–Q and East drops an honour, the jack or ten, on the second round. The odds are now about 2 to 1 in favour of finessing the nine!

The reason for the difference is that in (5) East, holding J–x–x, was *restricted* in his play to the earlier rounds: he had to retain the jack. In (6) East, supposing he held J–10–x, was not restricted on the second round: he could have dropped either the jack or ten. *The fact that he has played one card affords a presumption that he does not hold the other.*

As this proposition meets a good deal of resistance from people who hear it for the first time, it may be helpful to give an example from another sphere. Imagine that someone holds two billiard balls, which may be both red or may be one red and one white. You ask him to hand you a ball at random, and this ball turns out to be red. Now it is more likely that he began with two red balls. If he had held one red and one white, he might have given you a white one.

The principle has a bearing on the play of many very familiar combinations.

(7)    A 10 8 6 4           (8)    Q 9 7 6 4 2
        K 7 5 3                  A 5

In (7) the king drops the queen (or jack) from East. The odds now favour the finesse rather than the play for the drop, the point being that there are two singleton honours which East could have been dealt but only one combination of Q–J bare.

In (8) South's lead of the ace drops the ten or jack from East. On the next round it is right (barring special indications) to finesse the nine, playing East for K–J or K–10 rather than J–10. In short, *you assume the defender not to have had a choice rather than to have exercised a choice in a particular way.*

The principle can be applied to quite different problems. South plays in 6NT, no suit having been mentioned, and West leads a club from what turns out to be 7–5–3. Later in the play South has to decide whether in diamonds, say, West holds three low cards or three to an honour. It is perfectly logical to reflect along these lines: " If West had held the same cards in diamonds as in clubs he might have led a diamond. The fact that he chose a club affords a presumption that he has not the same holding in the two suits."

Every player has met this hazard at some time:

7 4

3 led               K played

Q 10 5

South plays in notrumps and West leads the three. East wins with the king (or ace) and returns the two. Big decision: should South put in the ten or the queen? The ten is right for this reason: if East had the A–K–x–x and intended to underlead on the second round, he might have won the first trick with either the ace (a well-known gambit) or the king; with A–J–x–x (or K–J–x–x) he would have had no choice. Assume, as always, that East did not have a choice.

In discussing the play of these various combinations we have assumed that declarer has little or nothing in the way of outside indications. Of course, if there is reason to place a particular opponent with considerable length in one suit it is natural to play his partner for the majority of cards in any other suit.

## Discovery Play

Some detectives in fiction solve their problems by brainpower alone. Thus Hercule Poirot just sits at home, exercising his little grey cells. Others, like Sherlock Holmes, go out on the job and seek out all the clues they can find. The successful bridge player belongs to the second school. His aim is to discover the lie of the cards as soon as possible, and this cannot always be done by relying on facts already to hand. Imagine the post-mortem as Doctor Watson shows his old friend this hand:

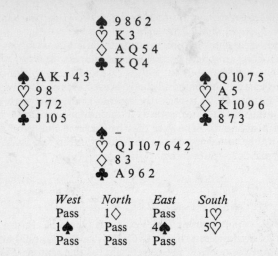

|  | ♠ 9 8 6 2 |  |  |
|---|---|---|---|
|  | ♡ K 3 |  |  |
|  | ◇ A Q 5 4 |  |  |
|  | ♣ K Q 4 |  |  |

| ♠ A K J 4 3 |  | ♠ Q 10 7 5 |
| ♡ 9 8 |  | ♡ A 5 |
| ◇ J 7 2 |  | ◇ K 10 9 6 |
| ♣ J 10 5 |  | ♣ 8 7 3 |

|  | ♠ – |  |  |
|---|---|---|---|
|  | ♡ Q J 10 7 6 4 2 |  |  |
|  | ◇ 8 3 |  |  |
|  | ♣ A 9 6 2 |  |  |

| West | North | East | South |
|------|-------|------|-------|
| Pass | 1◇ | Pass | 1♡ |
| 1♠ | Pass | 4♠ | 5♡ |
| Pass | Pass | Pass | |

" Confound it, Holmes," says the Doctor. " There's nothing I dislike more than a blind guess.

" On this deal the opponents pushed me to 5♡. I ruffed the spade opening, forced out the ace of trumps, and ruffed the spade return. After drawing the outstanding trumps I took the diamond finesse, which lost. Another spade came back and now I needed the balance.

" I cashed ♣K–Q and West dropped the jack on the second round. After anxious consideration I decided to finesse the nine next, playing West for ♣J–x, and thus I went down a trick. I don't hold it against you, Holmes, but I seem to remember you telling me this was the right play when a defender might have had a choice. Didn't work here, though. No use holding good cards if they always go badly, eh? "

" My dear Watson, it would be more accurate to say that it's no use holding good cards if you always play them badly, A simple form of discovery would have solved the case.

" After losing the diamond finesse and ruffing the spade return you should play a diamond to the ace, ruff a diamond, enter dummy with a club and ruff the last diamond.

" In this way you discover that West has three clubs! He has shown up with only three diamonds and two hearts, and cannot have more than five spades in view of East's bidding. Accordingly, you simply play out the top honours in clubs and claim the contract.

" In the same way, if West showed up with four diamonds you could be sure that he had only two clubs. Elementary, my dear Watson."

The principle of play is clear: when possible, *defer the play of a critical suit until you have discovered all you can about the lie of the cards.* Note that declarer is usually in a better position to test the lie of the suits in a trump contract than in notrumps, especially when he has a really strong trump suit, as in the last example.

An equally important form of discovery occurs when declarer is bent on identifying high cards, rather than suit patterns, in the opponents' hands. In this case the principle is first to *force out the high cards that do not affect the contract.* In the process, clues may be gained as to the remaining high cards that do affect the contract. For example:

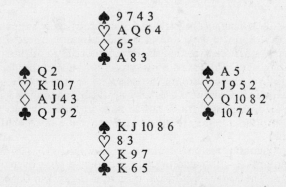

```
                  ♠ 9 7 4 3
                  ♡ A Q 6 4
                  ◇ 6 5
                  ♣ A 8 3
  ♠ Q 2                            ♠ A 5
  ♡ K 10 7                         ♡ J 9 5 2
  ◇ A J 4 3                        ◇ Q 10 8 2
  ♣ Q J 9 2                        ♣ 10 7 4
                  ♠ K J 10 8 6
                  ♡ 8 3
                  ◇ K 9 7
                  ♣ K 6 5
```

South opens with a semi-psychic 1♠ in third position, West passes, North raises to 3♠, and all pass. West leads ♣Q.

It may seem natural to tackle trumps first, but since South has a choice of plays in the trump suit he should plan to defer the guess. If ◇A is on the wrong side there is nothing to be done about it, so the first move should be to win with ♣A and lead a diamond to the king as a form of discovery. West wins and plays another club to the declarer's king. South finesses ♡Q, which holds, and leads ♠7 on which East plays low.

South reflects now that West has turned up with ♡K, ◇A, and ♣Q–J. Holding ♠A as well he would probably have entered the bidding. Holding a singleton spade he might have doubled the opening bid, so South goes up with ♠K and returns a spade, making the contract when the queen and ace fall together.

Discovery plays are rare in defence. The commonest example is seen in this deal:

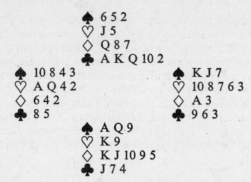

♠ 6 5 2
♡ J 5
◇ Q 8 7
♣ A K Q 10 2

♠ 10 8 4 3
♡ A Q 4 2
◇ 6 4 2
♣ 8 5

♠ K J 7
♡ 10 8 7 6 3
◇ A 3
♣ 9 6 3

♠ A Q 9
♡ K 9
◇ K J 10 9 5
♣ J 7 4

East is defending against 5◇ and West leads ♠3. Suppose East puts up ♠K, loses to ♠A, and then finds himself on lead with the ace of trumps. He can see that the defenders need to take two more tricks straight off, but he has no way of knowing whether to return a spade, playing his partner for the queen, or to shift to a heart.

The dilemma can be avoided very neatly by playing ♠J on the opening lead, trusting partner not to have underled an ace. If the jack loses to the queen East will know later that a heart shift is the only hope.

An analogous situation occurs when a defender has bid a suit consisting of A–Q–10–x and the player on his left has overcalled in notrumps. The opening lead from partner is the two or the equivalent, and the dummy goes down with one or two low cards. Now the opening lead may be from 9–x–x or J–x–x or from four cards. The queen will not clarify the position of the jack; the defender's best play is the ten, so that he will discover whether the declarer sits over him with K–x–x or K–J–x.

### Inferences from the Bidding

There are many inferences that every player draws from time to time. A player who has passed is unlikely to hold as many as 13 points or a strong distributional hand. As the play progresses it is often easy for the declarer to say to himself, " West has turned up with an ace and two kings, but he didn't open the bidding, so the remaining king must be on the other side." Easy, but often neglected. The important thing is never to misss the obvious—to form an unvarying habit of building up a picture of the opposing hands. Very often the inferences will be significant even though not conclusive. A defender who has passed and turns up with an ace, a king and a queen has room for another queen at least, but it is still sound reasoning to credit the other defender with the rest of the high cards.

Most players notice when an opponent turns up with more than his share of the honours, but general inferences about distribution are often overlooked. If the opponents have entered the bidding on minimum values declarer should expect bad breaks. If the opponents have not bid when it is apparent that they hold fair values, the reason will be that they both have balanced hands. This is especially true when opponents enter the bidding, find a fit, and then drop out below the three level. The inference here is that declarer's long suits are likely to break evenly; if either opponent had held a singleton or void he would have been more likely to push to the three level, which is usually the critical point in part-score deals.

This hand illustrates the other side of the coin:

    ♠ K Q 10 4
    ♡ A Q 9 7 2
    ◇ 10 4
    ♣ 10 7

    ♠ A J 8 6 5
    ♡ K 6 4
    ◇ Q 7
    ♣ A 8 4

South plays in 5♠ after the opponents, at equal vulnerability, have contested up to 5◇. The defenders take two rounds of diamonds, then switch to a club. The trumps are drawn in two rounds and declarer lays down ♡K. If West follows to the next heart South should put in dummy's nine.

This is because, if the opponents are competent bidders, it is most unlikely that the hearts will be 3–2. Playing in diamonds, East–West would lose at least two spades, one heart and one club, with ◇Q to find as well. They can hardly have five top losers, so the hearts must be 4–1, and South, needing five tricks from the suit, should play on that assumption.

367

## Inferences from the Opening Lead

Opening leads are most informative. We have noted in Chapter 22 the conclusions that can be drawn from the Rule of Eleven. Negative inferences are no less valuable. A defender leads the three of a suit against notrumps and the declarer, seeing the two in dummy, places him with a four-card suit. Very fine, but he should not stop there. Presumably the leader has no four-card suit headed by a sequence of honours, and presumably he has no longer suit. Here is a deal that brings into focus several of the points we have noted so far in this chapter:

```
                    ♠ J 9 8 7
                    ♡ 7 3
                    ◇ Q 7 2
                    ♣ A K 10 5
   ♠ K 6 3                          ♠ Q 10 4 2
   ♡ A 5                            ♡ 10 9 8 6 2
   ◇ 10 8 6 4                       ◇ A 3
   ♣ 8 7 6 2                        ♣ 9 3
                    ♠ A 5
                    ♡ K Q J 4
                    ◇ K J 9 5
                    ♣ Q J 4
```

| South | West | North | East |
|-------|------|-------|------|
| 1NT   | Pass | 2♣    | Pass |
| 2♡    | Pass | 3NT   | Pass |
| Pass  | Pass |       |      |

West leads ◇4 and East wins with ◇A. What should he return? Not very difficult when you see all the hands, but the question is, can East logically make the dangerous return of a low spade?

It should not be too hard for East to form a picture of the distribution. As ◇2 and ◇3 are in sight, West presumably has only a four-card suit, and this marks the declarer with four also. South bid hearts in response to Stayman, so he must hold four of them. If West had held five clubs he might have led one in preference to a diamond, so it looks as though South has three clubs. That leaves him with only two spades, and in that case a spade switch must be a sound notion.

There is much to be harvested from the reflection that the player on lead has made what appeared to him to be the *best* lead. We have already noted one example—that when a player has led from a four-card suit against notrumps it is reasonable to assume he has no better or longer holding, at any rate in an unbid suit. Other examples of the same kind of reasoning are:

Defending against notrumps, a player leads from a short suit. *Inference:* perhaps your side has bid his longest suit; watch out for that. Alternatively, he may be very weak and playing for his partner's hand.

Defending against a trump contract, a player leads from what turns out to be three small cards. *Inference:* he has no doubleton or singleton, which would have been a more dynamic opening. He is probably balanced.

Defending against a suit contract after a competitive sequence, a player does not lead the suit which his partner has bid. *Inference:* he has the ace and does not want to risk giving up a trick to the king.

Defending against a suit contract, a player leads from a dangerous holding such as K–J–x. *Inference:* he has made an attacking lead because he doesn't think he will beat the contract by sitting back. This means he is unlikely to hold a singleton trump or four trumps or length in a critical side suit.

A defender leads a trump. *Inference:* this may have been chosen for safety, but if either the declarer or the dummy has shown signs of holding a strong side suit there is a distinct probability that the suit is not going to break well. (A player with a balanced hand will not make a neutral lead if he thinks the declarer will have no problem in drawing trumps and establishing his side suit.)

### Inferences from the Play

The play to the first trick (and, indeed, to most subsequent tricks) always gives rise to certain inferences. Some are very obvious, some need a little thought. Compare these two situations:

| (1) | | Q 7 3 | | (2) | | Q 7 3 | |
|---|---|---|---|---|---|---|---|
| 5 led | | | 6 played | 5 led | | | 6 played |
| | | A 4 | | | | A J 10 9 | |

In (1) the five is led against a suit contract and dummy's queen holds the trick. No doubt at all that West holds the king.

In (2) the same lead is made and again the queen holds the trick. Who holds the king? If East is a good player it is not by any means certain. If he holds something like K–8–6–2 he will gauge that the lead is from a short suit and will not simplify the declarer's task by playing the king. So in this situation South must reserve judgment about the lie of the king.

It would be impossible to cover the whole range of inferences that can be drawn from the play to the first trick. The important thing is to appreciate that there are always currents below the surface.

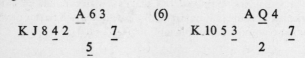

(3)    Q 10 4    (4)    9 6 2
8            J    Q        K
A 6 3           A 8 4

In (3) West leads the eight against either a notrump contract or a suit contract. As the lead might be from K–J–9–8 South puts in the ten from dummy, and East covers with the jack. Now the odds are that West has led " top of nothing ", and in that case it will probably be good play to let the jack hold. Admittedly, it is also just possible that West has led from K–9–8; but one must generally go along with the probabilities.

In (4) West leads the queen and East overtakes with the king. With K–x–x East would play the middle card to encourage. The king is surely from K–x.

In the remaining examples the critical inference is drawn by the opening leader.

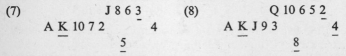

(5)      A 6 3    (6)     A Q 4
K J 8 4 2   7    K 10 5 3   7
      5           2

The cards played to the first trick are underlined. In (5) West leads the four against a trump contract and the ace is played from dummy. It is obvious that East holds the queen; West can bank on this well enough to underlead his king later.

In (6) West leads low and dummy's queen wins the trick. Again, West should assume that East has the jack, as with J–x or J–x–x declarer would let the lead run to his own hand.

(7)      J 8 6 3    (8)    Q 10 6 5 2
A K 10 7 2   4    A K J 9 3   4
      5           8

Figure 7 shows a common and important situation. West leads the king against a suit contract and the cards fall as shown. The missing cards are the queen and nine. With 9–4 East would begin an echo with the nine. So, East must hold the singleton four or Q–4 or Q–9–4. In any event, it is safe and correct for West to continue with a low card. The ace might crash the queen, establishing dummy's jack as a winner.

In (8) West leads the king and East plays the lowest outstanding card, the four. Assuming normal signalling methods, who has the missing seven? Holding the 7–4 East might not want to encourage his partner to follow with the ace, but it is still his duty to echo with a doubleton. Partner cannot always tell who holds the missing card, but this time he can. The seven must be held by South and it may well be good play for West to continue with a low card so that partner can ruff; this will prevent declarer from later leading up to the queen and establishing it as a trick.

(9)             J 4          (10)            J 7 5
    K 9 7 5 3       Q          Q 9 6 4 2       10
                A                          K

In (9) West leads his fourth best against a notrump contract and the jack is headed by the queen and ace. How should West play when next in the lead? With A–10–x South would assuredly have played low from dummy, so he must hold either A–10 alone or A–x or A–x–x. West's proper play is to lay down the king, trusting partner to unblock if he holds Q–10–x.

In (10) West's lead of the four runs to the ten and king. When West gains the lead it is safe to continue the suit, for with A–K–x South would have put in dummy's jack; probably he holds A–K alone.

Of course, one's estimate of the opposition often comes into it, as it does also in the next chapter. That is part of the challenge of any game. The great Botvinnik once said: " If Tal offers you a pawn, take it. If Petrosian offers you a pawn, decline it. If I offer you a pawn, think it over."

# CHAPTER 27

## Deceptive Plays

*Concealing information – Putting on the pressure – Plays to hide strength or weakness – Deception by the defenders – Deception around the trump suit*

STOLEN tricks are undoubtedly even sweeter than those which are won by force. The possibilities for misleading the opponents during the play of the hand at bridge have long engaged the attention of the keenest minds and a great number of attractive manoeuvres have emerged as a result. Some are in common use, while others may occur no more frequently than the visitation of a rare comet, but there are two considerations to be always borne in mind. One is that a certain smoothness or fluency will greatly improve the chances of success. The other is that the degree of artifice employed must not exceed the capacity of the opposition to absorb it. It is a waste of effort to be too subtle against opponents who do not notice what cards you play.

Deceptive plays may be employed equally by the declarer and by the defenders, although the declarer, with no partner to worry about (at least until the hand is over) has a somewhat freer hand. We begin with the cases where deception takes the form of simply withholding information, which sometimes is all the declarer can do.

### Concealing Information

It very often happens that the declarer, in winning a trick or in simply following suit, has a choice of cards to play and that the choice makes no difference in a logistical sense. In such a case one card may be less informative to the opposition than another. Here are two very common holdings:

(1)           8 5          (2)        8 5
   6 led         J played    6 led        J played
       A K 4               K Q 3

In (1), should South win with the king or the ace? There is no single answer: it depends on whether he intends to win the first trick or the second, and whether he is playing at notrumps or in a suit.

Suppose, first, that he is playing at notrumps and intends, for tactical reasons, to win the first trick. Now the king is less informative than the ace. From East's point of view the king might be from K–x–x or from A–K–x. On the other hand, if South plays the ace, East will place him with the king as well, because with A–x–x it would be normal to hold up. But if South elects to duck the first trick he should win the second with the ace, which may possibly leave East in doubt about the king.

At a suit contract South will surely win the first lead, and now the ace is less informative than the king. If South plays the king both defenders will know he has the A–K, since neither would underplay the ace at a trump call.

The situation illustrated in (2) is likely to occur only at notrumps. It is normal to play the king, as this will leave West uncertain about the queen. It is worth remarking, however, that if declarer expects East to gain the lead first, the queen is a better card as East may well conclude that South holds A–Q.

When following suit, also, one card may be better than another. A declarer who does not habitually play the right card in the following situations will make life easy for his opponents.

(3)                Q 6 3          (4)              Q 6 4
   A K 10 8 7      J 9 4              A K 10 8 7      5 2
         5 2                                      J 9 3

In each case South is playing a trump contract and West, who has bid the suit, leads the king. Suppose that in (3), when East drops the four, South would be happy for West to play off the ace, setting up dummy's queen. To encourage a continuation declarer should play the five, leaving West to wonder whether his partner has started a normal high-low with 4–2. (4) shows the other side of the picture. When East plays the five on the opening lead South's best card is the three, after which West has to reckon with the possibility that East has J–9–5.

There is a simple rule to follow in these positions: do what you would do if you were the *partner* of the leader. Thus, assuming that opponents are using normal signalling methods, declarer should play his lowest card when he does not want the suit continued. When a continuation would be welcome he should play a card just above the card played on his right.

There is an art in smoking out the opponents' high cards in situations like the following:

(5)    7 4 2           (6)    A Q 9 4
        K Q 8 3                 J 10 3

In (5) the declarer is playing notrumps and wants to test the suit but also does not want to run into two or three losers. He leads the two from dummy and East plays the five. Players tend to put on the king when they want to discover whether West has the ace, but a wily defender will place the declarer with K–Q and will hold off. After all, he will reason, declarer is likely to have better things to do than lead early towards an unsupported king. On the whole, the queen is the better card, as now West may fear to lose a tempo if South has Q–J–x. Similarly, in the common situation when declarer leads towards K–Q–10 in the closed hand, the queen is more likely than the king to establish where the ace lies.

In (6) the declarer is playing a side suit and wants to know before drawing trumps whether the finesse is going to win. If he leads the jack and it holds, he will not be very much wiser. East may be holding up because he can see that it cannot cost to do so, and it may be dangerous to attempt to settle the question by taking a second finesse. It is better to lead low to the queen originally, as East will not then hold up the king.

## Putting on the Pressure

There are many ploys whereby declarer can put the opponents under pressure and in that way increase the chances of a defensive error.

(1)    K J 5 4          (2)    K 8 6 3
         6 3                   Q 5

Many contracts depend on the finesse position shown in (1). Sometimes the declarer can use the type of discovery technique described in Chapter 26. At other times, and especially in a slam contract, there may be no scope for this. In such a case the best the declarer can do is lead the suit early on—at trick two if possible. This may put West under a good deal of strain. Declarer may have a singleton in this suit and a certain loser outside. There will be a temptation for West to play the ace if he holds it, so if West plays low without a tremor the declarer will have grounds for finessing the jack.

In (2) the declarer, hoping to establish two tricks, begins with a low card to the queen, which holds. Now he could duck the next round, hoping to find East with A–x–x and to ruff out the third round, but it is better play to make the next lead from the table. If East holds, say, A–10–x–x he must cater for the possibility that South holds the jack, and he may decide to go in with the ace. Here are two more examples on the same theme:

| (3) | K 9 7 5 2 | (4) | A Q 6 3 |
|---|---|---|---|
| Q J 6 3 | A 10 4 | J 10 7 2 | K 9 4 |
| | 8 | | 8 5 |

In (3), if East is marked with the ace, it is good play to lead low from dummy; East may be nervous of a singleton queen. In (4) a declarer needing two tricks, but able to afford an immediate loser, should start the suit by leading low from dummy. The finesse can be taken later if necessary, but meanwhile East may go in with the king.

Defenders do not have X-ray eyes and it is often possible for declarer to induce an unwise cover. There are some time-honoured plays which still succeed more often than they should, such as leading the queen from dummy when the trump holding is Q–J–x–x–x opposite 10–9–x–x–x. There are also many less obvious ways of tempting an opponent into an indiscretion.

| (5) | Q 6 3 | (6) | 9 6 3 |
|---|---|---|---|
| A | K 10 8 | J | Q 10 8 5 |
| | J 9 7 5 4 2 | | A K 7 4 2 |

South in (5) is tackling the trump suit. The standard play is to start by leading low towards the queen, a manoeuvre that offers the best chance of holding the opponents to two tricks. Suppose, however, that declarer can afford to lose only one trick. If he can be certain that East has not a singleton he should try the effect of leading the queen from dummy. In (6) the nine from dummy will save a trick when West has the singleton eight; as the cards lie in the diagram, East may cover, and again the defence can be held to one trick.

Finally, there are ways of slipping a trick through an unsuspecting defender. One well-known manoeuvre is to lead the jack from J–x–x

375

or J–10–x towards a singleton king in the closed hand. These are two examples relating to the play of a plain suit:

| (7) | A Q 8 4 2 | | (8) | | J 4 | |
|---|---|---|---|---|---|---|
| 10 7 | | K 6 5 3 | | Q 9 7 3 | | 10 8 6 5 |
| | J 9 | | | | A K 2 | |

Suppose that in (7) West opens with the ten. As the finesse is almost certain to lose, South should go up with the ace and drop the jack from hand. When later he leads a low card from dummy, East may deem it advisable to play low.

With the type of holding shown in (8), declarer could no doubt ruff his losing card in dummy. But it may be that he can afford to lose the first round of the suit because he can recover the trick by later discarding a loser from dummy in another suit. In such a case it costs nothing to start by leading low towards the jack, hoping West may duck; a trick is gained if that happens.

### Plays to Hide Strength or Weakness

When the defenders open up a suit which is to the declarer's liking, he has many ways of encouraging them to pursue the attack. We have already noted the simple false card that may cause an opponent to think his partner is signalling. These are more striking examples:

| (1) | K 6 | | (2) | | Q 10 4 | |
|---|---|---|---|---|---|---|
| J 9 5 4 | | 10 7 | | K 9 7 5 3 | | 8 2 |
| | A Q 8 3 2 | | | | A J 6 | |

In (1) West leads a suit which South, playing in 3NT, has concealed in the bidding. South may think this is most welcome, to be sure, but he should not necessarily go up with the king and clear the suit. It may be possible to extract further advantage by playing the six from dummy and the eight from hand! East will surely continue the suit and South will have gained a tempo.

When West leads the five in (2) the best deceptive play is to go up with the queen in dummy and drop the jack from hand. If West gains the lead early on he may play a second round, placing declarer with A–J alone.

Sometimes the best way to avert a damaging shift is for declarer to win the first trick with a higher card than necessary. The stratagem is well known, but it is undeniably effective in a hand like the following:

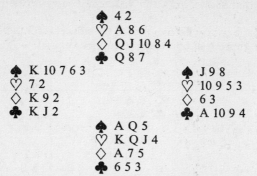

♠ 4 2
♡ A 8 6
♢ Q J 10 8 4
♣ Q 8 7

♠ K 10 7 6 3
♡ 7 2
♢ K 9 2
♣ K J 2

♠ J 9 8
♡ 10 9 5 3
♢ 6 3
♣ A 10 9 4

♠ A Q 5
♡ K Q J 4
♢ A 7 5
♣ 6 5 3

South plays in 3NT after West has overcalled in spades and has been supported by his partner. West leads ♠6 and East plays the jack. It is good play for South to win with the ace, not the queen. He enters dummy with a heart and leads ♢Q, losing to West's king. West may continue with a low spade instead of switching to a club.

The same sort of play may be made with these holdings:

(3)             7 5          (4)              K 8 5
   4 led         9 played       3 led             10 played
          A Q 10                 A J 4

In (3), it can hardly be wrong to win the first trick with the queen rather than the ten. If West gains the lead early on he may play low again from K–J–x–x; if East gains the lead it will make no difference whether South has kept A–Q or A–10. In (4), let us assume that a switch to another suit would be dangerous. Declarer therefore captures the ten with the ace, not the jack. The trick may come back if West gets in and again underleads the queen.

This is a more daring, and less familiar, example of the same stratagem:

(5)             9 3        (6)            9 3
  A Q 7 4 2      10 8 5      A Q 7 4 2     J 10
        K J 6                 K 8 6 5

In (5), West leads the four, East plays the ten and South the king! If East is going to win the first defensive trick South's king will be a dead duck in any event, but if West has the first entry he may well continue with a low card. From his point of view, the distribution might be that shown in (6), in which case it could be fatal to do otherwise.

One of the most effective moves to induce a continuation is to create the impression of a loser where none exists.

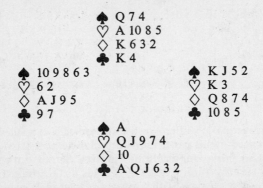

West leads ♠10 against 6♡ and declarer contributes the queen from dummy! East covers with the king, and when he comes in with ♡K he may try to cash a spade instead of playing a diamond. Now dummy's losing diamonds go away on declarer's clubs. The same sort of play is sometimes worth attempting with J–x–x in dummy opposite A–K alone. If dummy's jack is covered by the queen and ace the opponents are likely to think they have the scent.

When the defenders appear to be on the right track, many stratagems are open to the declarer. Bold action is sometimes needed to prevent an impending ruff:

(7)              J 7 4        (8)       10 7 4 2
    A Q 10 8 6 3 2       9         Q           A J 9 8 6 5
                 K 5                    K 3

In (7) West, who has pre-empted in this suit, leads the ace. Suppose that South can dispose of the second card if there is not an immediate ruff; in that case he should drop the king under the ace. (8) presents another aspect of the same play. When East, who is marked with a six-card suit, overtakes the queen with the ace, South drops the king.

Another useful move is the false hold-up.

(9)            Q 10 4       (10)          J 10 4
     7 led                       7 led
             A 5                     A 5

In (9) West leads the seven, which declarer reads as "top of nothing". His best plan (unless he thinks that West has no entry) is to cover with the ten and play low from hand. East may well fail to continue the suit, lest declarer started with A–x–x. In (10) dummy's ten is covered by the queen and South ducks as before.

Declarer can sometimes deflect the opponents from a dangerous suit by pretending to unblock.

(11)        J 7              (12)       J 6 3
     K Q 9         A 8 6 3 2   Q 10 7 5 2    A 9 4
           10 5 4                  K 8

In (11) East leads the three to West's queen. Declarer gravely plays the jack from dummy and West, placing him with A–10–x, may fail to continue the suit. In (12) West leads the five and East plays ace. When declarer coolly drops the king East will place him with K–Q and may switch.

There are also ways of forestalling an attack on a suit where the declarer is weak. South's stratagem on this deal is well known but none the less effective:

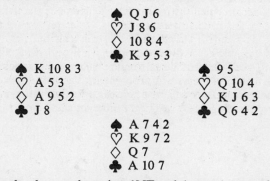

               &spades; Q J 6
               &hearts; J 8 6
               &diams; 10 8 4
               &clubs; K 9 5 3
&spades; K 10 8 3                  &spades; 9 5
&hearts; A 5 3                     &hearts; Q 10 4
&diams; A 9 5 2                 &diams; K J 6 3
&clubs; J 8                       &clubs; Q 6 4 2
               &spades; A 7 4 2
               &hearts; K 9 7 2
               &diams; Q 7
               &clubs; A 10 7

West leads a low spade against 1NT and dummy's queen holds the trick. At trick two there is really nothing better than a low diamond to the queen. The opponents may then open up some other suit to the declarer's advantage. The same effect can sometimes be obtained by leading a high card. For example, suppose the declarer at no-trumps holds A–K–x of a suit in his own hand, x–x–x on the table. It is a natural suit for the opponents to attack, but if the declarer lays down the ace at a very early stage the opponents may be mesmerized into thinking that he is preparing to develop the suit himself. Even bolder is the lead of the ace from A–x–x opposite dummy's 10–x–x. If the cards lie favourably the opponents may form quite the wrong impression.

One other way of preventing a dangerous attack is to mislead the opponents into thinking that time is on their side.

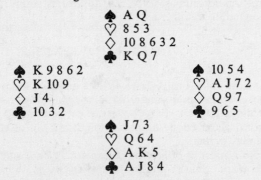

West leads a low spade against 3NT and dummy's queen holds the trick. If declarer plays three rounds of diamonds the defenders will be more or less forced to attack hearts. Declarer should attempt to conceal his strength in diamonds by ducking the first round, or perhaps by leading a diamond to the ace and ducking the next round. If the defenders do not realize that the diamonds are due to produce four tricks they will probably lead a second spade.

Sometimes declarer can best conceal his weakness in a particular suit by pretending to be weak in a different suit.

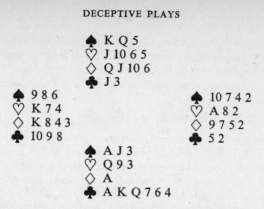

With two top losers in hearts, South arrives in 6♣ and is favoured by a club lead, which he wins in hand. He cashes ◇A, crosses to the jack of trumps, and leads ◇Q for a ruffing finesse; When East fails to cover, South can give himself an extra chance by discarding not a heart, but a spade. West may then try to find his partner with ♠A.

In a final example declarer conceals his strength in spades until the defenders have made a fatal move.

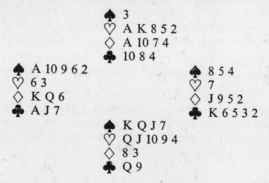

West opens the bidding with 1♠, North doubles for takeout and South eventually becomes the declarer in 4♡, against which West leads a trump. This seems only a temporary reprieve, for as soon as declarer attempts to dislodge ♠A the defenders are likely to take their club tricks and leave him with an unavoidable diamond loser.

The best shot is to lead a spade from dummy at trick two and

381

cover East's four with the seven! West wins with the nine but may not credit declarer with such strong spades. If he returns a " safe " trump, declarer can win in his own hand, take the ruffing finesse in spades, and subsequently discard two of dummy's club losers.

## Deception by the Defenders

The defenders have more opportunities for deceptive play than the declarer. This is true especially of manoeuvres within a single suit. Most of the plays described in this section are available only to the defenders; they would not work for the declarer because the fact that the dummy hand is exposed destroys the possibility of illusion. It is a long list, with many variations, and we describe the plays quite briefly, under these headings:

(a) Plays that create an option for declarer.
(b) Playing the card you are (or shortly will be) known to hold.
(c) Deceptive ways of opening up a new suit.

(a) *Plays that create an option for declarer*

The object here is to afford declarer a choice of plays in a situation where he would otherwise be bound to make a winning play. These are sometimes called " obligatory false cards ", for unless the defenders do something special the declarer has no chance to go wrong.

(1)       A J 8 6 4      (2)       A Q 7 5 3
   K 3           10 9 5      K 10          8 6 2
      Q 7 2                 J 9 4

In (1) South leads the two and puts in dummy's jack. To present declarer with a choice of plays, East must drop the nine or ten. In (2) South leads the four. If West plays the king, South may finesse the nine on the way back.

(3)          4      (4)        K J 8 7 3
  J 10 5      A 6     10 9 6 5      A Q 4
    K Q 9 8 7 3 2          2

In (3) declarer leads low from dummy and wins with the king. West must drop the ten or jack so that South will have the option of returning the queen or a low card. In (4) South leads the two and finesses the jack, losing to the queen. On the next round of the suit he ruffs dummy's three. West must play the nine or ten, so that on

the third round South may be tempted to lead the king, which would
be the winning play if West had 10–9–x.

(5)        A Q 10 8    (6)        K J 7 3
   J 9 5 3         2         4        A 10 8 5
        K 7 6 4            Q 9 6 2

In (5) South leads low to dummy's queen. If West plays the three
or five, declarer's next lead will be back to the king, exposing the
position. West therefore must play the nine on the first round,
affording South the chance to guard against J–x–x–x in either hand.
If unfamiliar with the deception declarer will surely guess wrong and
play the ace next. In (6) South leads low to dummy's jack. If East
takes the ace, declarer will lose no more tricks. East must play the
eight, giving declarer the choice of playing West for A–10–x–x.

(7)        A J 4    (8)        K J
   3          K 10 8 5  Q 10 9 4       3
        Q 9 7 6 2        A 8 7 6 5 2

These are two kindred plays. In (7), when South plays low to the
jack East must drop the eight. In (8) South leads low, intending to
finesse the jack. The nine (or ten) from West may cause him to
change his mind, as if this is a singleton the best play is to go up with
the king and return the jack through East's supposed Q–10–x–x.

The combination J–9 in a defender's hand presents many possibilities for deceiving the declarer. Here are two of them:

(9)        Q 10 8 6 3  (10)       K 10 4
   K 5 4 2      J 9      A J 9       7 5 3
        A 7             Q 8 6 2

In (9) South leads the ace. If East plays the nine a competent
declarer will always go up with the queen on the next round, the
correct percentage play because it helps to find J–9 more than K–9.
But if East plays the jack on the first round South will be inclined to
finesse the eight next, playing West for 9–x–x–x and East for K–J
alone. (A sidelight on this combination is that when East holds
K–9–x over dummy's Q–10–8–x–x it is good play to drop the nine
under the ace, encouraging the declarer to go up with the queen
on the next round.)

In (10) South leads the two. If West plays the nine, declarer will
finesse dummy's ten and the only trick he will lose is the ace. However, if West, knowing that his jack is dead in any event, plays it on

the first round, South will win with the king in dummy and may return the ten, losing to the ace. Now, on the third round of the suit, declarer will very likely lead from dummy and finesse the eight. It is a surprising fact that to play the jack from J–9 or K–J–9 or A–J–9 will very seldom lose and will often gain a trick.

(b) *Playing the card you are (or shortly will be) known to hold*

When West, in (10), made the deceptive play of the jack from A–J–9 in front of dummy's K–10–x, he was playing a card that was due shortly to be revealed by declarer's next play (a finesse of the ten). The first-round play of the jack was in line with an important principle: *When it does not sacrifice a trick, play the card that you are already, or shortly will be, known to hold.* These are all very common situations:

(1)             A J 5        (2)           A Q 10 6 3
     Q 10 4          8 3 2       K J 8 5       7 2
          K 9 7 6              9 4

In (1) South leads the six, successfully finesses the jack, and continues by laying down the ace. At this point West must not fail to drop the queen, the card he is known to hold. Declarer will then have to decide whether to play for the drop or finesse the nine. If the queen is not played he has no problem.

Figure (2) shows a side suit at a trump contract. The declarer, who is contemplating a crossruff, finesses the queen and lays down the ace. West must drop the king, for until the king is played the declarer will know that there is no fear of an overruff.

(3)             A 9 7 4       (4)          A 10 5 3
    K J 6 2          8 3       K J 4         7 6 2
          Q 10 5             Q 9 8

Figure (3) illustrates a different aspect of the principle we are discussing. Dummy leads low to declarer's ten. If West wins the jack, declarer's next move will be to lead the queen from his hand, and inevitably he will make the remaining three tricks in the suit. Knowing that his king is a dead card which will be exposed on the next round (assuming that declarer holds the queen), East should win declarer's ten with the king. Thinking that the position of the jack is " proved ", South will later play off the queen and ace.

Figure (4) shows another possibility from the same sort of combination. Lacking entries to attack the suit twice from his own hand, the declarer begins by leading low from dummy and putting in the nine. Knowing that his king can be picked up by a finesse on the next round, West plays it on the nine. When next in dummy declarer will probably finesse the eight, to take care of the possibility that East holds J–x–x–x.

(5)        K J 10 8     (6)       A Q 10 7

  Q 7 2          A 9 4      J 9 4         K 5 2

        6 5 3                8 6 3

In (5) South leads the three to dummy's ten and we will say that East holds off. When South regains the lead and plays another low card it is routine deception for West to play the queen, the card he is known to hold. If this is headed by the king and ace South may place East with the 9–7 and perhaps attempt some ill-starred throw-in.

Figure (6) is a variation of the same play. South leads the three to dummy's ten and this time we will say that East wins the trick. When South later leads the eight West plays the jack, the card he is marked with. The declarer may thenceforth play on the assumption that East began with K–9–x–x.

(7)         7 5       (8)        8 5 3

  K Q          10 6 4     A K         J 9 4

     A J 9 8 3 2         Q 10 7 6 2

Figure (7) shows one of the most important plays of this kind. Suppose the contract depends on losing only one trick in this suit. Declarer begins by finessing the nine and West wins with the king or queen. When declarer next leads the suit from dummy East must not fail to play the ten, the card he is known to hold. If he doesn't, South will know that his only chance to avoid a second loser is to drop the outstanding honour. The possibility of East holding K–10–x or Q–10–x will have been excluded.

Figure (8) shows another position where East must aim to protect his partner's doubleton honour. Declarer begins by leading from dummy and finessing the ten. Suppose that on the next lead from dummy East lazily plays the nine. Then, from declarer's angle, West is known to have had either A–K alone or a singleton; either way, it cannot lose to duck the second round, for the next lead can be made through East's A–J if necessary. If East makes the correct play of the jack on the second round it will be normal for South to play him for K–J–x and to cover with the queen.

On a slightly different plane, surprising effects can be obtained by playing high cards which will be exposed on the next round.

(9)        Q 10 6 4 2        (10)            A 7 4 2
    K 7            J 9 5          10 9 5              Q 6
        A 8 3                        K J 8 3

In (9) South, intending to develop the suit at notrumps, leads the ace from hand. West drops the king—not to unblock, but simply as a bluff. If South forms the conclusion that the king is a singleton he may abandon the suit altogether.

Figure (10) shows the trump suit. When the ace is led from dummy it can hardly cost for East to drop the queen. If this convinces South that the trumps are 4–1 it may alter his entire plan of play.

### (c) Deceptive ways of opening up a new suit

There is often scope for deception when a defender opens up a new suit. As we shall see in the next chapter when discussing the defence to throw-in play, with Q–x–x or J–x–x it is usually right to exit with the high card. These are less well known situations:

(1)        Q 8 4            (2)        Q 8 4
    J 6 5            A 10 7 3      A 6 5            J 10 7 3
        K 9 2                        K 9 2

Suppose that East is constrained to lead the suit shown in (1). The only way to give declarer a guess is to lead the ten. South will let this run to the queen and on the next round he will have to decide whether to play the king or the nine. From his point of view, East could have led the ten from the combination shown in (2).

(3)        K 7 4            (4)        K 7 4
    A Q 9 2            J 6 5      Q J 9 2            A 6 5
        10 8 3                        10 8 3

In (3) the queen from West is the only card that will put South on the rack. He may play low, expecting the situation to be more like that shown in (4).

Many players would select the play of the queen in (3) but would miss the corresponding opportunity in the next diagram:

(5)        10 7 4            (6)        10 7 4
    A Q 2            J 9 5 3      A 3 2            Q J 9 5
        K 8 6                        K 8 6

In (5) East should lead the jack (and equally, of course, the queen from Q–9–x or Q–9–x). South may play low, which would be the winning play if East held Q–J–9–x, as in (6).

There are interesting possibilities in this situation:

(7)           J 9 5      (8)         J 6 5
    Q 10 7 2       K 8 4       Q 10 7       K 8 4 2
          A 6 3              A 9 3

If West has to open up the suit in (7), the queen, in most cases, will offer better prospects than the low card. South will win with the ace and may play West for K–Q–x–x. (8) shows a related position. If East leads the king (or the queen from Q–x–x) South may well duck, placing East with K–Q–10.

However, the best play in these situations varies according to the declarer's estimate of his opponent. Consider, for example, this familiar position:

(9)             J 9 5
     K Q 7 2               10 8 4
         A 6 3

Suppose that West has to open up the suit shown in (9). Most players would lead low, expecting the declarer to put in dummy's nine. Declarers usually do, but against a strong opponent South may say to himself, " If West held K–10–x–x or Q–10–x–x he would lead the top card. Therefore it's more likely that he holds the K–Q." True, the expert defender against the expert declarer may attempt a double bluff, leading the queen from K–Q–x–x; but here we enter the field of Optimum Strategy, a complicated subject which would be of practical value only if one played endlessly against the same opponent.

In terms of overall strategy, the defenders' most useful form of deception is the simple one of failing to cash winning tricks in circumstances where it would be normal to cash them. A single example will show the effectiveness of this form of play.

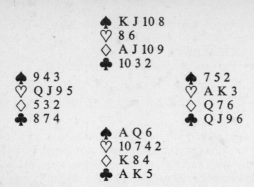

East is defending against 3NT after South has opened 1NT and rebid 2♡ in response to his partner's Stayman inquiry. West leads ♡Q and East can see that despite this favourable start nine tricks may still be made. West is marked with four hearts to the Q–J and nothing else, and the contract is bound to succeed if declarer takes the winning position in diamonds. Is there any way in which he can be persuaded to take the losing position?

Overtaking West's ♡Q with the king, East cashes ♡A and then shifts to a club, just as though he had no more hearts. Greatly relieved, South wins and takes the diamond finesse "safely" into East's hand. Now East produces a third heart! " Sorry, it got tucked away among my diamonds."

## Deception around the Trump Suit

Apart from false cards in a single suit, the defenders have many opportunities for tactical deception at trump contracts. One case occurs when a defender gives a false echo to tempt the declarer to ruff unnecessarily high.

```
              ♡ Q 4
              ◇ Q 8 3
                            ♡ 10 6 2
      ♡ K led                ◇ 10 9 7 5
```

East is defending against 5◇ and West, who has bid hearts, leads the king. East plays the ten and the two on the first two rounds, and when West plays a third round the declarer (if he started with

388

three hearts) may be tempted to ruff high in dummy, establishing a trump trick for East.

The stratagem is fairly obvious here, because of East's trump holding. It may still gain a trick if East holds, say, two small trumps and his partner holds J–x! Once the declarer, holding Q–x–x opposite A–K–10–x–x–x, has been persuaded to ruff with the queen, he has to find the jack and may decide to play East for J–x–x.

Some striking results can be produced by a defender who holds a doubleton trump and ruffs unnecessarily high to create the impression that this is his only trump.

```
              ♠ 7 4
              ♡ A 8 5
              ◇ K Q 6 3
              ♣ 10 6 4 2
♠ Q 3                          ♠ 9 8
♡ K Q J 9 6 3 2                ♡ 10 4
◇ 7                            ◇ A J 10 9 5 2
♣ 9 7 5                        ♣ Q 8 3
              ♠ A K J 10 6 5 2
              ♡ 7
              ◇ 8 4
              ♣ A K J
```

West is defending against 4♠ after having opened 3♡. He leads a diamond to the king and ace, and East returns a diamond. West ruffs with the *queen* and exits with ♡K. In dummy with ♡A, South has to choose between attempting to cash ◇Q and finessing ♣J. West's deceptive ♠Q, apparently a singleton, may push him in the wrong direction.

By pretending that a ruff is imminent, a defender can often persuade declarer to abandon a winning finesse in the trump suit. This form of play is a mighty saver of overtricks, if not of game contracts.

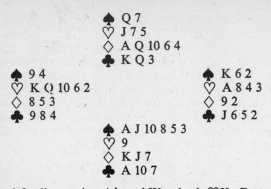

♠ Q 7
♡ J 7 5
◊ A Q 10 6 4
♣ K Q 3

♠ 9 4           ♠ K 6 2
♡ K Q 10 6 2    ♡ A 8 4 3
◊ 8 5 3         ◊ 9 2
♣ 9 8 4         ♣ J 6 5 2

♠ A J 10 8 5 3
♡ 9
◊ K J 7
♣ A 10 7

East is defending against 4♠ and West leads ♡K. East overtakes with the ace and returns ◊2. Apprehensive of a ruff, the declarer may now refuse the trump finesse, allowing East to make his king.

An effective defensive manoeuvre is to win with a higher card than necessary when declarer has the chance for a ruffing finesse.

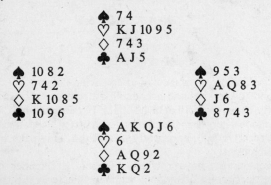

♠ 7 4
♡ K J 10 9 5
◊ 7 4 3
♣ A J 5

♠ 10 8 2        ♠ 9 5 3
♡ 7 4 2         ♡ A Q 8 3
◊ K 10 8 5      ◊ J 6
♣ 10 9 6        ♣ 8 7 4 3

♠ A K Q J 6
♡ 6
◊ A Q 9 2
♣ K Q 2

East is defending against 6♠. A club is led and South wins in hand. He draws trumps and leads a heart on which West plays the two and dummy the jack. East can see that if he wins with the queen his ace will later be ruffed out. He therefore wins with the ace and leads a diamond. As a diamond finesse will not see him home, the declarer will probably go up with the ace, enter dummy with a club and play ♡K, followed by the ten. When East plays low South will ruff, hoping to bring down the queen.

The declarer's grip on the trump suit can sometimes be weakened by causing him to ruff unnecessarily before he knows that he cannot afford it. The commonest setting for this type of play occurs when the defenders control a side suit such as this:

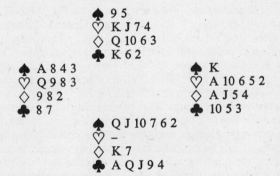

$$Q J 10 7 3$$
$$9 8 6 \qquad A K 4 2$$
$$5$$

East, who knows that the declarer's trump length is open to attack, leads the ace and continues with a low card. South ruffs and later finds that he cannot control the trump situation.

Here is a deal where the declarer was tormented by an agile defence:

♠ 9 5
♡ K J 7 4
♢ Q 10 6 3
♣ K 6 2

♠ A 8 4 3          ♠ K
♡ Q 9 8 3          ♡ A 10 6 5 2
♢ 9 8 2            ♢ A J 5 4
♣ 8 7              ♣ 10 5 3

♠ Q J 10 7 6 2
♡ –
♢ K 7
♣ A Q J 9 4

South played in 4♠ after having shown a two-suiter. West led a diamond on which East played the ace and South the seven. Judging that declarer must be void of hearts, East led a low heart at the second trick, which South ruffed. When East won the first round of trumps he led another low heart, and again South ruffed. At this point West and South had three spades each and South was due to go down a trick whatever he did. In practice, when West won the next spade lead with the ace he led a low heart and a desperate declarer went up with the king. In the end, West was left with a good trump and ♡Q, to put the contract down two. " You were lucky I didn't have the fifth heart ", said West.

# CHAPTER 28

# Endplays

*The throw-in – The ruff-and-discard – Eliminations – A partial elimination – Defence to eliminations and throw-ins*

ONE of the earliest and greatest writers on bridge, Milton C. Work, proposed that the title of E.P.D. should be granted to all who studied his chapters on the end game. The initials stood for Emptoris Pontis Doctor, which was the doggiest of dog Latin for Doctor of Auction Bridge. However, he went on to say, quite rightly, that endplay was not the most difficult part of bridge. There are certain ideas that should first be grasped, after which the ability to produce these highly satisfying plays comes quite readily with experience.

The endplays which we discuss in this chapter are the throw-in, which is not very frequent, and the elimination, which in many ways is the king of endplays. In both, the declarer's object is to place a defender in the lead and force him to concede a trick that the declarer could not have made on his own.

## The Throw-in

It is well known that in many situations the side which opens up a suit is liable to lose a trick in it. The object of the throw-in is to exploit that fact.

Q 6 3

J 8 5                    K 9 7 2

A 10 4

If South, the declarer, has to tackle this suit himself, he makes only one trick, but if either West or East has to make the first play declarer is assured of two tricks regardless of the location of the outstanding honours. The principle is that, faced with a combination of cards that are not in sequence, declarer should examine the possibility of forcing the opponents to lead the suit, which will often produce better results.

Sometimes a throw-in can be foreseen quite early in the play, as here:

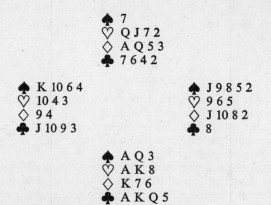

The contract is 6NT and West leads ♣J, which South wins. There would be no problem if either of the minor suits were favourably divided, but when declarer plays a second round of clubs East shows out, discarding a spade, and when declarer tests the diamonds East shows up with four of them. Now a throw-in against West is marked. Declarer cashes four heart tricks, discarding a spade, and then plays a third and fourth round of clubs, throwing West in and forcing him to return a spade into the A–Q.

Not every throw-in is as tidy as that, of course. Very often the declarer has only an approximate picture of the opposing hands and has to do some guesswork.

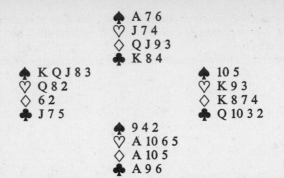

```
                    ♠ A 7 6
                    ♡ J 7 4
                    ◇ Q J 9 3
                    ♣ K 8 4
♠ K Q J 8 3                        ♠ 10 5
♡ Q 8 2                            ♡ K 9 3
◇ 6 2                              ◇ K 8 7 4
♣ J 7 5                            ♣ Q 10 3 2
                    ♠ 9 4 2
                    ♡ A 10 6 5
                    ◇ A 10 5
                    ♣ A 9 6
```

South is in 2NT and West leads ♠K, followed by ♠Q. Declarer takes this trick as there is no point in holding up further; indeed the third spade may come in useful later as a card of exit. The queen of diamonds holds the next trick and a low diamond is won by the ten. On ◇A West discards a club.

Where is the eighth trick coming from? It may be possible for South to do something with the hearts, but it would be far more satisfactory if the defenders could be forced to open up that suit. Is it possible to execute a throw-in?

To judge from the fall of ♠10 on the second round, West began with five spades. He has shown up with two diamonds and could have a doubleton heart and four clubs. In that case a throw-in would not work (West would have too many winners) and a low heart from hand would be the best move at this point. On the other hand, West might have begun with three hearts and three clubs. If South decides to play on that assumption he should cash ♣A–K, then exit with a spade. After taking his spade winners West, as the cards lie, has to lead a heart. South captures the king with the ace and returns a heart, making his eighth trick in this suit.

It is generally easier to plan a throw in after the opponents have entered the bidding. Here an opening bid by West is sufficient to point to the right play.

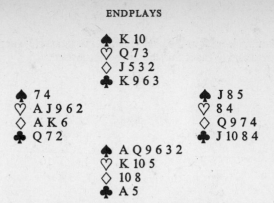

South plays in 4♠ after West has opened the bidding with 1♡. The defence begins with three rounds of diamonds, South ruffing. Trumps are drawn in three rounds, West discarding a heart. This leaves the cards as follows:

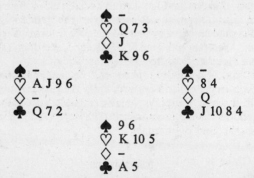

From declarer's angle the chances are that three rounds of clubs will exhaust West of that suit, and accordingly he plays ♣A–K and another club, ruffing. He could play East for ♡J, of course, but from the first he has had his eye on a superior chance. He leads ♡K from hand; West wins with ♡A and then has to lead into the divided tenace.

### The Ruff-and-discard

One does not need to have played bridge very long before learning, if only through partner's wrath, that it tends to be greatly to declarer's advantage to be able to ruff an opponent's lead in either hand, while discarding a loser from the other hand. For example, suppose clubs are trumps and West is on lead in this situation:

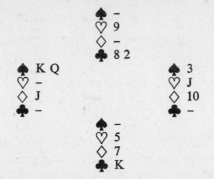

Declarer has a losing heart in each hand but West is unable to lead a heart. If West, having failed to keep track of the hand, should happen to lead a spade, declarer takes the remaining tricks by ruffing the spade in dummy and discarding a losing heart from his own hand. West should lead ♢J instead, avoiding the ruff-and-discard and forcing South to lose a heart trick.

In that type of situation, therefore, the defender tries to avoid offering declarer a ruff-and-discard while the declarer aims to leave him no alternative. Endplays which are based on obtaining a ruff-and-discard are called eliminations. They are much more common than any other kind of endplay.

### Eliminations

Eliminations are usually easier to produce than throw-ins, since it is not necessary to force the opponents to lead a particular suit. They are thrown in at a point where they must either lead into a tenace position or concede a ruff-and-discard.

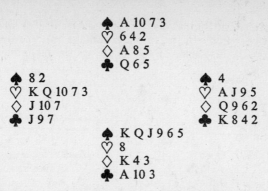

The contract is 4♠ and hearts are led. South ruffs the second round, draws the opponents' trumps, and notes that, with an inescapable diamond loser, he must avoid losing two club tricks. It was observed earlier in the chapter that, with this particular club combination, declarer can be sure of a satisfactory outcome if the opponents can be obliged to lead the suit. That may not be easy to arrange and in fact is not essential. It will be far easier to present the opponents with the choice of leading a club or conceding a ruff-and-discard, and the result will be equally satisfactory.

In this hand success is certain. After drawing trumps, declarer ruffs dummy's last heart and plays out three rounds of diamonds. At the point where he leads the third diamond, this is the position:

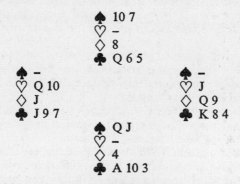

Declarer loses only one more trick no matter what the opponents do. Either they must open up the club suit or allow a ruff-and-discard.

397

The declarer will not always be on a sure thing as in the last example, but it may still be to his advantage that the opponents should make the first lead. In the following deal the critical suit is diamonds.

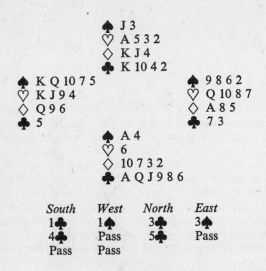

|       | South | West | North | East |
|-------|-------|------|-------|------|
|       | 1♣    | 1♠   | 3♣    | 3♠   |
|       | 4♣    | Pass | 5♣    | Pass |
|       | Pass  | Pass |       |      |

West leads ♠K and South wins with the ace. As the fate of the hand will depend on how many diamond tricks South loses, he plans to force the opponents to open up the suit or concede a ruff-and-discard.

South plays, therefore, to eliminate the hearts and throw the lead with a spade. He plays a heart to the ace, ruffs a heart, enters dummy twice in trumps and ruffs the remaining hearts. Then he exits with a spade to West's queen.

If West plays a diamond now, declarer must assume he has led away from the queen. South plays low from dummy, covers East's eight with the ten, and finesses ◇J on the next round, thus losing only one trick in the suit. If West leads a spade instead of a diamond, declarer discards a diamond from dummy, ruffs in his own hand, and then leads a diamond towards the K–J. In this case also he should place West with ◇Q, partly because West, holding ◇A, would not have conceded the ruff-and-discard, and partly because with an additional ace he would have doubled 1♣.

Declarer's handling of the trump suit is often influenced by the possibility of an elimination. See how South makes a certainty of his part-score contract on the following hand:

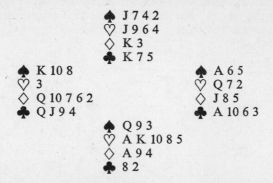

```
              ♠ J 7 4 2
              ♡ J 9 6 4
              ◇ K 3
              ♣ K 7 5
♠ K 10 8                        ♠ A 6 5
♡ 3                             ♡ Q 7 2
◇ Q 10 7 6 2                    ◇ J 8 5
♣ Q J 9 4                       ♣ A 10 6 3
              ♠ Q 9 3
              ♡ A K 10 8 5
              ◇ A 9 4
              ♣ 8 2
```

The contract is 2♡ and the defence begins with three rounds of clubs. South ruffs the third round and lays down ♡A, to which all follow. In the ordinary course of events declarer would continue with ♡K, the normal percentage play, but the possibility of an elimination suggests a different course of action. Declarer plays out the diamonds, ruffing the third round in dummy and creating this position:

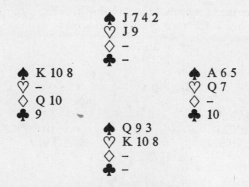

```
              ♠ J 7 4 2
              ♡ J 9
              ◇ –
              ♣ –
♠ K 10 8                        ♠ A 6 5
♡ –                             ♡ Q 7
◇ Q 10                          ◇ –
♣ 9                             ♣ 10
              ♠ Q 9 3
              ♡ K 10 8
              ◇ –
              ♣ –
```

The jack of hearts is led from dummy and East plays low. Now a finesses guarantees the contract; either it will succeed or West will win and become the victim of an elimination in which he has to open up the spades or concede a ruff-and-discard. It is an instructive hand, for a player with no grasp of elimination play would try vainly to drop ♡Q and then finesse ♣9, losing to West's ten.

For an elimination to succeed, it is essential to have a trump in each hand at the time when the opponents are placed on lead. Sometimes this object is achieved by deliberately surrendering a trick which an uninitiated player might have ruffed.

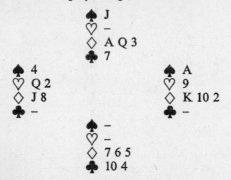

Clubs are trumps, declarer needs four of the remaining tricks, and the lead is in dummy. Declarer plays ♣J from dummy. He could ruff the trick and take the diamond finesse, but the superior play is to discard a diamond, leaving East to lead away from ◇K or concede a ruff-and-discard.

A deal from the European Championship provides a good example of the versatility of this type of elimination play:

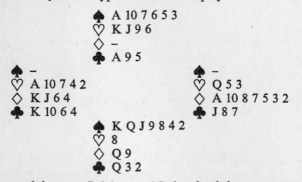

In a match between Belgium and Switzerland the contract at both tables was 6♠, after bidding that marked West with most of the outstanding strength. At the first table West led ◇4. Declarer ruffed in dummy, entered his hand with a trump and led ♡8. If West had put up ♡A, declarer would have been able to ruff a heart and discard two clubs on ♡K–J. West therefore played low and ♡K won the trick. South now ruffed the second and third round of hearts and his remaining diamond. Then he led the fourth heart from dummy, discarding a club from hand. West was obliged to lead a club or concede a ruff-and-discard.

At the other table North was the declarer and East led ◇A. Declarer ruffed, entered dummy with a trump and led a heart to ♡K, West ducking in approved fashion. Declarer could now have followed the same plan as the declarer at the other table, but instead he ruffed all his hearts and threw the lead to West with ◇Q, discarding a club from the North hand. West was left on play in much the same position. There was thus a loser-on-loser elimination at both tables, but in different suits.

The reader will by now, we hope, agree that we were not exaggerating when we said that elimination play could be quite easy as well as highly effective. This is because in many cases declarer has no need to visualize the opponents' holdings: he knows from his own hand that it will be possible to obtain a ruff-and-discard or force a favourable lead into one of his tenace holdings. There is another type of hand, requiring more luck as well as more effort of imagination, where declarer's holding in the crucial plain suit is not robust enough for him to benefit from a lead into it, and where only a ruff-and-discard will really help his cause. For example:

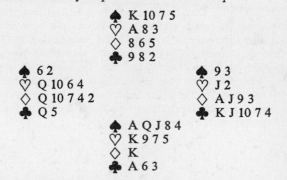

South is in 4♠ and West leads a low diamond to his partner's ace. The fall of declarer's king establishes that no more defensive tricks are available in this suit; in any case it is natural for East to shift to a club, and he leads ♣J.

South should duck this trick on general principles. It is extremely unlikely that the ace will be ruffed on the next round, and by ducking South restricts communications between the opposing hands. East continues ♣10 to declarer's ace, West dropping the queen.

South appears to have four losers—two in clubs, one in hearts and one in diamonds. What can he do about it?

Almost the only hope lies in obtaining a ruff-and-discard that will take care of dummy's heart loser. To prepare for this, it is essential to eliminate the diamonds. After ♠ A and a spade to the king, South ruffs a diamond. Then he plays a heart to the ace and ruffs a third diamond. The position is:

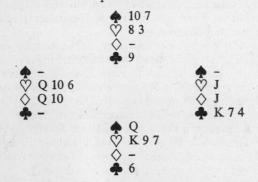

South cashes ♡K, then leads his losing club. East wins this trick, but having no heart left he must lead a club or a diamond, enabling the declarer to ruff with ♠Q and discard dummy's heart.

Note the two preparatory moves: the duck of the first round of clubs to restrict communications, and the elimination of dummy's diamonds. Also South has to envisage the possibility of one player being short in clubs and the other in hearts.

In the next example the declarer's picture of the distribution is helped by an opponent's pre-emptive opening.

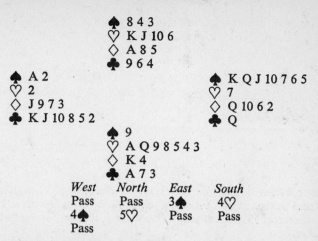

|       | ♠ 8 4 3        |       |        |
|-------|----------------|-------|--------|
|       | ♡ K J 10 6     |       |        |
|       | ◇ A 8 5        |       |        |
|       | ♣ 9 6 4        |       |        |

♠ A 2              ♠ K Q J 10 7 6 5
♡ 2                ♡ 7
◇ J 9 7 3          ◇ Q 10 6 2
♣ K J 10 8 5 2     ♣ Q

|       | ♠ 9            |       |        |
|-------|----------------|-------|--------|
|       | ♡ A Q 9 8 5 4 3 |      |        |
|       | ◇ K 4          |       |        |
|       | ♣ A 7 3        |       |        |

| West | North | East | South |
|------|-------|------|-------|
| Pass | Pass  | 3♠   | 4♡    |
| 4♠   | 5♡    | Pass | Pass  |
| Pass |       |      |       |

West begins with ♠A and another spade, South ruffing. Both opponents follow to a round of trumps and South is left with the problem of holding his club losers to one.

Most players would lead out several rounds of trumps, and it must be admitted that many contracts are made that way. However, the only genuine chance lies in a ruff-and-discard elimination involving the black suits. Declarer's first move is to eliminate the diamonds, ruffing the third round. Then he lays down ♣A, on which East drops the queen.

One possibility now is to cross to dummy, ruff the third spade, and lead a second club, playing East for K–Q alone, but there are two objections to this. One is that East, who has already turned up with strong spades, is unlikely to hold ♣K–Q as well; the other that, as the play has gone, East has had an opportunity to discard ♣K and has not taken it. There is another, and better, chance. Study the position after South has crossed to dummy at trick eight:

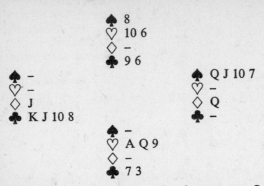

Our old friend, loser-on-loser play, wins the contract. South leads ♠8 from dummy, East covers and is allowed to hold the trick. Now East must concede a ruff-and-discard and declarer's second club goes away.

This was by no means an easy hand. South had to foresee the possibility of the loser-on-loser elimination and had to form a picture of the distribution.

## A Partial Elimination

In all the examples so far the declarer has been able to eliminate the hand and still have the essential requirement of at least one trump in dummy and one in his own hand. Quite often he has not enough trumps to do this. In such a case he may try for a partial elimination at the end of which there is still one trump at large. Here is an example which calls for good technique:

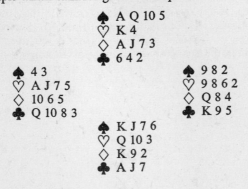

South opens 1NT and becomes declarer in 4♠. West leads a low club to the king and ace. There is no hurry to draw trumps; feeling his way, South leads a heart to the king and returns a heart to the ten and jack. West exits with a trump and South wins in his own hand.

The play to the first trick has marked West with ♣Q, and the contract may seem to depend on the diamond finesse. South can give himself an extra chance by ruffing ♡Q and drawing a second round of trumps, arriving at this position:

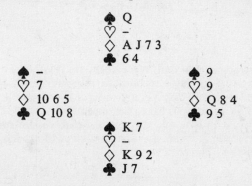

Declarer leads a club from dummy and covers East's card. He is hoping that West does not have the outstanding trump and that East can be kept from leading it. The partial elimination succeeds as West, after making his two club tricks, must either concede a ruff-and-discard or open up the diamonds. If West had a trump left he would exit with it, of course, and South would have to take the diamond finesse after all.

### Defence to Eliminations and Throw-ins

The first requirement in defending against any form of endplay is to understand what the declarer is trying to do. From that point there are three main lines of defence.

First, the defenders must not help declarer in the preliminary stages of elimination. There is no point in forcing a declarer to ruff unless this will weaken his control of the hand. Often, when a defender has won the first trick, it is good play to make a neutral lead. West has to follow that strategy to prevent declarer from getting home on this hand:

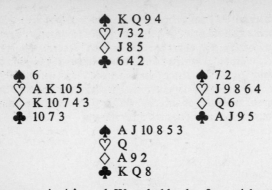

♠ K Q 9 4
♡ 7 3 2
◇ J 8 5
♣ 6 4 2

♠ 6                    ♠ 7 2
♡ A K 10 5            ♡ J 9 8 6 4
◇ K 10 7 4 3         ◇ Q 6
♣ 10 7 3             ♣ A J 9 5

♠ A J 10 8 5 3
♡ Q
◇ A 9 2
♣ K Q 8

The contract is 4♠ and West holds the first trick with ♡K. Suppose he were to play a second heart; South would ruff, lead a spade to the king, and play a club from dummy. East plays low and the king wins. A trump is led to the queen and a second club is led; East goes up with ♣A and exits with a club to declarer's queen. South enters dummy with ♠9 and eliminates the hearts by ruffing the third round. The position is:

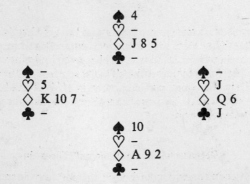

♠ 4
♡ –
◇ J 8 5
♣ –

♠ –                    ♠ –
♡ 5                    ♡ J
◇ K 10 7             ◇ Q 6
♣ –                    ♣ J

♠ 10
♡ –
◇ A 9 2
♣ –

Declarer has two possible chances of avoiding a diamond loser. He may lead a low diamond from his hand, hoping that West has ◇K–Q–x; or he may play ace and another diamond, hoping that an opponent with a doubleton honour will have to win the second round and concede a ruff-and-discard. For a number of reasons, the more promising line on the present hand is to play the ace and another. It would not help East to unblock, and after winning with the queen he must concede a ruff-and-discard.

How can the defence prevent this? Only by leading a trump at trick two instead of a second heart. West can hardly foresee the end game but he can see that South may be short of entries to dummy. He should therefore do nothing to help him.

The second aim of the defenders is not to be caught with isolated honours. This, too, sometimes calls for foresight—or at least, for a highly developed instinct. Consider the diamond situation in the previous hand, where South held A–x–x opposite J–x–x, and suppose the full distribution to be:

```
                  J 8 5
      K 6                      Q 10 7 4 3
                  A 9 2
```

The declarer, if planning an elimination, may be astute enough to play off the ace quite early in the hand. In this case, it may be essential for West to unblock. Moreover, the play is safe enough, for with A–Q–x declarer would not be laying down the ace.

It is especially necessary to guard against being stranded with a singleton honour in the trump suit. A defender who holds the singleton ace of trumps should always consider playing it at an early stage. An original holding of A–x can also prove a trap, for declarer, with J–10–x–x opposite the K–Q–9–x–x, will often lead the jack from dummy as though contemplating a finesse. If second hand plays low from A–x, declarer will promptly proceed to eliminate the hand before playing a second round of trumps. As a rule, therefore, it is wise to go up with the ace in this situation. If this happens to clash with partner's singleton king, *c'est la guerre*.

Another aspect of unblocking appears in these two diagrams:

```
(1)          7 4 2           (2)          7 4 2
    K J 9           10 6 3       A J 10           Q 8 6 3
          A Q 8 5                       K 9 5
```

In each case declarer plays from dummy, proposing to duck the lead to West and force a favourable return. To prevent this, East must go up with a high card.

Finally, the last line of defence against an elimination is for the defender who is left on lead to select the correct card of exit. This is a common situation:

```
(3)                  K 9 4
        J 8 6 3                      Q 7 2
                     A 10 5
```

Whichever defender has the lead must play an honour, not a low card. Then at least the declarer has a guess. The next two situations are less common but are also worth noting:

(4)          K 7 4      (5)         J 8 3

    J 6 2         Q 9 5 3     A 7 5        Q 9 4 2

        A 10 8              K 10 6

If East has the lead in (4) he must play the queen, no other card. This gives the declarer no chance to win three tricks. (5) illustrates a different type of defence. Say that the declarer leads the jack from dummy, East covers with the queen, and South plays the king. Unless he has a safe exit in another suit, West must not take this trick. Provided he ducks, the defence will always win two tricks by force.

Against a throw-in, the best form of riposte is an early attack on the declarer's tenace combinations. When that is impractical it may be possible to escape the lead by unblocking. If that, too, fails, the defender who is thrown in should give thought to exiting with an unsupported high card. Suppose West is obliged to lead away from the K–x–x, through dummy's A–Q–x; he should lead the king rather than a low one. If declarer has J–x–x, he will make three tricks whatever the defender does, but if he has only J–x the lead of the king may cause entry problems.

Finally, much can be done by clever discarding—in particular, by unguarding high cards. The defenders on the following hand had one genuine and one sporting chance to beat the contract, but they stood still and allowed themselves to be end-played.

           ♠ A Q 4
           ♡ Q 7 4 3
           ◇ K 6
           ♣ K 9 7 3

♠ J 9 7 2                   ♠ K 10 6
♡ K 9                     ♡ A J 10 8 6 5
◇ 9 4 3                   ◇ 8
♣ Q 10 6 2                ♣ J 8 5

           ♠ 8 5 3
           ♡ 2
           ◇ A Q J 10 7 5 2
           ♣ A 4

| West | North | East | South |
|------|-------|------|-------|
| Pass | 1♣ | 1♡ | 2♢ |
| Pass | 2NT | Pass | 4♢ |
| Pass | 5♢ | Pass | Pass |
| Pass | | | |

West led ♡K and East, who could see that it might be important to switch to spades, dropped ♡J, intending this as a suit-preference signal. West failed to take the message and continued with a second heart, which South ruffed. After a diamond to the king declarer ruffed a third heart, then played off three more rounds of trumps, arriving at this position:

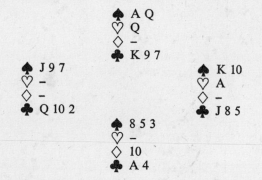

On the last trump West discarded a spade, North a club and East a club. Then came ♣A, a club to the king, and ♡Q, leaving East on play to lead up to ♠A–Q.

"It would have been easier in 3NT, but we get honours," remarked South.

"Couldn't you switch to a spade?" East demanded of his partner. "My ♡J was an unnecessarily high card."

"Why not simply play your lowest heart?" replied West. "It would have been obvious that you wanted a shift, and I would have been brilliant enough to work out that you wanted a spade rather than a club. Anyway, you could have made it more difficult for them at the end."

And so he could. From East's angle it should have been easy to see that a loser-on-loser throw-in was coming. On the last trump, or even earlier, he should have unguarded ♠K. Declarer might then have misjudged the end game.

409

A great many contracts can be saved in that way. When defending against 3NT, with an endplay looming, it is generally safe to unguard kings and queens. If there is a finesse position declarer will still take the finesse, and when the finesse loses the defender will have a nasty bag of surprises.

# CHAPTER 29

## Squeeze Play

*The simple squeeze and automatic squeeze – Double squeeze – Squeeze variations – How to defend against squeezes*

OCCASIONALLY during the later stages of a hand a defender may be somewhat disconcerted to find that whatever he discards will cost a trick. Such a situation may occur adventitiously, or as the intended result of the declarer's plan, but in either case the fact of the matter will be that the defender has become the victim of a squeeze.

Until quite recently a deliberate squeeze was seldom attempted by the average bridge player. Squeezes, when they occurred, tended to be regarded as the product of haphazard natural forces, dimly perceived. That was before the more serious type of player took to buying bridge books. Squeeze play is now much more widely understood and one is liable to encounter talk of Vienna Coups and extended menaces in almost any bridge game.

In the more exalted circles the possibility of a squeeze is considered whenever the contract cannot be made by straightforward methods. Every self-respecting expert has at least theoretical acquaintance with the exotic squeeze variations which we describe towards the end of the chapter, though not even the best of them can execute the more rare and difficult situations with faultless regularity. For all practical purposes, the basic squeezes which we now proceed to describe are by far the most important.

### The Simple Squeeze and Automatic Squeeze

Even a simple squeeze requires a certain amount of mental exertion, but it can lead to a successful outcome in contracts that are otherwise unmakable. To get down to cases, consider this quite ordinary type of hand:

411

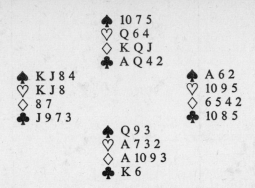

♠ 10 7 5
♥ Q 6 4
♦ K Q J
♣ A Q 4 2

♠ K J 8 4        ♠ A 6 2
♥ K J 8         ♥ 10 9 5
♦ 8 7           ♦ 6 5 4 2
♣ J 9 7 3       ♣ 10 8 5

♠ Q 9 3
♥ A 7 3 2
♦ A 10 9 3
♣ K 6

South plays in 3NT and the defenders begin by taking four rounds of spades. West then exits with a diamond. Declarer appears to have only eight winning tricks, in the shape of four diamonds, three clubs and a heart.

However, there is a good chance that dummy's ♥Q or fourth club can be promoted by means of a simple squeeze. Accordingly, declarer plays off his winning cards in the red suits, reaching this position:

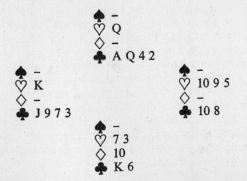

♠ –
♥ Q
♦ –
♣ A Q 4 2

♠ –            ♠ –
♥ K          ♥ 10 9 5
♦ –           ♦ –
♣ J 9 7 3     ♣ 10 8

♠ –
♥ 7 3
♦ 10
♣ K 6

On the lead of the last diamond West is obliged to give up the ghost; to be more precise, he is forced to give up either ♥K or his club guard. And dummy, of course, can select his own discard after West has played.

It could be said that declarer had not done anything very clever, and up to a point that would be true. However, a player with no grasp of squeeze play could easily have muddled it. For example, he might have played off three rounds of clubs early on. Then the squeeze would not work, as may be seen by ticking off the cards. The fact is that there is a certain technique in squeeze play and this is best studied in a methodical way, beginning with the terms used.

*The squeeze card.* To effect a squeeze you must be able to lead a card to which the opponent cannot follow suit, and to which he can discard only at the cost of a trick. This is called the squeeze card.

*Threat cards (or " menace " cards).* Any card that is not a winner can be said to be a threat card, in that its very presence obliges at least one opponent to keep a higher card. A squeeze works when one opponent controls two such menaces and cannot guard both of them when the squeeze card is played.

*Example 1*

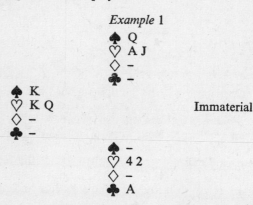

North's spades and hearts are menaces against West, who cannot guard both suits when the squeeze card, ♣A, is played. Thus if West discards a heart on ♣A North will keep ♡A–J and if West discards ♠K North will keep ♠Q.

*A two-card menace* consists of a winner and a loser in the same suit. In the above diagram, ♡A–J is a two-card menace. In all the common squeezes there must always be a two-card menace in the hand opposite the squeeze card. The importance of the two-card menace is that it provides communication. It is no use forcing your opponent to discard a winner if you have no way of entering the hand opposite the squeeze card.

*A single menace* is what the name implies—a single losing card. In the above diagram ♠Q is the single menace. Although the two-card menace must be in the hand opposite the squeeze card, the

413

single menace may be in either hand. In the above example the single menace, ♠Q, was in the same hand as the double menace, ♡A–J, but the squeeze would have worked just as well had it been in the same hand as the squeeze card. Thus:

*Example 2*

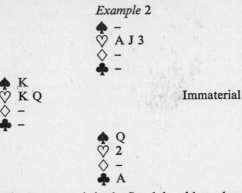

Here the single menace is in the South hand but when the squeeze card is played West is squeezed just the same. However, there really is a big difference between the two examples, for in the first case the squeeze would not have worked against East but in the second case it works against either opponent; transfer ♠K and ♡K–Q to the East hand and declarer still takes all the remaining tricks.

By now we are ready to define the simple squeeze and the automatic squeeze.

*A simple (or one-way) squeeze* is one where the two-card menace and the single menace are in the same hand, opposite the squeeze card. This squeeze works only when both menaces are controlled by the opponent who has to play next when the squeeze card is played (West in *Example* 1).

*An automatic squeeze* is one with a two-card menace in one hand and a single menace, together with the squeeze card, in the other (*Example* 2). When these conditions are met, the squeeze is effective against either opponent who controls the two menaces. Automatic squeezes, therefore, are more common than simple squeezes. In terms of practical play, the automatic squeeze and the basic double squeezes which we describe later are the most important.

*A divided menace* sometimes occurs in a simple squeeze. Observe the diamond situation in this diagram:

North's diamonds do not, by themselves, represent a two-card menace against West, because East's second diamond is higher than North's seven. But the combined holdings of North and South form a " divided menace " against West. When ♣K is led West must unguard his ◇Q to keep ♠A. A squeeze which depends on a divided menace is necessarily simple, not automatic.

Next, there is an invisible presence in the form of *timing*. The position must be " tight ", in the sense that when the squeeze card is played the defender must not hold any superfluous card which he can throw without damaging his hand. To use Culbertson's term, all his cards must be " busy ".

You may think that this kind of analysis is somewhat sterile and impractical, but there you would be wrong. If you just play out your long suits you will bring off a genuine squeeze from time to time, but you will miss a great many opportunities. Successful squeeze play depends on being able to visualize the end position in advance. In this diagram it is necessary to project the play to a three-card ending:

```
              ♠ K 7
              ♡ A Q 4
              ◇ -
              ♣ -
  ♠ J 6                      ♠ 10
  ♡ K 7                      ♡ J 8 5
  ◇ -                        ◇ Q
  ♣ Q                        ♣ -
              ♠ Q 4
              ♡ 3 2
              ◇ J
              ♣ -
```

South has the lead in notrumps and needs all the remaining tricks. He has only three sure winners and must therefore assume that the heart finesse is due to succeed. So, which are the menace cards? Not the spades, since they are all winners. The jack of diamonds must fill the role of the single menace (against whoever holds ♢Q) and the heart combination must provide the two-card (in this instance, three-card) menace.

South begins with ♠4 to ♠K and then leads 7♠ to ♠Q, squeezing East and taking the balance. Note that the squeeze would fail if South began by playing ♠Q. The reason for failure would be that South could not then reach a position in which the squeeze card was in the hand opposite the two-card menace.

The reader may wonder how, at the table, he can decide who controls which suit. Sometimes this will be obvious, and when it is not, the familiar process of assumption may be invoked. When a contract can be made only by means of a squeeze, and when the squeeze will be practicable only if East has, say, four diamonds and the king of clubs, you assume he has got those cards and you play accordingly.

Sometimes there is another possibility in the hand, but the squeeze is the superior chance. Consider this deal:

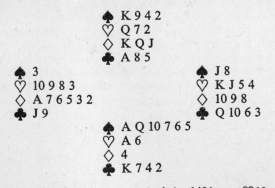

The contract is 6♠ and West leads ♢A, shifting to ♡10.

Dummy's diamonds will provide declarer with two discards, but that is not enough. A declarer who knew nothing of squeeze play would probably play ♡Q when West led ♡10, knowing of course that West was most unlikely to have led away from the king. Declarer should say to himself instead:

" No doubt East holds ♡K. If he holds four clubs as well he will not be able to guard both suits. The queen of hearts is a single menace and the clubs will supply a two-card menace."

Declarer plays low from the table, therefore, and wins with ♡A. He runs off six rounds of spades, enters dummy with ♣A, and cashes the two winning diamonds. The last two cards in dummy will be ♡Q and ♣8 and declarer will have ♣K–7 in his own hand. As East began with ♡K and four clubs, he will be squeezed.

Often it is necessary to make a special effort to bring about the conditions for a squeeze. One standard procedure is known as " isolating the menace ".

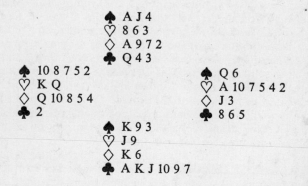

               ♠ A J 4
               ♡ 8 6 3
               ♢ A 9 7 2
               ♣ Q 4 3

♠ 10 8 7 5 2           ♠ Q 6
♡ K Q                ♡ A 10 7 5 4 2
♢ Q 10 8 5 4         ♢ J 3
♣ 2                  ♣ 8 6 5

               ♠ K 9 3
               ♡ J 9
               ♢ K 6
               ♣ A K J 10 9 7

The contract is 5♣ and West leads ♡K. East overtakes the second round and leads a third heart, which declarer ruffs.

At this stage the contract appears to depend on the spade finesse. However, after drawing trumps it will be sound tactics to take three rounds of diamonds, partly to gain a picture of the distribution and partly because this may place control of diamonds with just one opponent. This is the position after the diamond ruff:

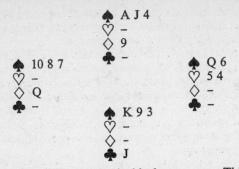

```
                    ♠ A J 4
                    ♡ –
                    ◇ 9
                    ♣ –
   ♠ 10 8 7                          ♠ Q 6
   ♡ –                               ♡ 5 4
   ◇ Q                               ◇ –
   ♣ –                               ♣ –
                    ♠ K 9 3
                    ♡ –
                    ◇ –
                    ♣ J
```

Declarer cashes ♠K and leads his last trump. This wrings a
spade from West and ◇9 is discarded from dummy. Declarer
leads a spade towards the A–J and now an interesting situation
arises: declarer knows that West's last card is ◇Q, so it cannot be
right to finesse ♠J. Declarer therefore goes up with ♠A and fells
East's now solitary queen. This is called a " show-up squeeze "
because the spade position is " shown up ".

If declarer had not taken the trouble to isolate the diamond
menace he would not have had such a clear picture of the hand and
might well have taken the spade finesse, especially as he would
place West with more spades than East.

One of the essentials for a squeeze, as we noted earlier, is correct
timing. In all the examples up to now declarer has had enough
winning cards to take " all the remaining tricks but one ". That
simplifies the play but it is not a necessary condition. Indeed, at
notrump contracts it is not uncommon for a squeeze to occur at a
time when several of the remaining tricks belong to the defenders.

```
                    ♠ 8 7 5
                    ♡ K J 2
                    ◇ K 9 6 4
                    ♣ A 10 3
   ♠ A Q 9 6 4                       ♠ J 2
   ♡ 10 7                            ♡ 9 6 5 4
   ◇ Q 10 5                          ◇ J 3
   ♣ K Q 2                           ♣ 8 7 6 5 4
                    ♠ K 10 3
                    ♡ A Q 8 3
                    ◇ A 8 7 2
                    ♣ J 9
```

418

South plays in 3NT after West has opened with 1♠. The six of spades is led to the jack and king. West can spare a club on the third round of hearts but on the next round he is undone. If he lets go a spade South has time to develop a trick in clubs or diamonds.

This squeeze is effective because when the fourth heart is played all West's cards are " busy ". No special effort is required on the declarer's part. On many hands, however, the defender will have one or more " idle " cards, and in such a case the declarer must manage the play in such a way that the idle cards are removed before the squeeze card is played. In this four-card ending the presence of an idle card enables the defender to escape the squeeze.

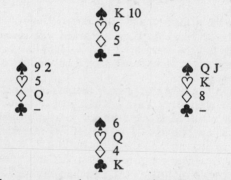

Declarer has a two-card menace against East in spades and a single menace against him in hearts. However, when South leads ♣K, East can comfortably spare a diamond and declarer can make only ♠K. He began with two tricks and he ends with two tricks.

Now suppose the declarer had contrived to get rid of the diamonds earlier in the proceedings. In that case the lead of ♣K would squeeze East.

To ensure that the defender to be squeezed has no idle cards is a very important part of squeeze preparation. The reader is invited to consider what South must do on the following hand, which he plays in 6NT after West has opened with a pre-emptive bid of 3♠.

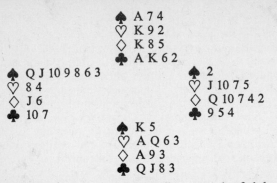

South wins the spade lead and takes three rounds of clubs, finding West with two of them. As West is marked with seven spades it is not at all likely that the hearts are 3–3. No doubt East has long hearts and long diamonds, in which case it should be possible to squeeze him in the red suits.

The difficulty lies in the timing. If South simply plays off all his winners in the black suits, East will discard two diamonds and will not be embarrassed. Declarer does not need to project the play in his mind to know that this is so; it follows necessarily from the fact that he cannot win " all the tricks but one ".

To put the necessary pressure on East, declarer must contrive to lose an early trick. To duck a heart or a diamond would achieve that object but it would also destroy the menace card in that suit. The solution, therefore, is to duck a round of spades, after which it will be possible to squeeze East in the red suits. The process of setting up the right timing is called " rectifying the count ". It is especially common in notrumps and, as we shall see later, the defenders must often resist the declarer's attempts to bring it about.

As the reader may have noted, 7♣ plays quite easily on this deal. After drawing trumps the declarer takes a spade ruff, which in effect is his twelfth trick, then crosses to dummy with one of the red kings and plays off the last club, to East's discomfiture.

## Double Squeeze

In all the examples so far, the declarer has squeezed only one opponent. There are, however, some common squeezes that operate against both opponents, either simultaneously or on successive tricks. They require menaces in three suits.

*A simultaneous double squeeze* requires the usual two-card menace in the hand opposite the squeeze card, plus an extra single menace, which must be in the same hand as the squeeze card.

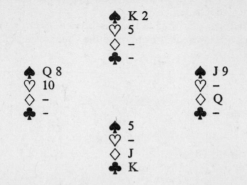

This is a classic simultaneous double squeeze. On the lead of ♣K West must unguard the spades to keep the master heart. Dummy's heart is then discarded and East becomes squeezed in spades and diamonds. For this type of squeeze it is essential that both single menaces should be favourably placed " over " the defender who holds the guard.

When these ideal conditions are not fulfilled there must be some kind of compensation. In the next example South holds both the single menaces, but the remaining suit, the suit that both opponents control, instead of being an ordinary two-card menace, is an " extended menace ".

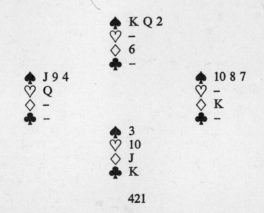

The extended menace is in spades. South needs just one card for communication opposite the three cards in dummy, and there is thus room for South to hold both the single menaces. So long as ♡Q and ◇K are in different hands, the opponents are bound to be squeezed when ♣K is led.

A different form of compensation is needed when both the one-card menaces are in the hand opposite the squeeze card.

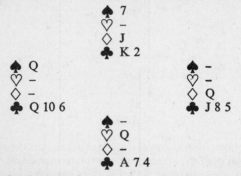

The situation is wrong for a classic double squeeze in that North's diamond menace is " under " the opponent whom it threatens. The squeeze still operates because of the additional entry in the pivotal suit, clubs. On ♡Q West must let go a club, the spade is thrown from dummy, and East is squeezed.

*A non-simultaneous double squeeze* occurs when the squeeze card or one of the menaces is badly placed and compensation exists in the presence of two two-card menaces—one in the pivotal suit, one in another suit.

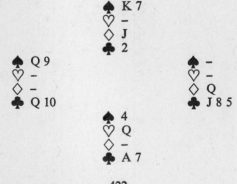

The situation looks all wrong for a double squeeze. The two-card menace controlled by both opponents, clubs, is in the same hand as the squeeze card, and furthermore ♢J is "under" the opponent whom it threatens. However, there is an additional entry in spades. When ♡Q is led West is squeezed and must throw a club. The seven of spades is discarded from dummy and East, under no pressure so far, lets go a club. The declarer follows with a spade to the king and now East feels the pinch.

Of the double squeeze positions, the classical simultaneous squeeze is both commonest and the easiest to execute. In this example, the declarer must prepare for the squeeze with the stratagem known as the Vienna Coup.

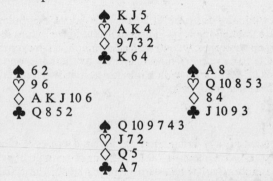

South is in 4♠ and the defence begins with three rounds of diamonds. South ruffs the third round and leads a spade to the king and ace. East exits with ♣J, which is taken by the ace.

Having lost three tricks, South must avoid a heart loser. He knows that dummy's fourth diamond is a menace against West, so that if West held ♡Q there would be a simple one-way squeeze against him. However, it is more likely that East, who is short in diamonds, has control of hearts. In that case the omens are favourable for a double squeeze. An essential preliminary is to play off ♡A–K, establishing ♡J as a single menace against East. Three rounds of trumps then lead to this ending:

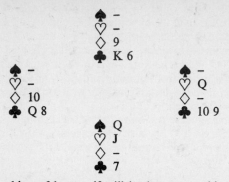

The ace or king of hearts, if still in dummy at this point, would simply be a stumbling-block. This is a useful hint: except in the rare case of a trump squeeze, which we describe later, it is never necessary or desirable to have more than one entry to the hand opposite the squeeze card. This rule is valuable because it will remind you to play off obstructive high cards.

## Squeeze Variations

There must always be an entry to the hand opposite the squeeze card, but this can sometimes take the form of a single high card instead of the more usual two-card menace. In this case there must always be a similar unprotected high card in the opposite hand. Observe how South, playing the deal below, puts pressure on West even though the menace card in clubs (the ten) does not appear to be well placed.

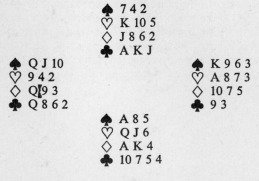

424

The contract is 3NT and West leads ♠Q. South holds up until the third round and then plays a low heart to the king. It would be good play for East to duck, but most players would win and cash the thirteenth spade. In this case South discards a diamond, West a heart and dummy a diamond. East exits with ♢7, which is won by declarer's ♢A.

Needing all the remaining tricks, South finesses ♣J and cashes ♣A. As there are still entries to both hands there is no hurry to play off ♣K. After a heart to the jack this becomes the position:

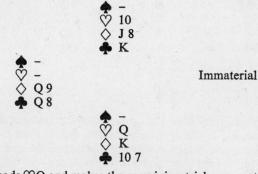

South leads ♡Q and makes the remaining tricks no matter which suit West unguards. This is a *criss-cross squeeze*, the characteristic feature being the two single controls in diamonds and clubs and the blocked position in both suits.

There is a criss-cross element in a trump squeeze, where the squeeze is possible only because of the ruffing factor. In this diagram diamonds are trumps:

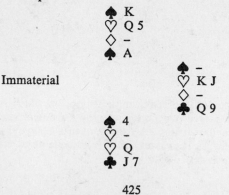

A spade to the king squeezes East. For this type of squeeze there must be two entries in the hand opposite the last trump. The second entry may lie in a suit where there is no menace card, as in the diagram above, or in one of the " menace " suits, as on the following deal:

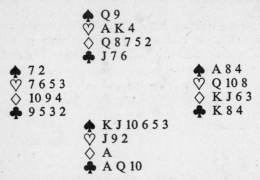

```
                    ♠ Q 9
                    ♡ A K 4
                    ◇ Q 8 7 5 2
                    ♣ J 7 6
     ♠ 7 2                              ♠ A 8 4
     ♡ 7 6 5 3                          ♡ Q 10 8
     ◇ 10 9 4                           ◇ K J 6 3
     ♣ 9 5 3 2                          ♣ K 8 4
                    ♠ K J 10 6 5 3
                    ♡ J 9 2
                    ◇ A
                    ♣ A Q 10
```

South plays in 6♠ after East has opened the bidding. The ten of diamonds is led to the declarer's ace and ♠A is forced out. East exits with a spade, which is taken in dummy. Declarer leads ♣J, picking up East's ♣K, and then plays two more rounds of trumps to reach this position:

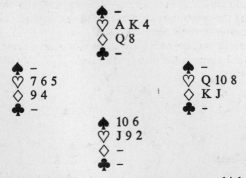

```
                    ♠ –
                    ♡ A K 4
                    ◇ Q 8
                    ♣ –
     ♠ –                                ♠ –
     ♡ 7 6 5                            ♡ Q 10 8
     ◇ 9 4                              ◇ K J
     ♣ –                                ♣ –
                    ♠ 10 6
                    ♡ J 9 2
                    ◇ –
                    ♣ –
```

The squeeze card is the penultimate trump, on which North discards a heart. Observe that, as always, there are two entries to the hand opposite the last trump. A trump squeeze is always automatic and is useful because it enables declarer to squeeze a strong hand sitting over the dummy.

The last variation we must look at is the progressive squeeze. The importance of this is that it wins two extra tricks against an opponent who is threatened in three suits. There is usually an extended menace in the hand opposite the squeeze card.

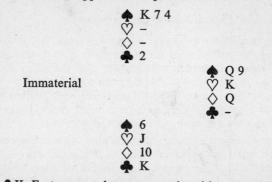

On ♣K East cannot let go a spade without establishing two tricks for North. If East throws a diamond or a heart, South follows with his established winner in that suit and squeezes him again.

When there is no extended menace the declarer will need two two-card menaces plus a favourably placed one-card menace, all lying against the same opponent, as in this diagram:

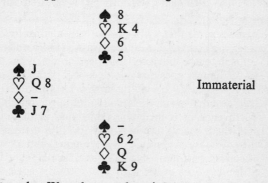

No matter what West throws when ◇Q is led, he can be squeezed again two tricks later.

Progressive squeezes are not common because they need a precise arrangement of entries and menace cards. But even when such an arrangement is not present, a declarer who is two tricks short of his contract should not despair. Defenders have been known to make the first discard from the wrong suit and so expose themselves to a squeeze that could have been avoided.

## How to Defend against Squeezes

Just as an ex-poacher makes the best gamekeeper, so a defender is likely to play the best defence against a squeeze if he understands the technique from the declarer's side. But the defender does not necessarily have to be able to visualize the squeeze ending that the declarer is planning. In practical play, a defender will often be able to judge that a squeeze is declarer's only hope, and in that case he may place his trust in certain well-known principles.

(1) *Discarding*. When declarer plays off a long suit and there seem to be menaces on all sides, a defender should follow these principles:

(a) When two double menaces are present, discard always the suit held on the left, keeping a guard against the menace on the right. (b) When there is a two-card menace which both defenders can guard, and a single menace which both defenders can guard, the defender on the right of the two-card menace should let go his guard in it and should keep control of the single menace. (c) Against a progressive squeeze, unguard a one-card menace held on the left. The squeeze (if imperfect) may then gain one trick for the declarer, but not two.

(2) *Killing menaces*. As has been seen, the declarer's aim is to establish menace cards that will lie exclusively against one opponent. The defenders can combat this in three ways: (a) By not assisting the declarer to isolate the menace. Suppose a defender leads from A–K–Q–10–x, dummy goes down with x–x–x–x, and it is clear that declarer has a singleton. It may be unwise to continue the suit, for this may help declarer to ruff the second and third rounds, establishing the fourth card as a menace against one hand only. (b) By extinguishing the menace; the best way to kill a menace card is to play the suit until none are left. (c) By arranging matters so that both defenders keep a controlling card. Thus, if a defender leads from A–K–x–x, dummy goes down with J–x–x, and it is clear from the play to the first trick that partner holds Q–10–x–x–x, the opening leader should continue with a low card, so that both defenders retain a card higher than dummy's jack.

(3) *Attacking entries*. Most squeezes can be defeated by an early attack on vital entries. This is true particularly of squeezes that

depend on a double menace with entries in each hand. All one can say on this subject is that a defender who has a good picture of the hand must foresee a possible squeeze and consider how to break up the entries.

(4) *Wrecking the timing.* For any squeeze the timing must be correct and we have seen how declarer will try to bring about a position where he can win all the remaining tricks but one with top cards. The defenders can often prevent this. At notrumps, in particular, a defender must beware of cashing a long suit when all the burden of the remaining defence will fall on his partner. Worse still, a defender must not play a card that squeezes his partner—a suicide squeeze.

In general, a player who is defending against, say, 3NT should hesitate to cash the fourth trick for his side unless he can see where the fifth trick is coming from. Remember that the declarer wants to be in a position where he can make " all the remaining tricks but one ". The task of the defence is to prevent the elastic from being stretched to that convenient point.

# CHAPTER 30

---

## Trump Coups

*Coup en passant – Trump reduction plays – Grand Coup, Devil's Coup and Smother Play*

THE PECULIAR properties of the trump suit can lead to many situations that appear to defy the normal principles of card play. For example, declarer or defenders may find as the hand progresses that a long trump holding can be an embarrassment as well as an asset, so much so that it is not unknown for a player to ruff his partner's tricks in an attempt to reduce his trumps. Other surprising situations occur where a player may deliberately underruff, or where the defenders may be denied a trump trick with some such holding as Q–x–x opposite J–x, and so on.

Some of these plays, of course, occur very infrequently. Others are well worth the attention of the practical player and we begin with one which is both useful and fascinating.

### Coup en Passant

This coup, the name of which means, literally, a blow in passing, often arises without deliberate planning, and the reader no doubt will soon recognize its characteristic feature. Nevertheless, a player with no experience of the coup might be quite surprised if told that it was a simple matter to make 4♠ on this deal.

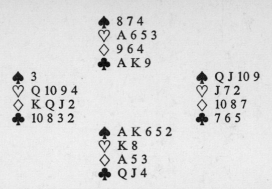

```
              ♠ 8 7 4
              ♡ A 6 5 3
              ◇ 9 6 4
              ♣ A K 9
♠ 3                         ♠ Q J 10 9
♡ Q 10 9 4                  ♡ J 7 2
◇ K Q J 2                   ◇ 10 8 7
♣ 10 8 3 2                  ♣ 7 6 5
              ♠ A K 6 5 2
              ♡ K 8
              ◇ A 5 3
              ♣ Q J 4
```

Against 4♠ West leads ◇K. Declarer wins and cashes ♠A–K, discovering the unfavourable break. It may seem as though declarer is due to lose two trump tricks and two diamonds, but in fact there is nothing the defenders can do to beat the contract. Declarer plays three rounds of hearts, ruffing, and cashes three clubs, arriving at this position with the lead in dummy:

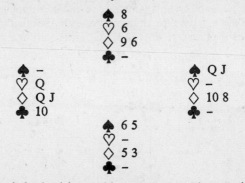

```
              ♠ 8
              ♡ 6
              ◇ 9 6
              ♣ —
♠ —                         ♠ Q J
♡ Q                         ♡ —
◇ Q J                       ◇ 10 8
♣ 10                        ♣ —
              ♠ 6 5
              ♡ —
              ◇ 5 3
              ♣ —
```

If East had the lead he could soon mop up the remaining tricks, but when ♡6 is led from dummy declarer comes to a trump trick, *en passant*, as it is called.

Sometimes the need for this type of play has to be foreseen before an unfortunate trump break has actually revealed itself, as in this example:

431

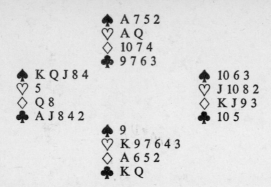

The contract is 3♡, West having overcalled in spades. West leads ♠K and declarer wins in dummy. If he plays in straightforward fashion, attempting to draw trumps, South ends up with only eight tricks. Since there will be no problem if the trumps break normally, declarer should take the precaution of ruffing a spade at rick two. He next leads ♣K, establishing a trick in this suit before the opponents can make any damaging discards. Suppose West wins and exits with a trump to dummy's queen. South ruffs another spade, cashes ♣Q, and returns to ♡A. The position is:

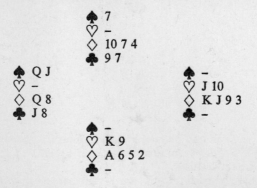

♠7 is led from the table. If East ruffs high, South will of course not overruff but will discard a losing diamond; if East does not ruff, then South makes a sixth trump trick by putting in ♡9.

Like other forms of trump endplay, this coup can work against the left-hand opponent also, though not exactly *en passant*.

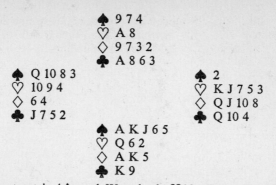

The contract is 4♠ and West leads ♡10. East wins with ♡K and returns a diamond to the declarer's ace. South takes ♠A, then crosses to ♡A and leads a low spade, on which East shows out.

It looks as though South must lose two spades and one diamond, but he continues with ◇K and three rounds of clubs, to arrive at this position:

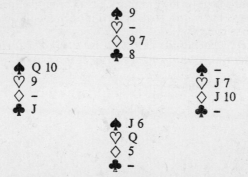

Declarer enters dummy again by the expedient of ruffing his own winning heart. Then he leads the fourth club and ruffs it for the tenth trick. This is the typical end situation, with the opponents' three winners falling together on two tricks.

### Trump Reduction Plays

The bridge player who protests that he has too many trumps might be thought, by the uninitiated, to be as unappreciative as the million-aire who complains about his tax problems. Nevertheless, such a situation is far from uncommon and we have already encountered it in this chapter. No doubt the reader, from time to time, has been obliged to ruff his own trick in this sort of ending:

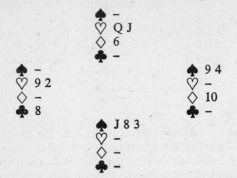

Spades are trumps, the lead is in dummy and declarer needs all the tricks. Hopefully he leads a heart winner from the table. East, of course, unless he has seriously miscalculated or miscounted, will not be so obliging as to ruff but will discard his diamond. Declarer then has to lose the last trick.

This unhappy conclusion can often be avoided if declarer takes steps to reduce his trump length earlier in the play. Consider this deal:

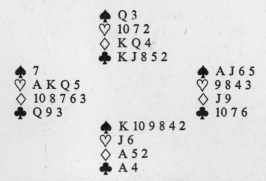

The contract is 4♠ and West begins with three rounds of hearts. South ruffs and leads a trump to the queen and ace. East does not want to help declarer to shorten his trumps again, so he exits with a diamond. South wins in dummy and successfully finesses ♠10.

Declarer has lost three tricks and knows that East still has ♠ J–6. However, all is not yet lost. South must endeavour to reduce his trumps to the same length as East's, so his first move is to take ♣ A–K and ruff a club. The position is then:

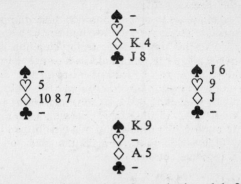

South crosses to ◇ K and leads a winning club from dummy. Declarer has achieved his object, for if East declines to ruff, another club will follow.

That was not too difficult a hand to manage because declarer did not have to form his plan until after the trump distribution had shown up. Many hands call for a degree of foresight, although it helps if declarer forms the habit of reducing his trumps as a matter of routine whenever he is endowed with considerable length in the suit. The following hand shows the value of this habit and shows also that the left-hand opponent can be endplayed as well as the opponent on the right.

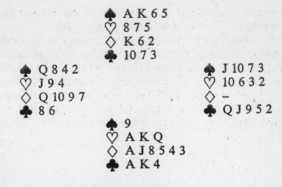

The contract is 6◇ and West leads a club. Suppose the declarer plays a diamond to the king; in this case he learns the disquieting news that the trumps are 4–0 and finds that it is too late to do anything about it. To endplay West he must reduce his trumps twice and he lacks the necessary entries.

The proper technique is to prepare for a possible trump reduction by leading a spade to the ace at trick two and ruffing a spade. Then a diamond is led to the king and the trump situation is revealed. Declarer cannot negotiate the hand unless he can take out all the plain suits and endplay West by leading a trump, so it is necessary to find West with four spades, three hearts and two clubs. Declarer cashes ♠K, ruffs a spade and takes his winners in hearts and clubs. Now he is down to ◇A–J–8 and simply exits with a low diamond.

Invariably the nub of the problem in this type of hand is how to time the play of the side suits. Here South made an expensive mistake in a grand slam contract:

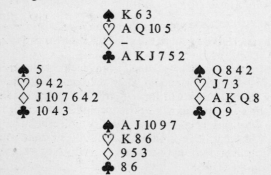

East opened 1◇ and South overcalled with 1♠. When East–West later defended in 7◇ over 6♠, North went to 7♠.

Declarer ruffed the diamond lead in dummy, took ♠K and finessed ♠J. This held, but East was left with the guarded queen. South played the high clubs from dummy and ruffed the third round, East discarding a heart. Thinking that all was for the best in the best of all possible worlds, South led a heart to dummy's queen and played an established club from the table. East discarded his third heart on this trick and a diamond on the next club. The position was now:

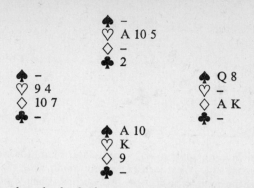

Declarer thought he had matters well under control, since all dummy's cards were winners and, if East ruffed, he could re-enter by overtaking ♡K. However, when ♣2 was led East discarded again and for the first time South realized that something had gone amiss. Whether he discards a heart or diamond on this trick, East will ruff the next lead and make either a trump or a diamond.

At the point where South led a heart to the queen he should instead have played ♡K and another heart, despite the danger of a ruff. Then he discards two diamonds on the fourth and fifth clubs and is down to a satisfactory holding of two spades and one heart when he leads the last club.

There is a little known formula that will save a declarer from mismanaging a hand of this type. After the trump reduction he had three good clubs left on the table and it was necessary, when he began to play the clubs, that he should have the same number of cards to discard if East did not ruff. He must come down to one heart and two diamonds, matching the three clubs in dummy.

When a trump reduction is on the horizon, the defenders, of course, should not assist in the process. Generally speaking, a defender who has long trumps, or who can judge that his partner has long trumps, should not help the declarer to make his own trumps by ruffing. This is a typical defensive situation:

```
            ♠ K 8 4
            ♡ 5
            ◇ 9 7 5 3
            ♣ A J 8 6 2
♠ J 9
♡ J 9 7 6 2
◇ A K 10 4
♣ 5 3
```

West is defending against 4♡, the declarer being marked with at least a six-card suit. West leads ◇K, on which East plays the six and declarer the eight. The declarer probably has a singleton diamond and it would be a mistake to continue the suit. West's length in trumps will soon show up and declarer will then use all his entries to dummy to enable him to ruff diamonds. To avoid giving him a good start, West should shift to one of his short suits at trick two.

A defender's own trump length will sometimes become such a liability that he must divest himself of one. This is a frequent type of end situation:

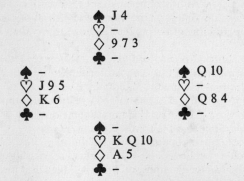

```
            ♠ J 4
            ♡ –
            ◇ 9 7 3
            ♣ –
♠ –                      ♠ Q 10
♡ J 9 5                  ♡ –
◇ K 6                    ◇ Q 8 4
♣ –                      ♣ –
            ♠ –
            ♡ K Q 10
            ◇ A 5
            ♣ –
```

Hearts are trumps and the lead is in dummy. The declarer, who knows that West has all the trumps against him, leads a spade from dummy and ruffs with ♡Q. If West throws a diamond, South will now lead ◇A and another diamond, and West will be forced to ruff and lead into ♡K–10. West must underruff, therefore, playing the five under the queen. When declarer then leads ◇A West must keep up the good work by dropping ◇K.

This type of play is perhaps more difficult to see in time when the

defender is in front of the declarer. On this hand from rubber
bridge two forms of defensive error occurred:

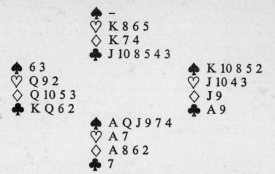

♠ —
♡ K 8 6 5
◇ K 7 4
♣ J 10 8 5 4 3

♠ 6 3                    ♠ K 10 8 5 2
♡ Q 9 2                  ♡ J 10 4 3
◇ Q 10 5 3              ◇ J 9
♣ K Q 6 2              ♣ A 9

♠ A Q J 9 7 4
♡ A 7
◇ A 8 6 2
♣ 7

South opened 1♠ and North responded with an uneasy 1NT. The
bidding then followed a predictable course:

| South | West | North | East |
|---|---|---|---|
| 1♠ | Pass | 1NT | Pass |
| 3♠ | Pass | 3NT | Double |
| 4♠ | Double | Pass | Pass |
| Pass | | | |

West led ♣K and continued with a low club, which declarer
ruffed. As we have noted, this was the wrong line of defence. West
should have switched to one of the red suits and not helped the
declarer to make cheap tricks by ruffing.

Even if nobody had doubled, it would have been natural for
South to play along the lines of trump reduction. After three rounds
of hearts and two top diamonds, this became the position:

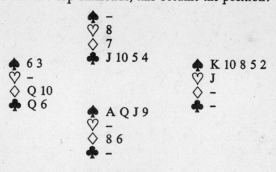

♠ —
♡ 8
◇ 7
♣ J 10 5 4

♠ 6 3                    ♠ K 10 8 5 2
♡ —                     ♡ J
◇ Q 10                  ◇ —
♣ Q 6                   ♣ —

♠ A Q J 9
♡ —
◇ 8 6
♣ —

If South had ruffed the last heart he could not have been prevented from making all his trumps, but instead he led a club. East discarded a heart and South ruffed with the nine. Now, again, it was easy to exit with a diamond and make three more tricks with ♠A–Q–J. Thus the contract was made and North, no doubt, felt that his bidding was entirely vindicated.

But see what happens if East, realizing that his trump length is a positive danger, ruffs low when the club is led from dummy in the diagram position. South overruffs and exits with a diamond, on which East discards his heart. East is obliged to ruff the next diamond, it is true, but with the K–10–8 of trumps remaining he is bound to make another trick.

## Grand Coup, Devil's Coup and Smother Play

These are famous plays which the authors feel bound to include in this work, though their practical importance is slight. The Grand Coup, despite its high-sounding title, need not detain us because it is nothing more nor less than a trump reduction play. The name dates from the days of Whist, when it was thought that a trump reduction achieved by ruffing a winner (the distinguishing feature of the Grand Coup) was deserving of a special name.

The other coups, by contrast, are very distinctive indeed. They involve situations where the defender's trump trick can be made to disappear in an apparently magical fashion. We will show only the end positions.

(1)

This is a classic example of the play known as the Devil's Coup. Hearts are trumps and the lead is in dummy. A combined defensive

440

holding of Q–x–x and J–x is normally considered impregnable, but in this instance it is not worth a trick when ◇4 is led from dummy. Declarer may try for this position when he has A–9–x opposite K–10–8–x–x and cannot afford to lose a trump trick, especially if the possibility of finding a defender with a singleton honour, or with Q–J doubleton, appears slight.

(2)

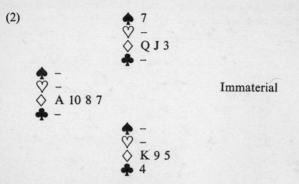

```
                    ♠ 7
                    ♡ –
                    ◇ Q J 3
                    ♣ –
  ♠ –
  ♡ –                          Immaterial
  ◇ A 10 8 7
  ♣ –
                    ♠ –
                    ♡ –
                    ◇ K 9 5
                    ♣ 4
```

This is a variation. Diamonds are trumps, and South has the lead. West may think he is on firm ground in anticipating two diamond tricks, but South leads a club and overruffs West's ◇7 with dummy's ◇J. One of West's trump tricks then disappears when declarer leads ♠7 from dummy and ruffs it with the king of trumps, taking two more tricks whether West overruffs or not. The same sort of endplay can be made against a defender who holds A–J–9 over declarer's Q–10–x, with the king in dummy.

(3)

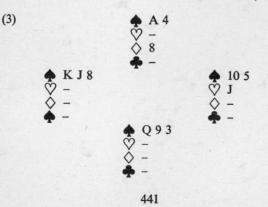

```
                    ♠ A 4
                    ♡ –
                    ◇ 8
                    ♣ –
  ♠ K J 8                      ♠ 10 5
  ♡ –                          ♡ J
  ◇ –                          ◇ –
  ♣ –                          ♣ –
                    ♠ Q 9 3
                    ♡ –
                    ◇ –
                    ♣ –
```

In this ending, also a form of Devil's Coup, spades are trumps and the lead is in dummy. The defenders would be bound to make two trump tricks against any form of direct assault, but are held to one trick when declarer leads ◇8 from dummy. It makes no difference whether East discards on this trick or ruffs with either ♠10 or ♠5.

Finally, the celebrated Smother Play, which has graced many problem hands and which the authors have not yet lost hope of accomplishing in practical play.

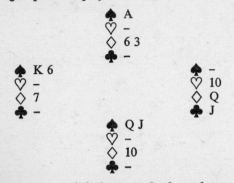

Spades are trumps and declarer, on lead, needs two more tricks. He must lose a diamond but does not have to lose a trump, despite West's holding of K–x in front of the singleton ace. Declarer exits with a diamond, which is won by East, and on the next trick West's king of trumps is smothered out of existence.

# CHAPTER 31

# The Play of the Cards at Duplicate

*The play in normal contracts – Unusual contracts – Sacrifice contracts – How the lead may affect your plan – Match-point defence*

CARD play at duplicate differs from rubber bridge in two important respects. First, the process itself is more exacting—you must contest every trick, whether it be the ninth in 2♣ or the thirteenth in a grand slam! Secondly, you do not aim at a fixed target. You cannot be sure that your principal objective as declarer is to make the contract or as a defender to beat it. Your fortunes may depend on whether you can avoid going down two tricks, or whether you can prevent an overtrick.

The declarer's first task is to consider, when the dummy goes down, what *sort* of contract he is in. The main distinction is between " normal " and " unusual " contracts.

## The Play in Normal Contracts

If you arrive in a normal contract, one which you assume most pairs will be in, your object is not primarily to make it, but to score more tricks than the other declarers. This does not mean you play for miracles. It means that when there are two alternative lines of play you go for the one that is likely to produce the most tricks on a majority of occasions. For example:

```
        ♠ K Q 7 3
        ♡ K J
        ◇ 10 8 4
        ♣ A 10 5 3

        ♠ A J 5
        ♡ Q 6 2
        ◇ A J 9 3
        ♣ K 9 6
```

The contract is 3NT and West leads ♡5, which is covered by the king and ace. East returns ♡8 and West follows with the four. At trick three declarer leads ◇8 from dummy, losing to West, who clears the hearts.

Declarer has nine tricks, and at rubber bridge he would cash them hastily. At duplicate he cannot rest so easily. He must risk the second finesse in diamonds, even though he will be defeated if it loses. The point is that he is in a normal contract, one that he expects to be reached at nearly every table. The chances of the second finesse succeeding are about 2 to 1 on, and such chances must not be spurned. Taking the second finesse (with chances of making eleven tricks) will lead to a good score twice as often as to a bad one. The fact that declarer stands to gain only 30 or 50 total points, and to lose 700, is irrelevant. It is a simple question of good score versus bad score.

The constant quest for a good score will lead a declarer to make many plays that are superficially hazardous but have a sound psychological expectancy of success. This is almost a standard example:

♠ Q 8 7 4 3
♡ A 8 2
◇ 10 5 4
♣ Q 4

♠ 10 6
♡ Q 10 4
◇ K 8 2
♣ A K J 7 3

South opens a weak 1NT and is left to play there. A low heart is led, dummy plays low, and East wins with ♡K. The heart return is covered by declarer's ten, West's jack and dummy's ace.

Instead of running for home with seven tricks, South should lead a low diamond at trick two and put up ◇K. This could result in one down, but (a) ◇A may be well placed, (b) if West has A–J–x or even A–x–x he may let the king hold, and (c) if West does play the ace on the king it is unlikely that he will return the suit. Remember, West doesn't know that South has five club tricks ready to cash. That is an important element in this play, which, at best, will produce only 120 instead of 90, but is still the right game.

Here is another example that shows how at duplicate the dividing line between safety and unsafety can become blurred:

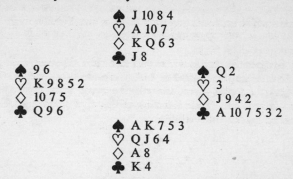

&spades; J 10 8 4
&hearts; A 10 7
&diams; K Q 6 3
&clubs; J 8

&spades; 9 6        &spades; Q 2
&hearts; K 9 8 5 2        &hearts; 3
&diams; 10 7 5        &diams; J 9 4 2
&clubs; Q 9 6        &clubs; A 10 7 5 3 2

&spades; A K 7 5 3
&hearts; Q J 6 4
&diams; A 8
&clubs; K 4

The contract is 4&spades; and West leads &hearts;5, which from declarer's angle might possibly be a singleton. At rubber bridge South would go up with &hearts;A, prepared to lose a heart, a trump and a club. At duplicate there is no room for such caution. Declarer finesses the heart, lays down the A–K of trumps, taking care to unblock dummy's eight and ten, then takes &hearts;10 and &hearts;A. Now back to &spades;7, ruff a heart, and return with &diams;A; play off the trumps, and claim thirteen tricks when East is squeezed on the last spade.

Just as the primary objective in a normal contract is not simply to make the contract but to make tricks, so it is often right to accept one down rather than risk two down when the chances for making the contract are not good. This is especially true when vulnerable, for minus 200 is always bad.

&spades; A J 7 5 4
&hearts; 8 6 3
&diams; Q 10 4
&clubs; K 8

&spades; 10 2
&hearts; A Q 7
&diams; J 9 6 2
&clubs; A Q 6 3

With both sides vulnerable West opens 1&hearts; and South becomes declarer in 3NT. West leads &hearts;4 and declarer captures East's jack with the queen.

Prospects are not great, but the contract will be reached elsewhere. It therefore becomes a question of which line of play will produce more tricks on the majority of occasions. Playing on spades will win nine tricks if West holds precisely K–Q–x but is much more likely to lead to minus 200. Therefore it is wiser to play on diamonds and be fairly sure of eight tricks.

On competitive hands where it is not clear whether your contract is normal or unusual, good or bad, there are two general rules: one is to play for a plus score, the other to avoid at all costs the kiss of death—minus 200. Your handling of this type of contract should be influenced by the vulnerability.

♠ Q 10 8
♡ Q 9 6
♢ Q J
♣ J 8 6 5 4

♠ 5
♡ J 10 7
♢ K 10 9 8 4 2
♣ A K 10

| South | West | North | East |
|-------|------|-------|------|
| *South* | *West* | *North* | *East* |
| 1◇ | 1♠ | 1NT | 2♠ |
| 3◇ | Pass | Pass | Pass |

A spade is led against your contract of 3◇ and dummy's ten forces the ace. A low spade comes back and the question is whether to ruff and try to make the contract or discard a heart and play for one down.

If you ruff, you may be held to seven tricks. The opponents will play spades every time they are in, and you will be in danger of losing control. Your only real hope of making the contract will be to draw trumps and lay down ♣A–K, hoping to drop the queen.

If you discard a heart at trick two, you can be reasonably confident of winning eight tricks. You cannot tell how many match points this will be worth; much will depend on how many tricks East–West can make at a spade partial.

In this close situation you should probably try to make the contract if you are not vulnerable, for in this case the difference between minus 50 and minus 100 may not matter much in terms of match points. Vulnerable, it would be advisable to discard the heart at trick two, settling for eight tricks. Remember that if you concede

200 you lose to all the pairs who have scored minus 110 or minus 140 when defending against a partial score in spades.

## Unusual Contracts

When playing an unusual contract, declarer should try to assess the likely score at other tables. Then he should go all out to try to equal or surpass it, even if he has to employ desperate measures. For example, if you are convinced that everyone else will be in 3NT, cold for ten tricks, your target in a contract of 4♠ is not ten tricks but eleven. Here this principle is demonstrated at a higher level:

    ♠ K 8 2
    ♡ A K 10 7 4 3
    ◇ A 5
    ♣ K 8

    ♠ A J
    ♡ J 8 2
    ◇ J 9 7 6 4
    ♣ A Q 4

North opens 1♡, South bids 2NT and North raises to 6NT. West leads ◇8. As there is no point in ducking, declarer wins with ◇A and plays ♡A-K, dropping West's queen.

It is obvious now that players who are in 6♡ will make seven by ruffing a spade in dummy. Therefore there is a case for finessing ♣J, playing for a 90 per cent score, as opposed to settling for a 25 per cent score by making just 6NT.

## Sacrifice Contracts

When sacrificing, you should follow the normal percentage most of the time. For example, suppose you have to tackle a trump combination consisting of A–Q–10–x–x–x opposite K–x. Suppose also that if the trumps are 3–2 your sacrifice will have been a "phantom". It would still not be clever to play for a 4–1 break. Your main concern when sacrificing is to win more tricks than players who are in the same contract. If you have indulged in a "phantom" there is nothing you can do against pairs who have registered a plus score.

Nevertheless, it may be correct to make an unusual play in an attempt to avoid a costly loss. The crucial question is: what is the danger level and can you keep the penalty below it?

Suppose that, not vulnerable, you buy the contract for 3♥ and see that the hand belongs to your opponents in a part score. You must direct all your attention to keeping the loss to 100. If you lose 150, that will be bad unless opponents can make ten tricks in spades.

At game level you can afford to lose 300 if opponents are not vulnerable, 500 if they are vulnerable. When playing an out-and-out sacrifice you must keep your eye very much on these figures, like a mariner watching his gauges.

♠ 7 6
♥ K 9 6 3
♦ K Q 10 8 4
♣ Q 4

♠ J 4 2
♥ Q J 10 8 5 2
♦ 7 5
♣ A 8

Suppose first that you go to 5♥, not vulnerable, sacrificing against 4♠ by vulnerable opponents. West leads ♠K–Q (from A–K–Q–x–x) and East plays ♠10 on the second round, a suit-preference signal asking for a diamond switch. West duly shifts to a diamond and East captures dummy's queen with the ace. If East returns a club you may as well let this run, even though you will probably lose 500, which won't be bad as not everyone will sacrifice.

Now suppose that you are in 5♥ doubled at equal vulnerability. After similar play it will probably be wise to go up with ♣A and finesse ◇10, the only chance of holding the penalty to two down. Few pairs will sacrifice at equal vulnerability, so to have a good board you must make your sacrifice against 4♠ a paying one.

## How the Lead may Affect your Plan

The opening lead is important in a sense that does not arise at rubber bridge. Suppose you get a favourable lead: then you must play to keep a step ahead of the field. Suppose that the opening leader strikes a particularly brilliant note: now you may have to perform some unusual feat of arms to hoist yourself out of the pit. First, an example where declarer's aim is to profit from a good start:

♠ A 9 3
♡ A Q 9 5
◇ 7 5 4
♣ K 8 6

♠ K J 7 2
♡ K 8 6 4
◇ A Q
♣ 7 3 2

The contract is 3NT and West leads ♠4. Declarer captures East's ten with the jack and returns ♠2, finessing ♠9, which wins. Declarer should appreciate that he has got off to a very fortunate start, as it is not certain that either 3NT or 4♡ will be made at other tables. Therefore, it will be wise to settle for nine tricks rather than to take the diamond finesse and risk a club switch.

Here, by contrast, is an example of the Doomsday syndrome:

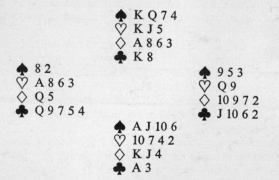

♠ K Q 7 4
♡ K J 5
◇ A 8 6 3
♣ K 8

♠ 8 2                              ♠ 9 5 3
♡ A 8 6 3                          ♡ Q 9
◇ Q 5                              ◇ 10 9 7 2
♣ Q 9 7 5 4                        ♣ J 10 6 2

♠ A J 10 6
♡ 10 7 4 2
◇ K J 4
♣ A 3

You are in 4♠ and West catches you with a low heart lead, the defenders taking the first three tricks. You win the trump switch at trick four and must seek a way to restore the situation.

You are in a normal contract and if the diamond finesse is right, other declarers in 4♠ will be making 650, while you bring up the rear with 620. Your only chance to come out with a 50 per cent score is to do something eccentric, such as dropping a doubleton queen of diamonds.

29 24pp.

## Match-point Defence

The tactics for the defending side at duplicate are similar to those for declarer, as seen in a mirror.

The defenders must dismiss from their minds the familiar injunctions about taking all possible measures to beat the contract. The object, as for declarer, is simply to take more tricks than other players who are in the same situation. Suppose, for example, that South opens a strong 1NT and North raises to 3NT. East has passed originally, and West, the opening leader, holds a featureless hand with 3 or 4 points. Clearly prospects of beating the contract are poor, and for a start West should select a safe lead in preference to a lead from an honour combination. Now suppose that dummy goes down with 12 points. Unless the opening lead has unexpectedly struck gold, the contract is sure to be lay-down, and both defenders must make it their objective to hold the declarer to ten or eleven tricks, as the case may be.

Suppose, next, that the defenders make a particularly bad start against a suit contract, perhaps by making a lead that presents the declarer with early discards. Thereafter they must seek to pull themselves up by their bootstraps through some daring or unusual play. Here, again, one sees a reflection of the declarer's tactics in a similar plight.

When you are defending after a competitive auction, the first objective is to obtain a plus score. This will generally ensure a score from 40 per cent upwards. When you see that a plus score is assured, the next step is to form an impression, if you can, of how your side would have fared had you been allowed to play the hand. If you see that you would have netted 110 or 140 in a partial, you must attempt to score 150 or better.

When you have sacrificed at game level you keep in the forefront of your mind the value of the game you are saving. If opponents are not vulnerable you may be happy to lose 300; if they are vulnerable you can afford 500. When it is the opponents who are sacrificing you must concentrate on obtaining an adequate penalty—500 or 700, depending on whether your own side is vulnerable or not.

So far, the problems for the defence have been the same as for the declarer, turned the other way round. There are, however, certain occasions in match-point play where the defenders have special opportunities. This arises from the fact that the declarer will be seeking to make the maximum number of tricks and not just to make his contract. Everyone knows the familiar situation where at trick twelve the declarer has the choice between going up with a winner to make sure of his contract and taking a finesse for an overtrick. Even when the finesse is odds-on to succeed, a declarer at rubber bridge will say " I am not going to look foolish ", and will take the money. At duplicate no declarer who is worth his salt will take that easy way out. There is therefore a premium on all those semi-deceptive situations in which a defender holds up a key card to a point at which the declarer begins to doubt its existence.

# PART VII

*Laws, Proprieties and Scoring*

# CHAPTER 32

# Laws and Proprieties

*The preliminaries – The auction period – The play period –
The proprieties*

THE INTERNATIONAL laws for both rubber and duplicate
bridge are promulgated jointly by the Portland Club, London, the
European Bridge League and the American Contract Bridge League.
The present code for tournament play has been in force since 1975;
for rubber bridge, since 1981. Except in a few special areas such as
scoring and the duties and powers of a tournament director, the
Laws for rubber bridge and duplicate are substantially the same.

The official Laws\* are extremely well drafted and are a model of
precision and comprehensiveness. However, these very qualities
sometimes cause the non-specialist, desiring easy reference to a
simple situation, to become baulked and it may be helpful, therefore,
to give a more relaxed account; not of the whole code, but of the
most common irregularities and the provisions that apply to them.

## The Preliminaries

*Drawing for partners.* It is improper to draw one of the four cards
at either end of the pack, or a card next to one drawn by another
player. It is also incorrect to turn up a card until all the players have
drawn.

*The deal.* There must be a redeal if any card is faced during the
deal.

## The Auction Period

*Asking for a review of the auction.* A player may ask for a review
only at his turn or at the close of the auction. This law is not always
observed in rubber bridge but is considered important in duplicate.

\* The Laws for Duplicate are published in Britain by Waddington Playing
Card Co. Ltd., Leeds 10, those for rubber bridge by Bibliagora, P.O. Box 7,
Hounslow TW3 2LA.

Strictly, only an opponent may give the review. For the defender, the right to ask for a review lapses after the opening lead; for the declarer, after dummy has gone down.

*Card exposed during the auction.* If a card below a ten is accidentally exposed, it becomes a penalty card. If it is a card of honour rank, or if it is exposed with intent to lead, or if more than one card is exposed, partner must pass at his next turn. All such cards become penalty cards.

*Correcting a call.* There is no penalty for correcting a call " in the same breath ". If a call is corrected not in the same breath, but before the next hand has spoken, the caller's partner must pass throughout. In addition, if the caller's partner becomes a defender he may be forbidden, when first in the lead, to lead the suit mistakenly named.

In this and all similar cases where a lead may be prohibited, the prohibition lasts for so long as the player retains the lead at this turn. Say that the bidding goes:

| South | West | North | East |
|-------|------|-------|------|
| 1♣    | 4♠   |       |      |

Before North has spoken, but not in the same breath, West says " I made a mistake, I meant to say four hearts." The correction is allowed, but East is barred for the rest of the auction. If North–South obtain the contract, East, when he first has the lead, may be forbidden to lead a spade, the suit of the misnomer.

If the mistaken call was in notrumps the caller's partner, at the opening lead only, may be required to lead a specified suit.

*Insufficient bid.* An insufficient bid is condoned if the next player calls before attention has been drawn to it; otherwise it must be corrected either by a pass or by making the bid sufficient. A double or redouble is not a permissible amendment (see below, Illegal double or redouble). The penalties for an insufficient bid depend on how it is corrected, as will be seen from this example:

| South | West | North | East |
|-------|------|-------|------|
| 3♠    | 2♡   |       |      |

After attention has been drawn to the insufficient bid, West may:
(1) *Amend to* 4♡, " the lowest sufficient bid in the same denomination ". There is then no penalty.
(2) *Pass.* In that case East must pass throughout, and if East–West

become defenders East may be required or forbidden to lead a particular suit. (The reason for this " required or forbidden " clause is that if declarer calls for the lead of a suit and the player is void, the penalty lapses; declarer may prefer not to take that risk and may instead prohibit the lead of a particular suit.)

(3) *Make any other legal bid.* In this case East is barred throughout.

*Pass out of turn.* There are three situations to consider:

(1)

| South | West | North | East |
|-------|------|-------|------|
| Pass  |      |       | Pass |

Here East has passed out of turn *before anyone has made a bid* (as opposed to a pass). The bidding reverts to the proper player, West, and East must pass at his next turn. The same would apply if any player were to pass before the dealer had spoken.

(2)

| South | West | North | East |
|-------|------|-------|------|
| 1♠    | 2♡   |       | Pass |

Here East has passed when it was the turn of his right-hand opponent to call. The penalty is the same as in (1). The bidding reverts to North, and East must pass on this round.

(3)

| South | West | North | East |
|-------|------|-------|------|
| 3♣    |      |       | Pass |

Now East has passed when it was the turn, not of his right-hand opponent, but of his partner to call. This attracts a more severe penalty. First, East must pass throughout. Secondly, West may pass or bid at this turn, but may not double (or redouble). Thirdly, if West passes and subsequently has to make the opening lead, declarer may require or forbid the lead of a particular suit.

*Bid out of turn.* Again, there are three situations:

(1)

| South    | West | North | East |
|----------|------|-------|------|
| (dealer) |      |       | 1♡   |

This is a bid out of turn before anyone has called. The bidding reverts to South, and West must pass throughout.

(2)

| South | West | North | East |
|-------|------|-------|------|
| Pass  |      |       | 1♡   |

South has called and East has made a bid out of turn when it was his partner's turn to call. West must pass throughout and if West has the opening lead the declarer may require or forbid the lead of a particular suit.

| | South | West | North | East |
|---|---|---|---|---|
| (3) | Pass | 1◇ | | 1♡ |

East has bid out of turn when it was the turn of the opponent on his right to call. Now, if North passes, East must repeat his bid of 1♡ and there is no penalty. But if North makes any call other than a pass, East may call what he pleases and West must pass on the next round. There may be a lead penalty; see *Correcting a call*, above.

*Double or redouble out of turn.* The procedure depends on whether it was the turn of partner or of the right-hand opponent to call.

| | South | West | North | East |
|---|---|---|---|---|
| (1) | 3♠ | | | Double |

East has doubled when it was his partner's turn to call. West must pass throughout. East, when his proper turn arrives, is not allowed to double 3♠, the bid he doubled out of turn. If West becomes the eventual leader, declarer may require or prohibit the lead of a particular suit.

| | South | West | North | East |
|---|---|---|---|---|
| (2) | 3♠ | Pass | | Double |

East has doubled when it was the turn of his right-hand opponent to call. The procedure now is the same as if East had made a positive bid: if North passes, East must repeat his double, with no further penalty; if North bids, East may make any proper call and West must pass on the next round. If West has the opening lead he may be required or forbidden to lead a particular suit.

*Illegal double or redouble.* There is a difference depending on whether the player doubles or redoubles a bid his side has already doubled or redoubled, or makes some other form of illegal double or redouble.

| | South | West | North | East |
|---|---|---|---|---|
| (1) | 3♡ | Double | Pass | Double |

East may substitute a legal bid or he may pass. If he substitutes another bid, say 3♠, West must pass throughout and if West becomes the opening leader he may be forbidden to lead a heart, the suit illegally doubled by East. Or East may pass; then West must pass throughout, his double may be cancelled, and he may be required or forbidden to lead a specified suit.

(2)

| | South | West | North | East |
|---|---|---|---|---|
| | 1NT | 2♣ | Pass | Double |

This is one of a variety of other illegal doubles or redoubles that may be made through inadvertence. East may make any legal call and West must pass on the next round.

*Bid, double or redouble when required by Law to pass.* Such calls are cancelled, both players of the offending side must pass for the remainder of the auction, and if the offender's partner becomes the opening leader the declarer may require or forbid the lead of a particular suit.

## The Play Period

*Dummy's status.* Dummy may intervene to prevent an irregularity, such as a lead from the wrong hand. When an irregularity has occurred he may state or inquire the law; for example, after a lead out of turn by an opponent, he may say to his partner, " Do you know your rights? " However, dummy forfeits his rights if he looks at his partner's hand or, uninvited, at an opponent's hand.

When dummy has forfeited his rights he suffers these disadvantages: (a) if he is the first to draw attention to an opponent's irregularity, no penalty may be exacted; (b) if he attempts to warn declarer not to lead from the wrong hand either defender may call on declarer to lead from a particular hand; (c) if he asks declarer about a possible revoke, and declarer has revoked, the revoke is corrected but the penalty for an established revoke applies.

If dummy improperly suggests the play of a card from dummy, either defender may require that such card be played; or may prohibit the play of that card, or one of equal value in that suit, or any card of that suit when dummy cannot follow suit.

*Card played.* A card is played by a defender when held so that partner can see its face. A card is played by declarer when held face up, touching or near the table. A card is played from dummy when touched (except to adjust). A card is played by any player when named as the card he intends to play, except that an inadvertent designation may be immediately corrected.

*Penalty card.* Any card exposed by a defender other than in the normal course of play becomes a penalty card. A card from the declarer's hand, or from dummy, never becomes a penalty card.

A penalty card must be left face up on the table and must be played at the first legal opportunity. If the partner of a player who has a penalty card is on lead he may be prohibited from leading the suit of the penalty card or may be required to lead that suit. There is a logical reason for this latter provision. Suppose a suit is divided as follows:

$$Q\,x\,x$$

$$K\,x\,x \qquad\qquad J\,10\,9\,x\,x$$

$$A\,x$$

East leads the jack, out of turn. Declarer treats this card as a penalty card. When West is next in the lead he may appreciate that declarer probably holds the ace. To prevent West from benefiting from his information, he may be required to lead the suit. When declarer requires or forbids a lead in these circumstances the penalty is discharged and the exposed card may be picked up.

When a defender has two penalty cards on the table, the declarer may require him to play either one.

*Opening lead out of turn.* Declarer may accept the lead, in which case dummy is laid down at once but declarer plays the second card to the first trick and dummy the last card. (If the declarer inadvertently begins to spread his hand the lead *must* be accepted and dummy plays the hand.)

If declarer requires the lead to be retracted, he has the rights described in the next paragraph.

*Defender's subsequent lead out of turn.* Declarer may accept the lead. If he requires it to be retracted he has the following options:

(a) If it was the turn of the other defender to lead he may either treat the card led as a penalty card or require the other opponent to lead, or not to lead, that suit. In this case the penalty card is picked up.

(b) If it was the turn of declarer or dummy to lead, declarer may either treat the card led out of turn as a penalty card or may allow it to be picked up and, when the offender's partner next obtains the lead, declarer may require or forbid him to lead the suit of the card led out of turn.

*Declarer's lead out of turn.* The defenders may accept the incorrect lead, even if it was their own turn to lead. If they require the lead to be retracted, and it was a defender's turn to lead, there is no penalty. If declarer has led from the wrong hand, he must, if possible, lead a card of the same suit from the correct hand. If he fails to lead a card of the same suit from his own hand, when he could have done so, and fails to correct the error before he or dummy has played to the next trick, he is subject to the penalties for an established revoke.

*Premature lead or play by a defender.* If a defender plays out of turn in front of his partner, the partner may be required to play his highest or lowest card of the suit led, or to discard from a specified suit. The declarer may name only one such option, and if the defender cannot comply the penalty lapses. The penalty for a play out of turn cannot be enforced if the declarer has already played from both hands, but even in these circumstances a defender should not deliberately play in front of his partner.

If a defender attempts to lead to the next trick before his partner has played to the current trick, the other defender may be required to play his highest or lowest card of the current suit or to discard from a specified suit. If this results in the player winning the trick, his partner's attempted lead to the next trick becomes a penalty card.

*Corrected revoke.* A player may, and if aware of the error must, correct a revoke before he or his partner has led or played to the next trick. A correct card is substituted, whereupon the other side may change any card played by them after the revoke. In the case of a defender's corrected revoke, the card withdrawn becomes a penalty card.

*Established revoke.* A revoke becomes established when the offending side has led or played to the next trick, or when the offending side has made any claim or concession.

A revoke on the twelfth trick never becomes established. The correct card must be substituted and the offender's partner may be required to play to the twelfth trick either of two cards he could legally have played.

When a revoke has been established, two tricks are transferred at the end of play. These count exactly as though won in play. But tricks won before the revoke trick may not be transferred. For instance, if a declarer in 4♠ revokes after making nine tricks and subsequently makes only one more trick, then just this one trick is transferred and he is one down.

There is no penalty for a second revoke in the same suit by the same player; but it is improper for a player to revoke deliberately.

*Missing card.* A player who mislays a card is deemed to have held this card from the beginning (assuming it was correctly dealt to him) and may incur the penalty for an established revoke.

*Claim or concession by declarer.* Not only an open statement, but a remark such as " All you get is a heart ", or the act of facing the remaining cards, amounts to a claim or concession. A declarer who has so spoken or acted may be required to lay his hand on the table; either defender may face his cards without penalty and may suggest a line of play to his partner.

The declarer has a duty to make a statement of his intended line of play, from which he may not deviate, when he makes a claim. The problems arise when he fails to do so, or when his statement is inadequate. Because of the limitless variety of situations, the lawmakers have had difficulty in expressing their exact thoughts, or of devising a form of words that will give effect to them.

Taking the relevant passages of the rubber-bridge laws and the duplicate laws together, the situation may be described as follows:

The declarer may be asked to amplify his statement and may be required to play on. In this case he may make no play whose success depends on finding an opponent with or without a particular unplayed card. Thus he may not take a normal finesse (except towards a player who has shown void *before* the claim), nor any sort of ruffing finesse; and if he proposes to ruff any card led by an opponent he must ruff with a master trump when there is even a theoretical danger that he might be overruffed.

Close questions should be resolved in favour of the defenders. Thus a declarer who has not stated his precise intentions concerning the trump suit may be required to draw, or not to draw, a trump that he may have overlooked. This rule is generally not enforced when the declarer has ample trumps and there is no reason to think that he has forgotten the outstanding trump or trumps.

A problem arises here: declarer, barred from taking a finesse, successfully plays for the drop of an opposing honour when, if he had not made the claim, he would probably have finessed. In duplicate the director has a right to adjudicate such a point in favour of the defenders, for the overall intention of the Law, undoubtedly, is that a declarer should not in any circumstances profit from his negligence in making a claim that was not ironclad.

*Claim or concession by a defender*. A defender may make a claim or concession verbally or by showing his cards to the declarer only. If a defender exposes or names any cards to his partner when making a claim, then his *partner* may be required to expose all his cards and these become penalty cards. This is logical because it is the partner who has gained improper information.

*Concession nullified*. Players are protected from conceding tricks they have already won, or a contract they have actually fulfilled.

A player is also protected from conceding a trick he could not lose by any play of the cards. Suppose that dummy's last two cards are $\heartsuit$8 (a master) and $\heartsuit$5 (a loser until the eight has been led), and that declarer says, " I give you one trick ". This concession legally stands, but if $\heartsuit$8 and $\heartsuit$5 were both masters, in whatever order they were played, the concession would not stand.

A concession by one defender is not binding on the other. Suppose that East, misplacing the cards, says, " The rest are yours ". West may say, " No, play on ". But West may not say, for example, " No, lead a diamond ". That would be " a lead improperly suggested " and could be vetoed by the declarer.

## The Proprieties

These relate to ethics and etiquette. They are set down in the Laws, but no specific penalties are prescribed. In duplicate, however, the director has power to award an adjusted score for a breach of the proprieties.

There are three areas where misunderstandings commonly arise. These concern: the freedom to depart from an announced convention; the duty to bid or pass following hesitation; the duty to warn opponents of a conventional call or play.

*Departures from an announced convention.* Duplicate players very soon learn the guiding principle here, but rubber-bridge players never cease to write to bridge editors with tales of woe such as: " Our opponents announced they were playing Blackwood, but one of them responded 5$\diamondsuit$ with two aces."

The answer to this is very plain: a player may at any time depart from an announced convention, provided that he has no private understanding with his partner on the matter. To repeat an aphorism made by one of the present authors some thirty years ago, " A convention in bidding is an agreement between partners, not an undertaking to the opponents."

*Duty to bid or pass following hesitation.* It is, in general, *desirable* that a player who has given some indication of his type of hand by hesitating should either double or bid at the finish, but it is not in itself improper to pass. Suppose the bidding goes:

| South | West | North | East |
|-------|------|-------|------|
| 1$\diamondsuit$ | 1$\spadesuit$ | 4$\heartsuit$ | ? |

At duplicate North is directed to warn opponents of his intention to jump, after which East would be required to pause in any event. At rubber bridge this is usually not done, and East may need a little time to adjust himself to the unexpected happenings, at the end of which he may decide to pass. The obligation now falls on West not to take any action that might be influenced, or might even appear to be influenced, by his partner's hesitation. The same kind of obligation arises when partner has made a " slow double " or a double that opponents might consider a trifle eager: the partner must " lean over backwards " not to take any sort of advantage.

*Duty to warn opponents of a conventional call.* Players are exhorted to give a complete account of the conventions they propose to use before beginning play, but this is not always practical in the modern world. When a player makes any call whose significance the opponents might not understand, his partner should draw attention either by tapping the table or by mentioning that the call has a conventional meaning. The opponent may or may not then ask for an explanation.

To conclude, we touch on various situations where doubts sometimes arise as to what is fair or unfair. Some practices are entirely permissible; some are objectionable; some are positively unfair.

The following practices are entirely in order:

(1) Exacting a penalty even when the offence has brought no conceivable advantage. To waive penalties (unless one's own side has contributed in some way) leads to confusion and to wounded feelings when opponents on a later occasion feel unable to reciprocate.

(2) Warning partner against any irregularity he may be about to commit. A player also has the right to query an opponent's play which may possibly be a revoke.

(3) Maintaining silence about an offence committed by one's own side; but it is improper to take any abnormal action to cloak an infringement.

(4) Drawing inferences from an opponent's gratuitous hesitation or remark. But you do so at your own risk. Supposing you are in a slam contract and an opponent starts a small grumble, you are entitled to take finesses towards him. If he turns up with the queen of trumps and another critical king you may think bitter thoughts, but you have no redress.

The following practices, though some of them are tolerated in certain circles, are objectionable in the literal sense that an opponent has every right to object to them:

(1) Picking up cards before the deal has been completed.

(2) As dummy, exchanging cards with declarer before the play, or leaning over to look at a defender's cards.

(3) Failing to stack quitted tricks tidily, so that they can be easily counted.

(4) Detaching cards from the hand before the player's turn to play; the more so, when the card is a potential winner.

The following practices are in different degrees unfair:

(1) Drawing attention to the score, for partner's benefit.

(2) Drawing attention to the number of tricks won or lost, for partner's benefit.

(3) Deliberately committing an offence, even though prepared to pay the legal penalty.

(4) Either calling or playing in a special manner calculated to convey information to partner. This, of course, covers an extremely wide field. Taking note of such illegal information is equally reprehensible, though on occasions difficult to avoid.

(5) Attempting to mislead an opponent by any extra-curricular activity, such as a fumble when there is nothing to think about.

Lastly, criticism is deprecated by the lawmakers and players are enjoined " to maintain at all times a courteous attitude towards their partners and opponents "; a pious aspiration, indeed.

## International Match Point Scoring

| Difference on Board | IMP | Difference on Board | IMP |
|---|---|---|---|
| 0–10 | 0 | 750–890 | 13 |
| 20–40 | 1 | 900–1090 | 14 |
| 50–80 | 2 | 1100–1290 | 15 |
| 90–120 | 3 | 1300–1490 | 16 |
| 130–160 | 4 | 1500–1740 | 17 |
| 170–210 | 5 | 1750–1990 | 18 |
| 220–260 | 6 | 2000–2240 | 19 |
| 270–310 | 7 | 2250–2490 | 20 |
| 320–360 | 8 | 2500–2990 | 21 |
| 370–420 | 9 | 3000–2490 | 22 |
| 430–490 | 10 | 3500–3990 | 23 |
| 500–590 | 11 | 4000 & upwards | 24 |
| 600–740 | 12 | | |

# Rubber Bridge Scoring

**Score below the line for tricks bid and made:**

| | | |
|---|---|---|
| Spades or hearts | 30 per trick | If doubled: |
| Diamonds or clubs | 20 per trick | multiply by 2 |
| Notrumps | 40 for first trick | |
| | 30 for each | If redoubled: |
| | additional trick | multiply by 4 |

100 points wins game, but no separate score is recorded.

**Score above the line:**

*Overtricks*

| | Not vulnerable | Vulnerable |
|---|---|---|
| Undoubled | Ordinary trick value | Ordinary trick value |
| Doubled | 100 per trick | 200 per trick |
| Redoubled | 200 per trick | 400 per trick |

**Making doubled or redoubled contract:**
    In addition to all other scores: 50

**Honours:**

| | |
|---|---|
| 4 trump honours in any one hand: | 100 |
| 5 trump honours in any one hand: | 150 |
| 4 aces in any one hand at notrumps: | 150 |

**Slams:**

| | Not vulnerable | Vulnerable |
|---|---|---|
| Small slam | 500 | 750 |
| Grand slam | 1000 | 1500 |

**Penalties:**

| | Not vulnerable | Vulnerable |
|---|---|---|
| Undoubled | 50 each trick | 100 each trick |
| Doubled | 100 for first trick | 200 for first trick |
| | 200 for each | 300 for each |
| | additional trick | additional trick |
| Redoubled | Twice the above | Twice the above |

**Rubber bonus:**
    When the rubber is won in two games: 700.
    When the rubber is won by two games to one: 500.

**Unfinished rubber:**
    Bonus for a side that is game up: 300.
    Bonus for a part-score in an unfinished game: 50.

# Index